How to Succeed with
Your Own Construction Business

by

Stephen & Janelle Diller

Craftsman Book Company
6058 Corte del Cedro, Box 6500
Carlsbad, CA 92008

ACKNOWLEDGMENTS

The authors wish to express their appreciation to the following individuals and companies for furnishing materials used in the preparation of various portions of this book.

Robert Bowman, Computer Specialist

Bradford Publishing Company, Lakewood, Colorado

Community Development

First American Bank, George Lenz

Haley Property Management Company

G.K. Helzer Construction, Valerie Helzer

Holme Roberts & Owen, Brent Rychener

The Insurance Center, Nancy Bramstedt and Connie Stevenson

Melvin Jantz, General Accounting & Tax Preparation

Neighborhood Housing Services, Terry Allen

Remodeling Magazine, Washington, DC

In addition, we greatly value the excellent resources of two other outstanding industry magazines: *Professional Builder* and *Qualified Remodeler.*

Our greatest appreciation goes to our parents, Ivan and Doris Diller and S. Milford and Rosie Roupp. Over the decades, they have set an example of honesty, integrity, and competence that we aspire to. Further, they have instilled in us an entrepreneurial spirit that is the foundation of our enthusiasm for owning our own business.

Library of Congress Cataloging-in-Publication Data

Diller, Stephen.
   How to succeed with your own construction business / by Stephen & Janelle Diller.
       p.   cm.
   Includes index.
   ISBN 0-934041-59-8 : $19.50
    1. Construction industry--Management.   2. New business enterprise--Management.   I. Diller, Janelle.   II. Title.
HD9715.A2D49   1990
624'.068--dc20   90-48956
                                     CIP

CONTENTS

1

Taking the Plunge

*I*t's hard to swing a hammer on a contractor's payroll and not dream of running your own construction company some day. You know you could do it faster, better, and make better money. So why let someone else make the profits while you work for wages? Why not take the risks and get the rewards yourself?

If that's what you've been thinking, keep reading. This book can help you make the big step from wage earner to contractor — in the shortest time possible and with the best possible chance of success. We're going to explain how to take the plunge, step by step, and in the clearest language possible.

Most new contractors quit their regular construction jobs because they have good prospects for making it on their own. A strong economy and a few good leads may provide all the courage needed to step out on your own. As long as the economy stays robust, you can keep busy moving from one job to the next. You feel good about all the money going through your bank account. For a while that may seem like prosperity — until you get a notice from the Workers' Compensation Board or the IRS that you're delinquent on some payment required by law. Or your suppliers start calling to find out where their money is. Or a client threatens suit because of some work you did or didn't do. Worse yet, the bottom may drop out of the local economy — leaving you with all overhead and no income.

What happens then? Do you quit and go back to work for your old boss (if the job's still open)? Do you declare bankruptcy? Or do you stop and rethink where you're headed, how you got there, and what your options are?

We hope you're reading this book before you reach the point of desperation. But even if you're desperate, what you learn here should be well worth the time you invest scanning these pages.

Maybe you're just starting to explore the idea of construction on your own. If so, you're lucky. Not everyone is so far-sighted. Nearly one-third of all new businesses fail in their first year. Only half survive two years. The statistics don't have to be so grim. You can overcome most problems. We'll show you how. You don't have to discover all the dead end streets, blind alleys and potholes yourself. Let this book be your road map.

Learning the Hard Way

Before beginning, we'll offer some personal history so you understand our perspective. We're a husband and wife construction team. We both grew up in the construction industry. Steve's father owned his own home-building business for 45 years. Janelle's dad owned a ready-mix concrete plant and plowed his profits into real estate. We saw our fathers work long hours and come home dirty and tired. Their struggles in running businesses — even successful ones — didn't appeal to us. The money looked good enough, but we weren't sure we wanted the customer hassles or the hard work. A construction company seemed like the last thing we wanted to do.

Still, construction was what we knew best. And everyone needs a career. So we tried to make a living in the home renovation business, fixing up old houses for sale in Colorado Springs. We might have made a living at it, except that home loan rates zoomed to 18 percent and the local economy went into a tailspin before our first home was done. Fortunately, a couple of jobs dropped in our laps and we were "contractors," whether we'd planned to be or not. Even more unexpected, we liked it!

Those first jobs rolled in so easily that we thought others would quickly follow. Those first jobs came from casual acquaintances who knew we had some construction skills. Of course, as luck (or logic) would have it, the phone didn't ring again for six months. Fortunately, we had very little overhead and a second income that kept us afloat.

Our success story would be more persuasive if we could say that some serious reading and a few changes solved all our problems. Unfortunately, that wasn't what happened. We discovered ways to make a good living in the construction business. But we never found a magic formula. Maybe there isn't any. What we discovered was the hundreds of mistakes nearly any contractor can make in this business — and a few ideas and ways of doing business that seemed to work again and again.

That's what we're going to share with you — information to make your first few years a lot easier than ours were. We'll tell you how to estimate and schedule jobs, set up books and run your office, dig up business and close the sale. Of course, you have to add the real magic that makes a business succeed: hard work, construction know-how, and management skills.

The Big Picture

The construction industry is the nation's largest in terms of the number of people employed. It touches the lives of everyone, either as a consumer or as a producer. Until just the last decade or so, new construction was the glamorous part of the industry and remodeling was the ugly duckling. Home renovation and remodeling were like crumbs left on the table after all the prime jobs had been swept up.

That's not true any more. The remodeling and renovation industry is growing much faster than new construction. Experts predict that remodeling work will continue to thrive because our nation's housing stock is getting older. A home is built only once. But most will be remodeled several times before they're finally demolished. For many homes, the cumulative cost of remodeling and repairs will far exceed the original cost of construction. That makes home remodeling, renovation and repair a very promising business.

Of course, new construction may seem more glamorous. You don't have so many unexpected problems. You don't have to work around a house full of people. And you don't have to deal with the eternal problem of knowing where to start and where to finally call it quits. Fortunately for the consumer, most remodelers see those as minor inconveniences in a very challenging and rapidly growing industry.

For the first few years we planned to move up to the "real" contracting business some day, putting up new buildings instead of just making them better. Gradually though, we began to realize that remodeling had major advantages. Once we stopped apologizing for being on this end of the industry, it was easy to get more respect. Most important, we found ourselves getting more business and more recognition as specialists in the construction industry.

Here's Why We Concentrate on Remodeling

1) Most remodeling and repair work is financed by savings or the settlement of an insurance claim, not proceeds from a loan. When new

construction is being strangled by high loan rates, repair and remodeling work tends to keep humming. In a weak business market, many prospective new-home buyers opt to remodel instead of buy. The market ups and downs aren't nearly as dramatic or dangerous to the remodeler as they are to the contractor who does mostly new work.

In 1985, *Professional Builder* reported that from 1979 to 1983 residential construction dropped about 60 percent. In the same period, inflation-adjusted dollars spent on remodeling dropped less than 13 percent.

According to *Qualified Remodeler*, in 1978, 16.2 percent of National Association of Home Builders (NAHB) members said remodeling was an important part of their operation. By 1982, that percentage had more than doubled to 36.8 percent.

In fact, this shift presents a problem. Most builders wouldn't touch a remodeling project when times are good. But they're more than anxious to bid remodeling jobs when work is slow. Because they don't have the unique skills that remodeling takes, they botch a couple of jobs and then get out. In the process, they leave behind one more blemish on the reputation our industry carries. Remodeling requires better management, scheduling, and public relations than new construction. Unfortunately, too many builders don't discover that until they're knee-deep in a tricky job.

2) The remodeling industry tripled in size between 1975 and 1985. By 1984, more money was being spent on remodeling and repair work than on new construction. Industry experts project total remodeling dollars to triple again by the year 2000, reaching nearly $300 billion a year. That compares with about $100 billion spent in 1989. About 40 percent of those dollars will be spent on additions or alterations. The rest will be spent on maintenance and repairs.

Asbestos removal by itself will become a big business. *Remodeling* magazine projects as much as $200 billion will be spent on eliminating the health risk from asbestos over the next ten years. And within the next few years, many states will probably require a radon test before houses can be sold. Detecting and correcting radon problems will become a nice sideline for many remodelers.

Predictions are that the industry will average 10 to 15 percent annual growth through the 1990s.

3) Remodeling takes less money and less risk than new home building. What you need is some equipment, credit from your suppliers and subcontractors, and cash to meet payroll until receipts catch up with expenses.

New-home builders need lots more. Many try to get started by putting up a speculative house. They find a bank to finance them, build the house, and hope that it sells. They also hope to get enough leads so building another spec house isn't necessary. Spec building is risky. Especially in suburban areas where big, publicly-held developers are active. They're masters at the fine art of getting more square feet of floor for less money.

Remodeling, by its very nature, lends itself well to a mom and pop company. You don't need a showroom or a fancy sales office. You can work out of the back of your truck. Plenty of good remodelers started this way and have chosen to stay this way.

Four-fifths of all remodeling companies have ten or fewer employees. But there are few very large remodeling companies. Most of the giants are in a single line of work, such as siding, roofing, or window replacement. *Qualified Remodeler's* 1988 listing of the 500 top remodeling companies in the U.S. included only five full-line remodelers in the top 25 companies. The number one company grossed over $120,000,000 doing siding and decks. Many in the top 500 were full-line remodelers with gross sales over $1,000,000 in 1987.

Some new-home builders hire subcontractors to do nearly all the work, from digging the foundation to decorating. All you need are competent subs. Construction becomes a matter of putting the many parts together like a giant jigsaw puzzle. Every house may have a different set of plans, but the parts go together the same way.

Not so with remodeling. Your first job may be enlarging porch windows and painting the exterior. Your second may be adding a sun room; your third, updating a kitchen. Unless you specialize, no two jobs are ever the same. As a result, most remodelers know a lot about most construction trades. It's hands-on skill that helps a remodeling company build a reputation in this industry. Good construction skills are essential. But as the company grows, good management skills become just as important. The remodeler who built the company with construction know-how has to master the fine art of running a construction office. That's not easy, as maybe you've already discovered.

4) Remodeling is a people business, not a product business. Turning clients into friends is one of the things that we like best about the business. If you don't like dealing with people, you might as well stop reading. Your success depends, at least in part, on how well you can get along with clients. Remember, they're trusting you with their most valuable possession, their home. Home renovation can be very stressful for homeowners. The mess, noise, and general disruption to their schedule is a nuisance for anyone. It's your responsibility to help clients survive while you build and remodel.

5) There's always room for someone who can do it better. The Better Business Bureau reported over 47,000 complaints against the home improvement industry in 1986. That was an increase of 31 percent over 1985 and accounted for 10 percent of all consumer complaints. Home

improvement ranked second highest in number of problems of all the business categories.

Those statistics aren't meant to scare you off. We've never had a complaint lodged against us; we've never spent a day in court or even with an arbitrator. We know lots of remodelers who can say the same thing. We also know several remodelers who got more than their share of those 47,000 complaints.

There's plenty of room for anyone who can do it better. If you do quality work, are willing to work hard to build a reputation, and can get along with people, the industry needs you!

6) Remodeling can be very profitable. We know that's true. But we won't mislead you. It can also be very unprofitable. If you can control your overhead and if you're consistently good at estimating costs, you can make good money on almost every job. Most remodelers who leave the business haven't been able to do either.

It certainly helps to do a high volume of business, but volume alone won't make you profitable. Some high volume remodelers we know aren't making much money. And we know some low volume remodeling specialists who consistently make good money. Profit margin is usually more important than volume. Be a remodeler who earns a healthy margin regardless of volume, not a remodeler who takes all the work available regardless of price.

Your reputation as an experienced remodeler should help open up some other opportunities in specialty markets. If you have any doubts, get a quote on having some asbestos removed.

7) Owning your own business is very satisfying. True, our bias is showing. We grew up in families that appreciated the flexibility, variety, and challenge self-employed people enjoy. We think running a remodeling company gives us a sense of pride that few businesses could. Looking back over the last ten years, we're proud to have survived changes in the local economy and to have grown and prospered as we accumulated experience. It feels good because we did it ourselves!

But Is It Right for You?

How do you know if you're cut out to run your own business? There's no sure way to know without actually trying it. But answer the following questions to get at least an initial impression. The first set of questions explore your general attitude toward being self-employed. The second set of questions is more specific. It covers the kinds of personality traits needed to run a remodeling business.

Neither test asks questions about your actual constructions skills. We've done it this way for three reasons. First, we assume that if you're reading this book, you have most of the construction skills needed in the remodeling business. You can either do the work, know who to hire to get the job done, or you've got an armload of books to fill in your gaps.

Second, testing your skill as a remodeler can't be done in half a page. In fact, maybe it can't be done on paper. Besides, you probably know already if you have the building skills needed to go out on your own.

Third, construction skills probably aren't as important to a remodeler as business smarts. We know several very average remodelers who have strong companies because they have good employees and they keep tight control on the business end. We also know some highly skilled craftsmen who have had trouble as remodelers because they couldn't estimate accurately or run an efficient construction office.

Here's the test. Take a minute to read the following statements. If you strongly agree with a statement, give yourself 4 points; if you generally agree, 3 points; if you disagree somewhat, 2 points; if you strongly disagree, 1 point.

1) I am very confident of my skills. _____
2) I would gladly hire someone like me to do a job. _____
3) I'm not a clock watcher. In fact, I find it hard to forget about my work outside of working hours. _____
4) Hard work — not luck — builds businesses. _____
5) I'd rather work with a difficult, highly-skilled person than an easygoing, less skilled one. _____
6) If I put my mind to it, I can do just about anything. _____
7) I like being in charge. _____
8) I rarely feel helpless in dealing with life's problems. _____
9) I'm not as motivated by making a lot of money as I am by being good at what I do and being successful in my field. _____

If you scored between 27 and 36, you're probably motivated enough to run your own business. But what about running a remodeling business specifically? Do you have the temperament for it? Take the next test and score it the same way.

1) I am able to delegate responsibility. _____
2) I try hard to tackle the parts of a task I don't like first so I can get them out of the way. _____
3) I like the challenge of keeping on schedule with a job or task, and I'm usually able to meet the deadlines I've set. _____
4) I don't mind doing "cold" or follow-up calling on a prospect. _____
5) I'm organized in most things that I do. _____

6) I usually make a good impression on people and I'm able to maintain it. _____

7) I'm somewhat of a perfectionist and I take pride in my work. _____

8) I demand high quality work out of others. _____

If you scored between 24 and 32, you'll probably like running a remodeling company and probably can develop the business skills needed. If you scored much lower, be careful. If you still think you're perfectly suited to running your own business, at least look for a likeable partner who would ace the test.

The Good Side

If you scored high on both tests, you have a lot to look forward to. As we've already said, there are plenty of pluses to owning your own remodeling company.

Remodeling is far less volatile than new construction. Because of that, it promises to be a strong growth industry throughout the 1990s. It's cheaper to get into and stay in than new construction. Yet, if you run your company right, it can be very profitable.

Owning your own business can be satisfying as well as profitable. Your hours are more flexible than when you work for someone else. There's never an end to the variety and challenge you'll find in remodeling. And you also have a chance to deal with the public every day.

Last, but certainly not least, if you're honest and capable, the industry needs you!

The Bad Side

Of course there is one. But this is the only time we're going to mention it. There are a number of things that can be and have been very frustrating to us.

Remodeling, especially in the early years, doesn't give you a steady income. In fact, there can be plenty of times when you have no income at all! Twenty thousand may come in one month and nothing the next. If you don't know what your true expenses are, you can find yourself in one of those financial sinkholes we mentioned earlier.

In the decade we've been in business for ourselves, we've seen our Workers' Compensation costs go from 9 percent of every dollar paid to over 30 percent. Our liability premiums have gone up over 500 percent. Add to that the paperwork required by federal, state and local government and it can get pretty discouraging. We get really tired of being tied to a desk when we should be on the job site.

Anyone who's self-employed will tell you about their long work days and weekend work. The extra hours are especially discouraging when they're the result

"Your turn to do the paperwork this week."

of an estimate that was too low. You planned to hire a crew to do the work but ran over budget. So you're doing the work yourself.

Even if you're making great money on a job, you're probably the first one on the job in the morning and the last to leave. Every day. Every week. On every job.

The part we like best — the people part — can also give us the most headaches. You'll find yourself dealing with an interesting variety of people, some of whom are a bubble off plumb. Even if you can spot them ahead of time — and there are usually some warning shots fired — you may not always be able to turn down the work, especially in the beginning.

Maybe most difficult of all, when you first set up shop, you're the bookkeeper, estimator, carpenter, personnel manager, salesman, and diplomat. And you have to be good at all of them. Some people like the various hats, some hate it.

Don't despair, though. This book is going to explain how to avoid the most common problems.

Are You Up to the Challenge?

How do you take advantage of the pros without being burned out by the cons? It's not an easy question to answer. But let us offer four suggestions from some professionals who have been in the business a long time.

1) Keep an upbeat attitude by trying to look at the larger picture. Try not to sink down in the day-to-day grind. Remember that you're building a business. Good ones don't happen overnight. If you can make it past the first two years, you've done better than 50 percent of the people who try.

2) Educate yourself. Take advantage of seminars, trade books, and even local college business courses. The more you can learn about what you're doing, the better off you, your business, and your clients will be. None of it will be wasted, even if you should decide down the road that running your own company isn't for you.

3) Plan, plan, plan. Industry experts stress the importance of a game plan. Where do you want your company to be in a year? In five years? How can you get from here to there? It also helps you keep that larger picture in sight.

4) Don't take work home with you. We know this must sound like strange advice. But we believe it's important. If your office is in your home, it's hard to resist working on an estimate at night or getting your shop ready for the next day. Tell yourself that after 6 o'clock, your day is done. Do something that will energize you for the next work day. You shouldn't have to eat, sleep, and dream construction.

The Next Step

The next step is to actually set up your business. The first choice is the form of business ownership. There are three alternatives:

1) Sole proprietorship
2) Partnership
3) Corporation

Each has its own legal and tax distinctions. The following will give you a general idea of which legal form is best for you. Every state has slightly different requirements. Before you make the final decisions, talk with an attorney and an accountant.

Sole Proprietorship

A sole proprietorship is a business owned by one person. As the owner, or proprietor, all of the company income and expenses appear on Schedule C of your federal tax return. Company profit is your income and you pay tax on it every year. You're legally responsible for all company debts. As owner, you assume all liability not only for your actions, but also the actions of your employees.

In the past, the "actions of your employees" has usually meant what happens while your employees were working. If your foreman drops his hammer and gouges the floor, you're responsible for repairing it. If a careless toss of his lit cigarette burns down the house, you're liable. If he has an accident driving from one job site to another, you again are responsible.

Recently, though, that interpretation has been broadened. In 1987, an Oregon contractor was held liable to a third person who was raped by an employee. The employee had been under a lot of stress and had been taking illegal drugs. During his working hours he became "disoriented," forced his way into a house, and raped a woman. The court held the contractor responsible because he should have been able to see that the employee wasn't stable and was a danger to others.

This chilling example should tell you two things. One, your liability for employee actions is very broad. It's more than most of us might consider even logical. And two, until the courts interpret the law differently, you must be very careful about who works on your jobs and what instructions they are given.

There are four main advantages to running a sole proprietorship.

1) You have total control of all business decisions.
2) All of the profit goes directly into your pocket.
3) Setting up a sole proprietorship is quick and simple.
4) Business losses are completely deductible.

The disadvantages are these:

1) You're legally responsible for all company debts.
2) You're liable for all company acts and omissions, including those of your employees.
3) If your business income is high, you'll pay more tax than if the income was kept in a corporation.

Partnership

A partnership is a business owned and operated by two or more people. The partnership is formed by an agreement negotiated between the partners. There may be a large number of partners — 50 or more, or as few as two. Each partner owns a percentage of the business. It doesn't have to be an equal percentage, although it can be. One may own 50 percent, one 30 percent, and one 20. Profits and losses are usually divided based on the same percentage as ownership.

Each partner is also personally responsible for the company's debts. Liability is *not* proportionate to each partner's percentage of ownership. Sadly, this means that if the business goes under and your partners are broke, you may have to pay any debts the company still owes, even if your share of the business was very small.

Usually, each partner contributes something to the business in the form of money, skills, or property. It's up to the partners to decide what each partner has to contribute and what each partner receives in return.

Note this very carefully about partnerships. Unless the partnership agreement says otherwise, each partner can act as an agent for the business. Any partner may hire, fire, borrow money, sign contracts, or make any business decision. All of the other partners are bound by these actions, whether they were aware of them or not.

As a result, if you choose to set up a partnership, it's extremely important that your partnership agreement cover all rights and obligations of each partner. Usually you'll want to have an attorney draw up an agreement that covers all the issues. Even partnerships among good friends and relatives can end in acrimony and lawsuits when the agreement omits some important point. We've seen it happen and it isn't pretty. Sometimes it's harder — both financially and emotionally — to break up a partnership than it is to end a marriage. The more you plan ahead, the smaller your risk if things fall apart.

Partnerships work well for some people. But they aren't ideal for a construction business. You have all of the disadvantages of a sole proprietorship and few of the advantages of a corporation. Consider very carefully whether your prospective partners will be bringing into the company enough to make the risk worthwhile. At the very least, try to find someone who can provide something you don't have, like money, contacts, carpentry experience or sales skills.

Again, the advantages:

1) The sum is usually greater than its parts. With one or more partners, you should have plenty of capital and expertise.

2) If you lack startup capital or management skills, bringing in partners may be the quickest and easiest way to get the business going.

3) Except for the contract between the partners, it's a very simple form of ownership.

And the disadvantages:

1) All partners are liable for all company debts.

2) Business losses may be deducted only to the extent of your investment.

3) You're legally responsible for the actions of your employees.

4) You're responsible for the business decisions of the other partners whether you know about them or not.

5) A partnership is dissolved after a partner's death and must be reorganized.

6) If your business income is high, you'll pay more in taxes than if you operate as a corporation. The partnership files only an "information" return showing income and expenses. Whatever profit is earned is divided among the partners and each pays tax on those earnings.

Corporation

A corporation is legally separate from the people who own and operate it. It's like a third invisible person. It can bid, make contracts, receive loans, and will pay taxes on its earnings. It goes on living even when shareholders sell their stock or managers leave the company or die. A partnership, on the other hand, is dissolved on the death of a partner. A corporation makes it easy to continue business from year to year. Although it's a very minor benefit, in some states it's also possible to pass on a construction license within a corporation.

Most corporations raise money by selling shares or stock. If you decide to incorporate, be sure to authorize far more shares than you ever expect to issue. From that point on you can sell any of the shares that have been issued.

You may own all of the shares, in which case you control the business. However, if you want to raise additional money for your company, you may sell shares to others. In doing so, you're also selling part of your control. As long as you keep over 50 percent, though, you have the votes to control the company. Of course, most investors want some voice in how their company is run. Raising money will be easier if you're willing to share control.

If you incorporate, you become an employee of the corporation. Both your salary and the fringe benefits you receive will be expenses to the corporation — part of the cost of doing business. The corporation doesn't have to pay taxes on that money. But, of course, you do. The corporation pays income tax on the profits it makes every year, even if that money is used to buy equipment or vehicles or to carry inventory or accounts receivable. If part of that profit is distributed to stockholders, it's taxed twice, once as profit to the corporation and once as income to stockholders. That's one major disadvantage of incorporating.

Most companies choose to incorporate for two reasons. First, corporations are taxed differently and usually at a lower rate than individuals. As of this writing, corporations pay federal tax of only 15 percent on the first $50,000 of net income (profits). If you took that same $50,000 as additional personal income, your federal tax rate would probably be 28 percent. Keeping profits in the corporation lowers the tax so you can accumulate the money needed to run your company. Of course, that money isn't in your pocket yet. If and when the money does reach your pocket, you'll still have to pay the tax.

There's another reason why so many companies incorporate. Unlike sole proprietorships and partnerships, your personal liability is probably limited to what you've invested in the company. Both the tax advantages and limited liability need more explanation. First, taxes.

Tax Differences

There are two kinds of corporations. Although there are a few characteristics that distinguish the one from the other, for all practical purposes, the choice is usually based on tax considerations. The two types of corporations are type C corporations and type S corporations.

In a C corporation, the corporation pays taxes on its profits. When the corporation distributes some of those profits to shareholders in the form of dividends, shareholders pay a second tax on the distribution. That's why most small corporations don't pay dividends. It's double taxation. It saves tax to pay a larger salary (a deductible business expense to the corporation) and no dividends.

An S corporation blends the advantages of a partnership with the advantages of a corporation. You still have the legal protection from personal liability. But all income and losses are passed through to the stockholders who then have to pay the tax, even if they didn't actually receive any money. Stockholders pay tax on their share of profits at their regular tax rate. That's the same rate as would apply if the company were run as a proprietorship or partnership. In effect, you escape the double taxation problem that you would have in a C corporation.

Limited Liability

A corporation can sue and be sued. If it's set up and run correctly, the corporate shell protects shareholders from liability. To have this advantage, though, it's very important that you separate personal finances from corporate finances. If you don't, a court may decide that you and your corporation are one and the same, exposing you to personal liability for corporate debts.

Which Corporate Form Is Right for You?

Unless you expect to make a lot of money or have more than the S corporation's current legal limit of 50 shareholders, we recommend an S corporation over a C corporation. Most small, and certainly most new, corporations are not profitable enough to make it worth their while to choose a C over an S. The tax advantage of being an S over a C is less than it used to be with the most recent tax changes. Have both your attorney and your accountant make a recommendation. The IRS allows one switch from C to S or the reverse. After that, you need IRS approval to change again. With good advice, you can choose the one right for you and stick with it from the beginning.

The Final Word

Incorporation doesn't make you a better remodeler. It won't make your company any more profitable. In fact, we would suggest putting off the decision to incorporate until you've been doing business for a few years. There's no hurry. Your banker will insist on getting your personal guarantee on loans whether you're incorporated or not. So you'll probably be personally liable for most corporate debt anyway.

	Sole Proprietorship	Partnership	S Corporation	C Corporation
Financial liability limited to your investment?	No	No	Yes	Yes
Business losses may be deducted? Only to extent of investment.	All	All	All	All
Where does startup money come from?	You	You and partner	Shareholders	Shareholders
Easy to form?	Yes	Yes	No	No
Ease of succession?	Hard	Hard	Easy	Easy
Can license be passed on?	No	No	In some locations	In some locations
Who is legally responsible for decisions made?	You	You	Corporation	Corporation
Who is legally responsible for employees' actions?	You	You	Corporation	Corporation
Tax status?	Pay as individual	Pay as individual	Pay as individual	Pay as corp. & individual

Figure 1-1

Forms of ownership

There's another reason to delay incorporation. It's expensive, usually a thousand dollars or more. Better to spend your money on what will bring in more money than on legal formalities. Wait a few years until business is good and getting better. Then spend some money to form your corporation.

Figure 1-1 compares the three forms of ownership. Use it to compare the advantages and disadvantages of each form.

Choosing Your Name

No matter what form of business you choose to set up, there are some things a new remodeling company has to do. The first is probably choosing your company name. Does that sound easy? Choosing a name can be surprisingly hard. Consider the following.

1) You want a name that isn't already being used.

2) You want a name that identifies the kind of work you do.

3) You want a distinctive name that people remember.

4) Ideally, you want a name that has all three of the above.

Still think it's easy? Try this exercise. Look in your local Yellow Pages under home improvement and read through the listings. Now close the book and try to remember as many company names as you can. Do any stand out? If any have, try and figure out why. If none do, maybe you can better understand how difficult it is.

For most remodelers, the easiest solution is also the most common. How many company names included the name of the owner: John Doe Remodeling? A name like this satisfies the first two elements listed above, but doesn't do much for three and four. How many were Miller Kitchens? Or White Construction? The first is so specific a homeowner might wonder if you do baths or additions. The latter is so general you wonder if they do a little of everything — and none of it well. Nevertheless, you're probably better off being too general rather than too specific, especially if you're like most remodelers and you do all kinds of remodeling and some new construction. Certainly for your new construction work, a name that has *remodeling* in it wouldn't be a good choice.

Good names are hard to find. One of the few we know of is used by a highly successful competitor in our area. His last name is Klass and he goes by Klass-ique Remodeling. It's a clever play on his name that's worked well for him. For some reason, the same contractor uses the name "The Remodeler." We don't know the history of that, but suspect that more than once he's regretted the clumsiness of using two company names. His combined name neatly fits criteria 1, 2, 3, and 4: A unique name that identifies the scope of work and is easy to remember.

If you live in a small town, choosing a unique name for your business probably isn't very important. Most people are going to be calling Tom Smith, not Best Remodeling. In fact, they may be confused if you do choose a name that doesn't directly identify you. In an urban area, your company name may be far more important. And while a name alone can't sell a job, if it sticks in the consumer's mind, it may get you in the door to bid a project.

Of course, even the worst name won't sink your company. But it can be a handicap. One tendency we've noticed is that remodelers often end up using their own name one way or another, even if they've chosen a completely neutral name for their company. If Tom Smith has a good reputation, potential clients will probably hear and remember his name and not Best Construction. Best Construction may be a nuisance for Tom Smith because it confuses potential clients.

The solution? Choose one name and use it. Put it on your stationery, vehicles, business cards, caps, all your advertising. If you know who your company is, the public will have an easier time knowing too.

One last note. Don't worry about choosing a name that will be listed first in the Yellow Pages. As we'll discuss in the next chapter, a Yellow Pages listing is more a courtesy to your clients who already know you. Very few remodelers get much work from the Yellow Pages; certainly not enough to merit an awkward name.

Registering Your Company Name

Once you've selected a name, your next step is to claim it officially as yours. Now's the time you'll probably run across the letters *DBA*. DBA is short for *doing business as* and refers to your business name. Only sole proprietorships and partnerships are identified this way. Corporations are chartered by each state and don't need a DBA.

If your company is a proprietorship and the name is Best Remodeling, for legal purposes you're Tom Smith, DBA Best Remodeling.

The DBA information informs the public of the person (or persons) responsible for the business. Not all states or counties require you to register your DBA. If you live in one that does, registering a DBA usually requires only payment of a fee and completing a simple form. Usually you'll have to run a small ad in the local paper giving notice to the public of the name you're using. Check with your county clerk and with your state's Secretary of State office.

You can't use a name that's being used by another business. Likewise, once you have registered your name, no one else in your area of registration may legally use that name. If you find the name you've chosen is already registered by someone else, don't give it up immediately. Check with the business that registered the name. If they're no longer using the name, they'll probably be very willing to release it.

Corporate names have to be unique too. The Secretary of State or Department of Corporations in your state probably keeps a register of names currently in use. They probably have a phone number where you can check the availability of a name and have that name reserved while your corporation is being formed.

An Employer Identification Number

Once you have a name, you'll need an Employer Identification Number (EIN), sometimes called a Taxpayer's ID number. An EIN is required if you have employees. If you don't have employees, you may use your Social Security number. However, if you plan to ever hire anyone, you might as well file for one right away. It saves the hassle and confusion of changing over later.

It's very easy to get an EIN. Either visit your local IRS office or call the toll free number listed in your phone book. Ask for Form Number SS-4. See Figure 1-2. They'll ask whether you plan to set up a proprietorship, partnership, or corporation. If you're still thinking it over, they'll send you a packet for each. Fill out the right form and you'll be sent an EIN. Use this number when you pay federal taxes or need to correspond with the IRS. Many states use your federal EIN on state tax forms. Check with your state revenue service to see if you need a separate state number. If you do, you should be able to get a form from that office.

Getting a Business and Contractor's License

You may or may not need a business license to operate. Although most cities require a license for retail businesses, not all will require one for construction or remodeling companies. Check with your city or county clerk to see if you need one. Again, this license is easy to apply for and the fee minimal.

Form **SS-4**	**Application for Employer Identification Number**	Offical Use Only
(Rev. August 1988) Department of the Treasury Internal Revenue Service	(For use by employers and others. Please read the attached instructions before completing this form.) Please type or print clearly.	OMB No. 1545-0003 Expires 7-31-91

1 Name of applicant (True legal name. See instructions.)

2 Trade name of business if different from item 1

3 Executor, trustee, "care of name"

4 Mailing address (street address) (room, apt., or suite no.)

5 Address of business, if different from item 4. (See instructions.)

4a City, state, and ZIP code

5a City, state, and ZIP code

6 County and State where principal business is located

7 Name of principal officer, grantor, or general partner. (See instructions.) ▶

8 Type of entity (Check only one.) (See instructions.)
- ☐ Individual SSN _____
- ☐ Plan administrator SSN _____
- ☐ Partnership
- ☐ REMIC
- ☐ Personal service corp.
- ☐ Other corporation (specify) _____
- ☐ State/local government
- ☐ National guard
- ☐ Federal government/military
- ☐ Church or church controlled organization
- ☐ Other nonprofit organization (specify) _____ If nonprofit organization enter GEN (if applicable) _____
- ☐ Farmers' cooperative
- ☐ Estate
- ☐ Trust
- ☐ Other (specify) ▶

8a If a corporation, give name of foreign country (if applicable) or state in the U.S. where incorporated ▶ | Foreign country | State

9 Reason for applying (check only one)
- ☐ Started new business
- ☐ Changed type of organization (specify) ▶
- ☐ Hired employees
- ☐ Purchased going business
- ☐ Created a pension plan (specify type) ▶
- ☐ Created a trust (specify) ▶
- ☐ Banking purpose (specify) ▶
- ☐ Other (specify) ▶

10 Business start date or acquisition date (Mo., day, year) (See instructions.)

11 Enter closing month of accounting year (See instructions.)

12 First date wages or annuities were paid or will be paid (Mo., day, year). **Note:** *If applicant is a withholding agent, enter date income will first be paid to nonresident alien. (Mo. , day, year).* ▶

13 Enter highest number of employees expected in the next 12 months. **Note:** *If the applicant does not expect to have any employees during the period, enter "0."* ▶

Nonagricultural	Agricultural	Household

14 Does the applicant operate more than one place of business? . . . ☐ Yes ☐ No
If "Yes," enter name of business. ▶

15 Principal activity or service (See instructions.) ▶

16 Is the principal business activity manufacturing?. . . ☐ Yes ☐ No
If "Yes," principal product and raw material used. ▶

17 To whom are most of the products or services sold? Please check the appropriate box. ☐ Business (wholesale)
☐ Public (retail) ☐ Other (specify) ▶ ☐ N/A

18 Has the applicant ever applied for an identification number for this or any other business?. . . ☐ Yes ☐ No
Note: *If "Yes," please answer items 18a and 18b.*

18a If the answer to item 18 is "Yes," give applicant's true name and trade name, if different when applicant applied.

True name ▶ Trade name ▶

18b Enter approximate date, city, and state where the application was filed and the previous employer identification number if known.

Approximate date when filed (Mo., day, year)	City, and state where filed	Previous EIN

Under penalties of perjury, I declare that I have examined this application, and to the best of my knowledge and belief, it is true, correct, and complete. | Telephone number (include area code)

Name and title (please type or print clearly) ▶

Signature ▶ Date ▶

Note: *Do not write below this line. For official use only.*

Please leave blank ▶	Geo.	Ind.	Class	Reason for applying

For Paperwork Reduction Act Notice, see instructions. ✴U.S. Government Printing Office: 1988-523-133/00332 Form **SS-4** (Rev. 8-88)

Figure 1-2

Application for Employer Identification Number

Licensing is a hot issue for remodelers all over the country. About one-half the states currently require contractors to have a license. Some licenses are not much more than a business license: fill out the form and pay the fee. Others are much more demanding. Some require extensive testing, bonding, and proof of Workers' Compensation, liability insurance, and financial stability. And the test and application fees can be steep. To put teeth into the law, some states won't allow unlicensed contractors to sue for payment under a construction contract that exceeds $600. A few states use part of the license fee to help consumers who have claims against insolvent contractors.

Florida is one of the more regulated states. The license exam is a two-day, 16-hour open book test. Less than a third of the people who take the test pass the first time around. The Florida system is also one of the more expensive. Books for the test cost $630, an application costs $175.

Many remodelers object to licensing laws. They feel government control of the industry is heavy-handed and the industry could do a better job of regulating itself. Many also believe that licensing is too costly for the small remodeler. And these costs are eventually passed on to the client. Others complain that the tests don't do any good. They don't test a remodeler's character or his construction skill. More important, states don't enforce the license law. There are too many unlicensed contractors running around making good money.

But there's another side to this debate. Licensing can help increase professionalism in the industry and can help to weed out the fly-by-nighter. Usually, states with solid testing and enforcement have more qualified construction contractors and fewer marginal operators.

In spite of the negatives, licensing is here to stay. If testing and enforcement are credible, then licensing is probably good for the industry. If they're not, licensing is just another burden you have to carry.

If you live in an area or state which requires a license, check with your local building department, county clerk, or contractor's license board for information on how to get licensed. All the tests we're aware of are open book, but you still need to study the material so you know where to look for answers. Take the requirements seriously, even if the testing authority doesn't. Passing the exam will make you a more qualified professional in the industry.

The Certification Option

If you don't live in an area that requires a license, you have another option. Both the National Association of the Remodeling Industry (NARI) and the National Association of Home Builders (NAHB) Remodelor's Council offer certification programs that may interest you.

The NARI program is for an individual, not a company, and must be renewed every year. The exam, which is open book, covers 21 areas of remodeling. Testing is scheduled several times each year in major cities. Again, this isn't cheap. The initial cost runs $340 for NARI members, and $600 for non-members. Re-certification costs $75 and $225 respectively.

In addition to the exam, you must have at least seven years' experience in the remodeling industry. You must also prove that your business dealings meet NARI standards.

The Remodelor's Council certification program is similar. For more information on either certification program contact the executive director of NARI or the executive director of NAHB Remodelor's Council. Their addresses are listed in Chapter 16 at the end of this book.

Opening a Business Checking Account

Banks love accounts opened by remodelers. They usually come with high cash flow, operating loans, and construction loans. Some bank in your community will probably offer very good terms on a checking account if you ask. At the very least, ask for free checking and no holds on local checks. You may also want a line of credit and a check guarantee.

You'll probably find that a small bank will serve you better than a large one. The first six years in business we banked at one of the largest banks in town. We had only one account with them — our company checking account. But they could never seem to understand that we were a business and had special requirements. In fact, they didn't seem to understand what we needed from our bank. We switched to a smaller bank and were amazed at how helpful our banker could be. Another advantage of a small bank? Once they got to know us, they sent a considerable amount of work our way.

Getting Bonds and Insurance

Although bonding is a form of insurance, it has one very important difference. Insurance policies cover losses that you can't absorb yourself. A bond, on the other hand, guarantees that money is available to do what's required. A bond is the bonding company's promise to pay. That makes getting a bond like getting a loan. You'll get a bond only for about as much as you could borrow. In a sense, the bond fee is like a loan commitment fee. A bonding company won't agree to back you unless it knows you're good for the money. If you don't perform as promised, the bonding company has to make good. Then they'll try to recover their loss by suing you.

Unless a state requires a bond to get a license, many small remodelers will go through their whole career without getting bonded. Bonds are usually required for certain kinds of government work and most larger commercial and industrial jobs.

There are several types of bonds.

1) *License bond* — This is the most common kind of bond. Many states now require a small license bond. This bond usually guarantees you'll do work according to code. It does not guarantee anything about completion or payments. Although the cost for a license bond may vary from state to state, it'll run around $50 and will need to be renewed every year.

2) *Bid bond* — On larger jobs the contract documents may require that either a bid bond or a certified check for 5 percent of the contract price be submitted with the bid. Usually the bid bond has to be for 10 percent of the bid total. The check or bid bond guarantees that if you win the bid, you'll sign the contract for your bid amount. A bonding company won't issue a bid bond for a job unless they're willing to write performance and payment bonds for the same job.

   If your bid is the lowest but you're not willing to sign the construction contract, the measure of damages may be the difference between what you bid and the next lowest bid. This amount usually won't be more than your bid bond.

   Bid bonds are usually written without charge because the bonding company has little or no liability until you win the bid. Then they get paid for the performance and payment bonds you need.

3) *Performance and payment bonds* — The performance part of the bond covers the owner if you don't complete the project according to specifications. The payment bond guarantees that all of your labor and material bills will be paid so there's no supplier or mechanic's lien on the project. If you're bonded through an insurance company, the cost of these bonds will usually be 1 to 2 percent of the total contract price. If you can't qualify for a bond with commercial insurance carriers, the Small Business Administration (SBA) has a program that may qualify you for bonding. The usual cost is from 2 to 3 percent of the contract price. If the job total is $100,000, your bond cost will be $1,000 to $2,000 with an insurance company or $2,000 to $3,000 with the SBA.

4) *Maintenance bond* — This bond assures the owner that you'll fix all defects in your work and materials for a period of time after work is completed. The usual period is no more than three years.

5) *Supply and subcontractor bonds* — These bonds are like the contractor's payment bond. They guarantee that the sub's labor and material bills will be paid. The bond is paid for by the sub or supplier and is included in the cost of their bids.

Your insurance agent can help you get bonded. There is no up-front charge for this, but there *is* a lot of paperwork — about like applying for a loan. If the insurance company approves you, you'll be charged only for the bonds you require. Figure 1-3 shows a sample application form. As you can see, applying for a bond isn't easy. The process usually takes from three to six weeks to process.

Liability and Workers' Comp Insurance

These are very important to your business. Even if the law doesn't require you to carry general liability insurance or Workers' Compensation, you'd be crazy not to. Every remodeler has a high level of exposure to risk. If you don't pay an insurance company for coverage and something happens, you'll lose everything you have. And maybe more.

We'll explain both of these in more detail in a later chapter.

The Final Checklist

Here is a brief checklist of the things necessary for starting your own remodeling business.

1) Choose a business form (proprietorship, partnership, or corporation).
2) Select a name.
3) Register the name.
4) Get an Employer Identification Number (EIN).
5) Get a business license.
6) Get a contractor's license or NARI certification.
7) Open a business checking account.
8) Get the bonds you need.
9) Buy business liability insurance and Workers' Compensation coverage.

What About a Franchise?

We can't end this first chapter without talking about franchises. A franchise is the right to market a product or service under a specific name in a given area. A franchisor is the one who sells the rights; a franchisee is the one who buys the rights. It's an option that has some attraction, especially if you feel really unsure

CONTRACT, BID OR MAINTENANCE BOND APPLICATION   Bond No. _____

STATE SURETY COMPANY

_____
Agent

NOTE

(a) Copy of contract, applicant's current financial statement (Form 2545) and contractor's information blank (Form 2592) must accompany this application, if not previously furnished.

(b) All questions must be answered fully.

(c) The Company reserves the right to decline this application and to withhold reason for declination, as all information relative thereto is regarded as confidential.

1. Full Name of Applicant (If corporation, give exact title)

2. Business Address (Street, City and State)

3. Name and Address of Obligee to Whom Bond is to be Given

4. Concise Description of Proposed Work and Location

5. Contract or Bid Price   Date Bids to be Opened   Date of Award

6. The following kinds and amounts of bonds are required:

Bid Bond	Performance Bond	Labor, Material Bond	Maintenance Bond	Other
$	$	$	$	$

7. Time for Completion | Penalty for Delay | Terms of Payment and Retained Percentage

8. List all other bids, including highest and lowest. (If more than four bids, tabulate on separate sheet and attach.)

NAME	ADDRESS	AMOUNT OF BID

9. Name and Address of Architect or Engineer in Charge

10. His Estimate of Cost of Work   Your Estimate of Cost

11. Will you sublet any part of the work? If so, state nature and amount. _____

_____
(Tabulate on separate sheet if necessary)

12. Will subcontractors be required to give bonds? _____

13. Terms and duration of guarantees of efficiency, maintenance and repairs, if any, in contract or specifications _____

_____ Is bond to cover this? _____

SSC 2506 (Rev. 7/77)   (OVER)

Figure 1-3

Contract, bid or maintenance bond application

Page 2

NOTE: If a fully completed application has been previously furnished us, only question 16 need be answered.

14. Number of Years Experience as a Contractor   (For Yourself)   (For Others)

15. List the most important contracts you have completed during the past five years:

KIND OF WORK	LOCATION	NAME AND ADDRESS OF ARCHITECT OR ENGINEER	CONTRACT PRICE	YEAR COMPLETED

16. List of contracts now being performed, with location, amount and percentage completed, including outstanding bids.

NATURE OF WORK AND OWNER	LOCATION	CONTRACT PRICE	% COMPLETED	EXPECTED COMPLETION DATE

17. Have You Applied to Any Other Company For This Bond? (If so, state when, to whom, and with what result?)

18. Have You Furnished Bid or Performance Bonds Before? (If so, give names of surety companies and state what bonds are now outstanding)

19. Have You Ever Failed to Complete Any Work Awarded to You? (If so, give details)

20. Have You Received Financial Assistance From Your Present or Previous Surety?

21. References. Give name of your banker, an architect or engineer, an owner, also supply houses who have granted you credit.

NAME	OCCUPATION	ADDRESS (Give Street Address, Town, State and Zip Code)

22. Have you, or if a firm or corporation, has said firm or corporation, ever been bankrupt or insolvent? _____

Figure 1-3 (cont'd)

Contract, bid or maintenance bond application

Page 3

AGREEMENT

THIS AGREEMENT entered into by and between State Surety Company, Des Moines, Iowa hereinafter called the "Surety" and the principal and other signatories herein sometimes called the "Indemnitors".

WITNESSETH:

In consideration of the surety executing the bond or bonds herein applied for or procuring the execution thereof, the principal and the indemnitors, hereinafter referred to as "Indemnitors," for themselves, their heirs, their executors, their administrators, their successors and assigns, jointly and severally convenant and agree as follows:

1. That the statements contained in the foregoing Application are represented by the indemnitors as true and correct and are made without reservation for the purpose of inducing the surety to become surety on the bond or bonds herein applied for.

2. If the application is for a bid bond and the principal is awarded the contract, that said principal shall not be obligated to secure the final bond or bonds from the surety nor shall the surety be obligated to sign or procure such bond or bonds.

3. The indemnitors will pay to the surety at its home office the premium, or premiums, including all additional premiums, if any applicable to the bond, or bonds, herein applied for, in the amount or amounts set forth at the rate or rates filed with the State in which the bond or bonds were executed.

4. The indemnitors will indemnify and save the surety harmless from and against every claim, demand, liability, cost, charge, judgment and expense which the surety may incur or be obligated to pay as a consequence of having executed, or procured the execution of such bond or bonds, or any renewal or continuation thereof or substitutes therefor, in making any investigation on account thereof, in prosecuting or defending any action brought in connection therewith, obtaining a release therefrom and enforcing any of the agreements herein contained, including and not limited to attorneys' fees and expenses of attorneys. Indemnitors further agree to pay the reasonable fees of attorneys in bringing any action for the enforcement of indemnitors' liability to the surety arising under this agreement. In the event of payment by the surety the indemnitors agree that the voucher or other evidence of such payment shall be prima facie evidence of the propriety thereof and the amount thereof.

5. If the surety shall set up a reserve to cover any claim, suit or other liability arising under such bond or bonds, the indemnitors will, immediately upon demand, deposit with the surety a sum of money equal to such reserve or securities acceptable to the surety. That in such property, the surety shall have a security interest and the surety shall have the rights of a secured party under the Uniform Commercial Code, as adopted by the state of Iowa, and it is further agreed that reasonable notice shall be satisfied by giving to the person who deposits such collateral security, five days' notice of any contemplated action or disposition.

6. The Surety is authorized and empowered, without notice to or knowledge of the Indemnitors to assent to any change whatsoever in the Bonds, and/or any contracts referred to in the Bonds, and/or in the general conditions, plans and/or specifications accompanying said contracts, including, but not limited to, any change in the time for the completion of said contracts and to payments or advances thereunder before the same may be due, and to assent to or take any assignment or assignments, to execute or consent to the execution of any continuations, extensions or renewals of the Bonds and to execute any substitute or substitutes therefor, with the same or different conditions, provisions and obligees and with the same or larger or smaller penalties, it being expressly understood and agreed that the Indemnitors shall remain bound under the terms of this Agreement even though any such assent by the Surety does or might substantially increase the liability of said Indemnitors.

7. The company shall have the right and is hereby authorized, but not required:

(a) To adjust, settle or compromise any claim, demand, suit or judgment upon said bond or bonds or any of them, unless the indemnitors shall request the surety to litigate such claim or demand, or to defend such suit or to appeal from such judgment, and shall deposit with the surety at the time of such request, cash or collateral satisfactory to it in kind and amount to be used in paying any judgment or judgments rendered or that may be rendered, with interest, costs and attorneys' fees; that such collateral shall be held as provided in paragraph five hereof;

(b) To fill up any blanks left herein, and to correct any errors in the description of any of said bond or bonds, or in any name or names, it being hereby agreed that such insertions or corrections, when so made, shall be prima facie correct.

8. The surety is hereby authorized, but not required to, make or guarantee advances or loans for the purposes of the contract without the necessity of seeing to the application thereof; it being understood that the amount of all such advances or loans, unless repaid with legal interest by the principal to the surety when due, shall be conclusively presumed to be a loss hereunder.

9. Indemnitors do hereby convey and assign unto the surety any and all payments, funds, money or property due or to become due the indemnitors under the contract and general intangibles which arise during the performance of the contract which required the bond or bonds applied for, and the indemnitors do hereby assign, transfer and set over to the surety all their right, title and interest in and to all subcontracts let in connection therewith, all machinery, plant equipment, tools and materials which shall be upon the site of work or elsewhere needed for the performance of such contracts including all material ordered for such contracts and the indemnitors do hereby authorize the surety to endorse in the name of the payee and collect any check, draft, warrant or other instrument made or issued in payment of any such sum and to disburse the proceeds thereof.

10. In the event the principal under any bond written as a result of this application:

(a) Abandons, forfeits, or breaches the contract or (b) breaches any bond given in connection therewith or any other bond or bonds executed or procured by the surety or (c) fails, neglects, or refuses to pay for labor and materials used in the prosecution of the contract or (d) if an individual dies, absconds, or cannot be found by the usual methods of communications, or is incarcerated or (e) have proceedings instituted alleging that the principal is insolvent; or (f) have proceedings initiated, the effect of which may be to deprive the principal of the use of any part of the equipment used in connection with the work under the contract so as to hinder, delay or impede the normal and satisfactory progress of the work; the surety shall have the right, but not the obligation, to take possession of the work under the contract and at the expense of the indemnitors to complete the contract or cause or consent to the completion thereof.

11. The surety, and its designated agents, shall, at any and all reasonable times, have free access to the books and records of the indemnitors.

12. The surety shall have the right at any and all reasonable times to ascertain from the bank, banks, or other depository with which the indemnitors do business, the amounts standing to the credit of the indemnitors, and the indemnitors' indebtedness to such bank, banks, or other depository and such are authorized and directed to supply the surety with such information.

13. Separate suits may be brought hereunder as causes of action accrue and the bringing of suit or recovery of judgment upon any cause of action shall not prejudice or bar the bringing of other suits upon other causes of action, whether theretofore or thereafter arising. Said actions may be commenced at the discretion of the surety in the Courts of the County or judicial district wherein the Capitol is located of the State wherein the indemnitor against whom action is brought resides.

14. Nothing herein contained shall be considered or construed to waive, abridge, or diminish any right or remedy which the surety executing such bond or bonds might have if this instrument were not executed. Should any clause or any part of this agreement be held to be void or unenforceable, such finding shall not invalidate the remaining covenants contained in this agreement.

15. If the surety procures the execution of such bonds by other companies, or executes such bonds with co-sureties, or reinsures any portions of such bonds with reinsuring companies, then all the terms and conditions of this Agreement shall apply and operate for the benefit of such other companies, co-sureties and reinsurers as their interests may appear.

16. The undersigned expressly agree and stipulate that their homestead(s) shall be liable for any and all indebtedness hereunder and that their homestead(s) may be sold on execution to satisfy any indebtedness arising under this agreement or any judgment rendered thereon.

17. The word indemnitors, or personal pronouns used to refer to said word, shall apply regardless of number or gender, and to individuals, partnerships or corporation as the circumstances require.

18. That this agreement contains the whole of the agreement of the parties hereto, and any subsequent agreement of the parties hereto shall be only in writing, and signed by the President, a Vice-President, Secretary or an Assistant Secretary of the Surety.

19. The Indemnitors do hereby waive the benefit of any statutory limitation of liability of indemnitors as contained in the statutes of any state.

Continued on page 4

Figure 1-3 (cont'd)

Contract, bid or maintenance bond application

Page 4

AGREEMENT – Continued

20. That this Agreement shall constitute a Security Agreement to the Surety and also a Financing Statement, both in accordance with the provisions of the Uniform Commercial Code of every jurisdiction wherein such Code is in effect and may be so used by the Surety without in any way abrogating, restricting or limiting the rights of the Surety under this Agreement or under law, or in equity.

21. Waiver of Exemptions. Each of the Undersigned does, jointly and severally, bind his or her property and does hereby release and abandon, as to the Surety all right to claim any property, including their homestead, as exempt from levy, execution sale or other legal process under the law of any state, province or other government, as against the rights of the Surety to proceed against the Undersigned for indemnity hereunder. The Undersigned also waive the provisions of Sec. 204.075 of the Wisconsin Statutes and any similar provision in any other jurisdiction.

PLEASE BE SURE application is dated, witnessed or attested, signed and notarized in full.

This Agreement shall be effective this _____ day of _____ 19_____.

APPLICANT

_____ (SEAL)

Witness or Attest:

_____

NOTARY ACKNOWLEDGMENT of applicant's signature.

By _____
(Officer's Name and title if a corporation)

State of _____

County of _____ } SS

Subscribed and sworn to before me this_____day of _____ 19 _____ NOTARY PUBLIC

(SEAL)

INDEMNITY

In consideration of the aforesaid Surety executing the bond or instrument herein applied for, the undersigned join or joins in the foregoing indemnity agreement, and agree or agrees to be jointly and severally bound thereunder, and by all of the terms, covenants, and conditions thereof; the undersigned admits and declares that it has a material, substantial, and financial interest in the performance of the obligation which the bond or instrument applied for is given to secure, or in execution of the bond or instrument applied for, and asserts that if a corporation or a partnership is fully empowered to obligate itself hereby.

INDEMNITORS:

WITNESS: _____

_____ (SEAL)
Signature

_____
Address

WITNESS: _____

_____ (SEAL)
Signature

_____
Address

WITNESS: _____

_____ (SEAL)
Signature

_____
Address

NOTARY ACKNOWLEDGMENT of Indemnitors' Signatures.

State of _____

County of _____ } SS

Subscribed and sworn to before me this _____ day of _____ 19____ _____ NOTARY PUBLIC
(SEAL)

WITNESS AND NOTARIZATION MUST BE COMPLETED FOR INDEMNITORS' SIGNATURES

Figure 1-3 (cont'd)

Contract, bid or maintenance bond application

about your entry into the remodeling market. After all, what worked for McDonald's and 7-Eleven might also work for construction!

If this book had been written five years ago, there might have been a full chapter on franchising. Five years from now, it may not be mentioned at all. At least, that's the direction we see it heading.

In the early 1980s experts predicted that remodeling franchises would swallow up a large part of all remodeling business. Nearly one-half the new construction businesses fail in the first two years. The survival rate among franchises is usually above 90 percent. It seemed like franchising was just what the remodeling industry needed.

Somehow it never happened. After nearly a decade, there are at most 2,000 companies nationwide that have bought franchises. That 2,000 includes everything from remodeling to gutter cleaning companies. Out of the 200,000 to 300,000 home improvement companies in the U.S., that isn't much. Nor do they have much impact in any market area.

Remodeling franchises haven't spread like wildfire because the public hasn't gone for it. People may be willing to tolerate large, faceless companies to build their houses, but they seem to prefer a small, hands-on kind of company to do their alterations. People eat at McDonald's because they know it's going to look, taste, and cost about the same no matter if they're in Matoon, Illinois, or Garden City, Kansas. But renovating a home isn't like catching a quick bite. You don't do it that often, so you better find someone who can do it right.

Most of those who predicted the spread of remodeling franchises were experts on franchising and marketing. They knew very little or nothing about the difficulties and quirks of remodeling. As a result, most of the early boom fizzled fast. It turned out that teaching a teenager to flip hamburgers or run a cash register was very different from teaching someone to patch drywall or trim.

Mr. Build is one of the biggest franchisors, with hundreds of franchisees. It was started by the same people who started the Century 21 real estate franchise. While marketing and sales are vital to real estate, they are only a small part of remodeling. No matter how much help the parent company can be in those areas, it's much harder to standardize construction techniques and regulate quality when the home office is 2,000 miles away.

There are some advantages to franchising. A good franchisor will offer good training on marketing and management. You'll get good quality advertising and an effective referral system. Unlike the early franchise operations, most of the companies now franchising in the remodeling field are run by true remodeling experts — people who have built successful remodeling companies. Most have experience and good advice to share.

Keep in mind, though, that most franchisors now try to avoid new startup companies. They prefer to sign up well-established firms. They want established successes, not companies that require time, energy and training. That alone says a lot about the value of a franchise to you.

The biggest advantage a franchisor can give you is access to information. But that information will cost you. Some franchises charge as little as $1,000 for the name, but then several thousand more to cover setup costs, and either a flat fee or a percentage of your gross take each month for advertising and management. Others will charge as much as $100,000 plus the monthly fees. For money like that you'll get a "turn-key" operation. One that should have retail space, trucks, computers, and a well-trained staff.

Remember that the franchise fee is in addition to your normal startup cost and regular overhead. How much will you have to add to bids to cover the extra overhead? Can you be competitive in your area if you have to charge this amount?

If you're still interested in buying a franchise, consider the options carefully. At the end of this chapter you'll find names, addresses and a brief sketch of some of the more solid franchisors. If you contact these people, ask some of the questions listed below. Don't be satisfied until you get some straight answers. After all, you're entitled to know what you're buying. Be especially wary of new or very small franchisors. Of the two dozen or more remodeling franchisors that have been started in the last ten years, probably only half are still around. Of those, only two have more than 100 franchisees nationwide. Eight report fewer than 25.

Questions to get you started:

1) How long has the franchisor been in business?

2) How many active franchisees are there?

3) How many franchisees are no longer with this franchise?

4) How much is the initial fee?

5) What additional fees are there? Will they go up?

6) What do I get in return for these fees?

7) What kind of information will I get? (Can you get the same information cheaper at the library, bookstore, or from a construction book publisher such as Craftsman, Walker, or R.S. Means?)

8) What kind of training will I get? (Can you get the same training at NARI or NAHB seminars or local college night classes?)

9) What are my ongoing costs?

10) If the franchisor goes under or pulls out of my area, will I get my money back?

11) What does this franchise have to offer that others don't?

Here are names and addresses of franchisors that were active at the time this book was written (Fall 1990):

Paul W. Davis Systems
5111-6 Baymeadows Road
Jacksonville, FL 32217

Contact them at (904) 730-0320. Specializes in insurance restoration work. Most franchisees are located in the eastern half of the U.S. Cost is an initial cash investment of $20,000 with additional $25,000 needed for operating capital. Monthly fees start at 2.5 percent of gross.

Four Seasons Greenhouses
5005 Veterans Memorial Highway
Holbrook, NY 11741

Contact them at (516) 563-4000. Sells franchises for design and remodeling centers and specialty trade franchises (plumbers, electricians, carpenters, etc.). The initial cost is $50,000 to $100,000 for design centers and $3,000 for specialty trade franchises.

Mr. Build Handyman Services, Inc.
Glastonbury Corporate Center
628 Hebron Ave.
Glastonbury, CT 06033

Phone (203) 657-3607. Mr. Build franchisees cover a whole range of services in addition to remodeling. Fees start at $3,000 with $600 or more in monthly service and advertising fees.

2

Knocking on Opportunity's Door

You're all set up. You've chosen your business form and your name and obtained the needed licenses and insurance. Now all you need is work.

Waiting for the phone to ring can be the most frustrating part of running your own business, especially in the beginning. For most established remodeling companies, anywhere from 75 to 95 percent of their business is repeat or referral business. That's great if you've been around five or ten years, but what do you do the first few years when you need the business the most? Advertising and public relations efforts will help, but even before you spend money on them, there are some places to go looking for jobs. And before you go looking, there are some things you'll need to do.

People like doing business with people they perceive as being like themselves.

The Professional Look

You may be the best remodeler in town, but if you look like you just stepped off the job site, the people with the best jobs won't take you seriously. Any time you meet with a client or a potential client, take a minute first to think about how you look. There is a certain image that you want to project. What is it? Are you doing it? What subtle messages are you giving the client?

How Are You Dressed?

Many people think a remodeler is nothing more than a handyman. A handyman is just fine if that's what you truly are. But people don't hire handymen to do a $25,000 kitchen remodel or a $50,000 addition. They hire someone who sounds and looks like he runs a successful remodeling company. They hire someone who looks like he's been around a few years and plans to be in business a few more. If you wear dirty jeans, a shirt half tucked in, and work boots that are scuffed and worn, what image are you projecting? Do you look like you would do a clean, meticulous job? Or do you look like your best skill is demolition? Would you hire someone who looks like you?

You don't have to wear a three piece suit when you call on a client. In fact, in many parts of the country, that might seem just as out of place as dirty, torn jeans. You should, however, always wear clean, neat clothes. Your hair, including beard and mustache, and nails should be clean and neatly trimmed. In the summer, you won't go wrong in slacks and a knit or cotton shirt. In winter, throw on a sweater. The further east you go, the more formal you can dress without looking odd. In the Midwest and West, you can stay casual. When in doubt, dress up rather than down.

Always consider who your client is. If you're meeting with a banker to do work on his repossessed properties, a tie and a sport coat wouldn't be out of line. He'll view you as a peer, instead of some guy who's willing to crawl under a house to fix the foundation — even if that's what you'll be doing. If you're meeting with a rancher, clean jeans and cowboy boots would make both of you more comfortable. He's not going to give you the time of day if you look like you're afraid to get a little mud on your shoes. People like doing business with people they perceive as being like themselves.

How Do You Sound?

While your personal appearance is the most obvious part of the impression you make, there are other areas you need to be aware of as well. Your voice tone and quality will be remembered long after the client has forgotten the main points of your pitch. Be sincere and you'll sound sincere. Be respectful and you'll sound respectful. Never call a woman "honey" or any other endearment. Such condescensions will lose you even the chance for an appointment, let alone the chance to give an estimate or do the work.

Poor grammar or swearing also leave an impression. Both suggest a less educated, less professional person. True or not, they also suggest less competence. As in the way you dress, the high-end client may not see you as a peer and will find someone he *does* see as a peer to do his work.

If you have trouble speaking standard English, pick up a self-help grammar book and work on it. You have nothing to lose by doing it. You'll never miss out on a job because you use better grammar than your potential client, and you'll have a better shot at the high-end work.

Swearing is another whole issue. You may think that swearing adds color and character to your speech, but many people are offended by it. Others, who may even use profanity themselves, may see it as less professional in you. If it's so much a part of your speech that you can't stop swearing altogether, at the very least, make an attempt to do it less than the client does.

Likewise, a little humor always helps, but never use off-color jokes. That kind of humor is not only unnecessary, but it can be highly offensive. Even a client who always has a dirty joke ready won't necessarily accept it as professional conduct for you to do the same.

What Kind of Paper Trail Are You Leaving?

Just as it's important for you to look and sound professional, it's equally important for your company literature to look good. This is what the client will have in hand after you've left. If it looks good, he'll be more likely to call you.

You'll want to hand a business card to the client at some time during the meeting. Whatever you leave with him, be it a well-designed brochure or a folder of information, it should have a business card stapled or inserted in it as well.

Whether you use a brochure or folder, it should clearly explain the kind of services you offer and what makes you unique in your ability to provide those services. Include, too, a resume and several letters of recommendation. All of this will be explained in more detail later in the chapter.

How's the Rest of the Picture?

Even your vehicle makes a statement about you. It doesn't have to be the newest, the best, or the fanciest, but it should be clean and in reasonably good shape. Some clients won't like it if you're driving a brand new, expensive truck or a Mercedes. It implies that you're making a killing in construction, and who wants to be someone's victim? Other people like the idea they're doing business with a successful company. The flashier the vehicle, the better. Most of your potential business will probably fall into the former group. If you find yourself doing business with the Mercedes crowd, go ahead and drive one. But be aware that you'll be losing the bottom 99 percent of the market.

How do all the other incidentals look? Is your briefcase in good shape? Are your literature, contracts, and drawings clean and neat or do they look like they've been riding around on the floor of your truck for a week?

Are you organized? Did you come prepared for the meeting or do you have to borrow a pen or paper? Even these little things leave a subtle impression. Make sure you're leaving the right one.

The Extra Edge

Membership in the professional organizations of the remodeling industry can also give you an extra edge over the competition. The Remodelors' Council of the NHBA, NARI, and, if you specialize in kitchens and baths, the National Kitchen and Bath Association (NKBA) are all respected organizations. The Better Business Bureau and the local Chamber of Commerce can also give you more credibility. Membership in these groups will tell your client that you are serious about being a part of the remodeling industry and that you support your community.

Even if you don't join, though, you can take advantage of the many seminars and industry shows that the remodeling organizations promote. They vary in value from area to area, but overall tend to be useful. If you do decide to join any of them, keep in mind that they're also the political arm of the construction industry. These are the groups that lobby for legislation favorable to remodelers. Sometimes that politicking gets in the way of industry education.

Do You Make the Client Feel Respected?

Finally, all of the above will get you nowhere if you don't return phone calls or aren't punctual. Make it company policy from the first day you're in business to return calls the same day they come in, even if it's only to say you haven't had a chance to work on an estimate. If you don't return calls, you're telling potential clients you don't care whether you have their business or not.

Likewise, if you're late for appointments, you're telling a client you're more important than he is. Don't kid yourself — you're not. Try to be at every appointment five minutes before the starting time. Those few minutes will give you a chance to go over your notes and catch your breath. If you're running late, stop and call. The extra two minutes it takes is worth the message it sends: you know how valuable a client's time is. This is especially true when you're meeting someone with a busy schedule.

The Bottom Line

The first impression you give is going to be the most lasting. It will also be the hardest to change. The bottom line, then, is to appear to be as professional as you can. Right or wrong, a client will perceive that the work you do will only be as meticulous as you look and sound. If you don't care about how you look, he'll wonder if you'd care about the finer details of his job.

People like to do business with successful companies. They see it as a reflection on themselves. Looking professional and successful won't guarantee you a contract, but it never, ever will prevent you from getting one.

What Do You Have to Offer?

You may think you're ready to hit the streets, but you're still not. Before you call on your first potential client, you'd better know what you're selling. Of course, you know all about remodeling and repair. Of course, you're honest and competent and reasonable in your prices. You know all of that, but how can you convince anyone else? Better be prepared for some tough questions.

"Why should I put you on my contractors' list?"

"What makes you think you're better than the guy I'm already using?"

"What kind of experience have you had doing this kind of work?"

"Why do you think you can do it better for less money?"

"How do I know I can trust you with my projects?"

Can you answer these questions convincingly? If *you* can't think of good reasons why you're better, you'll certainly never convince anyone else that you are.

You're selling your company; you're selling your services; and most of all, you're selling yourself. You'd better know the product well!

To help you think through the questions, sit down and sketch out your work history. What were your strengths and weaknesses for each kind of job you were hired to do? Don't limit your thinking to specific employers. What did you learn about yourself at various jobs you did for your past employers? Don't forget about your non-construction experience. Were you an office manager? Did you do retail sales? What strengths and weaknesses surfaced in those jobs?

Were you good at public relations? Were you able to figure out solutions to tricky remodeling problems? Did you always bring jobs in on time? Within budget? Those are the kinds of things a potential client wants to hear. You'll have to tell him though; don't assume he'll know.

The Next Step

Usually, a remodeler hopes that work will come knocking on his door. But there are several kinds of business you can go out and bring in. To do it, though, you will have to appear very professional and very capable. Anything less, and your competitor will win instead of you.

Property managers, bankers, architects, and insurance adjusters all are ready sources of business. Each one will have varying amounts of work and there will be varying hassles with each. But if you can cultivate these sources, you may never have to go looking for any other jobs.

Before you go out and make even your first contact, remember that you'll be dealing with women as well as men. If you have any stereotypes about talking to women about construction, get rid of them! In all of the following professions, there are many competent women who are the decision-makers. If you're unable to treat them with respect, be prepared to lose their business to a competitor who will.

Property Managers

Property managers are people who manage the property of others. They may manage huge apartment complexes, single homes, or commercial properties. The owners may live in another state or they may live in the same community as the property they own, but just don't want the hassles of having to take care of it themselves.

Whatever the reason, a property manager is responsible for taking care of their real estate for them. Some managers have enough properties that they have their own maintenance crews to do repairs. Others don't. Even those that have crews usually aren't able to do larger repairs caused by fire or storms.

Advantages and disadvantages

Working with a property manager has its pluses and minuses. You'll need to be able to handle a variety of jobs, from a little drywall or fence repair to renovating a house gutted by fire. You'll need to be able to get to the work and quickly complete it so the house, apartment, or commercial space can be rented again. Every day you lose is money lost by the property owner and manager. If you're able to do the small jobs, you'll be called on to do the big ones as well.

The plus side is that price won't be much of a consideration. As long as you charge a fair amount and do good work, the manager isn't going to shop around. In fact, she'll be willing to pay a little more just to have the work done right the first time with the least amount of aggravation.

The other plus is that you shouldn't have any trouble getting paid within a matter of days. Generally, you won't be asked to do the work until the owner has put money in escrow to cover your costs. If an insurance company is involved, they, too, will be putting the total amount in escrow. Either way, the money should be released by the property manager as you complete your work. Be prepared, though. It doesn't always work that smoothly. Sometimes, either because of incompetent managers or because the property management company doesn't have the same concerns about your cash flow that you have, you'll have a harder time getting paid quickly. We'll give you some tips in a later chapter to shorten the process.

Introducing yourself

If you have the range of needed skills and the ability to get to jobs quickly, your next step is to visit with the property managers in your community. You'll have a much better chance at getting in if you know their names. If a name isn't listed in the Yellow Pages, call the property manager's office and find out from the secretary who you should talk to.

When you have the name, call the manager and briefly introduce yourself and your company. Find out if she's using an outside firm for maintenance and repair work on her properties. Whether she is or isn't, ask her for a few minutes of her time so you can come in and talk further. Tell her you'd like to explain in more detail what services you and your company have to offer her.

Most managers are willing to give a few minutes, but if you call one who's happy with her repair people already, or is especially busy, she may not want to take the time to listen to you. If she refuses, thank her for her time anyway, and ask if it would be all right for you to send her a price sheet for standard repairs and a brochure (or business card, or whatever you may have in the way of literature) for her to keep on file for future reference. Rarely will anyone turn you down on this request. Ask too, if it would be okay for you to check back in six months to see if her needs have changed. Again, you'll be turned down only occasionally.

Send the promised information and a brief thank you for her time on your company letterhead. If you have nice handwriting, it'll look and feel more sincere if you handwrite the note. If your writing looks like chicken scratches, type it and sign it. Six months later, call her and repeat the process. If in the meantime, you've done any work for other property managers in the area, tell her so. It may get you an interview. If not, repeat the thank you note and information.

As long as you are polite and professional each time, she'll treat you the same. Eventually, it may be enough for her to send some work your way. But even if she doesn't, you haven't lost anything but a few minutes' time and a little postage.

On the other hand, she may be willing to give you an appointment the first time you call. If so, remember to look and sound professional. Be punctual. Firmly shake her hand and again thank her for seeing you for a few minutes — and only take a few minutes. Briefly explain your experience and what your company can do for her and her properties. Stress that you will be dependable, reasonable, and competent. Ask for any work she can send your way.

When you leave, again shake her hand and make sure you give her your company literature. Send her a follow-up thank you note with a business card attached. If after several months you haven't heard from her, politely call her and ask if she's needing any work done. Whether she does or doesn't, as long as she treats you courteously, follow up again in several months. Eventually, if she sees you as a professional, chances are good she'll decide to try you out.

Do the job right

If she gives you a job, no matter how small, *do it fast and do it right.* Let her know that you're the professional you told her you are. A small job done right will lead to any big jobs that come across her desk. If you mess up on the first job, don't expect to get another chance. There's no shortage of your competitors out there willing to do the same work for the same price. One of them will get called the next time.

Once you've established a working relationship with her, don't be afraid to ask her for names of other property managers she thinks might need your services.

If you live in a small town, you may know who owns a lot of rental properties. In less urban areas, owners usually manage their own properties. Go to them directly and ask for their business. Use the same procedure as outlined for the property manager.

Once again, the steps to follow:

1) Call property manager and ask for an appointment.

2) If you can't get an appointment, thank her for her time and ask if you can send her your business card to keep on file. Send a short thank you note on your company literature. Call and try again in six months.

3) If you can get an appointment, keep it short and give her your literature.

4) Send her a follow-up thank you note.

5) If the manager expresses interest but you haven't heard from her in several months, call to see if she's needing any work done.

6) If she gives you a job, no matter how small, handle it as though your business depends on it. It does.

The Banking World

A good banker can be your best friend in many ways. In a strong economy he can send your way any leads he may hear about. In a weak economy he can be even more important. In a recession, a bank will have any number of repossessed properties. Some will be in good enough shape to put right back on the market. Most, though, will be in need of sprucing up — if a person thinks he's going to be losing his house, he doesn't offer to do paint touch-ups. This is the real estate your banker needs help with.

Start with your own bank. If you have a loan officer, contact him. Find out if the bank is in need of a repair crew for any of its properties and who you should contact for more information. Then follow the steps we suggested above for getting a foot in the door with a property manager.

Remember, it's essential that you look and sound professional. Briefly explain your experience and what your company can do for the bank's repos. Stress that you will be dependable, reasonable, and competent. And don't forget to ask for any work he can send your way.

If you have your account at a small bank, you should have a good shot at doing their work. If you're banking with a large institution, it'll be a lot tougher, but it's still possible. It'll just be that much more important to appear to be 100 percent professional.

Repeat the process at other local banks starting with the smaller ones and working your way to the larger ones. The bigger banks will of course have more properties that have been repossessed, but they'll also have a much longer chain of command. With the smaller banks, you will often deal directly with the bank president himself.

The pros and cons are much the same as when you do work for a property manager. You'll need a wide range of skills and the flexibility to get to a job fast and get it done quickly. On the plus side, a bank may be more concerned than a property manager about price, but its main goal is still going to be to get the job done right and fast. The best part, though, is that a bank can and will hand you a check the day a job is done. And you can be sure it won't bounce!

Insurance Repair

Insurance work is one of the best areas to choose for a specialty in the remodeling industry. It's not tied to the local economy so it stays pretty much the same from year to year. Although you won't get any money up front, you'll never have to worry about getting paid. As long as the insurance company accepts your price, you'll get your money — eventually. Often, a homeowner will decide to do extra work in addition to the insurance work. The repair is a good foot in the door for that. Best of all, because of the special problems involved in this kind of work, the money tends to be really good. You don't even have to be low bidder. If the homeowner and the adjuster feel your price is fair you can still get the work.

So why doesn't everyone do insurance work? Mostly because, like every other part of the industry, it has its down side. Even more than property managers and bankers, you'll need to be able to get to the job fast and get it finished quickly. If you were called by the adjuster, she'll expect you to be there within hours to secure the property against further damage and to put together an estimate. You'll be expected to do the $50 jobs as well as the $50,000 jobs.

Also, just because the adjuster calls you out for an estimate doesn't mean you'll automatically have the job. You'll probably end up with half the work you bid, and you won't get a dime for any of the estimate work. Even more so than in other work, your estimates must be detailed and thorough. Don't plan on going back for a change order unless you expect this to be your last job for the adjuster.

Fire damage is especially hard to do. The smoke odor and the mess of water and ashes can actually make you sick. There are good products out on the market for removing the smoke smell, but the fumes from them can almost knock you out if you're working in a small space. In short, your employees will hate the work, even if you love the profit.

Added to the mess, you'll be dealing with a client who's extremely upset. Immediately after a storm or fire, a homeowner will be in a state of shock. He'll appreciate and be reassured by someone taking charge. Within a day or two, though, those feelings will change to anger and mistrust. By the end of a week, he'll be going nuts living in a motel room with spouse, kids, and pets under his feet. He'll want his house fixed yesterday! Remodeling clients can sometimes be pretty crazy under the best of circumstances. Add the stress of having a partially destroyed home, and you'll understand why even a 30 to 50 percent markup isn't good enough for some remodelers.

In spite of all of these problems, probably the biggest drawback to doing insurance work is the difficulty of getting a foot in the door. In urban areas, you won't even have a shot at bidding the job unless you know the homeowner, the adjuster, or the agent. Of the three, the adjuster often has the most influence in the choice. In fact, unless the homeowner is firm in his choice of contractors, the adjuster's choice is usually the one used.

To up your chances of being called by the adjuster, follow the steps suggested previously for contacting property managers and bankers. In addition, take along before-and-after photos of jobs you've done. If you've done insurance work for a homeowner, take along a letter of reference. There are far fewer adjusters than managers or bankers, so the competition for their work will be a lot stiffer. Again, it's essential that you appear to be 100 percent professional. An adjuster is going to be far more concerned about getting the job done right and fast than even a property manager. Her reputation with the insurance company is on the line every time you do a job for her.

Once you have your foot in the door, you'll need to work hard at keeping it there. Each job should be treated as though it's your first. One complaint from a homeowner can end all calls from an adjuster.

Architects

One final profession to contact is architects. It's surprising how many established architects don't have a good remodeler to turn work over to. All but the newest offices will have a list of builders, but few of even the best firms in town will know who to turn to for a tricky renovation job.

Traditionally, architects and remodelers have not gotten along well. Each profession harbors suspicions of the other; some are justified, others aren't. Even though there are incompetent people in both fields, there are plenty of competent ones as well.

Architects tend to think remodelers can't design jobs themselves. They resent it when they aren't used and the job turns out ugly and not very functional. And rightly so.

Remodelers, on the other hand, think that architects don't know the first thing about construction. They say architects specify expensive, even unavailable products, and then complain that the contractor can't keep the job within budget. There's truth to that, too. An even worse problem is when an architect has vague or incomplete specs. You can't bid apples and build oranges without losing your shirt or angering the client with change orders.

In spite of these problems, an architect can offer some of the most exciting renovation projects you'll find. High-end customers use architects. They're the customers who want something beyond function and they're willing to pay for it. They'll demand high quality and efficient scheduling for their dollar.

If you can meet these demands and can respect the architect's role, your next step is to scout out one or more architects you can work with. This will be a different kind of relationship than you'll have with any of the other professionals discussed in this chapter. A banker, insurance adjuster, or property manager will just want to get the job done fast and right for a fair price. An architect who has invested time in designing a project will feel as much ownership in the job as you will. He'll be much more concerned about detail and quality and less concerned about speed or cost.

Remember that you'll have something to offer him as well. Remodeling requires greater design skill than many new construction projects. Unless you're able to do your own drawings, you'll need the services of an architect from time to time. Keep in mind that not everyone who does architectural work is a licensed architect. Some will be designers, which means they aren't licensed and may not even have a degree. Not being licensed has nothing to do with artistic skills or structural competence. You'll find architects with neither and designers with both.

The license will only make a difference with building departments and insurance companies. A licensed architect will be able to put his state stamp on his drawings. A designer won't be able to stamp any of his work, and so he's less liable for any problems. Most residential work, and even some commercial, won't require a stamp. When it's not required by a building department, an architect will rarely be willing to use his stamp, for obvious reasons.

Even if you do have a stamped drawing, you as a contractor still may not be free from liability if a structure proves to be unsound. The courts assume that you're professionally competent. Consequently, you can be held liable for any obvious design flaws. Instead of correcting major blueprint problems yourself, you should ask the architect to do it. Oddly enough, he may or may not be willing. If he's not willing to do it unless you sign a disclaimer to release him of responsibility, go to the homeowner and explain the situation. A disclaimer should be signed by your client which releases you of responsibility if you make the needed changes without the architect's approval. Of course, you'll want to avoid having to do work for that particular architect ever again.

As a result of all of this, the best architect to work with is one who has construction experience. He's more likely to be in tune with your needs as a remodeler if he's known firsthand the hassles of the building side of the profession. He's also less likely to have design problems in his drawings. But even if you use an architect without construction experience, if you can find one who will respect you and who is a competent designer, you should be able to work together.

Finding architects to work with

Begin looking for architects by calling and dropping off literature. When you find one who needs a remodeling contractor, spend some time with him. Both of you will need to make clear what your needs are. The following issues are a few of the essential ones you'll be concerned about.

1) You'll need clear and specific specs to bid from.

2) You'll want to be able to deal directly with the client and not have to do everything through the architect.

3) When there *is* a design problem, you'll want the architect to take responsibility for it. Make clear that if there is a construction problem, that responsibility is obviously yours.

Of course, he'll want to make sure of a few things himself. Most of all he'll want to be certain that you have the construction skills to carry out his ideas. When you interview him, be sure to take along your resume and references as before. Also take along before-and-after photos of jobs you've completed. If you have a job in progress, invite him to visit the job site. Your emphasis should be on your ability to do high quality work.

Home Inspections

Home inspection is one of the fastest-growing areas of the remodeling market. This, again, is work you can go after by making some calls and dropping off your literature. One difference with this work, though, is that ethically, inspection work can't be used to get repair work. You'll need to keep your remodeling business and your inspection business separate.

According to *Remodeling* magazine, in 1987 there were 3,000 companies doing property inspections. They project that within five years that number could grow to 25,000. Texas already requires an inspection for real estate transactions and several other states are close to that point. Most of the inspectors will come out of a remodeling background. That's logical enough — remodelers are the troubleshooters of the construction industry. If they can't spot potential problems, who can?

It takes an hour or two to do a thorough inspection. Charges will run around $150 to $200 including a written report. Most of the report can be set up on computer software so that an 18 to 20 page personalized report would take very little time to put together.

Home inspections have one serious drawback: liability insurance is so expensive that most inspection companies don't carry it. Instead, they budget up to 5 percent of their gross take for claims. In addition, most require homeowners to sign a pre-inspection agreement releasing the inspector of liability. The written report is also full of disclaimers.

The field is new enough that it isn't clear how much the release of liability and the disclaimers would cover you if a client takes you to court. If you're not familiar with all aspects of remodeling — heating, plumbing, electrical, roofing, and so on — it's probably better to stay out of the inspection market until it's a safer risk for you.

A less obvious drawback is that you'll get most of your work from real estate agents. Whether the agent is representing the seller or the buyer, she'll want a favorable report so she doesn't lose the sale. The buyer, on the other hand, will want to know every blemish the house has. Since he's the one who pays for the inspection, your legal obligation is to him. Unfortunately, it's the real estate agents you have to keep happy. It's an uneasy relationship, but if you're competent and have integrity, you'll still be able to build a good home inspection business. It may take you a little longer, but it's really the only route to take — especially if you want to sleep well.

If all-around troubleshooting is what you do best and you think you can handle the seller-agent relationship, home inspection can be an easy, lucrative market. If you're interested, more information is available from the national organization of home inspectors. You can write to them at:

ASHI
1010 Wisconsin Ave, NW
Suite 630
Washington, DC 20007

In the meantime, start contacting real estate agents. Again, use the steps outlined for the other professions.

Even if you don't want to go out and solicit home inspection business, you still may be asked to do it from time to time. Former or current clients who respect your remodeling skills may ask you to look at a property they're thinking of buying. With this kind of inspection you should stress that you accept no liability if you don't catch everything, and that you won't provide a written report. For an hour of your time, you can walk through the property and point out trouble spots, items needing general repair, or give advice on how expensive it would be to remodel the property. Depending on how valuable the client is, you might be willing to do this for free. It's not unreasonable, though, to charge $50 to $100 for this service. After all, your expertise is valuable, as is your time.

Redevelopment Organizations

All of the above options are good ones to get you started. However, all of them require that you have enough self-confidence to sell yourself. If you aren't quite that courageous yet, there is one other excellent option. In fact, if it hadn't been for this option, we wouldn't be in construction today. We survived our first few years of business doing jobs for a couple of redevelopment organizations, Neighborhood Housing Services (NHS) and Community Development. The first is a nationwide, private funding source; the second is funded with federal, state, and local money.

Urban Renewal is also an arm of Community Development. Its emphasis is on larger urban projects.

A redevelopment organization provides low-interest money to homeowners and businesses to fix up their properties. The house or business must be in certain geographical or "target" areas to qualify. And the client must meet certain criteria to qualify for the loans. Both organizations, and others like them, even have interest-free loans. They also have loans that in very special situations don't have to be paid for until the property is sold.

The advantages

The good thing for you about these organizations is that they're a great place to pick up work without having to go out and dig up your own clients. It works like this:

1) The home or business owner applies to the redevelopment organization for help.

2) A construction specialist visits the property and does an inspection to see what's needed.

3) Specs, drawings, and an estimate are put together. The owner is pre-qualified for a loan to make sure he meets the criteria for the loan amount he'll need.

4) A contractor or contractors are called in to give a bid.

5) A contractor is chosen and the loan process is finalized.

As you can see, the contractor's part comes late in the process. You don't have to worry about finding the client or getting financing for him. And if you bring a client to the organization, you won't even have to bid against other contractors. It's a good place to start for a remodeler just going out on his own.

The disadvantages

But it's not perfect. In fact, the process has enough flaws in it that most contractors eventually cut back or completely stop the bidding they do with these groups. Its biggest problem is also its biggest asset: anyone who has liability insurance, workers' insurance, and the necessary licenses can bid. You don't need to be good. You don't need to be fast. As long as you meet the minimum quality standards, they'll let you bid and get jobs again.

As with any bid situation, the quality of the specs has a big effect on the bidding process. If the specs are clear and complete, it can be an excellent training ground for someone just getting into construction. However, if the specs are poorly written, it'll result in a wide range of bids. Little can be more frustrating to a new contractor. Occasionally, it can be devastatingly expensive as well. When in doubt, bid an item to ensure you're covered. It's far better to lose the bid and be solvent than to get the job and go broke. If you find yourself consistently on the high end of the bidding, you can always tighten your bids to pick up more work.

Another frustration is that, like many government programs, the system works slowly. A job that's let for bid in July may not start until October. The pay can come equally slowly. Draws may take two to four weeks and the final payment can take even longer. If you make sure every "i" is dotted and every "t" is crossed, you'll be on the shorter end of that time span. If you trust them to be responsible for that thoroughness, expect the long end. And last but not least, your files will be twice as fat from all the paperwork.

In spite of these drawbacks, it's still a good place to start. Although most urban areas have a Community Development office, the program isn't based on population but on need. As a result, Community Development can be found in rural areas as well as cities. But even if you don't have a redevelopment organization locally, you still may be able to benefit from their programs. The money for the loans is provided by the Department of Housing and Urban Development (HUD). If you're in an area that would qualify for such a program, your first contact should be with them. They'll be able to direct you to the closest office that covers your community. Write to them at the following address:

> Department of Housing and Urban Development
> Assistant for Community Planning and Development
> 451 Seventh Street, SW
> Washington, DC 20410-7000
> (202) 755-6422

If HUD funds aren't available, the other option is to look for private redevelopment organizations such as NHS. Their address and phone are:

> NHS, Inc.
> 1325 G Street NW
> Suite 800
> Washington, DC 20005
> (202) 376-2400

To pursue redevelopment work, you won't need even so much as a business card. Nor will you have to worry about photos or letters of reference. You'll still make a better impression if you're dressed neatly and sound professional, but it's not as critical because usually the jobs are awarded to the low bidder. However, never assume that it isn't important. The first job we ever bid for NHS we got because the homeowner thought we looked and sounded the most competent. Little did she realize we were probably also the least experienced.

Redevelopment organizations will want you to show proof of liability and Workers' Compensation insurance. In some areas you'll need to be licensed and bonded, too. They'll also want you to provide information on your credit history and your construction experience. Don't be worried about the last two items. They just want to make sure you pay your bills and have enough remodeling expertise to do the jobs you bid.

Other Ideas

All of the areas discussed in the chapter so far are just places to start. Don't limit yourself to them. You might also find work from home improvement centers that sub out installations. Check with kitchen and bath centers or custom cabinet makers. Like the property managers, many of them will have hired their own crews, but others will sub out whatever they can.

Another good place to look is in new home subdivisions. Homeowners often add decks or finish out basements within the first year or two after purchasing. Although you'll probably have better luck going door to door, you might try mailing information to neighborhoods. Once you get your first job, others can quickly follow if you take advantage of some simple and inexpensive advertising ideas discussed in the next chapter.

If you have some money to work with, you might invest in a property to renovate. A lot of remodelers use this approach. Try spending the extra money to make it a distinctive, quality job, then use it as your sales office. Invite prospective clients to your house and give a tour. Let them see firsthand what you're able to do. Use the tour as a chance to show off your craftsmanship and your sense of design. A lot of contractors use this approach in a move-up real estate game. By buying, fixing up, and selling, you can really fatten your yearly profits — until you and your family finally get tired of living in a construction site.

Last, but not least, make sure that you really make the most of any unique remodeling skills you may have. One area that's been extremely helpful to us in building our business is our design skill. We like to meet the challenge of turning dull tract houses into something interesting and functional, without making them look out of place in the neighborhood. Blending the old with the new on turn-of-the-century Victorians also takes an eye for design that not every remodeler has.

Our clients like the idea of dealing with one person from the start of an idea to the finished product, instead of having to use an architect along the way. An added plus is that when we work with a client from the very beginning, we never lose the client to another contractor when the job is about to start. We build trust and loyalty, which serves us in referrals long after the job is finished.

3

Digging Up Business

*I*n the last chapter we explained where to go looking for work. You might pick up enough jobs from property managers, bankers and architects simply by doing what we suggested. It's also possible you won't get a single job from these sources. Most likely, you'll get some business from these sources, but not enough to stay busy. You'll need more good leads, more inquiries, more people asking you for bids. How do you get them? The answer is obvious: a good advertising program.

We think every professional remodeling contractor should advertise. But understand this clearly. *Advertising alone won't keep you busy — ever.*

As we pointed out in Chapter 2, the most successful and profitable remodeling companies depend on repeat business and referrals for most work. But even so, they advertise. They have broad circles of satisfied customers who provide a steady stream of leads. That's exactly what you want to develop. But until you've been in business a few years, you'll have to find customers the expensive way — by advertising for them.

We'll also emphasize another point: if you think advertising will bring in all the work you need, you're going to be very disappointed. Owens-Corning Fiberglas conducted a survey among several hundred homeowners who had shingles installed by roofing contractors. Each owner was asked how he or she found the contractor who ended up doing the work. More than 70 percent of the homeowners said they got a referral from a friend, neighbor or relative. Almost half did not select the lowest bidder to do the work.

But roofing jobs aren't like remodeling jobs. They're smaller and usually don't interfere with the daily activities of the occupants. Remodeling is much more expensive and much more disruptive. We'd want a remodeler we could trust. Someone who had the recommendation of a friend, neighbor or relative. Choosing a good remodeler is a little like selecting a good doctor. How comfortable would you be finding a doctor in the Yellow Pages or through a newspaper ad?

Most people are more concerned about who comes in their home than who provides their health care. Keep that in mind when planning your advertising.

The best advertisement for a remodeler is always a job well done. Every customer you have will spread the word about your work — one way or the other. That means you can't afford to have even one unhappy client, especially in a small community. If your work is good and you charge a fair price, your name will get around. If you do shoddy work and ask for top dollar, that word will get around too. Unfortunately, bad news usually travels farther and faster — and for longer — than good news.

As you study the various advertising options in this chapter, keep this in mind: every advertisement that emphasizes your specialty or special skills has more impact, especially when it's directed at those who need your service most. Whether your specialty is kitchen design or building for the handicapped, or anything in between, focus on what you do best in messages delivered to those who need it the most.

One final point to remember. A good advertising plan shouldn't just dump tons of leads in your lap. In fact, that may be the worst thing that can happen. If lead quality is poor, you may have to hire new people to service those leads. Good advertising should bring in *quality* leads at a measured rate. Prospects should need what you do best, not what any other remodeler can do just as well and for less money. Turning down leads is bad business. It creates ill will. Find a way to solicit only the leads you really need.

Remodelers new to this business sometimes think good advertising, and plenty of it, should help them build the biggest remodeling company in town. We think that's foolish. Instead of trying to be the biggest, aim for being the best — and most profitable. Being the best may eventually make you the biggest. But size by itself isn't a very good measure of success. Don't emphasize quantity over quality. It's a little like driving two nails with two hammers at the same time. A nice trick, but who needs it?

Study the suggestions in this chapter. Some are easy and inexpensive. Others are more appropriate for a remodeling business that's been around for a few years. None of them will work well if you don't provide quality service at a fair price. That's the best way to build a successful business.

Creating a Logotype

A logotype, or *logo* as it's more commonly called, is an identifying symbol. It might be the way a product name is written, such as the famous Coca-Cola script. Or it might be a design, like the golden arches of McDonald's. An attractive logo used consistently can become as familiar as the company it represents. The best logos identify the company and service and need no further explanation.

Even if you've been in business for several years, creating an effective logo should be the first step in your new advertising plan. The logo should go on your vehicles, every piece of literature, business cards and all advertising. You want the public to recognize it and connect it with you. Remember three things about a logo:

1) It should be well-designed and distinctive. An awkward, complex, or trite logo is worse than useless. Your logo should reflect the quality and individuality of your company. It should show that you recognize good design and have the ingenuity to create a distinctive style. If your company symbol is bland or hard to figure out, you're not sending the message you want to project.

   Make sure your logo doesn't look like every other builder's logo. The hammer and framing square and house under construction have been done and redone many times. Don't you want to be a little more unique?

2) Simple is better. A well-designed logo should be easy to understand and easy to remember. Complex images are harder to remember and tend to be more expensive to create. Remember, you're going to reproduce the logo hundreds of times. A more elaborate logo will probably cost more to design and almost certainly will cost more to reproduce on your truck, signs and brochures.

3) The most effective logo will include your company name *and* identify your business. Your company name and your logo are probably the first contact your clients have with you. You won't ever sell a job on the strength of your logo, but it may help clients feel more familiar with you even before they meet you. If a logo reinforces the image of you as a true professional, you're starting off on the right foot. Figure 3-1 shows a couple of sample logos that we designed. We think they're distinctive, simple and effective. But your ideas will be better for your business.

Designing a good logo isn't easy. That's why many remodelers never get around to creating one. Some think they can't afford it, or that they have to come up with something themselves. Neither is true. If you can afford to be in business, you can

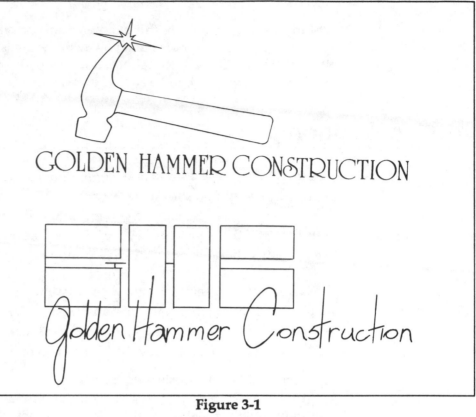

Figure 3-1

Two typical logos

afford a good logo. If you don't have a clue about what your logo should look like, get some ideas from a designer or artist. Most ad agencies can create a logo for $300 to $1,200. But the price drops if you have some rough sketches that only need to be refined.

If that sounds steep, there are cheaper alternatives that can be just as good. If you have a general idea of what you want, a graphic artist can produce a camera-ready product (which is what you'll need for reproduction) for as little as $25 to $50. Many printers also offer graphic design services. If you bring in an idea, a printer may be able to create a camera-ready logo for $25 to $50. Some may even do it for free if you're a good customer. In theory, you'll get a more distinctive design from an ad agency. In practice, $50 may buy you $500 worth of art service.

Suppose $50 is all you can afford and you don't have any ideas for a logo. What then? Go to your local community college graphic arts department. Offer a $50 honorarium for the best logo design. At best, you might get exactly what you want. At worst, you'll pay $50 for some ideas that may simply need more refining.

If you decide to use an agency, you'll get more for your money if you've done your homework. Think first about the kind of style that should represent your company. What do you want your symbol to say about you? Do you want to convey old-fashioned craftsmanship and quality? Do you want to appear to be on the modern, cutting edge of the industry?

Designing a good logo isn't easy.

While you're planning a logo, think about the direction you want your company to take. Do you want to emphasize commercial work? The elderly? Your flair with tract houses? The type of customer you want to attract should influence the design of your logo.

Gather brochures, business cards, flyers, advertisements — anything that has a look that you like. Sketch logo ideas from TV commercials or billboards. If you find one you especially like, call the company and find out who did it for them. Ask other contractors to recommend someone they've used. Try to find an agency that has other construction contractor or remodeler clients. At the very least, find an artist who will listen. Then help that artist create something that fits your needs and style.

Don't be shy about asking prices before you get started. Either get a firm quotation or set a budget limit. Don't get surprised with a bill that's several times what you expected. You want the best logo at the best price, not the best logo regardless of price.

There's always a danger that the artist you hire won't come up with a logo you like. If that happens, both your time and money may be wasted. Here's how to make that unlikely. First, write up a paragraph or two about your company, your specialty, and the customers you want to attract. Suggest a few guidelines for the logo: color, size, shape, style, etc. Then describe anything you would consider unacceptable. Finally, describe or show some examples of what you *do* like. Give all this information to the graphic artist of your choice. Then make your artist this offer: $50 for three or four rough pencil sketches. You'll pay the $50 even if all are rejected. With each sketch, the artist should include a bid for producing the finished product, camera-ready art on artboard at least 8 inches by 12 inches. Finally, make it clear that everything the artist produces is your property to use any way you want without further payment to the artist. Don't forget this last part.

The Tag Line

A tag line is a word picture. Much like the logo, it's a phrase that's repeated on advertising so much that it becomes associated with your company name. General Electric has used the phrase, set to music, "GE . . . we bring good things to life," so much that you only need to hear the tune and the words come to mind. In the last few years, Ford has used the tag line, "Quality is job one." The tag line is what the advertiser wants you to remember most.

Tag lines aren't as common as logos, and they may change from year to year or even from ad campaign to ad campaign. They shouldn't be overlooked, though. Tag lines are a powerful tool in keeping your company firmly etched in the consumer's mind — especially if they're set to a catchy tune.

Developing a good tag line is not like designing a good logo. An artist has to create a logo. You may be able to create a tag line without any professional help. If you have trouble coming up with something that's distinctive yet easy to remember, get help from an ad agency. If you hire an agency to develop a complete advertising program, they should be able to work up at least one catchy tag line. Even if you're not hiring an agency for a major advertising campaign, they may be able to create a distinctive phrase for you. It should cost less than having a logo designed. Expect to pay at least $50 whether or not you use their suggestion.

Before you pay someone to do your thinking, try a little brainstorming yourself. You'll be surprised at what you and your crew might come up with. It's easier than you think.

The following examples appeared in the November, 1986 issue of *Qualified Remodeler*:

▌ For a specialist in kitchens— "Best Remodeling Kitchens Are Wife Savers."

▌ For a specialist in insurance work— "Best Remodeling Helps Heal Hurt Homes" or "In Case of Fire, Call Best Remodeling."

▌ For general remodeling— "Best Remodeling: Rebuilding Colorado Since 1975" or "We Do It Right the First Time!"

Here are some suggestions if you want to develop your own tag line:

1) Lead from strength. Emphasize just one point, your major advantage over the competition. Quality? Old-fashioned craftsmanship? Design skills? Choose one and hammer it home.

2) Keep it short and simple. A tag line is never more than a sentence long and is usually less. Any more than seven words is clumsy. Keep it full of punch.

3) Set it to music for the electronic media. Again, keep the music as simple as the phrase. Use only one or two instruments or the phrase will be overwhelmed by the accompaniment.

Institutional vs. Promotional Advertising

Advertising comes in two broad categories: institutional and promotional. Institutional ads help people remember your name. They remind the public that you're there. They may identify your skills, professionalism, reliability, and experience. They don't create a sense of urgency that results in a sale. Figure 3-2 is a typical institutional ad for a remodeling contractor. And notice the tag line: *Solid Gold Quality.*

Figure 3-2

Typical institutional ad

A promotional ad, on the other hand, should create some urgency. It should motivate the potential client to buy now. Promotional ads quote prices and discounts and offer limited time specials. They make it easy to order. Retail stores use promotional ads almost exclusively.

In contrast, most remodelers use only institutional ads. The reasons for this are obvious. Because you're selling a highly-customized service, every sale is different.

How can you offer a 20 percent discount if there's no way to determine the full price?

Sometimes you'll see ads for remodelers claiming a 20 percent discount. As a practical matter, very few remodelers make a true 20 percent profit on any job (after all bills and your salary are paid). But you'll still see claims of big discounts. If it isn't just advertising puffery, it probably means that the contractor's usual markup was much higher than average. Even after a 20 percent discount, the competition's bid may be higher than your usual bid. It's the actual cost, not the percent of discount, that counts.

Of course, it's frustrating to lose even one client to a contractor who claims 20 percent discounts. What makes it worse is the impression it leaves with the public: Contractors are making a killing if they can give a 20 percent discount and still make money.

If you see an ad claiming 20 or 25 percent discounts, you don't have to sit back and steam. Call the remodeler and remind him that he's not doing a favor to the industry. Then call your local NARI, NHBA Remodelor's Council, and the BBB. All these organizations have advertising standards. While they can't require anyone to change an ad, they can educate a contractor on ethical advertising. If the remodeler's advertising is truly fraudulent, call your district attorney. A phone call from the district attorney may produce the quickest results of all.

Advertising professionals will warn you that institutional ads, while necessary and effective, produce much slower results. It may take several years before you see a lot of work. But unless you're a major or exclusive dealer for some product, most advertising will simply promote your company name. This kind of advertising can be very effective and well worth the time and money.

In our community there was a cabinet refacer who advertised heavily on TV. The commercials were mostly short institutional spots. They emphasized skilled craftsmanship and quick turn-around time. And every ad ended with the entire crew pointing at the camera saying, "Call Alliance *because we do good work*!" Hardly the most inspired line, but it was effective. They were the busiest cabinet refacers in town.

Institutional ads can work. They can have punch and purpose and make your phone ring. Even if you don't try electronic (TV and radio) or print (magazines and newspapers) advertising, do some institutional advertising to keep your name in front of the public. The more familiar your name to a client, the better your chances of being invited to bid.

But institutional ads can be a trap for small companies. Every dollar you spend on advertising should produce measurable results, and the sooner the better. Put an ad with a coupon in the newspaper or run an ad in the Yellow Pages and you'll know right away if it's working. If it isn't, you can pull it and do something else. Run an institutional ad and you're never sure if it hit home. The benefits can't be measured precisely and may not come in for years.

We recommend buying very little institutional advertising. But that doesn't mean you should avoid all institutional ads. Some institutional promotion is either very cheap or free. How? We'll explain.

The Value of Institutional Ads

Institutional promotion is anything intended to give the public a better impression of your business. We call that *image enhancement*, making you and your company look good in the community. Fortunately, there are hundreds of ways to do that at little or no expense. Some of these are great, cheap ways to advertise. It may be as worthy as heading up the local food drive for needy families or as fun as sponsoring a softball or volleyball team. Image enhancement might be as direct as writing a remodeling column for your local paper or as subtle as being photographed with the mayor.

Whatever you do, you'll probably find that image enhancement will give you low-cost, high-quality leads. Compare that with paid advertising that costs plenty and usually produces high-cost, low-quality leads. People will call you because they know your name and admire the work you've done. They want to be identified with a winner.

There are many ways to enhance your public image. Some imply to the public that you're available and active in the community. Others are more direct: "I'm the best remodeler in town. Call me instead of anyone else." Most fall somewhere in between. All can be productive.

Being active in church and community activities is a good place to start. As long as it's appropriate for your skills, you can never go wrong with volunteering to chair committees or fund drives for worthy causes. The exposure reminds people that you're there and you're competent. Be sure to wear your company shirt when doing volunteer work. Pass out your business card when introduced to anyone. Maybe even donate services or products to be auctioned off.

Of course, your primary goal is to help in your community. But in doing that, you'll increase your circle of contacts and your company visibility. To protect yourself, don't volunteer unless it's a project you feel is worthwhile and one you can put your heart into.

Rubbing shoulders with community leaders is another way to increase your exposure and credibility. The Chamber of Commerce, Rotary Clubs, Kiwanis, and Lion's Clubs are just a few of the many service organizations you might consider joining. Although all have a service side, most members will admit that they use membership to build business contacts.

And, of course, as we mentioned in the last chapter, belonging to construction industry organizations adds to your image, both within the industry and beyond. Most clubs are happy to have anyone volunteer time and leadership skills.

Although it means work on your part, it can pay off. When the media wants to interview an "industry spokesperson," these are the groups they call. They're more likely to interview the president or the vice-president of a NARI chapter than someone with no official position in the industry. They want someone in a recognized position of authority, speaking for the organization, not just for himself.

If you don't get calls from the local media, call them. When you have a unique project, such as renovating a local historical landmark, call the local newspaper or TV station and let them know just how interesting it is. Bob Vila from *This Old House* got his start just that way. He was renovating a local landmark that just happened to be across from the home of a politician. Since reporters were often in the area, Vila decided to take advantage of the situation. He had a sign made that explained the historical significance of the building and described what was being done to it. His name, as contractor, and phone number were displayed as well. Before long, a reporter called him and wanted to do a story on the house. The story was eventually picked up by a national magazine. Within a year Vila was hosting a popular TV show.

Not every remodeler needs to host a TV show — or wants to. But maybe you see some of the opportunities. A more realistic possibility is that you would be identified as an expert in the field by the news media. For example, you could do weekly 60-second spots or regular columns on remodeling information for the consumer. Whether or not you're paid for this work, it's great advertising that few companies could afford to buy.

But don't abuse your connection with the news media. If your first call to the news media isn't really about something newsworthy, your second call will be ignored. Don't ask for press coverage until you have something unique enough to catch the public interest.

If the local media puts together a story on one of your projects, send a copy to national magazines such as *Better Homes and Gardens, Country Living,* or even industry magazines like *Qualified Remodeler* or *Professional Builder.* And if you get one of the magazines to do a story on your project, send a copy to the local newspaper. Contact the real estate editor and the lifestyle section editor.

It's easier to get into print than on TV or radio — but television has high impact and will increase your credibility very quickly. If you look good and sound good in your first interview, you'll get more calls.

We'll recommend one more way to get lots of publicity for very little money. Many trade organizations and publications sponsor various competitions which often go begging for entries. Some are free; most require an entry fee. If you can win or even be a runner-up in one of these, the local newspaper will almost certainly want to run the story. To enter, write for the entry requirements. Be sure to follow the instructions closely. Have a *professional* photographer take "before" and "after" pictures of the job. Snapshots you might take won't do your work justice. Write your summary clearly and concisely. Make certain your grammar and spelling are flawless. Make your entry as professional as humanly possible.

Emphasize the following:

■ *Project uniqueness*— What distinguishes this project from the countless others out there? Were there special challenges you had to overcome in design or construction?

■ *Construction details*— Describe completely what you did to the property. How did you overcome the challenges you described in point 1?

■ *Specifics*— Include all the data from the project: the square footage, remodeling costs, and other statistics.

■ *Major products*— Some competitions will want to know the brand names of materials you used. They may even want copies of the receipts if you have them. This helps the magazine promote their advertisers' products. If you win and you've used major brand names, you may be able to get extra publicity from the manufacturers.

Don't assume the competition is too stiff in national contests. Look at the winners in remodeling magazines. Some competitions are won by remodelers who did little more than take the time to enter — and had the good sense to get great photography. Competitions are never won by even the best and most capable in the industry if they don't take the trouble to enter.

Low-Cost Essentials

Increasing your visibility in the community is much easier if your name is already visible. Site and vehicle signs, company shirts, hats, and jackets will all remind the public that you're there. None of these is very expensive, but all can be very effective.

It's cheap and easy to have your company logo printed on clothing. There's a one-time setup charge that runs around $10 if you already have camera-ready art. A simple T-shirt printed with your logo and company name costs as little as $6. Hats cost even less. Most silk screen shops will do any number of items, from a dozen to a thousand, for about the same price per unit. Consider printing some shirts or hats in all sizes and handing them out to clients or their children when a contract is signed. That's an inexpensive way to get high-visibility advertising.

Your employees will be glad to wear company uniforms if you provide them at little or no charge. As long as they feel good about working for you, they'll be proud to wear what you provide.

Site and vehicle signs are a little more expensive. Both are available for under $75 and should last for several years. Instead of having your logo and company information painted on your truck, consider using vinyl lettering. When you sell the vehicle, you can peel off the lettering and buff out the paint. That makes repainting unnecessary. Consider using lettering that glows in the dark. Your signs should work 24 hours a day. The extra cost is minimal.

Business cards and stationery are also cheap and effective advertising. They're inexpensive and add a lot to your image. Five hundred business cards shouldn't cost much more than $30 or $40. Good quality stationery and envelopes will cost only a little more. A printer will help you design something tasteful and striking. Of course, your logo should be part of whatever you have printed.

When you have stationery printed, also print presentation folders, thank you notes, and postcards. Use the folders whenever you present a bid. Inside, you would have the bid, your resume, and several references from previous clients, as well as credit references the client can check. We'll explain more about this in the next chapter.

Send thank you notes every time you get a chance. They're a great form of advertising. Everyone likes to be thanked for doing something thoughtful. Always send a note when a job is finished. Customers will appreciate your thoughtfulness — and remember you when they, or someone they know, needs remodeling work.

Postcards make good advertising. Whenever you're working on a job, even one that will only take a few days, send announcement postcards to all the homeowners on the street. The message might be:

Dear Homeowner,

Pardon our mess while we work on your neighbor's house at_____.
We'll do our best to keep the mess and noise at a minimum. If you should have
a question, let us know. We'll try to help.

Of course, if you've been thinking about doing any remodeling, we'd be glad to
sit down and help you plan and design whatever project you may have in mind.

In the meantime, ask your neighbor how we're doing. We're proud of the work
we do and would be pleased to show you examples!

Tom Smith
Best Remodeling

Postcards make an effective, cheap way to introduce your company to neighbors. The cards should be reinforced by on-site signs and vehicle signs. That's what neighbors will see every day. The postcard also helps them understand that you're trying to be courteous and minimize the disruption, mess and noise. If neighbors have complaints, they can be taken care of quickly while they're still small problems, not major disputes. Most likely, though, you'll get fewer complaints because homeowners understand that you're trying to be courteous.

Of course, when you invite neighbors to check on your job, you'd better be doing good work. Otherwise you've lost more business than you stand to gain.

Do your best to keep the job site clean. Tidy up every day. Make sure your employees look professional. If your foreman insists on wearing torn jeans, dirty T-shirts, and playing his radio at a deafening level, you're better off keeping your company name a secret!

Summing It Up

As you can see, good institutional advertising doesn't have to break your budget. The total cost of all the institutional ads we've recommended so far in this chapter will cost well under $500. That's all you should pay for a year's supply (or more) of hats, shirts, business cards, and stationery.

Most businesses don't spend even this much to spruce up their image. But they may spend far more on advertising that won't be as effective. Keep in mind that spending more won't necessarily get you more.

High Dollar Advertising

When putting your money into any type of advertising, go for quality, not just quantity. We feel that a few well-directed ad campaigns will give you much better results than blanketing a neighborhood with ads, shotgun fashion. Don't try to saturate the media. First, you can't afford it. Second, you'll end up with loads of worthless leads.

Here are a few more tips:

▪ Don't put all your eggs in one advertising basket. Instead, make lots of small-scale tests. Most won't work. Some will. Stop doing what doesn't work and do more of what does.

▪ Don't ever rely on a single campaign to produce a miracle. Very few do.

▪ Target the audience you want to reach.

Unless you're trying to dig up community development jobs, you'll want to aim for homeowners over 30, with family incomes over $40,000 or a home equity over $10,000. As you study the information that follows, keep this in mind. For instance, hard rock radio stations usually have the lowest advertising cost per thousand listeners. But buying time on one of these stations is almost certainly a mistake for anyone in your business. Very few listeners have high incomes, are over 30 and own homes.

Remember, too, that women make the key decisions about a house. They initiate the work and make most of the buying decisions. Target a portion of your ads at women, either by placing them where women will read them or with a message that will appeal to women.

As the calls come in, keep a record of how many leads each ad produces. Also, keep track of which leads turn into signed contracts. For instance, newspaper ads may give you 25 new leads a week. But only one or two may convert to new work. Radio spots, on the other hand, may only give you five leads a week, but three or four of them may lead to signed contracts. If the jobs produced by each advertising method have the same contract price, radio would be the better buy, even if it produces fewer leads.

We've found that some types of advertising produce higher dollar value jobs. If newspaper leads become $20,000 kitchen remodels and radio leads tend to be $1,000 handyman jobs, your money should go for newspaper ads, even if it means wading through more poor-quality leads.

The only way to be sure which ads are working is to keep track of your conversion ratio: how much must you spend on advertising to produce each $1,000 in new business? When you know that number, you know where to plan more advertising.

Remember that it takes time to produce results. Several months will usually pass between the time you place an ad and the time you begin work on a job produced by that ad. That's normal. It's also why you have to permanently identify the source of each new customer. In the file folder for each job, make a note about the advertisement or referral that brought that customer to you.

Also remember that repetition pays in the advertising business. That's another reason why you have to be patient when evaluating advertising results. Most people have to see or hear an advertisement many times before they remember it — before it becomes familiar to them. Some of the most effective ads have run so long that the companies using them can't believe that anyone is still listening. That's not the way advertising works. Ads that produce good results the first time tend to keep pulling good results, time after time after time. Ads that bomb the first time tend to do the same the second. When you find an ad that works, stick with it. Let repetition of the message work for you.

Your Advertising Budget

How much should you budget for advertising? Remodelers differ widely in their opinions about this. Here's how two successful companies handle their advertising.

Ben Singer is an award-winning remodeler. He began the local Remodelor's Council and has served at the national level in various remodeling organizations. When the press has a remodeling question, he's the first person they call. He's had write-ups in the local paper, trade magazines, and even the *Wall Street Journal*. He's good and he's successful by any standard.

Singer has never advertised. He doesn't even have an in-column ad in the phone book. The most he's done is to put site signs on the properties he's remodeling — when the homeowner gives him permission. His gross sales of over $2,000,000 in one year were based entirely on referrals, repeat business, and all the free press he's received over the years.

But recently, Singer's sales dropped to about a third of what they were at their peak. The local economy is poor, and doesn't look like it's going to improve for a year or more.

He still doesn't intend to spend a penny on advertising this year. He points to a half dozen competitors who have advertised heavily in the past year, but are no longer in business.

By contrast, Jake and Sam Davis spend nearly $4,000 a month in advertising. That's 5 percent of their monthly gross sales of $80,000. They put about half their budget into phone book ads, the rest into television spots. In addition, they've always had their name on their vehicles, site signs, shirts, caps, and anything else that moves.

The Davis brothers aren't sure how effective their advertising is. They know the phone doesn't ring as much when the TV ads aren't running. But they also admit that the leads the ads produce aren't always good quality ones. They're convinced the phone book has been their bread and butter. But they still cut the budget in half to use some for television.

The brothers have seen some decline in their gross sales, but it hasn't been nearly as dramatic as Ben Singer's. They agree the problem lies in the lousy economy. Their response is to beef up their ad budget.

These two remodeling companies have opposite views of the role advertising should play. Still, each company has been relatively successful in spite of — or because of — its approach.

Wise advertising management probably falls somewhere between these extremes. Singer was fortunate to have all the free publicity. Even so, an occasional well-designed ad campaign might have boosted his sales. The Davis brothers should be a little more scientific in their approach. They might discover that the entire ad budget should go back in the Yellow Pages. They also might discover that they're spending far more than they need to for advertising.

What's right for your company? We recommend you put the bulk of your budget into long-lasting items such as site and truck signs, shirts, and caps. We also like small promotional gifts like mugs. Your truck, which people see around town every day, has far greater impact than a newspaper ad that's tossed by noon. And it will probably cost considerably less. Print and electronic media have their place. But it's smart to spend cautiously until you know how they work for you.

Most remodeling companies spend about 2 to 3 percent of gross revenue on promotion. If your company is taking in $1,000,000 a year, that yields $20,000 to $30,000 for advertising. Use 2 to 3 percent as a starting point for your first advertising budget: $250,000 gross times 2 percent (or 3 percent) is $5,000 (or $7,500). $500,000 times 2 percent (or 3 percent) is $10,000 (or $15,000).

Realistically, if you gross under $100,000, it'll be hard to budget $2,000 or $3,000 for advertising. Do try, though, to spend at least the minimum amount on the items described earlier in this chapter. That's where you get the most visible results for your advertising dollar. Keep spending more as long as you get good results. The more innovative and creative your advertising program, the more effective it will be, and the more you should be spending.

Of course, whatever amount you spend will be part of your overhead costs. If you spend 5 percent on advertising and your competition spends nothing, all other things being equal, your bids have to be about 5 percent higher. This doesn't mean that you still won't get the job. It does mean, though, that you'll have to sell yourself harder to earn it. That's why it's important to get the most for your advertising dollar. Otherwise, you're simply increasing your overhead without any benefit.

In practice, advertising should help you find more jobs, keep your crews busier, and spread your overhead thinner over a greater volume of work. When that happens, advertising is a benefit both to you and your clients.

Many manufacturers offer to help stretch your ad dollars by sponsoring co-op advertising programs. The manufacturer reimburses you for some or most of the cost of ads that feature that manufacturer's products. Your name and phone number appear in the ad along with the manufacturer's product. One major advantage of co-op ads is that the manufacturers provide ready-made ad copy and illustrations prepared by advertising professionals. That relieves you of most of the creative burden.

To find out about co-op programs, contact your building material distributors. Several kitchen cabinet, flooring, plumbing fixture and siding manufacturers have co-op programs you may want to investigate.

Larger advertisers usually turn their advertising budget over to an advertising agency. If you're spending $1,000 a month on advertising, an agency will help you get the most for your money. Ad agencies make most of their money in commissions paid by the media. So your cost of using an agency won't be much more than you would pay to place the same advertising without an agency.

Unfortunately, there may be as many bad advertising agencies as there are bad contractors. Don't just hire the first one you interview. The way to find the best agency is the same way your clients find a good remodeler: get referrals. Find out what each has done and can do. Then select the one you like best. Just as you did in looking for a good logo, collect brochures, flyers, and newspaper ads. Also, watch and listen to commercials on TV and the radio.

When something catches your eye, call the company to find out who put the advertising together. Find out if they were satisfied with the service and the price of the agency. Ask, too, if they're getting good results from the ad. If they aren't, don't automatically write off the agency. There are many reasons why an ad doesn't work. Maybe the product is bad or the price too high. But if an ad isn't working, a few red flags should go up. No matter how attractive an ad is, if it doesn't get results, it can't be that good.

No matter whether you use an agency or place ads yourself, have a plan and a budget. Sketch out your direction for the coming year. Try to stay on the plan and within budget. Don't fall for special deals offered by whoever happens to call you first. Be consistent. Advertising is most important when business is weak. It's least important when there's more work on your plate than you can handle.

Comparing Apples to Apples

There are good buys and bad buys in advertising. How do you know which is which? How do you compare the value of radio spots to newspaper ads or to billboards? Of course, each medium has its own advantages and disadvantages. Yet all are different. That makes direct comparisons almost impossible.

Cost per thousand (M) exposures or *CPM* is a rough measure of advertising cost. Of course, this isn't the best measure of advertising value. But it's a good place to start comparing costs. You'll still have to decide if the *demographics* are right. Is your message going to appeal to people of the age, sex, income, and education level in the prospective audience?

Many newspapers, magazines and broadcast stations can supply good information on their audience: the percentage blue collar or professional, their ethnic classification and marital status, and the percentage of homeowners.

To find the CPM, you'll need to know the advertising cost and the circulation or listening audience of the medium. For instance, suppose station KAAA has a weekday, drive-time audience of 17,500 and charges $150 for a 60-second spot.

17,500 divided by 1,000 = 17.5 (listeners in thousands)

$150 divided by 17.5 = $8.57 (cost per thousand listeners, or CPM)

Let's compare radio station KBBB. It has a weekday, drive-time audience of 24,200 and charges $180 for a 60-second spot. What's the CPM?

24,200 divided by 1,000 = 24.2

$180 divided by 24.2 = $7.43

The CPM for station KBBB is $7.43.

As you can see, station KBBB charges more per minute but less per listener because the listening audience is larger. That's your clue that it may be a better advertising value. You still have to decide if KBBB reaches your audience, though. If KBBB is the local hard rock station, it's probably not a good buy for you even if its CPM is half the next lowest station.

Be sure to compare the same time slots on the same days. It's unrealistic to compare KAAA's Monday through Friday drive-time cost with KBBB's 7 p.m.-to-midnight slot.

Television CPM can be figured using the same formula. Be careful, though, in using CPM alone to judge advertising value. Television has a much higher impact than radio. It will also have a larger audience than even the top radio station.

To find the CPM for newspapers, use the cost per column inch for the whole ad you plan to place. In the following examples, we've used an ad that takes 36 column inches.

The News has a daily circulation of 42,000. It charges $8.75 per column inch:

42,000 divided by 1,000 = 42

36 (column inches) times $8.75 = $315

$315 divided by 42 (thousand) = $7.50

That's the CPM for our proposed ad.

The Times has a daily circulation of 75,000 and charges $19.50 per column inch.

75,000 divided by 1,000 = 75

36 (column inches) times $19.50 = $702

$702 divided by 75 = $9.36, a higher CPM than *The News*. But maybe *The Times* has better demographics. If so, it may be a better buy even at the higher cost.

Figuring the cost of mailings is fairly easy. Add the printing cost per thousand to the cost of mailing per thousand. Direct mail advertising always has a much higher CPM, usually at least $300 per thousand. Why, then, do so many remodelers use direct mail? Because direct mail lets you pinpoint even a small audience very precisely and supply each with a handy order form.

Billboards are harder to evaluate. A different measurement is used: Gross Rating Points, or GRP. We'll discuss billboards later in this chapter.

As a rule, billboards will consistently reach the most people at the lowest cost per thousand. Except for direct mail, television will cost the most per thousand. However, as we've tried to explain, CPM is only one way to predict advertising effectiveness.

A Final Checklist

Whether you're using print or electronic media, billboards, or home shows, ask yourself the following questions.

1) Is the ad aimed at the buyer you want to reach?
2) Does it grab and hold the buyer's attention?

3) Is it well positioned or is it buried on a back page, poor time slot, or back road?

4) Do you know what you're selling? Is the message clear?

5) Is it well designed? Attractive? Distinctive? Well written? Memorable?

6) Is it honest? Is it in good taste?

7) Does it look professional? Does it add to your image, or does it detract?

8) Is it producing enough good-quality leads to pay for itself?

Your Media Choices

In the following pages, we'll take a look at the advertising choices you'll have to make. Keep in mind that no one choice is right for every remodeler 100 percent of the time. With some good advice and a little experience, you'll find the right mix for your company.

Yellow Pages

Even if you don't do any other kind of advertising, you'll probably have a listing and at least a small ad in the Yellow Pages. If you believe the phone book's sales force, you'll end up with a full page ad and still wonder if you have enough. Better yet, follow your own common sense: Do what your most successful competitors are doing and you won't waste money.

The Yellow Pages are great when you're price shopping for tires, insurance, sporting goods or thousands of other consumer goods. You call four stores and select the one with the lowest price. For doctors, stockbrokers, contractors, lawyers and nearly any service, the Yellow Pages are only a starting place. You want more than the lowest price. You need to know more than which vendor placed the largest ad.

Our company has been listed in the Yellow Pages for over ten years. During that time, our ad has generated only four new clients. That's in spite of trying several sizes and types of ads. Two of those chose us because we were in their neighborhood. One chose us because our ad listed handicapped renovations as a specialty. We have no idea why the other one selected us over all of the others listed.

Obviously, if we had to depend on the Yellow Pages to survive, we would never have made it through the first ten years. Fortunately, we haven't spent too much for our ads. So we judge the ad cost as money well spent.

For many remodelers, anything more than a bold print listing or small, in-column ad probably won't pay for itself. This is especially true if you live in an urban area. Yellow Page prices vary with ad size and number of copies distributed.

Figure 3-3 shows what you can expect to pay for an ad in the Yellow Pages. All prices shown are monthly charges. Prices for color will be higher. Leaf through the Yellow Pages and notice how your eyes go right to color ads. Yellow Pages sales people will tell you that color increases readership by 50 to 60 percent. If you decide on a larger ad, we recommend buying an in-column ad rather than a display ad which is separate from the alphabetic listing.

Population size	2,000,000	400,000	15,000
In-column ad 1/2 inch	$ 33.50	$ 18.00	$ 5.70
1/4 column	164.60	78.00	20.20
Color 1/4 column	263.40	124.80	32.30
Display ad 1/2 page	1,415.60	663.00	172.90

Figure 3-3

Yellow Page ad costs

Consider very carefully how much business an ad will have to generate to pay for itself. Suppose you live in a community with a population of 400,000. You decide to go with a quarter-column ad that costs $936 for the year. While it's true that one good job would pay for the ad, it's also true that $936 spent in newspaper ads or radio spots might bring in *ten* good jobs. How would you rather spend your advertising budget?

To increase the effectiveness of Yellow Pages advertising, try listing your company in more than one category. Home improvements, kitchen and baths, remodeling, and general contractors are all possibilities. Or get even more specific, under headings such as siding, roofing, or decks. For your customers' convenience, you might pay extra for bold print or even superbold, which is both darker and larger type.

No matter what size your ad, even the half-inch size, make your message unique. What's your specialty? How many years of construction experience have you had? Are you a member of NARI or the Remodelor's Council? Tell the reader as much as you can. Don't assume prospects already know all about you. And don't forget to include your logo and tag line.

As long as you have a business phone, your company name will be listed in all the Yellow Pages directories. Rather than wasting your money in several phone books, put your ad in the one that's the biggest and has been published the longest, even though it will also be the most expensive. It costs more because it's used more.

Newspapers

Circulation, placement, ad size, and ad frequency determine the cost of newspaper advertising. The more times you run an ad, the less you'll have to pay for each insertion. Also, if you run on the back page of a section or in a special issue, the price may be higher. As in Yellow Pages advertising, color will add to your cost but it will also add to your readership. We've found that several small, well-placed ads return more for our money than a single large ad.

Newspapers sell two kinds of advertising: display and classified. Display ads are sold in an endless variety of sizes. They're measured in width by column and in length by inch, or agate line, with 14 lines in a column inch. Classified ads appear in the classified section and are sold either by the column inch or the agate line. Until a few years ago there was no standard number of columns on a page. Now nearly all daily newspapers use a six-column page. Tabloids generally use five columns.

Some remodelers advertise in the classified section because it's so much cheaper. But you get what you pay for. Exposure in the classified section is much more limited. Most of your potential consumers would never think to look in the classified section for a remodeling contractor. One of our competitors tried running an ad in the "Services" column of the classified section. In three months he got only one call — to fix a door knob. The ad was very cheap, but the money was wasted.

One advantage of newspapers is that they appear every day. Unless you're advertising in a special issue or the TV magazine or comics, the ad you submit today can probably be in tomorrow's paper. Rarely will your ad have to be turned in more than a week before it appears. And most papers will either help you put an ad together or do it for you, charging only for the type and artwork they prepare. Many have books of camera-ready clip art you can use in the ad at no additional cost. If you do just the occasional ad and aren't using an agency, that can be a big help.

Probably the biggest disadvantage of newspaper advertising is the short shelf life, not much more than one day for daily papers. Weekly papers are usually cheaper and tend to pull responses for a longer time. That helps stretch your advertising dollar. The free weekly "shopper" throwaway papers fall in this category. They have nothing but ads. People reading them are looking for interesting ads. That's an advantage. But what they're looking for is probably a baby crib or a good buy in a used car, not your offer of remodeling services.

Many of the larger dailies let you choose the section where your ad will appear, whether sports, lifestyle, local news, or the business section. Even those that allow you to select a section won't guarantee that's where you'll end up, although they'll probably do their best. Some papers will guarantee position only for their best customers.

In large, urban areas, you're probably better off buying space in one of the small, neighborhood weeklies. You can target the specific region you want to reach for a lot less money. Figure 3-4 should give you some idea of what you can expect to pay for newspaper display ads. The circulation and cost per column inch figures shown are for weekdays. Sunday circulation and rates are usually higher.

Paper	A	B	C	D	E	F
Circulation (in thousands)	3	50	9	54	105	405
Daily/weekly	W	W	D	D	D	D
Number of columns	5	7	6	6	6	6
$ per column inch	$5.00	$7.20	$7.50	$19.15	$27.40	$53.00
$ extra for color	$60.00	N/A	$35.00	$200.00	$254.00	$700.00
Ad cost (6" x all column ad)	$150.00	$302.40	$270.00	$689.40	$986.40	$1,908.

Figure 3-4

Comparing newspaper ad costs

Where there's little competition for your business, rates will be higher. Where two dailies compete for the same market, you'll pay less for the same space. Keep in mind, too, that the costs in Figure 3-4 are *open rates*, what you'll pay for a single insertion. *Contract rates* for multiple insertions are lower. The contract rate for even as few as two insertions may be 10 to 40 percent less.

As you can see, there's a huge range in the CPM. But as we said earlier, the CPM is only one indicator. The numbers seem to say that the CPM of paper F makes it an unbeatable value. Paper A looks like it's vastly overpriced. Now look at the demographics in Figure 3-5. See if it doesn't help you decide which is the best buy.

Paper	A	B	C	D	E	F
Average income (in thousands)	46.8	28.9	34.0	32.0	35.0	38.0
% professionals or managers	57.0	32.0	42.0	35.0	46.0	48.0
Average years education	14.8	12.2	13.3	12.9	14.2	14.7
% own homes	84.0	55.0	74.0	63.0	64.0	68.0
Average age	37.0	44.0	39.0	43.0	41.0	42.0

Figure 3-5

Comparison of readership demographics

In spite of its CPM, paper A would probably be the best buy. It has by far the highest percentage of homeowners as well as the highest average income. Then look at the education level and the average reader's age. Those make it look even better. Since it's a weekly, it has a longer shelf life than the dailies. That's another advantage.

Paper F also has good demographics. But when you look at the cost of the ad size we're using for comparison ($1,908), your risk becomes much greater. At that price, you could use your entire ad budget and not get a single call. And next week you could be back at work for your old boss.

Paper C has the next lowest CPM. But you'll probably avoid using it. This paper is the free "shopper" that's distributed to everyone in the community. If you're selling a house or truck, this paper is a great buy. You can't beat the CPM. If you want to appeal to homeowners with high incomes, it's the worst value.

Not every paper can supply demographics on their readership. In that case, make an educated guess. Drive down the streets of their delivery areas. Are the people in these homes good potential customers? Do they look prosperous? Are the homes well kept? Are home values increasing? Are the vehicles new and in good shape? Remember, the junkiest neighborhoods need your service the most. But the people who live there have other things to do with their money — like buying groceries.

Newspaper advertising has its own vocabulary. Here are some of the common terms:

Rate card— It lists the prices a newspaper charges for advertising space and the policies the paper observes.

Open rate— The rate charged for non-contract advertising. This is usually higher than even the smallest space contract.

Contract rate— If you're willing to commit yourself to several insertions, you can lock in a lower cost per column inch. Running only a small ad several times in a calendar year probably qualifies you for the contract rate.

Broadsheet— A full size sheet. Most dailies are broadsheet size.

Tabloid size (Tabs)— Approximately one-half of a broadsheet page. Many weeklies are tabloid size.

Inserts— When ads are printed separately from the paper and inserted after the paper is printed, there will usually be an inserting charge. Many inserts are a broadsheet folded in half.

ROP (run-of-paper)— An ad that may appear anywhere and in any section at the newspaper's discretion.

Double truck— An ad that runs across two facing pages. Papers usually have a minimum length and column width for these. An ad running across two pages uses an extra column. You'll usually pay for this column.

Reservations— It's wise to reserve advertising space ahead of time. To reserve space in a specific section, reserve four or five days in advance. For preprinted sections, such as the Sunday comics or the TV magazine, reserve three to four weeks in advance.

Layout— Also called a *dummy*. This is the first copy of the ad you turn into the paper. From this the paper will create a *proof* or checking copy.

Proof— A copy of the ad as the paper has laid it out for you. You make corrections and return the proof to the paper. If you turn in your layout too late, there may not be time to prepare a proof.

Tear sheets— Extra copies of your printed ad. If the ad is partially sponsored by a co-op advertiser, send a tear sheet to that advertiser with your request for reimbursement. The remaining tear sheets can go in your file.

Pickups— Ads that are repeated without any change. Many papers allow a substantial discount on pickup ads.

Copy— The text of your message.

Velox— When art work is the wrong size for an ad, it's photographed to enlarge or reduce it. The reproduction is called a velox.

PMT (photo-mechanical transfer)— Another name for velox.

Halftone— Look at a black and white photograph through a magnifying glass. Notice that blacks blend smoothly into grays and whites. Then look at a picture in a newspaper through the same magnifying glass. Notice that you see hundreds of tiny dots of black or gray instead of continuous tones. This dot pattern improves the quality of a printed picture and is made by laying a semi-transparent screen over a photograph when it's reproduced. This screened reproduction is called a halftone. Eighty-five lines per inch is standard screen for newspapers. Magazines have much higher quality photography and may use screens as fine as 250 lines per inch.

Line art— This is drawing or type that's all black and white without any tones of gray.

Magazines

Many communities now have magazines that are produced and distributed locally. These magazines usually have a much higher CPM than newspapers with a comparable circulation. And they also have a much longer shelf life — anywhere from one to six months. Generally, their demographics will be more like paper A in Figure 3-4. Readers have higher incomes, higher education level, and include more professional people.

Advertising in local magazines costs more because these magazines cost more to produce. That also means that production schedules are longer. Instead of the one- to five-day lead time that newspapers have, you'll have to deliver copy from one to three months before the ad is scheduled to appear. To get the most for your advertising dollar, you'll want a very high-quality ad, probably produced by an advertising agency.

Radio

Advertising on the radio is a little like advertising in a weekly neighborhood paper. Because stations offer a wide variety of formats, their listening audiences generally have very narrow demographics. Radio station formats are designed to appeal to a narrow audience. Think about the kind of format that would appeal to your buyers. All news? Classical? Oldies? Easy listening? Talk? Which do you feel would be best?

Radio advertising rates vary widely. Different time slots have different rates. *Drive time* is often considered the most valuable time for the age group you want to target. From 6 to 9 a.m. and 4 to 7 p.m. people are on their way to and from work and are listening to the radio.

Some stations have the largest audience from 10 a.m. to 3 p.m. because their format makes good background music for offices and stores. Obviously, that time will be most expensive. The least expensive will be the midnight to 6 a.m. slot. The 30-to 65-year olds are asleep then. This time slot will probably cost less than half the next lowest time slot. But is it going to do you any good?

Like the other media, the more you buy, the lower your rate. The rate charged a one-time buyer will be as much as one-third higher than the best customers pay.

Radio spots are sold in blocks of time. An advertiser usually buys 15-, 30-, or 60-second spots as a package. You have a choice on scheduling. Select the time slot you want and pay accordingly. Or you can buy a run-of-schedule (ROS) package. Like a newspaper's ROP, it means your spots will be scattered through the day and not concentrated in one time slot. If you buy an ROS package, make sure it has a good distribution in high-rating times and not just in the 7 p.m. to 6 a.m. stretch when the listening audience is way down.

Another alternative is to try public radio. Although public radio stations don't sell commercials as such, they do sell time. Businesses are asked to "underwrite" programs. For a reasonable fee, the business is identified as the program's sponsor. Sponsoring a month at a time gives steady exposure at very reasonable rates.

Again, you won't have the low CPM of a more expensive station. But you will have quality demographics. Public radio attracts a high income, professional audience that's very loyal. They appreciate not having a lot of commercial interruptions and are more likely to patronize the businesses that support their station. The other nice part is that you aren't competing with a lot of advertisers for the listener's pocketbook. Generally, you can buy either sole sponsorship or share it with a very limited number of other businesses.

Figure 3-6 shows rates for several radio stations. The CPM will help you decide which is the best value. But keep in mind that demographics are still the most important. All commercials in Figure 3-6 are 60 seconds except for station KAAA, which is a public radio station. Costs listed are for program sponsorships.

As we said earlier, KAAA is the public radio station and has excellent demographics for your purposes. Station KBBB is an AM station and plays hits from the '60s, '70s, and '80s. KCCC is an easy listening station that's popular background music for businesses. The last station, KDDD, is an all-talk station in a large, urban area. The announcers on KDDD often sound as if they do business with the advertisers personally. This adds a lot to the advertiser's credibility.

Station	KAAA	KBBB	KCCC	KDDD
6-10 a.m.	$10	$34	$54	$180
10 a.m. to 3 p.m.	10	30	67	175
3-7 p.m.	15	28	54	180
7-12 p.m.	10	30	51	160
Audience	1000	2,000	9,200	24,000
CPM at peak	15.0	17.0	7.28	7.50

Figure 3-6

Costs for 60 seconds in each time slot

Because all the stations have reasonably good demographics, what you can afford may make more of a difference than the CPM.

Many remodelers reject radio advertising without trying it because they think radio commercials are too expensive to produce. Actually, the cost can be fairly reasonable. To be sure, you can spend a lot. But a spot read live by an announcer can be just as effective.

Humorous radio spots can be very effective. If you can come up with a good script, you and a friend can produce a 30-second spot on a shoestring. In fact, if you're buying a good block of radio time, you can probably use the station's production facility at little or no additional cost. But don't sacrifice quality just to minimize cost. A bad commercial is much worse than no commercial at all.

Jingles add interest to a radio commercial and stay in the listener's mind long after the words are forgotten. When was the last time you heard "*J-E-L-L-O*" or "*See the USA, in your Chevrolet*"? No doubt you can still sing the jingles. But jingles are expensive to create and produce.

If you decide to spend the money for a jingle, remember that a jingle is just a tag line set to music. Keep it simple. People should call because they remember you, not because they want a copy of the lyrics. Keep the accompaniment simple, too. Use no more than two or three instruments. It's cheaper and the words don't get lost in the accompaniment. And finally, try to create a jingle that's different. It doesn't need the prettiest melody, just the most memorable one. Set it apart with a different rhythm or an unexpected turn in the tune. If it seems like most jingles are peppy, try one that's a little sleepy.

Radio advertising requires repetition to be effective. Don't buy radio unless you can afford repetition. And don't jerk a commercial just because your phone doesn't start ringing immediately after the first radio play. Give people time to react.

Just like newspapers, radio has its own vocabulary. Here are some of the terms you'll use.

Arbitron— The company that estimates the listening audience for both radio and television.

Average quarter-hour audience (AQH)— An estimate of the average audience that's listened for a minimum of five minutes within a specific quarter-hour.

Cume (Reach)— An estimate of the number of different households or persons within those households that listen at least once during the average week for five minutes or more.

Spot— Another word for commercial.

Run-of-schedule (ROS)— Commercials spread throughout the station's time slots instead of a particular time slot you request.

Talent— The actor/actress or announcer who has a part in the commercial.

Dubs— Copies made of a completed commercial.

As with any kind of advertising, there's no guarantee that radio will work for you. However, studying a station's demographics makes mistakes less likely.

Television

Television is an expensive stepchild of radio. Some of the same principles apply, but the cost will almost always be higher. By selecting the program when your spot is to run, you can target a very narrow group of consumers. For remodelers, cable stations may be a better choice. They're much cheaper and much more focused in geographic area.

Advertising on television will give you a broad exposure. It will also add to your credibility. You can look like a major company, when, in fact, you're just a little company willing to spend some money.

Television commercials can be much more expensive and difficult to produce than radio spots. A TV station, if you're buying a good block of time, will sometimes produce a very simple commercial at no charge to you, except for the talent and dubs. Even if they do charge, they'll probably do it for less than an agency would. So check with the station first. Most smaller stations will suggest a good advertising concept. Some may help you write the copy.

Just as in radio, you can buy a specific slot or you can buy an ROS package. Prices will vary widely from area to area. Just like newspapers, magazines, and radio, TV stations base their fees on estimates of the viewing audience. Rates vary so widely that it's hard give you any idea of typical costs. In a small market, a 30-second spot can run anywhere from $30 to $850, depending on program ratings.

In major urban areas, the high end can be ten times that. If you want to buy time during a specific program, expect to pay a premium for it. Of course, as in radio, the more commercial time you buy, the lower your rates will be.

Billboards

Almost all billboard advertising is institutional rather than promotional. You can't expect to put much urgency into a seven-word message. You can, however, make it memorable by adding wit and punch.

Outdoor advertising has a high initial investment. Dollar for dollar, it also has the highest number of viewers (reach) and will be seen the greatest number of times (frequency). Billboards are seen all day, every day. They can't be turned off like television, tuned out like radio, or discarded like newspapers or magazines. A billboard constantly reminds the public you're around.

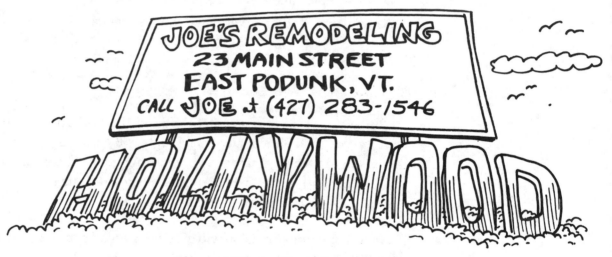

Choose billboard locations carefully.

By choosing billboard locations carefully, you can reach 75 to 80 percent of the market in a given area. If billboard space is available, you can target the right intersections and highways in the right neighborhoods.

Billboard value is measured in Gross Rating Points or GRP rather than CPM. This can be a complicated computation and we won't go into it. If you're interested, ask a billboard company to give you sample GRP ratings so you can compare the cost of outdoor advertising with other choices.

The easiest way to evaluate the effectiveness of billboards is to look at the *showing numbers*. Usually you'll buy a billboard ad by location and showing numbers: a number 50 showing, a number 100 showing, a number 200 showing, and so on. The showing number is just a percentage, 100 equaling 100 percent.

This number doesn't refer to the number of billboards. It indicates the percentage of the population in a certain area that will see the sign. If you buy a number 100 showing, the number of people who will see your sign every day is equal to the total population of an area. Some people may see it twice, some three times, some none at all. Simply put, if you're trying to reach a population of 50,000 and you buy a number 100 showing, your sign will have 50,000 viewings a day. If you buy a number 50 showing in the same area, your billboard should reach half the market, or 25,000 viewings a day. A number 200 showing would give you twice the market, or 100,000 viewings a day.

Of course, there's no single billboard that's going to give a number 200 showing. You get numbers that high by using several billboards. For example, 10 billboards might yield a number 100 showing and 20 might yield a number 200 showing.

How is the showing for each billboard calculated? Outdoor advertising agencies use traffic counts compiled by government agencies or their own count of the number of cars and occupants per car passing each location. In most communities, 10 to 20 percent of the roads carry 80 to 90 percent of the traffic. This is where billboards are located.

There are two common sizes for billboards. *Posters* are the smaller of the two and measure 12 feet by 24 feet. They're printed on paper and the paper is applied like wallpaper to a wood or metal backing on site. The printing cost of the poster will be in addition to the cost of renting the billboard space. Depending on the number of colors and the number of posters you order, you can expect to pay from $50 to $200 per poster.

Bulletins are larger and more permanent. Standard bulletin size is 14 x 48 feet. Bulletins are painted panels that are trucked to the site and mounted on the billboard frame.

With either, the company will require a minimum contract, usually 30 days for posters and 60 days for bulletins. For longer contracts, they'll rotate your posters every 30 days and bulletins every 60 so the same people aren't seeing the same message continually for three months.

Billboard prices vary. A good billboard in an urban area may cost several thousand dollars a month. Even within urban areas, costs will vary. Advertising agencies know which part of town is best for selling cars, liquor, or remodeling. Obviously, you'll pay more for the best space.

An outdoor advertising agency will drive you to the signs available so you can choose the billboard that's best for your purpose.

When creating a billboard ad, keep it as simple as possible. Don't bother with lots of artwork. It'll run up your printing and design costs and may even work against you. Billboards are seen at a glance over and over. If you're lucky enough to be at a heavily-traveled intersection, people stopped at red lights may spend time studying an involved ad, but don't count on it. Instead, use bright, eye-catching colors and distinctive but easy-to-read lettering. Don't forget to put your logo on it, too.

Keep your message brief and punchy, no more than five to seven words. Humor works well, as do tag lines. Always include your name and phone number. What prospects need to know most is how to reach you. Don't assume that everyone knows where to find you, even if your logo has been spread all over town for many years.

Assault by Mail

Many remodelers mail brochures, flyers and newsletters to prospective clients to generate business. This is called direct mail marketing by advertisers and *junk mail* by nearly everyone else.

Brochures and newsletters tend to be institutional advertising. Flyers are promotional. They're a good way of soliciting business in an area that's been hit by storm or fire damage. Both brochures and newsletters are good for selling prospects on performance, service, efficiency, and quality at a fair price.

Send a newsletter to past and current clients, people who have requested information from you, suppliers, architects, real estate agents, and the news media. A newsletter might include news about work you've been doing, news of interest to anyone planning to remodel, trends in the industry, and employee profiles. Sent at regular intervals, a good newsletter will keep your company name in the minds of potential clients.

Flyers are inexpensive single sheets sent by mail or hand-delivered to prospective clients in target neighborhoods. But even flyers should look professional. A flyer that's handwritten or produced with a copy machine won't have the impact of a well-designed piece printed in color on coated stock. Unless you have beautiful handwriting, use type from a typesetter or a letter-quality printer. Spend a little time on it.

Brochures may be anything from a simple black on white folder to a bound booklet done in full color. Like flyers, they should be mailed to carefully targeted areas. You'll also give the same brochures to prospective clients at home shows or when meeting for the first time with any client.

Brochures can be very expensive. Even the cheapest one you design can cost several hundred dollars to print. If you upgrade to a heavy paper, several colors, and photos or custom art work, you can expect to pay several thousand dollars for the same number of brochures. Figure $5,000 for 5,000 copies of a 4- to 8-page full color brochure, including design, photography, color separation, type, layout and printing. Add mailing costs, and you can quickly use an entire year's advertising budget.

Fortunately, there's a cheaper way. Free or low-cost brochures are available from NARI, the Remodelor's Council, or even from the government. These brochures usually have a place where you can stamp your company name, address, and phone number.

Brochures offered by the remodeling associations and government agencies usually give advice on remodeling and selecting a contractor. That doesn't help you sell the job. But don't underestimate the value of giving a little free advice. Even if you're not actively promoting your company, you'll be remembered. That, of course, is the point in the first place. If you can't afford an expensive brochure of your own, do the next best thing. Pass out brochures made by others but with your name, address and phone number.

The question, of course, is this: Will any of this advertising produce the desired result? Unless your newsletter, flyer, or brochure is unusually distinctive, or you're meeting an urgent need such as roof repair following a hail storm, you probably won't see any immediate result. However, there are several ways to increase your mailing's effectiveness.

1) Use the most current and accurate mailing list you can find. Weed out renters and homes in low-income areas. The average U.S. family moves every seven years, so an old list won't do you any good. Lists with good demographics can be bought from mailing list compilers and from sources such as local newspapers or magazines. Credit card companies and national magazines also sell lists, but expect to pay more. If you have time, the best list is almost free. Use the Polk directory from your local library to compile your own list. Polk directories show the names, addresses and phone numbers of residents on each street in a neighborhood. Most of these directories suggest average income ranges for each neighborhood. What more could you ask for?

2) Personalize the envelope. Use a postage stamp instead of a postage meter. Handwrite the name or type it instead of using a computer-printed label. That makes it more likely that the envelope will get opened. Address the envelope by name rather than Homeowner or Resident. It may or may not get opened if the name on the envelope is no longer at that address. But mail addressed *Occupant* gets tossed out with all the other junk mail.

3) Time your mailings. Homeowners are more likely to think of home improvement projects in the spring and fall. They're less likely to do anything over the holidays or the summer months. Target your mailings to catch people when they're already in the mood to do something.

4) Make your mailing as distinctive as possible. Choose a theme and build around that. The best mailing we ever received was an invitation to visit an open house in a new development called Stetson Hills. The invitation was printed on a handkerchief with a bandanna border. The name of the development is still vivid in our minds years later because of the unusual invitation. Try sending refrigerator magnets, odd sized or shaped pieces,

or messages on something other than paper. All will add to the cost, but they'll also add to the impact.

5) Give some incentive to respond. Credit old customers $100 for repeat or referral business over, say, a $5,000 minimum. Or if a supplier is promoting a product line, pass the sales incentive on to customers who sign a contract by a certain date.

6) Above all, make your mailing piece reflect quality and professionalism. If you or an employee can't do that, hire someone who can. What you send out creates an image for either better or worse. Do the best you can. Make it polished and memorable.

If you decide to try a mailing, you'll probably run across some of the following words:

Cheshire labels— Fan-folded mailing labels printed by a computer on plain paper. A machine made by the Cheshire company cuts the paper into strips and applies each label to an envelope or card.

Pressure sensitive labels— Labels that you peel off paper backing and stick on envelopes and cards by hand.

Self-mailer— A ready-to-mail piece that doesn't need an envelope. It must conform to U.S. postal regulations.

Above all, watch your own mailbox. What catches your eye? Which piece stands out from the rest of the junk mail you get every day? Keep this in mind. No brochure creates a need to spend $20,000 on a kitchen remodel. The homeowner had to have that idea already. But for the owner who's thinking about making some changes, a good mailing can turn the inclination into action.

Home Shows

Most larger communities have home shows or displays where the public can see what's new and interesting for homeowners. These shows are usually sponsored by the industry organizations, although local papers, radio stations and shopping malls sometimes will put together very successful shows. Many of the exhibitors will probably be remodelers or construction contractors.

Taking a booth or exhibit space will put you in touch with prospects who are already in the market to make some changes. You don't have to sell the idea of remodeling. All you need to sell are your ideas and yourself as the remodeler who can do the job.

Booth fees are usually very reasonable, often only a couple of hundred dollars. The cost of building the booth, staffing it, and buying literature to pass out will usually be much more. If you plan to do home shows more than once every few years, it's wise to design a reusable booth. The cost will be higher initially, but will be far less after several uses of the booth. You don't need an elaborate booth. But it should feel open and airy and be well lit. Use your best workmanship; no buyer will give you a second look if your booth is shoddy.

Use large "before" and "after" pictures to show off what you've done. Have some photo albums on hand that show other types of jobs.

Anyone who expresses interest in your work should be invited to leave a name, address and phone number. Note the kind of job each prospect wants and when the work will be done. Put this information on a file card. Until you've actually made an appointment with this prospect, file the cards by anticipated work date rather than alphabetically. In other words, if a prospect says he'd like to do something "next summer," file his name under the month of May and give him a call then. If he says then that he can't do anything until fall, file him again under August. Always be polite and friendly. If you're persistent, by the time he's ready to do something, you'll have a good shot at doing the work.

Don't waste your money on popcorn, balloons, or drawings. It's true you'll attract a bigger crowd. But, as in any kind of advertising, the number of leads isn't nearly as important as the *quality* of leads. If you have an attractive, interesting booth, serious buyers will stop even if you only have a nice brochure and a business card to hand out.

Staffing can be one of the biggest headaches in running a booth. You'll need someone who is courteous and knowledgeable. In fact, you'll need a minimum of two people each day so one can take breaks without leaving the booth unattended. Your representatives at the booth don't have to be sales people. A secretary or foreman work almost as well. But whoever runs the booth must look clean and be comfortable meeting the public. Otherwise, they'll drive work away rather than attract it.

Talking enthusiastically for hours at a time is a high energy job. Shifts shouldn't run more than two or three hours without a break.

Teaming Up with a Supplier

We've found several building material dealers who are willing to offer display space to their best contractor customers. A display at a lumberyard or hardware store can be a very effective and low-cost way to attract business.

A contractor in our town hit the jackpot with this idea: He built a wood deck at the edge of the parking lot of the biggest lumberyard in town. His name and phone number were prominently displayed on the deck. Initially, the deck was built as a "do-it-yourself" promotion. The lumberyard provided the materials. The contractor provided the labor and maintenance. Beyond that, no money changed hands. Both the yard and the contractor liked the arrangement. The display sold at least a dozen decks for the contractor in the past year. And the lumberyard has sold a lot more deck material since the display was built.

Suggest this to one or two of your best suppliers: you'll put together a home improvement exhibit in an unused corner or a display window of their store. The supplier may want a referral fee or a percentage of every job the display generates. But explain the obvious benefits. You buy most materials at that store already. The more business you do, the more business you can give the supplier.

Qualifying Leads

Until now we've been talking about finding prospective customers. If you've got a creative program, whether in one medium or spread across several, the phone should start ringing. Your job then is to separate the good leads from the window-shoppers. Many new remodelers make the mistake of giving red carpet treatment to every lead that comes across their desk. That's a mistake. You want to concentrate on the *quality* leads, the ones who need what you're offering and are willing to pay for what they want. It's still a good practice to qualify leads immediately by phone rather than wait until your first appointment.

Don't worry about turning off potential clients with a lot of questions. If you're courteous and professional, no one will mind. Anyone who's serious about having work done should be happy to cooperate. Anyhow, you'll need this information eventually. How you get it and when is the only question.

Keep a form like Figure 3-7 near your phone. Use it when you ask the following questions. When it's completed, put it in a folder marked *Leads*. If you begin negotiating with the prospect, staple the form in a new folder with the client's name marked on the outside. This way you'll have easy access to all the key information about the job.

1) Ask for the name, address, home and work telephone numbers. Ask if it's O.K. to call the client at work. Note this information on the form.

2) How did you hear about the company? If the caller was referred to you by another client, be sure to ask who made the referral. If some of your advertising prompted the call, find out which ad so you'll know which ad gets the credit for this lead. If you're swamped with calls, you'll need to set priorities. Referrals should generally come first, calls from ads next, and Yellow Pages last.

3) How long have you lived at your present address? If less than five years, there may not be much equity to borrow against.

4) What type of project do you have in mind? Listen carefully. This is important. Find out exactly what the caller wants. That's what you're going to sell. Does he or she have plans drawn yet?

5) When are you planning to do the work? Again, set priorities. If the caller says she's not in a hurry, but wants something done in the next few months, don't drop everything to rush out and talk to her. Take care of people who are in a hurry first.

Date_____ Appointment date, time_____

Customer name_____

Street address_____

City, state, Zip_____

Address of property if different from home address_____

_____

Directions_____

Home phone_____ Business phone_____

O.K. to call at work?_____ Yes _____ No_____

Lead source_____

Own home____ ____ _____ years

Scope of the project_____

Time frame_____

Budget for project $_____

How financed_____

Bid outcome: Date accepted_____

        Bid price_____

        Rejected, awarded to_____

Starting date_____

Figure 3-7

Lead form

6) Do you have a budget amount in mind? This is the most difficult question to ask, but it's also the most important. You can weed out a lot of tire-kickers with this one question. Most homeowners aren't good at estimating project costs. They know how much they can afford to pay. But they don't know what that will buy. If you don't get a good answer to this question, and you probably won't, gently probe a little deeper. For instance, suppose your prospect wants a kitchen remodeled. Explain that your company has done $5,000, $10,000, even $30,000 kitchen re-models. Suggest what that money would buy for each job. Then ask what the caller has in mind. Whatever you propose should fit in that budget. There's no use suggesting something your prospect can't possibly afford.

7) How are you planning to pay for the project? From savings? Or will it be financed? As we'll explain in later chapters, it takes time to get financing. Lenders don't normally hurry. That can delay start dates and cause complications. A little advanced planning can avoid most problems.

Some contractors also ask what other contractors are bidding on the project. That's a legitimate question. Don't settle for an evasive answer, especially if you plan to compete primarily on price. If you're selling craftsmanship, innovation, efficiency, and quality rather than price, the number of bidders won't be as important. Generally, a prospect who's getting a dozen bids on plans already prepared has one thing in mind: Get it done at the lowest possible price. You may or may not want to compete in that market. That's your choice. But know the rules before you jump into the game.

4

Making the Sale

Closing a sale is hard work. New remodeling contractors know that. It's the hardest part of making a business grow.

Our company had some serious sales problems in the early years. We understand now, though, that it wasn't our clients. It was *us*. We created most of our own sales problems. We didn't believe in ourselves. We didn't believe our price was fair. We didn't believe we could do the job. Even when we were low bidder and the customer raved about our quality work, we thought it was a fluke.

Gradually we developed more confidence. A well-run job is anything but a fluke. We make good money because we're good at what we do. Anything as complex and demanding as remodeling deserves a fair return for the effort, not just the lowest bid. Once we shook off the doubt and developed some self-assurance, we closed sales faster and easier. We still don't get every job that comes across our desk. We don't want to. But our closing ratio is way up, probably because prospective clients are reassured by the confidence they see in us.

We don't pay much attention to conventional selling wisdom, the kind you're likely to get at a sales seminar: *99 ways to overcome objections*, for instance. We don't try to be something we're not, just to meet the client's expectations. What we do is simpler and easier. We didn't learn it from a seminar or a book. We learned it through experience. This chapter is intended to share that experience with you.

A Hard Lesson

For us, the turning point came nearly ten years ago. It happened when we lost the Brown job. Ted and Tina Brown wanted to finish out a basement and redo a kitchen. They asked us to write up a proposal. Like most homeowners, they only had a general idea of what they wanted done. Their list included new kitchen cabinets, counters, flooring, and a new staircase upstairs. Downstairs they wanted a bathroom finished, the walls drywalled over furring, and carpet. They wanted a "medium" quality job. Not so cheap that it would fall apart and not too much for their budget. That's all the plans and specs we got.

Using their suggestions, we put together a very complete, detailed proposal. Our bid came to $22,000. The Browns seemed pleased with us and the price. We didn't ask them to sign a contract, but they told us to start the job when we were ready. Several days later, Ted called to say he had another price and wasn't sure what to do. The second contractor came in at just over $13,000. Ted wanted us to explain why our bid was $9,000 higher. Our only answer was that we obviously weren't bidding the same job. The Browns didn't understand that. The other contractor had given them a price for most of what was in our bid, but for about $9,000 less. Ted was worried we were gouging. In the end, Ted and Tina chose the other contractor.

Green as we were, we knew our price wasn't out of line. True, we might have figured 20 percent for profit and overhead instead of 10 or 15 percent. But we knew the extra 5 or 10 percent didn't make a $9,000 difference. We also knew we couldn't do the work for $13,000. No one could. Even if we had zero overhead and tradesmen who worked for $5 an hour, we couldn't do the job for $13,000. We explained that to Ted Brown, but all he could see was the $9,000 difference.

So, we lost the Brown job. I won't mince words. We were deeply frustrated — *and* discouraged.

Six months later a neighbor of the Browns called to ask for a bid on a small job. While talking to the neighbor, we got a description of what happened to the Browns. The contractor they hired was a low-ball change order artist. The final cost of the job was well over our price of $22,000. Adding insult to injury, he'd done such shoddy work that much of it would have to be redone when the Browns could afford it.

Don't Be a Low-baller

It's easy to low-ball unsophisticated homeowners. Just leave out of the bid (and contract) everything you think the owners won't miss. For example, if the owners want cabinets, list in your bid the cost of new cabinets. But leave the cost of breaking out the old cabinets, hauling them to the dump, resurfacing the wall, installing shims, cabinet hardware, cabinet finishing, cabinet tops and cabinet shelves. Your customers probably won't notice what you left out. Then, once you've started work, point out to your customers that they probably want the old cabinets taken off the walls before you put the new ones on, the walls repaired, shims, shelving, tops, hardware and finishing. Those are extra. And, naturally, you'll have to charge for those changes.

If you're going to install a header in a wall, list that header in your bid as a 2 x 6. Of course, a 2 x 6 header won't pass inspection. You know that. But your prospects don't. Later, when the inspector demands a 6 x 12 header, give your clients the bad news. You'll have to install a 6 x 12 header. That's going to cost extra — several hundred extra. After all, you bid a 2 x 6 header. It's not your fault that the code is so crazy and the inspector an ogre.

Our point is this: Every contractor in the business can think up a hundred ways to get paid extra on almost any job. And some contractors do exactly that. *But they don't do it for long.* Eventually the word gets around. No one wants to buy headaches and a lawsuit. And that's exactly what homeowners risk when they accept low-ball bids from change order artists.

Explain the change order game to your prospective clients. Warn them about what can happen if they accept a low-ball bid. Then assure them that your bid is as complete as you can make it. You can do the job described in the bid for exactly the price quoted. Other bids they receive may not be so complete. The only way to be sure is to compare bids item by item. Anything that's missing from a bid will probably be an extra charge if that bid is accepted.

That Important First Impression

As we pointed out in Chapter 2, how you look and sound is very important. Whether you get a chance to bid and whether your bid is taken seriously depends on how your client evaluates you as a remodeling professional. You want clients to respect you, your judgment and your character. The best way we know to earn respect is to show respect for those you deal with. By showing respect you build trust. Be prompt, courteous and professional at all times. There's no better way to build mutual trust.

New clients judge you by the first impressions you make. Unfortunately, what you say makes less than 10 percent of the first impression. Your appearance accounts for over half; your tone of voice for the balance. Look and sound professional. Look and sound capable and confident. Good posture, a firm hand-shake, and good eye contact are essential. Be enthusiastic!

Some experts on selling suggest that you put your hand on a client's shoulder or arm several times during the initial appointment. The purpose is to break down barriers between the two of you — to become more familiar quickly. The theory is that people are more likely to trust and buy from a familiar friend. We don't agree. Tactics like that seem insincere and inappropriate to us. They're more likely to get you a brush-off than close a sale.

More important, in our opinion, is finding the balance between formality and familiarity. The name you use when addressing a client can be a sensitive point. If you address clients as "Mr. Smith" and "Mrs. Smith," you may seem too formal and stuff. Using only a first name can seem disrespectful.

When First Names Are OK

Here's our recommendation. For people with professional titles, use their title: "Dr. Smith" or "Captain Jones." For people 20 or 30 years older than you are, Mr. and Mrs. is appropriate. For nearly everyone else, use their correct first name. But be sure you get it right. Listen to how they introduce themselves. If a man introduces himself as Tommy, don't call him Tom, or even worse, Thomas. If a woman introduces herself as Katherine, don't make the mistake of calling her Kathy. Nor should you assume that just because Katherine's husband calls her Kate that it's OK for you to do the same. Becoming too familiar too quickly can build unnecessary barriers. Selling is hard enough. Don't make it any tougher than necessary. And don't overuse names. If it doesn't sound natural, the client will sense it before you do.

Here's another mistake: selling the husband and ignoring his wife. We've taken work away from other contractors many times simply by listening carefully to what the wife wanted. Of course, every job is different, just as every marriage is different. But we've noticed a common division of responsibility between hus-bands and wives. The wife decides that remodeling is needed. The husband takes care of business arrangements for the work. The wife makes final decisions on design, brand names and colors. She'll probably have a veto over which contractor does the work. If she doesn't like you, if she doesn't like your proposal, forget it! There's no chance you'll get the job, no matter how low your price. If you want to do the work, listen very carefully to what she says about what she wants.

Even if a wife seems to be taking a back seat in decision-making, respond to her questions and solicit her opinions. The decision about which contractor to hire will nearly always be made in private between husband and wife. A wife who's reluctant to speak up in your presence may be very opinionated when you're gone. Work hard to earn the confidence of both husband and wife, even if it seems that a wife is leaving decisions up to her husband.

Sell Yourself Before You Sell the Job

Remember the Brown job we talked about earlier? That's the job that got away — mostly because of some major mistakes we made. Probably our first mistake was in not selling ourselves before we began selling the job. Ted and Tina Brown were friendly, pleasant people right from the beginning. We thought they knew about us and our reputation for good work and fair prices. We assumed they knew we stuck to our specs. We thought they understood about the change order game. We were wrong.

The Browns seemed to like us — and probably did. But that was all. They got our name from a casual acquaintance and actually knew very little about our work. If we had done a better job of selling ourselves, there might not have been a second contractor to bid against. And there certainly wouldn't have been a question of which bid to select.

Now, when we go out on our first meeting, we sell our company. We sell our skills. We sell our reliability. And we sell our fiscal responsibility. The easiest and best way to do this selling is with a presentation folder. See Figure 4-1. Inside the folder we include copies of our liability and Workers' Compensation insurance, job and credit references, and a resume. An album of "before and after" pictures helps our clients understand both the work we do and what we can do in their home. Many people have trouble visualizing the changes they plan to make. It helps if they can see pictures of the dramatic results of other remodeling jobs

Leave the presentation folder with your clients so they can call the references if they want to. Leaving the folder proves your confidence in what past clients will say about you.

It takes a lot of work to create a presentation folder. But it's well worth the effort. Some prospective clients will ask for references anyway. You might as well offer a list of satisfied customers before they ask. That helps create trust.

Every remodeler needs references. Make it a habit to ask for letters of recommendation from your most satisfied clients. Most people are willing, even if they don't enjoy doing it. You need three or four current letters of recommendation, preferably dated within the last year. Keep your file of recommendations current by asking each client to write a letter when you finish their job.

Figure 4-1

Presentation folder

If you're just starting your business and don't have any former clients, ask your old boss, co-workers, neighbors or friends to write recommendations. It doesn't matter that you haven't completed a job for them. If they can honestly say you're a reliable, knowledgeable, honest, and skilled contractor, that's enough.

If the people you ask are willing but don't know what to write, offer a sample letter as a starting point. A letter like Figure 4-2 should work perfectly.

To Whom It May Concern;

I am pleased to have the opportunity to recommend Tom Smith, owner of Best Construction.

Best Construction was our contractor on a 3500 square foot renovation of our space at Skyway Plaza. I give Tom and his company the highest rating for the work that they did.

Best Construction was efficient, thorough, and conscientious. They began work on time, finished on time, and stayed within our budget. We especially appreciate the extra effort Tom and his staff took to reduce the inconvenience to our employees and employees of other tenants at Skyway Plaza.

I enjoy working with Tom and everyone at Best Construction and can recommend him highly to anyone who needs an experienced and knowledgable renovation expert.

Sincerely,

Take Five Sporting Goods

Alan Bartoli

Alan Bartoli

General Manager

Figure 4-2

Letter of recommendation

If you've done several jobs for the same company, Figure 4-3 would be more appropriate.

Your material suppliers are another good source of recommendation letters. If you pay material invoices on time and do a good volume of business with a particular supplier, request a letter of recommendation. A letter from a supplier won't be as persuasive to a potential client as a letter from another client, but it indicates that your company is financially sound.

Greetings:

As a property manager for Ace Management Company, I have had the opportunity to work with Tom Smith, owner of Best Construction, on numerous projects.

Tom is a highly competent remodeling pro and knows the construction business thoroughly. He maintains a high standard of quality in his work and demands the same from his employees and his subcontractors.

Tom consistently meets our high standards with only the minimum amount of supervision. I can trust him to treat the renters and property owners honestly and fairly and to do the job right the first time.

Not only is Tom an excellent contractor, but he is very congenial to work with. He has always kept a pleasant, yet professional, working relationship with everyone on our projects.

I would not hesitate to recommend him for any renovation or repair work.

Sincerely,

Ann Johnson

Ann Johnson

Property Manager

Ace Management Company

Figure 4-3

Letter of recommendation

Your Personal Resume

We feel that including a personal resume in our presentation packages gives us a major advantage. Putting a personal resume together takes more time, but is definitely worth the trouble. If you decide to include a copy of your resume with each proposal, note the following points:

1) Keep it brief. One single-spaced page is enough.

2) Organize the information on the page. Clients will spend no more than a minute reviewing it. Be sure anyone reading your resume will get the major points at a glance.

3) If you don't have a high-quality typewriter or a letter-quality printer, have a professional resume agency prepare your resume. The classified section of most major Sunday papers includes ads placed by companies that prepare resumes for a fee. The polished look will be well worth the few dollars it costs. Use your company stationery.

4) Make sure there are no misspellings, typographical or grammatical errors.

5) Keep sentences short and to the point. Use active rather than passive verbs. ("Responsible for scheduling jobs," not "Jobs were scheduled by me.")

6) Don't just offer job titles. Give a brief description of responsibilities. Keep it relevant, but don't worry if it isn't all construction-related. If you managed a clothing store for three years, it says you have management skills. Don't list every summer job, even if they were all in construction. Rather, lump them together into a time period. (Summers 1975-80: Worked on a variety of residential and commercial construction crews.)

7) Highlight awards, difficult jobs, special achievements.

8) Don't bother with unnecessary information such as height, weight, or marital status.

Figure 4-4 shows a resume that would help promote trust and confidence from prospective clients. The personal statement is optional. If you do it right, it can pull the information together in a warmer, more personal way.

If you look and sound competent and your presentation folder reflects your professionalism, you'll find that half the battle is won. You've sold yourself as a professional worthy of trust by the clients you serve.

Tom Smith
Owner of Best Construction
1111 Peak View Blvd. Colorado Springs, CO 80909
(719) 555-1111
Contractor's License: B 651

Work History

1988 to the Present   Started, owned and operated Best Construction

1984 to 1987   Foreman for Barnes Remodeling in Colorado Springs. Scheduled and supervised a crew of four. Responsible for design work from 1985 to 1987.

1980 to 1984   Worked for Gingerich Construction in Denver, Colorado. Supervised and scheduled a commercial framing crew.

Strengths

Design   At Barnes Remodeling, I designed an addition on the historic Bowman house, blending the old with the new while maintaining the integrity of the period.

Scheduling   Recognized for good scheduling skills. Strive to complete each job ahead of schedule without compromising quality.

Fiscal   Payments current with every supplier. Financial statement provided upon request.

Experience   Familiar with a wide variety of projects: additions, remodeling, new residential and commercial. Past clients have appreciated my skills and attention to detail.

Affiliations   A member of HBA's Remodeler's Council since 1988.

Education   BA from University of Colorado, 1988

Personal Statement   As a third generation building contractor, I've maintained the same high standards that made my father and grandfather respected professionals in their field. I enjoy my work, take pride in the projects, and strive to maintain high standards in my relations with suppliers, subcontractors, designers, clients and government officials.

Figure 4-4

Personal resume

Selling the Value of Remodeling

Usually you have only two sales tasks: First, selling yourself as a responsible professional in the field. Second, you have to sell your proposal as the one to accept. Once in a while you'll have a third task — convincing a client that remodeling is worth the trouble and expense. Usually your prospects will have decided on what they want done long before you arrive on the scene. For the client who's still undecided about doing anything, your task involves that third step.

Most remodeling makes good sense. Spend $20,000 on a car, use it for 10 years, and then try to sell it. You'll get a few thousand back, at most. Spend $20,000 on a remodeling project, use it for 10 years and then sell the home. With any luck you'll get more than the $20,000 back. Most people consider their home their best investment. And it's an investment they can use while it appreciates in value. Emphasize these points if your prospect is still undecided about proceeding.

If more convincing is needed, refer to one of the annual cost vs. value studies that many of the remodeling and home improvement magazines publish. For example, *Remodeling* magazine lists a percentage of return on investment for all kinds of remodeling projects. Their tables show, for example, typical costs for remodeling a kitchen or bath and how much that investment adds to the value of a home.

Use one of these studies to compile a page of statistics on remodeling projects. Know which types of work increase home values the most. These figures may help a client decide to put some extra money into a third bathroom or a fireplace. Professional advice like this is appreciated and will be remembered.

Whatever you do, don't try to memorize your presentation. You're not making a speech. You're selling yourself: your skills, integrity, and competence. If what you say sounds like a recording, you'll put your audience to sleep. Don't take that chance. Every sales call is and should be different.

Listen, Listen, Listen

It's easy to feel like an expert when you call on a client. Of course, you are an expert — but only at construction. You don't have the slightest idea what your clients want until they tell you. They're the experts on that. They have to pay for what you propose to build. They have to live with your finished product. No matter how much you personally dislike a conversation pit, if that's what the client wants, that's what you're going to build. Even if you're tired of earth colors and gag at the thought of beige carpet, remember, *you're not paying for it*. Let the customer make those decisions.

Listen to their needs and wants. Don't project your own prejudices into the conversation. When you think you understand what they want, repeat it back to them to be sure you're right. If you're wrong, try again until it's perfect.

We're not saying that you let clients make every decision. Only rarely will you meet a homeowner who knows exactly what he wants you to do. But, they'll all have a basic concept. Listen very carefully. Give suggestions if you have them. If they're rejected, don't take it personally. If a client wants to do something that would be unrealistically expensive, don't reject the proposal as impossible. Instead, make positive suggestions. Explain how to get the same result at a more modest cost.

If you tend to be too blunt, try using phrases such as these.

"Have you thought about this kind of an arrangement? We've done it before and it works well."

"Earth tones are still a solid choice, but since you're thinking of remodeling to sell the house, you might try some of the trendier colors."

"This arrangement might give you a better traffic flow. How does it look to you?"

"The entry you've suggested would give the house a dramatic look. But a few changes could reduce the cost by half."

You get the idea? Be tactful. Be agreeable. But make good suggestions. Your client will recognize both the advantage of what you suggest and your professionalism.

If Your Client's Taste Is Awful

If your client insists on doing something you think will be a disaster, there are only two choices. Either do it or bow out. As long as the client is simply making a design error, either will work. If he insists on something that doesn't comply with the code, find a different client. We've heard contractors insist that getting a signed release absolves the contractor of responsibility. But we don't believe it. You shouldn't either.

Listened carefully to what your client wants. That saves you time, prevents misunderstandings and makes the sale more likely. Of course, any client can have a change of mind. If that happens, you'll have to make changes. But in the meantime, you've established trust. You're a good listener who can carry out instructions.

Be wary, though, of the client who simply can't make up his or her mind. Either walk away from the job or allow 5 or 10 percent more as contingency for extra hassles and delays.

We had a client several years ago who simply could not make up his mind. Over the course of several months, we drew up three totally different plans. That should have been fair warning to us. We did the work anyway. Maybe that was a mistake. The client changed his mind on window sizes *the day we were setting them.* He changed his mind on the direction of the tub *after it was framed in and plumbed.* He added something or deleted something every week! You can see why we felt a little crazy by the end of the job.

In the end, change orders came to more than 15 percent of the job. We don't like to do business that way. Changes should be less than 5 percent on almost any job. Even if you get paid promptly for changes, they're still bad business. It's hard to keep subs happy and schedule accurately when the job description keeps changing. Jobs with lots of changes are usually low profit jobs because of all the delays and administrative hassles.

As long as it's the client who wants the change, it's only fair that he or she pay for it. If your normal markup on the job is 15 or 20 percent, charge 30 to 40 percent markup on changes. That isn't all profit, of course. More likely it just covers your overhead. Changes take a lot of time and interrupt the work flow. Better yet, avoid working for people who can't make up their minds.

Bid Specifications, Not Ideas

The second job we ever did was nearly our last. Half way into the job, the homeowner angrily insisted we were trying to cheat him by not doing the electrical work he'd wanted. It happened to be a job we'd bid through a redevelopment organization. So we sat down with the homeowner, the electrician, and the construction specialist from the redevelopment organization who had written the specs. It turned out that the homeowner thought he was getting his house rewired. Instead, he was getting some much-needed repair on his electrical system but nothing more. Where did he get such an idea? He pointed out that the specs read, "The wiring is an area of concern."

That was pretty bizarre. How could our electrician have bid such poorly written specs? It just shows how green we all were. Fortunately, we had several electrical bids on that job. All were within about $100 of each other. We could argue very sincerely that the other electricians must have interpreted the specs the same way as our electrician although we can't imagine how. We were lucky. We got through the job without digging into our pockets. It could have been much worse.

The Browns thought they were getting bids that compared apples to apples. They thought both contractors were pricing the same items. They weren't. There's a big price difference between cabinets at the top of the line and cabinets sold as "handyman specials." You have the same kind of difference between top quality and minimum quality flooring. Between top quality and minimum quality plumbing fixtures. Taken together, the difference can be thousands of dollars on a kitchen or bath job.

Ted Brown called us to explain that our bid was $9,000 too high. We're glad he did. Some clients don't have that courtesy. And when he called, that was our cue. We should have suggested that Ted compare what we were bidding with what the competition was bidding. There was no real comparison because there were no real specs. Our bid was based on quality materials and workmanship throughout. Our competition didn't feel the same obligation. Yours won't either. No wonder our bid was $9,000 too high!

The lesson? Easy. Bid only jobs that have good specs. If your client doesn't know enough to draw up good specs, offer to help him or her write them — even at no charge. Otherwise you'll never be sure all contractors are bidding the same job. If the client doesn't have a clear set of specs, the job will always go to the low-ball, cut-throat change order artist with the lowest standards.

We'll cover this in more detail in the chapter on estimating. In the meantime, don't get left out in the cold because your standards are higher than others. Do quality work and insist that the competition does the same.

Don't Let Money Do All the Talking

In our early years, we thought we had to be the lowest bidder to get work. We thought price alone was the major consideration for most of our prospective clients. That created two problems for us. First, if our bid wasn't the lowest, we didn't know how to explain the difference. Second, we tried to shave prices to the bare bones to be the low bidder. So, when we won bids, we made barely enough to cover our overhead and way too little profit.

We don't play that game any more. The Browns taught us that someone else will always have a lower price. That builder may not be in business six months from now, but that doesn't make any difference at the moment.

At one point, when we were doing a lot of work with Community Development, there was a contractor who was consistently the low bidder on most jobs. Usually, his bids were well below our cost — forget profit or overhead. With all of his jobs, he should have been running four or five crews just to keep up. Instead, he didn't have a single employee. He told us one day, "At these prices, you can't afford to keep a crew."

That's a funny story if you weren't a victim of this shark. Needless to say, he's not in the construction business any more. But he's still remembered — mostly by contractors, subcontractors, suppliers and homeowners who wish they'd never heard of him. Those of us who knew our overhead and wanted a fair wage for our time and skills suffered along with him.

The point is this: When you start working for nothing, that's what you're worth. Quality has its price. You can't get a BMW for the price of a Chevy. It can't be done in the automotive industry and it can't be done in the construction industry. You get what you pay for.

But how do you get that across to the client?

1) Talk value instead of cost. Don't refer to yourself as the most expensive contractor in town. Rather, you're the best buy. You offer *value*. You bring quality, knowledge, and honesty to the job. Do that and you don't have to explain why your prices aren't the lowest. Professionalism doesn't come free. Play like a pro and you won't have to worry about the amateurs. A contractor with a solid reputation for value and professionalism is worth a fair price — and always will be.

2) Don't assume too much about your client's taste. "Expensive" means one thing to one person, another thing to someone else. A car with a $20,000 price tag seems expensive to us. You may think a $40,000 car is cheap. Just because we're not willing to spend extra for high ticket plumbing fixtures, doesn't mean our customers won't. Don't apologize for a high price. Instead, offer options in several price ranges. Your client may think the high price choices are worth every bit of the cost.

3) Convince people to do less, but do it well. It's a rare client who doesn't have to worry about total cost. Encourage your customer to give up a little square footage or some frills they can add later. Instead, get a quality job in the first place. We've used this quotation many times: "When you buy quality, you only cry once. Cut corners and you may be sorry for many years."

4) Walk away from jobs when you can't make a fair profit. A homeowner who isn't willing to pay for quality and integrity is going to be a problem client. That same client will quibble over specs, change orders, and everything else. No matter how short you are on jobs, it's foolish to work for nothing.

What happens when your prospective client is obviously a price shopper? Here's what we do. We level with that client right from the start. We're not going to submit the lowest bid. We're not the cheapest contractor in town. We don't apologize, we simply make it clear that we don't try to underbid everyone in town. We also explain that we'll do the job right the first time and give top value for the dollar.

Of course, we're not the most expensive contractors in town either. Our bids are always within a few percent of other legitimate, quality-conscious contractors.

Overcoming Objections

If you follow the recommendations in this chapter, you won't have many objections to overcome. If you keep hearing, "I don't like this, I need this, I want this," or "I can't afford this," you haven't listened carefully to your client. If you've followed a client's requests and stayed within the budget, closing the sale is easy.

Sometimes contractors misunderstand the difference between an observation and an objection. Distinguish between each of the following:

1) Will these windows be energy efficient?

2) I want energy-efficient windows.

3) I don't like these windows because they're not energy efficient.

The first two are observations. They can be explained. The third is an objection. Maybe your client forgot to mention energy-efficient windows at the first meeting. Or maybe you weren't listening. Or maybe the client did, but the budget is so tight that energy-efficient windows are out.

Regardless of the reason, acknowledge the objection and find a solution. If you didn't realize the importance of energy-efficient windows to the customer, offer to call back tomorrow with the price difference on better-quality windows. If you knew it was a priority but had to work within a tight budget, give your client some options.

1) She can increase her overall budget to pay for better windows.

2) She can scale back the job somewhere else to get better windows.

3) She can give up energy-efficient windows and accept what you've offered.

Whatever choice a client makes, respect that choice and move on to the next objection. Treat each the same way: acknowledge the objection and offer a solution.

If your client still isn't sold, the problem may be that you haven't sold yourself. They may not be convinced you're a capable, honest, reliable professional. It's possible, too, that your customer is just a dreamer. Maybe he loves the excitement of thinking about a new rec room or den. But maybe he couldn't possibly commit to doing the project.

You won't get every job that comes your way. No one does. Sure, it's frustrating to invest time on drawings, estimates, and meetings, and get nothing in return. But that's part of the business. And sale or no sale, there's one benefit from a sales presentation. It's what you learn. When you don't get a job, *analyze what went wrong.* How could you have sold yourself better? How could you have understood the client's needs more clearly? Let each loss be a learning experience. Eventually you'll have fewer jobs that were lessons only.

Polishing the Proposal Folder

As we suggested earlier, take a presentation folder to your first meeting with a client. It should include certificates of coverage for liability and Workers' Compensation insurance, job and credit references, a resume, and some "before and after" job photos.

When you return for your second meeting, bring another folder. See Figure 4-5. This is a proposal folder. It should include detailed specifications for your bid, well-drawn floor plans and elevations, and a contract ready to sign.

The contents of the folder should be letter perfect. If you don't have a computer and printer, at least use a good-quality typewriter. For the contract, we recommend a letter-quality printer. Watch for misspelled words and grammatical errors. In a later chapter we'll explain what to include in the contract.

The drawings have to be good. They should look like professional plans, not sketches done on typing paper. If you don't know how to do simple drawings, learn. Most community colleges and night trade schools offer mechanical drawing classes. You could hire an architect or professional draftsman to draw plans for you. But it's quicker, easier and cheaper to learn mechanical drawing yourself.

Don't leave the original drawings with your clients. Instead, give them reprints. It's easy to duplicate the original plans for use by other bidders. Unless we've been paid to prepare plans, we consider the drawings we make to be our property until the job is finished. We resent it when another contractor bids from plans we've drawn. Maybe you do, too. As added insurance, we stamp all of our drawings with the following message:

This is an original design and layout and must not be released or copied in any manner in full or in part unless applicable fees have been paid or contract has been signed confirming the sale of this job with this firm.

There's no guarantee that our drawings won't be used by someone else. But the stamp makes the issue clear. Anyone who uses the plans without paying for them is a thief. Most people aren't that brazen.

There are several ways to price the work. Some remodelers list a single lump sum cost. Others price each area or room separately and show a total for the entire job. Another option is to list a price for each individual item. Generally, we show only a single price. That gives us a little room to maneuver with a client who's having trouble deciding. Pricing each line item gives the impression that a client can pick and choose what to include and what to exclude. It also creates confusion when pricing change orders.

You may want to include lien waiver forms in the folder. As you may already know, lien waivers are a hassle. We prefer avoiding them because we know we'll pay all of our bills. We've been around too long to let our good credit get tarnished.

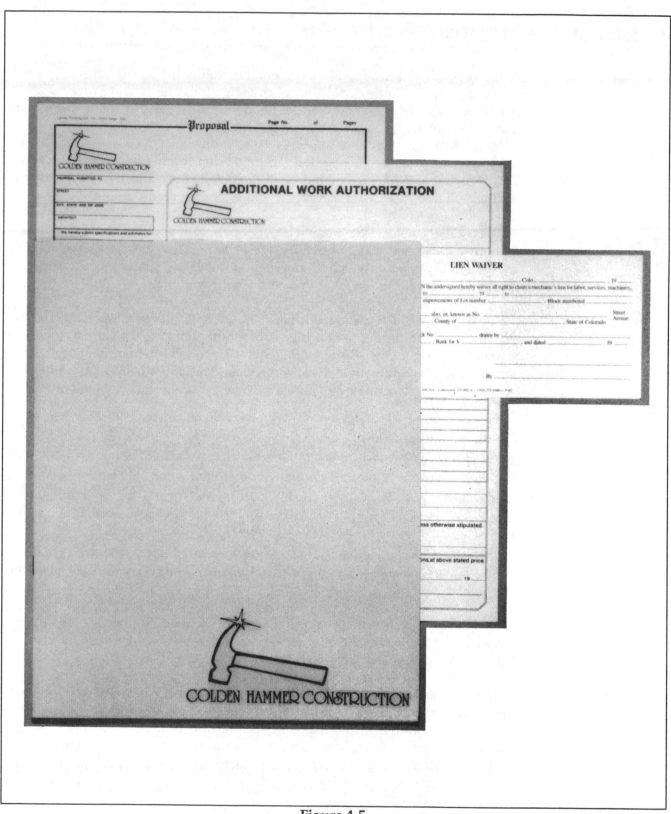

Figure 4-5

The proposal folder

But there are times when you should bring up the subject of liens. Suppose you're bidding against a contractor whose reputation is suspect. Maybe you live in an area where lien waivers are always used. Suppose your competition has a bad credit rating. Those are good reasons to include lien waivers in your proposal folder.

Suggest to your client that lien waivers be part of the contract. Don't openly criticize your competition, though. That's unprofessional. It's fair, however, to expect other bidders to meet your high standards.

The Final Step

At one time we thought the Brown job was sold. We had instructions on when to start and an oral agreement to go ahead. We could probably have locked up the job by taking one small extra step. We should have asked Ted and Tina to sign a contract. That's a simple, basic sales rule. And we broke it. When you've got an agreement, get it in writing. They were clearly ready to sign. We just didn't take advantage of the opportunity.

As we've already pointed out, when you submit an estimate, offer a contract ready for signatures. That's not high pressure selling. It's just careful preparation.

Once every few years we lose a job to a high pressure sales artist. But we win far more business with an honest, sincere, low-key approach. You don't have to be slick or even smooth — just professional.

We've heard salesmen insist that you shouldn't quit trying until the client has said "no" seven times. We don't agree. If you get to the second "no," it's because you didn't listen carefully in the first place. The customer has called you because work needs to be done. The need is established. *Understanding* the need is what gets you the work.

Don't be afraid to ask for the job. Make it clear you'd like to do the work. Be enthusiastic about it. If it's a particularly interesting job, *say so*. Clients are flattered to think you consider their job a special opportunity.

If the homeowner still hesitates, ask what you can do to get the job. What questions can you answer? What problems haven't been addressed? The objections may or may not have anything to do with you or your bid. Either way, *listen*.

If the customer wants some time to think, provide the time. That's everyone's right. Offer to call back tomorrow. If your client agrees, call as promised.

If more information is needed before your client can decide, provide it. Don't give your client a reason to delay a decision any longer!

Selling Is a State of Mind

Selling really isn't a matter of overcoming objections. It's just providing information. You can do exactly what's needed and at a fair price. You shouldn't have to twist any arms. You shouldn't have to worry about the competition. Just remember this:

1) Look and sound professional. Be knowledgeable, capable, and sincere.

2) Sell yourself to the client. If you do this first, you won't have to sell your price later.

3) Listen, listen, listen. And then listen some more. Most jobs are lost because you put together a project the client doesn't need, want, like, or can't afford.

4) Bid specifics, not vague ideas. Don't get caught bidding plums when the other guy is bidding prunes.

5) Talk *value* instead of cost. You're worth the price because you can deliver the job on schedule and within budget.

6) Acknowledge objections, provide solutions. Again, the key is to listen!

7) Polish your proposal folder. From drawings to specs to contract, make sure it's letter perfect.

8) Get a signed contract. Don't let the mood pass.

Everything we've suggested is easier if you have confidence in yourself. If you believe in yourself, so will the client. If you don't believe in yourself, why should anyone else?

Selling the Next Job Off This One

Look at each job as a referral for the next. If you can deliver all that you've promised, you'll have to sell yourself a little less to the next client.

The key to referrals is service and consideration. Remember that remodeling is a burden for every homeowner. It's a dirty, noisy inconvenience. Nobody likes living on a construction site. But living in a motel room for weeks can be worse. A little diplomacy can keep a client on your side. The lack of it can turn even the most patient, tolerant homeowner into an angry nitpicker. How you handle problems will make the difference.

Here are a few tips that can keep little problems from ballooning out of proportion and out of control.

1) Warn your clients about the dust and dirt. Suggest how long the disruption will last. Explain that dust will probably creep into the whole house, not just the part being remodeled. If the water or electricity will be turned off, give advance warning.

2) Clean up after yourself every day. Sweep, put tools and supplies in order and out of the way. It takes only a few minutes extra each day to run a clean, organized job. You'll save nearly that much time at the end of the job. Final cleanup will be easier and faster. Regular nightly cleanups also make for a quicker start in the morning.

3) Use only good quality material. Sort your 2 x 4s. Reject any that are splintered or bowed. Use #1 shingles, not #2's. Profits aren't squandered on good quality materials. Profits are sucked up by inefficient labor and poor scheduling. The quality of materials will be remembered in five years when the homeowner decides to remodel again. But if the soffit has buckled and the paint has peeled, you won't be the one getting the call.

4) Remember that you and your crew are guests. Take extra care not to damage shrubs or gardens, floors or woodwork. Keep the volume down on radios. Make it company policy that employees don't smoke in a client's home. Few things are as offensive to a non-smoker as the smell of stale cigarettes in their home. Explain this policy to everyone who works for you, preferably before you hire them. That should make enforcement easier.

5) Employees must not drink alcoholic beverages either before coming to work or during the work day. What employees do after work is their business. But they should leave the site before they open the first can of beer.

Insist on clean, neatly mended clothes and no offensive T-shirts. Above all, demand courtesy. Even if the client's kids are obnoxious, it's not part of the specs to set them straight.

We try to throw in a few unexpected extras on every job. The first day the kitchen's torn apart, give the family a coupon good for a large pizza at a local restaurant. When the dust has settled and work is nearly done, bring in a cleaning service for a few hours to remove most of the construction grime. Something like that costs peanuts compared to the total job cost. But it pays big dividends. Clients will brag to their friends about you for weeks. If you're worried about the cost of a large pizza or a cleaning service, include it as an expense in your estimate.

If you fix a leaky faucet or a loose step at no charge, your client will remember that courtesy for years. Do something extra that takes only a few minutes and costs only a few dollars. It leaves an impression that no remodeler can buy.

When the job is complete, leave some memento. A bottle of good champagne, fresh flowers, or homemade cinnamon rolls are good choices. Don't forget to take something that will be a lasting reminder as well. We leave a set of ceramic mugs with our company logo, a subscription to one of the home magazines, or a photo collage of the remodeling project. Anything like these will help keep your name in a client's mind for years. Don't forget to send a thank-you note as well. After all, you're thankful, both that you got the job and that it's finally over!

5

Dealing with Clients

*I*f you've read and understand the information in the previous chapter, you'll have no trouble mastering what we're going to say in this chapter. What you do to close a sale is about the same as what you do to keep a job going smoothly. Listen to your clients, treat them honestly and courteously. That's the key to keeping your customers. Of course, once in a while there's going to be a problem. In this chapter we'll suggest how to survive the most common client disputes, hopefully preserving your good humor and doing the minimum damage to your profits.

Any contractor who's been in business a few years has at least one customer horror story to tell. The worst clients often come in the early years when you're least able to recognize a potential problem. Even worse, you may see the problems looming, but you don't have the luxury of being able to turn down the work.

It's not easy to avoid problems with clients. Sometimes you just don't see the hassles coming — they don't show up until the job is well under way. Most problems are the result of surprises — surprises caused by poor communication: "I thought you said . . ." or "Why didn't you tell me . . ." Precise communication can prevent surprises like these and the disputes that inevitably follow. But even perfect communication won't prevent every conflict.

In the following pages we've listed the most potent troublemakers you should try to avoid. But be forewarned. Sometimes you're going to have to go a little hungry to keep clear of all these characters.

The Handyman

The most common hassle is the homeowner who wants to do some of the work himself. Often, he'll also want to buy products or services directly instead of ordering them from you. Rarely is he motivated by the sheer pleasure of swinging a hammer or tracking down the right carpet. Rather, he thinks he's going to save some money.

This can be a sensitive issue. Almost without fail, a homeowner who wants to work with you will disrupt the schedule because he doesn't get his share done on time. And he probably won't do it as well as your crew or subs would. Yet, it's your reputation that's on the line once the job is done.

Like some contractors, you can refuse the contract if the owner insists on helping. Or you can grit your teeth, add 20 percent to the schedule, and sign the contract. Realistically, it's hard to deny the client the right to work on his own house. To do it without making him mad is even tougher. Don't insult the homeowner, but don't automatically give in either. Try reasoning with him.

▌ Be sure he realizes how much work he has to do and what his time limits will be.

▌ Have a little "builder to builder" talk. Discuss whether the owner has ever done a job like this before. How long ago? How involved was it? Does he truly enjoy this sort of thing, or does he need to save some money?

▌ Does he have the right tools, or will he have to buy or rent them?

▌ Is he good enough at what he's doing so he'll be satisfied with the final product, or will he expect you to salvage it if he makes a mess of it?

▌ If he has to take time away from his regular job to finish his part of the work on time, would he be money ahead to pay your crew to do it?

*" My Jimmy wants to do the excavation work for the foundation.
How much will that take off the price?"*

We run into the handyman itch most often on demolition work and painting. Both seem to the homeowner to be simple jobs that take more sweat than skill. Many of the handyman paint jobs we've seen prove that's not the case.

And while it may not take a lot of finesse to demo a wall, you'd better know what you're up to, or you can do a lot of expensive damage. Because they're repetitive and dirty, both jobs can get old fast. If your homeowner-helper gets bogged down, there goes your schedule.

If the client still insists he wants to do the work, lay some ground rules before he ever starts.

1) Let him know exactly how much time he has to finish his part of the job. Be specific: "We plan to finish with the drywall on Thursday the fifth and want to begin trimming on Monday the ninth. The time in between is for you to paint."

2) Make it clear he has to furnish his own equipment. Just because you're acting as the general contractor doesn't mean he has free use of your tools.

3) If you have to repair or touch up his work, tell him you'll bill him and what the rate will be. Include your percentage for overhead in that rate.

These rules may sound harsh, but they're a good place to start. If it turns out you can work well with the client and he doesn't take advantage of your good will, you can always back down. It's a lot harder to get tough once things start to get sticky.

At the very least, make the owner responsible for entire blocks of the project. Unless you're billing for time and materials instead of a fixed contract, never allow him to help whenever he has the time. He'll value his time at a much greater level than you will, and he'll want credit against his bill accordingly.

To get around this problem, tell the owner your workers' compensation coverage won't allow you to work that way. (It probably won't.) Or use a sign like this one that hangs in our mechanic's shop:

Hourly rate:	**$30.00**
Hourly rate if you watch:	**$40.00**
Hourly rate if you help:	**$60.00**

It should work the same way for a contractor.

The Purchasing Agent

You can — and *should* be — firmer with homeowners who want to buy products or services without going through you. Often they'll want to buy their own carpet, kitchen cabinets, or other items that you count on for a good profit margin. For the more expensive products, point out that your contractor discounts are very generous. You can add a reasonable percentage to your cost for the product, and they'll still pay less than they will if they buy it retail.

Profit is only one reason to prevent homeowners from doing their own shopping. Time is the other. Often, clients will think they can get a hot deal through their own networking. Recently, we made the mistake of letting a customer buy her own carpet. She only needed a few square yards to match the existing flooring. She had bought the original carpet through a home buyer's club several years earlier, and they said she'd have the new piece in two to three weeks.

The carpet finally arrived six months later. The rest of the job had been completed for four months, but we had to wait for final payment until the carpet was installed. Fortunately, the homeowner acknowledged the holdup was no fault of ours, and she paid us all but the final few hundred dollars while we waited. Financially, it could have been much worse if she had held to the letter of the contract and waited to pay us the final 25 percent.

Sometimes it won't interfere with the job if you allow the owner to buy some of his own fixtures or accessories. One former customer liked antique lights, so we let him scavenge for his own fixtures. Our electrician charged him a preset rate to get them working again. Everyone was satisfied with the arrangement.

To be safe, set your policies and make them clear to the customer before you start the job. If you want to make an exception to your rules once you've gotten to know him, that's up to you. But don't let the client pressure you into something you don't want to do.

The Manipulator

Clients like this can be the hardest to spot before the job gets rolling. They can also cost you money. Manipulators won't usually come right out and cheat you, but they'll take advantage of you in lots of little ways if they get the chance. In the last chapter we gave the example of the homeowner who thought we should rewire his house for the price of some electrical repairs. That could have been an innocent assumption since he had no experience with the remodeling process. But this same client tried to squeeze us for more work on several other parts of the job. We suspect we were being manipulated.

"Now I see it all finished, maybe the toilet would be better on the other wall after all. It won't take you a minute to move it, will it? There's only two bolts."

Shortly after we went into the business, a client hired us to remodel her bathroom. She chose the color of the vanity top from a set of color chips. The color she chose didn't look right to us. It didn't blend with the rest of the bathroom. We tried to switch her to another color, but she stood firm. When the bathroom was finished, she saw that the vanity top was a disaster.

Her solution? We should replace the top at no charge. After all, anyone who saw the bathroom would think *we* had done a poor job. At the time, we were so green we gave in. She did pay for the materials, but we provided the labor at no charge.

Today, we work with a lot more confidence. That same client probably wouldn't have the nerve to suggest such a thing. We make it very clear which changes are our responsibility and which ones are the client's. Anything we damage or measure incorrectly, we pay for. If the client changes her mind about color, size, location, or quality, she pays for it.

It's tough to stand firm. Especially if there's a good profit in the job, it's easy to let a client nibble away. Maybe you feel a little guilty about your markup, or maybe the customer has become your friend. Either way, it's easy to start giving away your profit. Keep in mind that if the client signed a contract he thought was fair in the beginning, it's still fair to charge more when he wants to add a second sink in the master bath.

Your best defense with the manipulator is to start with iron-clad specs. If you simply say, "lighting fixtures included," be ready for trouble. Don't even use the phrase "medium quality light fixtures." Be specific about the budget: "Lighting allowance: $300." If the owner chooses fixtures that cost more, it's an add-on. If he stays under the allowance, it's a credit.

Better yet, list specific part numbers, but with one caution. Protect yourself with the phrase, "or like quality," in case you have trouble getting that particular item.

The Perfectionist

Some contractors claim they can spot a perfectionist half way down the block. True, some perfectionists give themselves away. They have an obsession for detail and try to iron out every problem that's likely to come up for at least the next ten years. You appeal to these people by selling high quality and attention to detail. But you better add at least five percent to the cost of the job to cover demands that no one could anticipate. If you have a reputation for first-rate work, the perfectionist will gladly pay the extra cost.

When you know in advance that you're dealing with a perfectionist, you have a fighting chance. When you discover that a client is a perfectionist two weeks into the job, it can be a nightmare. Oddly enough, some of the most demanding clients are people who can't produce quality work themselves. You cringe at their painting while they're complaining they can feel the joints in your trim work.

Often, the people who'll cause you the most trouble are the ones who are connected to the construction industry. Engineers and architects have the worst reputation. Unfortunately, these are the same people who can feed you work, so you have to tread extra carefully.

With the perfectionist, it's especially important to keep a clean job site. Listen to his requests and, as long as they're reasonable, follow through with them. If he starts to complain, describe in detail exactly what you're doing to provide top quality work.

The Deadbeat

There are two kinds of deadbeats. The first can't pay his bills and the second one won't. Both are a headache. Generally, we're more sympathetic toward the first, but still, the bank won't take sympathy in lieu of payment, so we have to collect.

Here are some rules to handle deadbeats:

Rule number one: Apply Pressure.

One of our clients had an accident just before we were to collect our final payment. Months after she should have been fully recovered, she still hadn't paid us. Finally, we sent her a polite letter telling her we would begin to charge her interest. We got a check for the full amount by return mail. We suspect she could have paid much sooner, but she didn't because we didn't put any pressure on her to do so. The money was earning her interest, and she liked it that way.

You don't have to be rude or angry. In fact, you'll have a lot more success if you're courteous. You must be persistent, though. The client with an unpaid bill is going to hope you've forgotten or have written off the charges.

Rule number two: Be Courteously Persistent.

Once we did a job for a husband and wife who were both M.D.s. They had a good combined income. They also spent it freely. They were turned down twice before they found a bank to make them a construction loan. I suppose their credit history was shaky. We should have seen what we were getting into.

During construction they kept adding on and upgrading. Although we got paid for each change in the following draw, at the end of the job they still had to come up with $5,000 more than the loan amount.

The couple really wanted to pay us. Unfortunately, they were both so bad at managing their money, they couldn't. This time we were smarter. We called them every few days to see if they were finding any way to come up with the money. We reminded them that we were getting pressure from our suppliers and we wanted to keep our credit good. Within 30 days they paid the full amount.

Rule number three: Don't Give Them a Reason Not to Pay.

In ten years of business, we've collected every dollar due us. We've never had to threaten a lawsuit or even charge interest. Almost every client has paid upon completion or within a few days. Our banker claims this is an unbelievable record. We think it shows that our clients are happy with our work and they like us. We also write a tight contract. We'll explain how to do that in the next chapter.

People Who **Won't** Pay

Far worse than the client who can't pay is the one who has no intention of paying. Maybe we've been lucky. There aren't many people who will purposely stiff you. But there are a few. So beware.

How do you avoid the cheaters? If anything seems suspicious, *don't take the job.* Here's one scheme we almost fell victim to.

Recently, we were offered a large repair job on a rented house. The out-of-state owner consented to the repairs, accepted our bid and told us to get started. We mailed the owner a contract, including a stamped return envelope. Six weeks passed and we still hadn't received the signed contract. The tenants called the owner who was surprised we hadn't done the work yet. He told his renters he'd send the contract right away, and that we should get started.

Instead, we sent another contract, this time with a provision that the owner escrow the money in our local bank. We haven't heard from him since. We might have been wrong about him. It's possible he would have put a check in the mail as soon as we finished the job. It's also possible we would have had to file a lien against his house. The profit on the job just wasn't worth the risk.

Always start with a solid, binding contract. Then, make sure your customers' progress payments come in on time. If you suspect trouble ahead, insist on an escrow account controlled by a third party. If the client refuses, don't start work. Period. It's just not worth it.

Whatever you do, don't fall into the trap of doing the next job to get paid for the last one. This problem plagues subcontractors more often. But it can happen to a general contractor, too. We know of a contractor who owes his electrician over a hundred thousand dollars. He's making it up by paying the electrician double for each new job. That's an honorable way to work off the debt. But we wonder why the electrician let him get that far behind in the first place.

Your common sense will help you avoid cheaters most of the time. When you do get stuck, there are some legal options which we'll explain in the next chapter. Don't be afraid to use them!

The Fall Crazies

For some unexplained reason, our worst clients have come in the fall. After a few years of this pattern, we analyze all our would-be clients to figure out which one might be our "fall crazy," as we not-so-affectionately call them. We recognized some as troublemakers right from the beginning. But we didn't spot them all. Some actually end up being easy to please. Others turn out to be real nuts.

The Alcoholic Client

A high proportion of our fall crazies were alcoholics. The hassles of remodeling — the mess, decision making, and dwindling bank account — all create unbearable stress for these clients. You can't always spot a drinking problem. But if you suspect you may be dealing with an alcoholic, avoid the job.

Once you're into a job and you realize you have an alcoholic client, try to deal with him in the mornings. That's when he's most likely to be sober. Start your work day at 7:00 a.m. and be off the job by 3:30 p.m. Even if it means dragging the job out an extra few weeks, stay on this schedule. You'll avoid a lot of tense confrontations.

Your customer's personal situation can affect both you and your job. It's the same whether a client is struggling with a family crisis or simply is a little looney. Avoid the "off center" ones if you can. But if you find you've got one, do your job as quickly as you can and get out. Don't play amateur psychiatrist. You've been hired for your building skills and nothing more.

The Pre-construction Meeting

Once a client has signed the contract, schedule a final meeting before you start work. Use this pre-construction meeting to go over the specs and drawings one last time. This gives you and the homeowner one final chance to settle questions or make changes. Also use this meeting to explain the schedule and repeat your policies for payment and change orders. The more homeowners know from the beginning about what to expect, the less likely they'll be to nitpick. You can take care of any problems that do come up while they're still small.

Give your clients a shopping list and schedule for their part of the process. Let them know when you'll be ready for paint, wallpaper, carpet, or light fixtures. Keep after them to make decisions early, and remind them that specially-ordered materials can take from one to six weeks to receive. Furnish them with paint chips and tile and carpet samples and suggest they start there with their selections.

Prepare Your Client

Don't assume the homeowner knows how much of a mess to expect while you're working. Of course, you'll do your best to confine it to the work area with tarps and sealed doorways. But warn your clients that they'll face extra cleaning and higher utility bills during construction. There's no way to avoid it.

Arrange for keys and make sure you're clear about the homeowner's expectations. Some people simply leave their doors unlocked and are comfortable with subs and inspectors coming and going. Others will want you or one of your crew members present when any third party comes. Still other customers will insist on always being there themselves. Whatever the homeowners choose, respect the decision. If you earn their trust, they may relax their rules as the job goes on.

Here are some other questions you'll want to clarify before you begin.

1) How should your crews treat incoming phone calls?

2) Where can your crew and subs park?

3) Where can you safely leave tools overnight?

4) Where should the dumpster be placed?

5) Is it all right to work evenings? Weekends?

6) How early can you begin work? How late can you stay?

As you can see, these are minor details. Yet, if you're insensitive about the little things, the homeowner may get upset and start looking for trouble. Set the tone for the rest of the job by communicating from the very beginning. And remember, the best way to keep the customer happy is to do good work and keep the job moving. If the homeowners have to look at a torn-apart kitchen or an unusable bathroom for too long, you'll bear the brunt of their frustration.

The Change Order

The pre-construction meeting is a good time to explain how you handle change orders. If you wait until you're well into the job, it looks like you're making up the rules as you go along. If your clients have any doubts at all about the job, they should be dealt with at the pre-construction meeting. Explain that now is the time to clear up any questions. They'll make much better decisions now than later when they're in the middle of a mess and under strain.

Change orders have the reputation among consumers for being the icing on the cake. People think that's where you make your profit. If that were true, many contractors would have fatter bank accounts.

The truth is, change orders add to your overhead. They interrupt the job while the change is priced, written up, and signed. If you have to order something, it can slow the schedule even further. Your labor costs go up because you often can't use your crew as efficiently. Explain all that to your customer. Make it clear that you like to avoid change orders if you possibly can.

Pricing Changes

It's hard to make a fair markup on a change order. If you charge extra to cover the cost of delays and other hassles, your client will suspect that you've over-charged for the whole job.

Some contractors charge an administrative fee of $25 to $50 plus the cost of the change. Another option would be to use a percentage figure — maybe 5 or 10 percent — over the cost of the change. If you prefer that approach, print the fee on your change order form and point it out at the pre-construction meeting. When a client decides to add something to the contract, you'll need to do three things.

1) Write the change order as clearly and specifically as the rest of your specs.

2) Show the total price, including any administrative fee you charge.

3) Don't proceed until your client has signed the change order. Unsigned change orders aren't admissible in court and can't be collected. If that makes you nervous, it should. It's a bother to wait for a signature. But remember, the signature is your protection — and that's more important than meeting a deadline.

Another good reason to get a signed change order is so you remember to add it to the total bill. It's easy to forget change orders when a job stretches out over several months.

Collect payment for change orders as you go, rather than tacking them on to the last payment. Either require payment upon completion of the change or at the next draw. Some contractors ask for payment before they start the change order. This may seem overly cautious, but do it if the client has a construction loan that won't cover the cost of the change. Otherwise you may have trouble getting paid.

Job Completion

A job completion form like Figure 5-1 ties up the loose ends when the work is finished. It also serves as a "punch list" for you and your client. Once everything on the list is finished, the client is obligated to pay the balance due. If the clients decide they want something else done, write a new contract. That way, they can't use additional work as an excuse to stall payment.

Go over the form at the pre-construction meeting. Then the client won't be surprised by the write-off process at the end of the job. Everyone concerned should know that the job is done when the list is completed. Your customer should understand when he'll be expected to pay.

(logo)

Job Completion Form

From: _____   Date: _____
           Owner's name

Address: _____

             _____

Please return by: _____
                  Date

     We have carefully and thoroughly examined the work Best Construction has done on our property. We are satisfied with everything, except for the following items:

_____

_____

_____

_____

_____

If more space is required, please use reverse side.

When these items have been corrected to our satisfaction, final payment will be made immediately upon completion.

We fully understand that no further work will be done and no further materials will be furnished after this statement is signed and the above list of items is completed. We also understand that all work performed and all materials supplied by Best Construction are guaranteed for one year from the date of this statement. We understand further that Best Construction will return only for work related to their guarantee or change order items.

Your contract has been completed and we will make payment in agreement with the terms of our contract. A retainer of $_____ will be held pending completion of this list, at which time it will be remitted immediately.

_____   Date _____
Owner

_____   Date _____
Owner

Figure 5-1

Job Completion Form

Summing It Up

If you find yourself having frequent run-ins or trouble collecting money, it's time to review what you might be doing wrong. Here's our checklist for smoother, more trouble-free jobs:

▪ Be honest and fair

▪ Do good work

▪ Mind your own business

▪ Get all change orders signed

▪ Keep the job moving

▪ Listen to your client

If you're faithful to these, your problems should all be small ones.

6

Making It Legal

*I*n the last chapter, we suggested how to handle clients under special circumstances. Remember that good customer relations always begin with a good contract. Your contracts should be a written record of what you've both agreed to. It should also cover every likely problem so there's no dispute when something unexpected happens. Your agreements shouldn't be traps that capture unwary clients. We've seen contracts like that — one-sided agreements that settle every issue in your favor. That's no way to do business. Your contracts shouldn't victimize your clients. They should prevent disputes by anticipating most of the situations likely to cause an argument.

In any case, a complete agreement and mutual trust are more important than an elegant, perfectly-written contract. Our experience is that more disputes result from poorly drawn plans or specifications than the construction contract itself. Even when we were vague about payment schedules and didn't get every change order signed, we still got paid because we followed some simple rules:

1) We get full and complete agreement on job specifications.

2) We work hard to merit the trust of our clients.

3) We avoid doing business with people we can't trust.

4) We make sure every customer is satisfied with the quality of our materials and workmanship.

There are exceptions, of course. A lawyer we know says that most people who refuse to pay the bill are just trying to beat the contractor out of a few bucks. He represented one contractor who had client that refused to pay because joists were 15-3/4 inches on center instead of 16. The tightest contract ever written couldn't have prevented that dispute. The client was just looking for a way to save a few dollars.

The Smart Contract

This chapter isn't going to cover much more than the essentials of contract law. Here's why. Contract law details vary from state to state. If you get into a dispute, you're going to need some very specific legal advice, far more than we're able to supply. What we can do here is offer some suggestions intended to help keep you out of court. That's preventative law, and it's probably the cheapest and best legal advice you're going to get.

Our first suggestion is this: Don't avoid written contracts because you're intimidated by the language or think they're too much trouble. Always put contracts over $500 in writing. Contracts are for your protection as much as for your customer's.

Think of a contract as the rules by which you and your customer play the game. It takes cooperation to get the job done. You do the work — they pay the bill. But contracts protect both sides. You can't expect a court to honor the terms of a contract when they're to your benefit and ignore them when they're not. For instance, suppose your contract says the customer must sign change orders. You make a mistake. You forget to get a signed order. Don't expect to collect the full price of the change.

Here are some general guidelines for writing contracts:

▌ A typewritten addition to a standard printed contract will be treated with the most authority because it was written last. A handwritten note on all copies will usually be given even more weight.

▌ Any changes made on the contract at signing should be initialed and dated by both you and the client.

▌ All copies of the contract must be legible.

■ Try to limit the contract to one or two pages. Then make the plans and specifications a part of the agreement by including the following statement in the contract:

Work will be done according to the drawings and specifications dated and attached hereto.

■ Date your contracts. If the contract is also a proposal, clearly state the period during which prices are valid. Thirty days is common. You don't want to get stuck with old contracts six months or a year later when material prices have jumped ten percent.

■ Both you and your client must sign and date the contract.

■ Keep copies of previous proposals with your copy of the final contract. You may need to jog your client's memory about something that was added or deleted prior to the final draft.

■ Check and double-check your contracts. Before signing any contract, go over it line by line. Review the specs on the work order and all the provisions of the contract. By doing so, you'll accomplish three things:

1) If the work order still doesn't describe exactly what the homeowners want, or they don't understand the contract's language, you can correct and clarify those issues before the job begins.

2) By clearly explaining your obligations and your customer's, you'll build trust. The customer will realize you have nothing to hide. You want the client to feel comfortable and know exactly what's going to happen.

3) The client's expectations will be realistic from the beginning.

In the following pages, we'll cover some detailed instructions that will help you develop a solid, workable contract form. If any of this isn't clear, get legal advice. Any ambiguity in the agreement will probably be interpreted against you, the person who wrote the contract. Know what yours says, and know how to enforce it.

Write Clear Specifications

Good job specifications help you two ways. First, they make it easier for you to bid accurately. Second, they make the job run smoothly. Vague descriptions create problems. Here's an example. Suppose your work description includes "repair front door" as an item. What does that mean to you? Probably not what the homeowner hopes it means. How much repair has to be done? You may intend to rehang the door so it closes and locks properly. Your client may think you're also going to fill the deep grooves the dog scratched into it, sand, and paint it. Be specific about what you'll do and what you won't do. Be sure to include any disclaimers. For example:

*"The bottom part is our standard disclaimer.
It says we're not responsible for anything."*

1) Front Door

a) Rehang door so that it closes and locks properly. Note: Because the foundation is shifting and because foundation repair isn't part of this contract, the door will likely need readjustment again within a year. We can't guarantee that further adjustment won't be needed because foundation settlement will continue even after the door is rehung.

b) Fill in dog scratches and sand as smooth as possible. Note: Because of the deep grooves and the difficulty of bonding a thick base of putty to the door, slight ripples may remain.

c) Prime door's exterior with Sears 10-year, exterior oil-based paint as specified by owner.

d) Homeowner has agreed to apply finish paint coat.

This isn't the same as saying, "Repair front door." You're giving an exact description of what you'll do, and the expected outcome. You've told the owner what materials you'll use and what you'll leave for him to do.

If the door isn't perfectly smooth after you've puttied and sanded, the owner has been warned. When he signed the contract, he acknowledged the door might not come out perfect. However, if you're able to make the door entirely smooth, he'll be pleased. It's better than you promised.

There's not much incentive to go back to a job and finish up the little nickel-and-dime items once we've cashed the check. But we use the "substantial completion" phrase for our own protection. Some owners come up with one petty item after another to delay that final payment.

On some jobs, particularly large ones where public money or an architect is involved, the buyer may hold back a percentage — usually 10 percent of your first draw — as a retainer until the job is complete. The client can hold the final payment for up to 60 days as a guarantee you've paid your suppliers and subs.

If your job requires a retainer, you're often entitled to hold back the same percentage from payments to your suppliers and subs. But we've found this isn't worth the extra book work. Weigh for yourself the advantage of the extra cash flow against the trouble of writing additional checks to each vendor. Be sure to let your subs and suppliers know ahead of time if you plan to do this. Some may not be willing to go along.

Start Dates and Completion Dates

Some states require that you include start and completion dates in your contract. It puts extra pressure on you to be bound by a time limit, so don't include it if you don't have to. If you must show this information, allow yourself a generous period beyond your estimated completion date. Getting an extension may be easy. But it's better if you don't have to.

Include a disclaimer if your client insists on naming the completion date. We recommend a statement like this:

Contractor is not responsible for delays caused by weather, acts of God, performance of suppliers or subcontractors, or anything else beyond contractor's control.

Be aware that even your client can cause a delay that's beyond your control. Remember the homeowner in the last chapter who ordered her own carpet?

Warranties

Express warranties and implied warranties both guarantee the quality of your work. An express warranty describes exactly what you will guarantee, and for how long. It can be specific, such as guaranteeing that materials you use are rated to a certain quality level. Or it can be broad, like saying you'll fix anything that goes wrong with your work during the first year.

Either way, express warranties can cover any work you do or materials you install. Unless you define exemptions as we suggested for the door in the house

Be careful with disclaimers, though. If you include too many, the client might think you can't do anything right. In this example, it was important to exempt the door from the warranty. Otherwise, the owner might expect to have the door adjusted every few months at no charge.

Getting Paid

Many contractors ask for 25 percent of the contract price either when the agreement is signed or when materials start arriving on the job. The balance may come due in three equal payments: the first two when a certain amount of work has been completed and the final payment when the job is done.

Some states severely limit the amount you can collect as a down payment. It can be as little as 5 percent, or $300, whichever is less. A few prohibit any advance payment. If your state has a law like that and if you violate the law, you may forfeit your right to attach a lien. You can thank the scam artists for these laws — those fine fellows who collect money up front and then disappear.

Truth-in-lending laws can further complicate collections. Some states require you to include truth-in-lending information in your contract, even if you don't charge interest. If you do intend to collect interest on past due balances, be sure to include that information in the contract. Otherwise a court may not award interest on the debt. Most states have a limit on the interest rate you can charge. In states where it's very low, you can sometimes get around the letter of the law by calling the interest "carrying charges."

Payment Schedules

Be very clear about payment schedules. "Second payment due when job is 50 percent complete," isn't specific enough. Tie your draws to a definite stage of the project. "Second draw due at the beginning of drywall application," is better.

Notice that it's better to ask for payment at the beginning of a certain operation, not at the end. Sometimes it's hard to tell when something is done. But no one can dispute that something has started. Many times you'll have a few details to complete on one phase even though you're ready to start on the next step. This is especially true if you've had last minute change orders.

The way you handle the final payment is even more important. Instead of asking for final payment "upon completion," say, "upon substantial completion." This phrase prevents the homeowner from holding back his final payment of $10,00 because a door latch has been back-ordered for two months.

Don't overuse this option, though. We've found it's to our benefit not to ask final payment until we've puttied every nail hole and removed every trash with the problem foundation, a warranty may cover all your work. Even if you make a specific exemption, you may still have trouble if your client decides to sue.

An implied warranty isn't expressed. It's assumed. For example, your client should be able to assume that the new roof you put on won't leak, even if you don't say so. Everything you install comes with an implied warranty of suitability for the intended purpose. Water pipes should hold water without leaking — at least under normal use and for a reasonable time after installation. If the pipes you installed last week spring a leak this week, there's a breach of the implied warranty. You might as well fix the leak with no questions asked.

Be explicit about the warranty period, otherwise your client may assume the warranty is longer than you intend. Some states require a one-year guarantee on all work whether you say so or not. Limit your warranty to one year if you can. Even if you're convinced your work will stand flawless for a decade, don't obligate yourself to more than what's legally required.

If you choose to do substandard work, the time limitation on a warranty won't protect you. You may remain liable for an indefinite period. If you decide to save some bucks by sinking footings 12 inches instead of the 30 inches your local code requires, a court can hold you responsible for cracks or shifting ten years from now.

A warranty also guarantees you'll fix problems even if you used top quality materials and followed accepted standards for workmanship. If the plumbing leaks under a sink, you'll have to fix it, even if it was installed correctly. If a front door lock jams, you'll have to replace it, even if it's the finest one on the market.

Don't guarantee that a job will be flawless. It's not reasonable to expect that you can do a $50,000 remodel without a single defect. Nor should you guarantee "customer satisfaction." Make every effort to please your clients, but you'll always run across someone who won't be satisfied, no matter what you do.

Instead, use the phrase "in a substantial and workmanlike manner" or "standard quality work." Legally, as long as you've done what a reasonable person would consider satisfactory, you've complied with the warranty.

What's satisfactory to a reasonable person? Unfortunately, there's not a set definition. If you rarely get complaints, you're probably doing standard quality work. But if you get complaints on nearly every job, maybe your work isn't up to standard quality.

Claims Against Your Warranty

When an owner calls with a problem that's covered under warranty, respond promptly, especially if it's something minor. There's a risk here. Some owners assume that as long as you're there, you're responsible for any problems they have during your warranty period. Gently remind them you've only warranted your work and materials, not their entire house.

As a gesture of good faith, call your clients just before the warranty expires. Stop by and tighten screws, touch up paint, repair drywall nail pops. While you're there, maybe you can sell them a basement finish! Even if they're not ready to do more work on their house, they'll be reminded to recommend you to their friends.

A Word About Waivers

Suppose a soils report calls for an over-dig and concrete pylons instead of a standard foundation. You're obligated to follow the instructions of the soils engineer. So far, so good. But your client insists on a standard foundation. You agree after he signs a waiver releasing you from all responsibility. Later, there's a settling problem. You wind up in court as a defendant. The judge will probably find you liable for the damage. Your client hired a professional contractor and should be able to rely on your skill and knowledge. You're expected to do professional quality work and comply with the building code, no matter what the owner demands.

Insurance

Your client is responsible for some kinds of insurance; you're responsible for others. The customer can assume some of your insurance obligations, but only if that's spelled out in your contract.

Homeowners usually carry insurance against wind, storm and fire damage. Those policies cover buildings on their property and work in progress. They also cover materials delivered to the site, even if the materials haven't been installed yet. Most homeowners, and even many contractors, don't know this. Be sure your customers understand. Suggest to clients that they check their policies to be sure they're covered for vandalism and theft.

As a contractor, you're responsible for liability and workers' compensation insurance. Put this in your contract. Sometimes a homeowner will act as his own contractor and may want to hire you as a sub. If you agree, he may also be willing to cover your workers' compensation. If so, make it part of the contract, and ask for proof of coverage before you begin work.

Cancellation or Rescission

Rescission or cancellation clauses in a contract give clients the right to back out after signing the contract. Federal law gives your clients the right of rescission for three days if the home secures payment of the debt. Even this can be waived if the job is an emergency, as long as the homeowner signs a waiver.

Some states have home solicitation laws that give a special right of rescission any time a contract is signed in the client's home. Your customers will never invoke this right unless you're guilty of arm twisting. However, if there's a conflict and you don't have a rescission clause in the contract, a court may permit a client to back out at a much later date. You might also have to return all the money the client paid you.

To be safe, include the right of rescission in your agreements. Stipulate when you're required to return deposit money. Don't start the job until after the three day cooling-off period. Otherwise, you could do some free excavation in your client's back yard.

Change Orders

Include a statement in your contract that any changes to the original specifications must be in writing and will result in an additional charge. If you charge an administrative fee for changes, include that too. Specify when changes have to be paid for. We don't recommend that you tack them onto the end of the contract. Collect as soon as the change is finished.

Personal Guarantee

On most jobs, you'll deal with the property owner. In some cases, you might deal with the owner's agent, or someone who represents himself as the owner but is not. Protect yourself. If you're dealing with an owner, include the following language in your contract:

The owner, upon signing this contract, represents and warrants that he or she is owner of the property located at _____.

If you're negotiating with an agent for an owner or a renter or lessee, use a personal guarantee clause:

The client, upon signing this contract, warrants that he or she is legally responsible for payment for improvements of the property located at _____.

This requires the person who signs the contract to be personally responsible for payment, even if he's not the owner. Keep in mind that this clause doesn't guarantee the signer is able to pay, only that he's legally responsible.

Hazardous Materials

Recent changes in codes may require that you remove hazardous materials if they're found during construction. Removing materials such as asbestos may be very expensive. You shouldn't have to absorb this cost. Include a disclaimer saying that removal and disposal of hazardous materials isn't covered by the contract price.

Mediation and Arbitration

Mediation is using an impartial third party to settle disputes. If the problems aren't major, mediation may work quite well. The main drawback — and it's a serious one — is that a mediator's decision isn't binding. Either party can still take the dispute to court.

Arbitration is like mediation in some ways. An impartial third party hears both sides of the dispute. But unlike mediation, courts will usually honor an arbitrator's decision. Arbitration also has several benefits over the usual litigation.

1) It's almost always faster than a lawsuit. Arbitration is less formal than legal procedures.

2) Because it's faster, it's also usually much cheaper than litigation. You pay the arbitrator and lawyers by the hour. The arbitrator's decision is usually binding and may have the same effect as a decision rendered by a trial court.

3) Arbitration hearings are private. Results aren't a public record.

4) The rules of arbitration are less strict than they are in a formal suit. Judgments are made according to the spirit rather than the letter of the law.

Put an arbitration clause in your contract. It assures that you can use arbitration as the first step to resolve a conflict. Without an arbitration clause in your contract, you can't force a client to arbitrate. As a rule, the courts favor arbitration. Neither party can bring suit if either party to the contract insists on arbitration under the terms of the agreement. Generally the courts are glad to be relieved of cases as long as justice is being served.

Several organizations offer arbitration services. The American Arbitration Association is probably the best known. It's the one named in most contracts. Specify which arbitration service you intend to use if the need arises. There's an arbitration clause in our sample contract in Figure 6-1.

CONTRACT AGREEMENT

Best Construction

111 Peak View Blvd.
Colorado Springs, CO 80909
(719) 555-1111

Date: January 10, 1990

Proposal submitted to: Ted Miller

Job location:
100 Colorado Ave.
Colorado Springs, CO 80908

1) We hereby propose to furnish all the materials and perform the labor necessary for demolition and improvements located at the above job address. Work will be done according to the drawings and specifications as described in the attached work order.

2) All materials and work are warranted to be of good quality, free from faults and defects for the period of one year from the day of the job's completion. The work will be performed and completed in a substantial and workmanlike manner for the sum of twenty-five thousand dollars ($25,000). Payment is to be made as follows: 25 percent due at start of job, 25 percent due at start of framing, 25 percent due at start of interior trim work, and the remaining 25 percent due upon substantial completion.

3) Work will begin within seven (7) days of signing the contract and will be completed within ninety (90) days of the start. Contractor is not responsible for delays caused by strikes, accidents, or delays beyond contractor's control. If additional time is needed due to change orders, the contractor may add a reasonable period.

4) Owner to carry fire, tornado, and other necessary insurance on above work. Workers' compensation and public liability insurance to be carried by the contractor.

5) Owner may cancel contract within three (3) days of signing for a full refund. Cancellation must be in writing and received by contractor within three (3) days of signing. A full refund will be returned within ten (10) days of receipt of cancellation.

Figure 6-1
Sample proposal and contract

6) Any alterations or deviations from the above specifications will be executed only upon written orders, and will become an extra charge over and above the estimate. Payment on change orders will be due with the subsequent draw unless otherwise specified.

7) The owner, upon signing this contract, represents and warrants that he or she is owner of the above property.

8) This contract does not include removal and disposal of hazardous materials which contractor may find during construction. If such materials are found, the removal and disposal will be treated as a change order.

9) Any problems or claims arising out of, or relating to, this contract, shall be settled by arbitration in accordance with the rules of the American Arbitration Association, and judgment may be entered on the award in any court having jurisdiction.

10) This agreement and the documents referred to in this agreement shall be the entire, full, and complete agreement between the owner and the contractor. There are no oral agreements that are not included in this contract. This agreement may not be changed or modified unless in writing and signed by both the owner and the contractor.

_____

The undersigned understand and agree to each of the terms set forth above.

(Owner) _____ Date _____

(Contractor) _____ Date _____

This proposal may be withdrawn if not accepted within 30 days.

Figure 6-1 (cont'd)
Sample proposal and contract

Complete Agreement

A complete agreement clause states that you're only obligated to do what's written down in the contract. Neither you nor the client can be held to any oral statements or unwritten promise.

This clause can work both for you and against you. Suppose your client verbally agrees to clear the house of furniture and personal possessions before work starts. He doesn't do it and then your crew breaks his favorite lamp. You may be liable unless your written contract includes the client's agreement to remove his belongings. The client's verbal promise isn't part of the contract and can't be enforced.

A Contract Checklist

It's not hard to put together or understand a smart contract. Here's a checklist to be sure you've included everything:

1) Clear specifications — Attach a detailed and accurate description of the job.

2) Payment procedures — Show how much you'll be paid, and when. Be sure to use the phrase "substantial completion." Include required truth-in-lending information.

3) Start and completion dates — Give yourself some slack beyond the maximum time you expect the job to take. Indicate that you won't be responsible for delays beyond your control.

4) Warranties — Limit your guarantee to one year. Promise standard quality workmanship, not customer satisfaction.

5) Insurance — Explain who is responsible for all required insurance. Make sure yours is up-to-date.

6) Cooling-off period — Include the cancellation and rescission clause.

7) Personal guarantee — Make sure the person who signs the contract is also the person who is responsible for payment.

8) Hazardous materials — Specifically exclude removal and disposal of hazardous materials, unless that's part of the specs.

9) Abitration clause — Won't absolutely prevent litigation, but will encourage a cheaper, faster alternative.

10) Complete agreement — The only agreement you have with the client is what's written and signed.

In Figure 6-1 we've put all this together into a sample contract. You can buy preprinted forms at office supply stores that cover almost every possible contingency, with more official-sounding language. Or you can use the form created by the American Institute of Architects. The AIA form is usually used when an architect is involved. Unfortunately, it seems to us to protect the architect first, the client second, and the contractor third. You're probably better off with your own form or one of the other preprinted ones.

For change orders, use Figure 6-2 as a guideline. Show the running contract total on the change order. That way, the homeowner always knows what the bottom line is. Some contractors operate on the theory that if a homeowner knows what a change order will do to his contract total, he won't want to do it. Those same contractors dread asking for the final check and often have trouble collecting it. Keep the surprises out. They don't belong in the contractor-client relationship.

Time and Materials Contract

Even if you're working by the hour and the owner is paying for materials, have a written contract. Your job and fiscal responsibilities may differ from the remodeler who contracts a total job, but it's just as important to protect yourself legally.

For a time and materials contract, you'll most likely drop or modify paragraphs 1, 2, and 6 of Figure 6-1. In their place, include paragraphs to clarify the following:

■ List the hourly rates for yourself and your employees. If the rates vary, itemize them for each worker.

■ Indicate any charges for estimating and consulting time. (Expect to do the initial consultation at no charge.)

■ Stipulate who is responsible for paying for materials. You'll order at least some if not all the supplies. Will they be billed to you or the homeowner? If you pay, specify when you expect reimbursement: You can request payment monthly or at specified stages during the project.

■ What markup percentage will you charge? Will it apply to labor, materials, or both? Will you add a percentage to the total job cost?

■ Agree to a payment schedule.

■ When will you stop work if payments are late? Be clear about that, and stick with it.

You can drop the change order clause. If the client changes his mind about something, you're still billing for time and materials. You probably don't need the cancellation clause either, but it won't hurt to leave it in.

Everything else stays the same. Dates, warranties, insurance, personal guarantee, arbitration, and complete agreement clauses all affect the remodeler who works by time and materials. Leave the hazardous materials clause in also. Otherwise, if you find an asbestos problem, the homeowner may accuse you of lowballing an estimate to get the work.

CHANGE ORDER

Best Construction
111 Peak View Blvd.
Colorado Springs, CO 80909
(719) 555-1111

Date: February 10, 1990

Owner's name:
Ted Miller
100 Colorado Ave.
Colorado Springs, CO 80908

Job location:
100 Colorado Ave.
Date of existing contract: January 10, 1990

Change order number: 1

We authorize Best Construction to make the change(s) specified below:

MASTER BATH

1) Install Swirl-Way almond whirlpool tub instead of American Standard 5' cast iron standard color tub.

Additional charge	$550.00
Previous contract amount	$25,000.00
Revised contract total	$25,550.00

The above prices and specifications of this change order are satisfactory and are accepted. All work to be performed is under the same terms and conditions as specified in the original contract unless otherwise stipulated.

(Owner) _____ Date _____

(Contractor) _____ Date _____

Figure 6-2
Change order

Collection Troubles

Years ago we knew of a bricklayer who laid a new chimney for a homeowner. The job was done right and completed on time. But for whatever reason, the homeowner couldn't or wouldn't pay the bill. The bricklayer waited several months before he finally decided to put a little muscle into his pleas.

One evening he stopped by the client's house and asked one more time for his money. The homeowner once again offered an excuse and shut the door. A few minutes later, the owner looked out the window and saw the bricklayer prop a ladder against the chimney and begin to climb up, lugging a battered old sledgehammer. The homeowner rushed out of the house yelling, "What do you think you're doing?"

The bricklayer calmly responded, "Since the chimney is mine anyway, I just thought I'd take it home with me." He left with check in hand.

That kind of client intimidation may not be realistic — you can't settle disputes with a sledgehammer. And anyway, it wouldn't always be effective. It's one thing for a bricklayer to take his work back. A painter can't do that. Neither can you. Don't even try.

Here are your options to avoid filing suit. Some work better than others.

- Arbitration

- Place a lien against the property

- File a claim in small claims court

- Barter, or discount the bad debt

- Help the client arrange financing

- You can even try a modified version of the bricklayer's solution. As long as you don't damage a client's property, you may be able to remove material that's already installed.

None of these solutions guarantee results every time. Every situation is different. Sometimes it makes sense to go directly to small claims court; other times arbitration or a lien against the property should be the first step. Still other times, your best bet will be to cut your losses and collect what you can, even if it's a reduced amount.

Whichever option you choose, a few basics will work to keep the judgment in your favor.

1) Write the contract clearly. Get all of the ambiguities out. As we've said, this is the best way to prevent disputes. Oral agreements breed misunderstanding. Get it in writing, and make sure it says what you want it to say.

2) Don't let problems fester. If you ignore a client's complaint until the job is finished, a minor problem can erupt into a volcano. Whether or not

you think the owner is justified, listen and acknowledge what's said. Do your best to fix the situation immediately.

3) Keep a journal of your work on the job. Have weekly walk-throughs with the owner. Take notes and have the owner initial them. Then give the homeowner a copy. If the owner agreed in writing in the third week that the framing looked good, he'll have a hard time six weeks later claiming that the framing was bad.

4) If a dispute comes up that looks like grist for a lawsuit, write down everything connected with the issue while it's still fresh in your mind. Take pictures and get statements from witnesses. Your plumber may swear that the homeowner saw the chip in the enamel tub and said it was OK. But your plumber's notarized statement will have a lot more impact if it's taken two weeks after the incident instead of two years later. Keep an accurate phone log, too. Notes you make about a phone conversation right after the conversation takes place tend to be persuasive in court.

5) Find an expert witness who will support your case. Look for someone who's an authority in the area of your dispute. Find a plumber or carpenter or contractor who is both respected and can communicate effectively. Use that person even before you go to arbitration or court. Expect to pay for his services.

6) Ask other contractors for names of attorneys who are familiar with construction litigation. Your banker or accountant may have suggestions, too. Your county bar association may have a referral service that can give you the names of lawyers who specialize in construction disputes. You'll get a referral but no recommendation. You have to decide about competency yourself. Once you contact a lawyer, furnish all the information you can, not just the part that makes you look good. Your attorney can only help you if you're entirely open.

7) Don't let the statute of limitations run out. Regardless of the type of dispute, you have a limited time to file suit.

Mechanic's Liens

A mechanic's lien is a charge against real property to pay for work done on that property. If your client won't pay, you can file a lien that isn't cleared until the debt is paid. Until that happens, your lien is like a mortgage. Any potential buyer (or lender) will insist that the lien be cleared before taking title to the property.

There's a complication here. The lien secures payment for anyone who does work on the property. What if your electrical subcontractor does the work, you get paid, but then fail to pay the sub? The electrician can file a lien against the homeowner — even if the homeowner has already paid the full contract amount. Because of this possibility, a client may require lien waivers from all of your subcontractors and suppliers. A lien waiver says that the sub or supplier has been paid and won't make a claim against the homeowner. As added insurance, the client may also ask you to sign a lien waiver at the completion of a job.

Figures 6-3 and 6-4 are sample lien waivers from Colorado. You can buy padded forms similar to these from your office supply store. The ones you buy locally should meet requirements in your state.

Both forms work the same way, but you might prefer to use one like Figure 6-3 for final lien waivers. It doesn't ask for a specific dollar amount. Instead, it uses

No. 1030. Rev. 3-84 RELEASE OF RIGHT OF LIEN   Bradford Publishing, 1743 Wazee St., Denver, CO 80202   (303)292-2500   4-84

———— ① ————, Colo., ② ————, 19 ③ ——

FOR A VALUABLE CONSIDERATION *the undersigned hereby releases unto the owner or owners of the hereinafter described property, and to the heirs, personal representatives or assigns of such owner or owners all right of the undersigned to claim a mechanic's lien for labor, services, machinery, tools, equipment, or materials heretofore furnished for the construction, alteration, improvement, addition to or repair of the structure or improvement on Lot numbered* ④ ———— *Block*

numbered ⑤ *in* ⑥ ———— *Addition,*

also known as No. ⑦ ————,
Street Address

in the City of ⑧ ———— *and County of* ⑨ ————
and State of Colorado.

———— ⑩ ————   ———— ⑪ ————

1 Your city
2 Month and day
3 Year
4 Lot number of the property you're contracted to improve*
5   Block number of the property
6 Name of the addition or subdivision where the property is located*
7 Exact address of the property
8 The city in which the property is located
9 The county in which the property is located
10 The name of the company that is waiving its right to lien (Ed's Plumbing, Springs Lumber, etc.)
11 The name of the person signing for the company in #10

* *You can find the legal description of the property at the county clerk's office or on a surveyor's map. You can leave these spaces blank as long as there's absolutely no question about the address of the property you're working on. In new construction, the lot and block numbers and the addition or subdivision name will probably be more important and more reliable than a street address.*

Figure 6-3
Sample lien waiver

LIEN WAIVER

_____(1)_____ , Colo., _____(2)_____ , 19 _(3)_

FOR A VALUABLE CONSIDERATION the undersigned hereby waives all right to claim a mechanic's lien for labor, services, machinery, tools, equipment or materials furnished prior to ___(4)___ , 19 (5) , to _____(6)_____

_____ owner

_____ contractor in the improvements of Lot number ___(7)___ , Block numbered ___(8)___ ,

Addition ___(9)___ also, or, known as No. ___(10)___ Street Avenue

in the City of ___(11)___ , County of ___(12)___ , State of Colorado.

This release valid on condition that check No. ___(13)___ drawn by ___(14)___

on the ___(15)___ , Bank for $ ___(16)___ , and dated ___(17)___ , 19.(18).,

is paid when presented.

_____(19)_____

By ___(20)___

No. 1030A. LIEN WAIVER   Bradford Publishing, 1743 Wazee St., Denver, CO 80202   (303) 292-2500   9-83

1 Your city
2 Month and day
3 Year
4 Month and day of statement from which you are paying
5 Year of statement
6 If you are writing the check, write your name here and circle "contractor."If the homeowner writes the check, put their name here and circle "owner."
7 Lot number of the property you're contracted to improve*
8 Block number of the property*
9 Name of the addition or subdivision where the property is located*
10 Exact address of the property. Circle "street" or "avenue" if it applies.
11 The city in which the property is located
12 The county in which the property is located
13 The number on the check you've written to the sub or supplier. Or, if you're the one waiving your right to lien, the number on the check the homeowner has written to you.
14 The person who has written the check. If you're paying a sub or supplier, your name goes here. If you've received a check from the client, the client's name goes here.
15 The name of the bank the check is drawn on
16 The check amount, or "Paid in full"
17 The month and day on the check
18 The year on the check
19 The name of the company that is waiving its right to lien (Ed's Plumbing, Springs Lumber, etc.)
20 The name of the person signing for the company in #19

You can find the legal description of the property at the county clerk's office or on a surveyor's map. You can leave these spaces blank as long as there's absolutely no question about the address of the property you're working on. In new construction, the lot and block numbers and the addition or subdivision name will probably be more important and more reliable than a street address.

Figure 6-4
Sample lien waiver

the phrase, "For a valuable consideration." This allows you to use your standard markup — or more — without having to explain to the homeowner why you need it.

If you use one like Figure 6-4, write in the amount paid to the sub or supplier for each draw. At the end of the job write "paid in full" rather than a dollar amount. That way, the homeowner won't have reason to complain about your markup on the subcontractor's charges.

It's obvious what to put in most of the blanks, but some of them are confusing, especially if you've never seen a lien waiver before. To help you fill out a waiver for the first time, there's a key following each form.

Lien rights aren't universal. Some states won't allow a sub or supplier to attach a lien to a property. Their only remedy may be to sue the contractor. Some states require that you follow the letter of the law in the rest of the contract. Otherwise you may forfeit lien rights.

In some places, you're required to notify the homeowner of your right to file a lien. If you don't notify them, you waive your right to file if the customer fails to pay you.

You have to send the pre-lien notice to the client within a short time after you've first delivered materials or performed labor on a job. Often the deadline falls before you expect to collect your first draw.

This requirement presents you with a sticky customer relations problem. You have to follow the law. Otherwise you give up one of your most effective tools for collecting overdue accounts. But sometimes clients are offended. They mistakenly think you're starting the lien process or that you don't trust them to pay. Warn your clients at the pre-construction meeting that the notice is required by law and is nothing to be alarmed about.

Most states have fairly short time limits within which you can file an intent to lien. If you don't receive your payment right away, don't let the owner string you along until it's too late to file. After that, you have to follow up with the lien statement, again within a specified period, and finally, the suit itself. If you miss any of these deadlines, you lose your right to sue.

Small Claims Court

Dollar limits for small claims vary between states from as little as $500 to as much as $10,000. The whole idea of small claims court is to provide a less expensive, less complicated and faster way to settle minor financial disputes. In most states the maximum amount for which you can sue has been going up much faster than the value of money has been dropping. Check the limits in your state. The clerk at your local small claims court will probably be able to answer most of your questions.

If your losses are higher than your state's limit for small claims, you can reduce your request and sue for the state limit. For instance, in Colorado the limit has been $1,000. If a client refuses to pay a $1,200 bill, we have two choices. First, we can sue in municipal court for the full $1,200. Fees and costs will probably be more than $1,200. The second, and better choice, would be to sue for $1,000 in small claims court.

Notice that you can't separate your claim into two parts and sue twice in small claims court. Suppose $800 of the bill is for changing some walls and $400 is for replacing the front steps. If both jobs were part of the same contract, you can't split the action into two parts to avoid the $1,000 maximum.

Although the amount you can sue for in small claims court is limited, the cost is minimal. Filing fees are low, sometimes as little as $5 and rarely more than $20. Some states allow you to notify the defendant by registered mail. Others require that he be served in person. Even then, the fee is usually under $40. In most states, you can't be represented by an attorney in small claims court. An attorney may sue or be sued, of course, but he may only represent himself just as you would represent yourself. This also keeps the costs down.

Appeal rights to small claims decisions also vary. Some states allow an appeal by either party. Some allow only the defendant to appeal. Some make appeals very difficult. Where allowed, an appeal must be filed shortly after the case is heard the first time, usually within 15 to 30 days.

Small claims court is a fairly simple option, but it's not without its drawbacks. There's no guarantee you'll collect any money if you win. It's up to you to enforce the court's decision, usually by finding property subject to levy. Good sources of payment include wages owed, money in a bank account or real property. In most cases, this is enough protection for a contractor. Rarely will you work for a client who doesn't own some property. However, a client in bankruptcy or foreclosure may have nothing to lien.

Despite the imperfections of small claims court, for small disputes it's still a faster, cheaper solution than filing in a higher court.

Arbitration

Arbitration is cheaper and quicker than litigation. And because there are no state-imposed dollar limits, it's an excellent alternative to a lawsuit if you're trying to collect more than the small claims limit.

Arbitrators have more flexibility than a court in listening to claims. The focus is on finding a win/win solution instead deciding who should win and who should lose.

Arbitration costs more than small claims court, but less than a lawsuit. In the June, 1987 issue of *Professional Builder*, Lester Wolff of the National Academy of Conciliators (NAC) reports that the average cost of settling a dispute by arbitration is about $250. In contrast, a plaintiff's legal fees in a construction dispute average around $12,000. If the contrast seems unbelievable, keep in mind that of the 16.5 million lawsuits filed in 1986, 90 percent cost more to litigate than the amount in question, according to the March, 1987 issue of *Qualified Remodeler*.

Rarely will it be worth your time and money to go to court. Of course, you can have a lawyer plead your case in arbitration. But arbitration goes so fast (90 percent of the NAC disputes are settled within 40 days according to Mr. Wolff), legal fees tend to be less. A case that drags on for years almost always generates large legal fees.

Arbitrated decisions are generally binding on the parties. Appeals are possible, but unless the court believes there has been fraud or collusion in the arbitration process, it will rarely overturn the decision.

A Better Alternative

You may be forced into court if the amount in question is too high for small claims, if your client refuses to arbitrate, or if your client initiates the claim. If the stakes are high enough, it may be worth your while to go to court. But a better solution is to write a tight contract and do the work you've agreed to do.

If you build a solid, trusting relationship with your clients, you'll rarely, if ever, have to use the court system or arbitration. If you're in litigation regularly, find out why. Maybe you've drawn some very unpleasant clients. Maybe you're doing something that justifies the dissatisfaction. Whatever the problem is, work to change it.

7

Financing

Should you care where your customers get the cash to pay your bills? Maybe you think it doesn't matter where they get the money as long as the draws are on time and the checks don't bounce. But what if they have trouble coming up with the cash? What if they have to delay the project until they have the cash on hand? What if you can get the job only if you can help the owners get financing? Let's face it, they don't all have the money they need. This is when your financial skills become very important.

Remodeling contractors have two types of problems with customer financing. The first is when clients can't qualify for a loan. Either they don't have enough income or they have a bad credit history. The second is when the customer needs emergency repairs and hasn't the time or ability to qualify for a loan.

If your client is in the first category, you're better off to let the job fall through even if you really need the work. That client will be worried about the cost of the job, picking your bid apart and haggling over every dollar.

It's tougher to make a decision about the second kind of client. They *must* have the work done. Maybe the roof has a big leak or the heating system is broken. If these people can't get financing, you might consider carrying the financing yourself.

If your client can qualify for a loan and isn't in a hurry to get the work done, there's a lot you can do to help clients get the financing they need. Plenty of homeowners are credit worthy, but they just don't know how to go about getting the best deal on a loan. If you know the financing ropes, you'll have one more arrow in your quiver, one more way to get the kind of work you want.

Money Sources

For small jobs, your client will only need a single loan. You'll take draws against the loan commitment while you're doing the work. When the job is finished, the client will repay the lender.

For larger jobs your client will need both a construction loan and a permanent loan. Construction loans have a time limit of six months to a year. The job must be finished and the loan converted to a long-term note such as a second mortgage by the end of the period.

If the value of the house is far more than the amount owed, many lenders will be happy to write a home equity loan — usually up to 80 percent of the property value.

It's better if your client can borrow the full amount needed without restriction on the use of funds. But many lenders prefer to write construction loans. They insist on disbursing funds as the work progresses and getting an appraisal when the work is done. If the work has been done poorly or the scope of the project has changed enough to reduce the value, a permanent loan may be refused.

Banks vs. Savings & Loans

Deregulation of the banking industry has reduced the distinction between what banks offer and what savings & loan or mortgage companies offer. Generally, banks provide construction loans and short-term permanent loans.

Permanent loans are amortized (have a payoff schedule) over 10, 15, or even 20 years. They'll almost always require a balloon payment in three to five years, when the entire note comes due. At that time, the owner can pay off the loan, or refinance it for another three to five years under a similar amortization schedule.

Banks treat these loans either as consumer loans or second mortgages. Consumer loans have a much lower initial cost but slightly higher interest rate than second mortgages.

As we write this, savings & loans rarely offer construction or consumer loans, although this may change with further deregulation and changes in the economy.

S&Ls specialize in home mortgage loans. These are permanent loans and don't require a balloon payment.

Mortgage Companies

Mortgage companies generally don't make construction loans. They might arrange one for your client through another lender, but they may add a finder's fee to the cost of the loan.

Lines of Credit

Banks and S&Ls also issue lines of credit based on a homeowner's equity. This kind of loan has more flexibility, but also brings a higher risk to the client. For some reason, consumers perceive a line of credit as cash, instead of debt. Even though it's usually cheaper to borrow against equity than to borrow on your credit cards, some people tend to abuse this type of credit.

If a borrower can pay off a loan in a couple of years, a credit line may be cheaper than a second mortgage, even though it carries a higher interest rate.

Your clients can usually get a consumer loan or line of credit quickly, sometimes in a day, and almost always within a week. A mortgage loan often takes anywhere from several weeks to two months.

Loan Rates

There's no way to know in advance whether a bank, savings & loan, or a mortgage company will offer the best deal. All charge competitive fees for their services. The fees vary from lender to lender. Presently, a line of credit or consumer loan costs only about $100. Mortgage loans cost considerably more. Both S&Ls and mortgage companies charge an application fee to cover an appraisal and credit report. When the mortgage is approved, they charge an origination fee, usually one percent of the total loan. The consumer also pays for title insurance, points, and recording and survey fees. A $50,000 loan can easily cost $1,500 or more.

Points

Points are what lenders charge for writing a loan. A point is one percent of the loan. For example, one point on a $10,000 loan is $100; one point on a $50,000 loan is $500. Sometimes a borrower can buy down the interest rate on a loan by paying additional points at the outset. For instance, a borrower who agrees to pay two points instead of one on a long-term loan may get an interest rate of 10.50 percent instead of 10.75 percent.

In this case, it would take about four years in lowered interest payments to make up for the cost of the added point. On a 20-year note, this saves the borrower money. But if the owner plans to move in five years, it's probably not worth the extra cost.

While fees are fairly stable, points vary from day to day. They may fluctuate wildly over several weeks, changing as economic conditions change. We've seen points vary from a high of 11 to a low of 2 in a month. On a $50,000 loan, that's the difference between $5,500 and $1,000. Remember, this is only the purchase price of the loan! There's still the interest to consider.

Interest rates

First mortgages always offer the lowest interest rate. A second mortgage will cost about half a percent more. Consumer and construction loans are usually 2 to 3 percent above prime.

Banks may quote their rate above prime or above base. The first pegs the interest to the prime rate. The second ties it to the bank's cost above prime. A rate pegged to prime won't necessarily be higher or lower than one that's quoted above base. Listen carefully. Don't be confused and assume that a rate pegged to the bank's base is less than one tied to prime just because the percentage figure they quote is lower.

Some lenders pay contractors a percentage of the origination fee for bringing a loan to them. They do this for their own good banking customers if the loan applicant is a good credit risk. Ask the loan officer at your bank if he'll work with you that way.

Loan to value

Whether your client chooses a line of credit or a second mortgage, financial institutions won't lend more than a certain percentage of the value of the property. The percentage depends on the total of loans already outstanding. Banks use a lower total percentage, probably 75 to 80 percent. Savings & loans and mortgage companies will likely go a little higher, maybe even to 95 percent.

In other words, for a house that's worth $100,000, a 75 percent loan would be $75,000. It doesn't matter if there's one loan, or three. But if there are too many loans already against the property, a lender may not be willing to get in line behind the others.

The loan-to-value ratio varies by location and with the economy. When the economy is strong and property values are rising, lenders may be willing to loan a higher percentage of the appraised value. If property values are flat or decreasing, ratios will be lower.

The value of the improvements you make should affect the appraised value of the home. Unfortunately, each dollar in improvements you make won't add a dollar in appraised value. But some types of improvements add more to the resale value than others. Here's an example:

Suppose your client wants to add a deck. Your bid is for $4,500. According to a local appraiser, the house will be worth an extra $2,500 once the deck is completed. The cost of the deck will be $2,000 higher than the value of the house. The lender doesn't care how much the deck cost, only the increase in value of the property.

City	Project	Job cost	Resale value	Cost recouped
Atlanta	Minor	$7,662	$8,107	106%
Madison	kitchen	7,639	7,213	94%
Colorado Springs	remodel	7,530	6,500	86%
Atlanta	Add a	$9,757	$10,844	111%
Madison	full bath	9,488	7,667	81%
Colorado Springs		9,874	9,250	94%
Atlanta	Replace	$6,259	$6,386	102%
Madison	windows	6,942	4,333	62%
Colorado Springs		6,398	5,500	86%

*Courtesy: **Remodeling** magazine, a Hanley-Wood, Inc., publication*

Figure 7-1

Loan-to-value ratios

Figure 7-1 shows how much various remodeling projects can be expected to add to resale values. The examples are from *Remodeling* magazine's annual Cost vs. Value Report, in their October 1990 issue. It's based on a mid-priced house in an established neighborhood where a lot of remodeling is going on.

Remodeling costs and values vary widely, so we've selected Atlanta, Georgia; Madison, Wisconsin; and Colorado Springs, Colorado as examples.

The same specifications were used to determine the cost in each city. Resale values were estimated by real estate agents and appraisers. Of course, all these values are only opinion. But notice that lenders usually won't lend the full amount of the property's increase in value. Percentages in the chart are related to job cost.

As you can see, values are subjective and vary from place to place. The amount a lender is willing to finance always depends on the perceived added value and the client's credit rating. They know that a bath addition in Atlanta won't always recoup more than its cost, or a window replacement in Madison just more than half its cost.

Here's a final point to consider on the subject of cost-to-value ratios. A lot depends on the neighborhood. If most of the homes on the client's street have four bedrooms and three baths, adding a fourth bedroom and a third bath to a small home almost always makes financial sense. But the opposite probably doesn't. Adding a fourth bedroom to a home in a neighborhood of two bedroom condos probably doesn't add much to the home's resale value. Remember that when counseling potential clients.

Finance Companies

Your clients will nearly always get the best deal at either a bank, savings & loan office or a mortgage company. But if they simply can't qualify for a loan at one of those institutions, you might direct them to a finance company. Finance companies are best known for consumer loans, though they also write mortgages. They'll charge for the same things as a mortgage company or savings & loan. Their fees may even be competitive. But their interest rates will always be several percentage points higher. If a mortgage company is charging 11 percent for a second mortgage, a finance company will probably charge 14 or 15 percent.

Finance companies charge higher rates because they make loans to a higher risk group. They expect to be paid for taking the risk. Of course, they'll secure the debt with whatever property is available. Lenders don't like to make unsecured loans for more than a few thousand dollars.

Steer your clients to a finance company only as a last resort. If this is the only way they can afford to do the job, suggest they wait until they can qualify for a better loan. You might lose an occasional job by your honesty. But we think that's better than getting work at the expense of your client's financial security.

Getting Paid

No matter what type of loan your client arranges, a lender will have standard procedures for paying you. Typically, once the loan is approved, you'll be given a form like Figure 7-2. This form shows your estimates of the job cost. Fill out the budget column, dividing the contract price between each of the line items. Most banks use the same form for new construction and remodeling, so it probably won't exactly match the line items in your own estimate. In fact, for renovation work, the form is missing some major items such as demolition and patch work. It also has several items that are important for new construction that you'll never need for remodeling.

It's not too important if the form doesn't fit your job exactly. What's important is to make sure you'll get timely draws against the loan. You may have to juggle your figures a bit to fit the line items, but as long as the numbers are logical and the bottom line is correct, a lender won't be too picky.

We've filled in Figure 7-2 to show the cost breakdown for a living room addition and kitchen remodel valued at about $40,000.

The lender won't care if individual line items aren't perfectly accurate. If you've put more than you need into the foundation material line and less than you need into foundation labor, they won't mind. Nor will they be concerned if the two combined don't completely cover your costs — as long as it appears that other line items make up for the deficit.

Lenders will look for logical proportions in the cost breakdown. They'll also be watching for front-loading. If it looks like you're arranging to get all your profit before the framing starts, they'll be very uneasy. And they should be. They may suspect you'll try to abandon the job after the foundation is in, or that you'll have serious cash flow problems at job completion. Either way, you'll sacrifice the lender's trust in your ability to complete the job.

Property address: **1000 S Nevada**   Builder: **Best Construction**   Date: **05-15-**

Buyer: _____   Builder signature: *Tom Smith*   Phone: **555-11**

Item	Budget	Draw I	√	Draw II	√	Draw III	√	Subtotal draws	D
1 Lot									
2 Plans & specs-arch. fee	500								
3 Water & sewer fee or well & septic									
4 Gas tap									
5 Building permit	200								
6 Insurance									
7 Engineering	500								
8 Appraisal									
9 Title & recording									
10 Loan fee									
11 Site preparation	200								
12 Excavation & backfill	600								
13 Foundation labor	1,950								
14 Foundation material	2,900								
15 Foundation waterproof	100								
16 Foundation drain									
17 Survey									
18 Flat work labor									
19 Flat work material									
20 Lumber-millwork	4,800								
21 Steel posts/beams									
22 Windows-sliding doors-sills	2,800								
23 Framing labor	3,700								
24 Siding labor	1,100								
25 Garage doors									
26 Gutters	375								
27 Roof labor	725								
28 Roof material	400								
29 Plumbing	650								
30 Water-sewer-gas lines									
31 Electric	750								
32 Heating									
33 Venting	80								
34 Insulation	850								
35 Drywall	2,150								
36 Masonry labor									
37 Masonry material									

Figure 7-2

Cost breakdown and construction progress schedule

Item	Budget	Draw I	√	Draw II	√	Draw III	√	Subtotal draws	Dr
38 Stucco									
39 Pre-built fireplace	600								
40 Finish carpentry labor	800								
41 Ornamental iron									
42 Painting	675								
43 Decorating									
44 Drapes									
45 Carpet	950								
46 Hard surface floors	800								
47 Ceramics									
48 Marble									
49 Cabinets	7,500								
50 Countertops	800								
51 Appliances	1,400								
52 Mirrors/shower doors									
53 Bath hardware									
54 Light fixtures	600								
55 Intercom									
56 Central vac									
57 Trash removal	200								
58 Final grading									
59 Landscaping									
60 Driveway									
61 Retaining wall									
62 Cleaning	100								
63 Misc. labor									
64 Breakage allowance									
65 Call backs									
66 Tool rental									
67 Const. utilities									
68 Const. interest									
69 HBA fees									
70 VA inspection									
71 Supervision									
72 Overhead									
73 Contingency expense									
74 Real estate commission									
75 Closing costs									
76									
77 Total	39,755								

Figure 7-2 (cont'd)

Cost breakdown and construction progress schedule

Lenders do their best to protect their money. A construction loan is generally set up with its own separate checking account. You (or the homeowner) write the checks to the subs and suppliers and to yourself for the scheduled draws. The bank countersigns the checks and mails them out. The checks have a lien waiver printed on the back so that endorsing each check is a legal lien waiver.

The lender may also do on-site inspections to make sure the job is really as far along as you say it is. This usually isn't necessary on remodeling jobs because the owner is unlikely to release funds unless the work is proceeding as agreed. It's almost always done on larger construction projects. In fact, the lender may hire a third party to oversee the job and be sure the work is being accomplished as stated and at an acceptable quality level.

Scheduling Draws

Draws from a lender are usually scheduled by date rather than by operations completed. Set the draw date so you can take advantage of tenth-of-the-month supplier discounts. You'll submit your draws on a form like Figure 7-3. It shows the draws for the remodeling project in Figure 7-2.

Items 5 and 7 were paid for before the draw. The amounts shown are to reimburse the contractor. The actual bills may be less than the amounts on the draw sheet, but you shouldn't have trouble collecting if the figures are within budget.

Figure 7-4 shows the lender's breakdown. By the first draw, the job is 50 percent framed. You can collect the total budgeted for the architectural plans, building permit, engineering, site prep and excavation, and all the foundation work. Charge all the framing materials to this draw, even though the framing itself is only half done. As long as the material is on the construction site, you may ask for payment.

If the windows, sliding doors, and sills had also been delivered, you could collect for those also, even though they won't be installed for another week. Don't abuse this policy, though. The longer supplies are on the job site, the greater the chance of theft, vandalism, or accidental damage. The homeowner is technically responsible for any items on site. But if you've contributed to a problem by having supplies delivered unreasonably early, you'll have trouble getting the owner to pay for any damage. And you'll certainly create a lot of bad will for yourself.

The rest of the lumber and millwork, including the exterior siding and interior trim material, hasn't been delivered. You'd charge those to the next draw following their delivery. You're entitled to payment for anything that's been delivered even if you haven't received your bill yet.

A second draw would look like Figure 7-5. You can see from the draw how the job is progressing. The exterior work is completed except for installing the gutters. The drywall is about 75 percent finished. Painting, finish carpentry and flooring haven't started yet. The plumbing and electrical are partially done, but none of the light fixtures have been delivered to the job site. The cabinets have been delivered

LOAN DISBURSEMENT REQUEST

Date: June 1, 1990

Builder: Best Construction

Property address: 1000 S. Nevada

Item no.	Name of payee	Purpose	Amount	Check no.	Lien waiver received
2	Sun Design	Plans	$ 500	4432	
5	Best Const.	Permit	200	—	
7	Best Const.	Soil Eng.	500	—	
11	Best Const.	Site Prep.	200	—	
12	Best Const.	Exc. and fill	600	—	
13	Best Const.	Labor	2504.52	—	
14	Springs Concrete	Found. mat.	2345.48	4456	
15	Best Const.	Waterproof	100	—	
20	Home Lumber	Materials	1447.93	4461	
20	Peak Lumber	Materials	684.06	4462	
20	Ranch Lumber	Materials	220.16	4470	
20	Best Const.	Misc.	33.82	—	
21	Best Const.	Labor	1850	—	

Total draw request $ 11,185.97

Certifications— Dispersal is hereby authorized on the above captioned construction loan. This is to further certify that all labor and materials above listed have been used exclusively in the construction of this house.

_____
Signature

LIP.............................$_____

Draw............................$_____

New Balance ....$_____

Balance from
last draw $_____

Property inspected_____
(Date)

Request approved_____
Loan no._____

Figure 7-3

Loan disbursement request - draw I

Property address: **1000 S. Nevada**   Builder: **Best Construction**   Date: **06-05-9**

Buyer: _____   Builder signature: *Tom Smith*   Phone: **555-111**

Item	Budget	Draw I	√	Draw II	√	Draw III	√	Subtotal draws	D
1 Lot									
2 Plans & specs-arch. fee	500	500	√						
3 Water & sewer fee or well & septic									
4 Gas tap									
5 Building permit	200	200	√						
6 Insurance									
7 Engineering	500	500	√						
8 Appraisal									
9 Title & recording									
10 Loan fee									
11 Site preparation	200	200	√						
12 Excavation & backfill	600	600	√						
13 Foundation labor	1,950	2,504.52	√						
14 Foundation material	2,900	2,345.48	√						
15 Foundation waterproof	100	100	√						
16 Foundation drain									
17 Survey									
18 Flat work labor									
19 Flat work material									
20 Lumber-millwork	4,800	2,385.97							
21 Steel posts/beams									
22 Windows-sliding doors-sills	2,800								
23 Framing labor	3,700	1,850							
24 Siding labor	1,100								
25 Garage doors									
26 Gutters	375								
27 Roof labor	725								
28 Roof material	400								
29 Plumbing	650								
30 Water-sewer-gas lines									
31 Electric	750								
32 Heating									
33 Venting	80								
34 Insulation	850								
35 Drywall	2,150								
36 Masonry labor									
37 Masonry material									

Figure 7- 4

Cost breakdown for draw I

Item	Budget	Draw I	√	Draw II	√	Draw III	√	Subtotal draws	D
38 Stucco									
39 Pre-built fireplace	600								
40 Finish carpentry labor	800								
41 Ornamental iron									
42 Painting	675								
43 Decorating									
44 Drapes									
45 Carpet	950								
46 Hard surface floors	800								
47 Ceramics									
48 Marble									
49 Cabinets	7,500								
50 Countertops	800								
51 Appliances	1,400								
52 Mirrors/shower doors									
53 Bath hardware									
54 Light fixtures	600								
55 Intercom									
56 Central vac									
57 Trash removal	200								
58 Final grading									
59 Landscaping									
60 Driveway									
61 Retaining wall									
62 Cleaning	100								
63 Misc. labor									
64 Breakage allowance									
65 Call backs									
66 Tool rental									
67 Const. utilities									
68 Const. interest									
69 HBA fees									
70 VA inspection									
71 Supervision									
72 Overhead									
73 Contingency expense									
74 Real estate commission									
75 Closing costs									
76 Total draw		11,185.97							
77 Total	39,755								

Figure 7- 4 (cont'd)

Cost breakdown for draw I

and are ready to install. The countertops will be delivered as soon as the cabinets are set.

Figure 7-6 shows the lender's progress schedule. You can see that some of the completed line items have money left in the budget. The price listed for each item should include both labor and material expense, of course, and a proportionate share of your profit. If you're installing the materials and don't have any other payroll, labor cost may show up on the overhead and supervision expense lines of the form.

Figure 7-7 is an example of the final draw. Figure 7-8 is the lender's breakdown.

Your lender may require that you show overhead (and maybe even profit) separately. You do that by reducing each line item by an amount that represents your overhead percentage, and totaling those amounts on the line for overhead. If that's the case, collect a proportion of your profit in each draw.

For example, suppose overhead is 15 percent of the job we've shown in the illustrations for this chapter. The total amount of the job doesn't change, and the draws won't either. Only the item breakdown would be different. You'd divide each line item by 1.15, total the line items, then show 15 percent of that total under "overhead." Line 72 would look like this:

Item	Description	Budget	Draw 1	Draw 2
72	Overhead	5185.44	1459.04	2274.86

If a lender asks you to itemize the job profit, it may be because he intends to hold back part or all of the profit until you finish the job. This is like a retainer and it's unfair to contractors. If you have a good reputation for completing jobs, there's no need to hold up payment of the profit margin.

Some additional items may be included in the draw sheet: lot costs, appraisals, title, and recording fees. Those will be paid to the client. Those are expenses the owner pays and won't be part of your contract.

Change orders aren't shown on the schedule unless the loan includes budgeted funds to cover the possibility. If change order money is included, it shows up on the line item for contingency expense. If these funds aren't part of the loan, make sure you promptly collect what's due from the client.

All of this can complicate the job tremendously. It puts you in the uncomfortable position of having to let your client see every bill that comes across your desk. It can also be a real paperwork hassle. Unfortunately, the construction industry has only itself to blame. A few dishonest contractors made this mess for the rest of us. But the trend is moving in this direction, and you have to live with it.

LOAN DISBURSEMENT REQUEST

Date: July 1, 1990

Builder: Best Construction

Property address: 1000 S. Nevada

Item no.	Name of payee	Purpose	Amount	Check no.	Lien waiver received
20	Peak Lumber	Materials	$1,240.60	4526	
20	Home Lumber	Materials	429.86	4527	
20	Best Const.	Materials	87.15	—	
22	Ace Windows	Materials	1,958.00	4532	
22	Best Const.	Labor	842.00	—	
23	Best Const.	Labor	1,850.00	—	
24	Best Const.	Labor	1,100.00	—	
27	Best Const.	Labor	645.00	—	
28	AAA Roofing	Materials	480.00	4529	
29	Al's Plumbing	Labor + Mat.	400.00	4528	
31	Miller Elec.	Labor + Mat.	200.00	4530	
33	First Heat	Labor + Mat.	68.00	4533	
34	Mike Brown	Labor + Mat.	720.00	4535	
35	Ace Drywall	Labor + Mat.	1,600.00	4536	
49	Scandia Cab.	Materials	5,820.00	4540	

Total draw request $ 17,440.61

Certifications— Dispersal is hereby authorized on the above captioned construction loan. This is to further certify that all labor and materials above listed have been used exclusively in the construction of this house.

_____
Signature

LIP.......................$_____

Draw.....................$_____

New Balance ....$_____

Balance from
last draw $_____

Property inspected_____
(Date)

Request approved_____

Loan no._____

Figure 7-5

Request for draw II

Property address: **1000 S Nevada** Builder: **Best Construction** Date: **07-05-90**

Buyer: _____ Builder signature: *Tom Smith* Phone: **555-1111**

Item	Budget	Draw I	√	Draw II	√	Draw III	√	Subtotal draws	Dr
1 Lot									
2 Plans & specs-arch. fee	500	500	√						
3 Water & sewer fee or well & septic									
4 Gas tap									
5 Building permit	200	200	√						
6 Insurance									
7 Engineering	500	500	√						
8 Appraisal									
9 Title & recording									
10 Loan fee									
11 Site preparation	200	200	√						
12 Excavation & backfill	600	600	√						
13 Foundation labor	1,950	2,504.52	√						
14 Foundation material	2,900	2,345.48	√						
15 Foundation waterproof	100	100	√						
16 Foundation drain									
17 Survey									
18 Flat work labor									
19 Flat work material									
20 Lumber-millwork	4,800	2,385.97		1,757.61					
21 Steel posts/beams									
22 Windows-sliding doors-sills	2,800			2,800	√				
23 Framing labor	3,700	1,850		1,850	√				
24 Siding labor	1,100			1,100	√				
25 Garage doors									
26 Gutters	375								
27 Roof labor	725			645	√				
28 Roof material	400			480	√				
29 Plumbing	650			400					
30 Water-sewer-gas lines									
31 Electric	750			200					
32 Heating									
33 Venting	80			68	√				
34 Insulation	850			720	√				
35 Drywall	2,150			1,600					
36 Masonry labor									
37 Masonry material									

Figure 7-6

Cost breakdown for draw II

Item	Budget	Draw I	√	Draw II	√	Draw III	√	Subtotal draws	D
38 Stucco									
39 Pre-built fireplace	600								
40 Finish carpentry labor	800								
41 Ornamental iron									
42 Painting	675								
43 Decorating									
44 Drapes									
45 Carpet	950								
46 Hard surface floors	800								
47 Ceramics									
48 Marble									
49 Cabinets	7,500			5,820					
50 Countertops	800								
51 Appliances	1,400								
52 Mirrors/shower doors									
53 Bath hardware									
54 Light fixtures	600								
55 Intercom									
56 Central vac									
57 Trash removal	200								
58 Final grading									
59 Landscaping									
60 Driveway									
61 Retaining wall									
62 Cleaning	100								
63 Misc. labor									
64 Breakage allowance									
65 Call backs									
66 Tool rental									
67 Const. utilities									
68 Const. interest									
69 HBA fees									
70 VA inspection									
71 Supervision									
72 Overhead									
73 Contingency expense									
74 Real estate commission									
75 Closing costs									
76 Total draw		11,185.97		17,440.61					
77 Total	39,755								

Figure 7-6 (cont'd)

Cost breakdown for draw II

LOAN DISBURSEMENT REQUEST

Date: Aug 1, 1990

Builder: Best Construction
Property address: 1000 S Nevada

Item no.	Name of payee	Purpose	Amount	Check no.	Lien waiver received
20	Peak Lumber	Materials	620.80	4598	
20	Best Const.	Materials	24.25	—	
26	Mt. Gutters	Labor & Mat.	380.00	4595	
29	Al's Plumbing	Labor & Mat.	175.50	4601	
31	Miller Electric	Labor & Mat.	475.00	4605	
35	Ace Drywall	Labor & Mat.	740.00	4599	
39	Heat Center	Material	398.48	4590	
39	Best Const.	Labor	250.00	—	
40	Best Const.	Labor	800.00	—	
42	Stan's Painting	Labor & Mat.	690.00	4602	
45	Floor Master Car	Labor & Mat.	950.00	4606	
46	Floor Master Car	Labor & Mat.	775.00	4606	
49	Best Const.	Labor	1,800.00	—	
50	Form Fit Counters	Labor & Mat.	740.00	4609	
51	T's Appliances	Material	1,040.80	4615	
51	Best Const.	Labor	350.00	—	
54	Range Fixtures	Materials	620.00	4597	
57	Best Const.	Labor	200.00	—	
62	Best Const.	Labor	100.00	—	

Total draw request $ __11,129.83__

Certifications— Dispersal is hereby authorized on the above captioned construction loan. This is to further certify that all labor and materials above listed have been used exclusively in the construction of this house.

_____
Signature

LIP.............................$_____
Draw.........................$_____
New Balance ....$_____

Balance from
last draw $_____

Property inspected_____
                     (Date)

Request approved_____
        Loan no._____

Figure 7-7

Final draw

Property address: **1000 S Nevada** Builder: **Best Construction** Date: **08-05-90**
Buyer: _____ Builder signature: _____ Phone: **555-1111**

Item	Budget	Draw I	√	Draw II	√	Draw III	√	Subtotal draws	Dr
1 Lot									
2 Plans & specs-arch. fee	500	500	✓						
3 Water & sewer fee or well & septic									
4 Gas tap									
5 Building permit	200	200	✓						
6 Insurance									
7 Engineering	500	500	✓						
8 Appraisal									
9 Title & recording									
10 Loan fee									
11 Site preparation	200	200	✓						
12 Excavation & backfill	600	600	✓						
13 Foundation labor	1,950	2,504.52	✓						
14 Foundation material	2,900	2,345.48	✓						
15 Foundation waterproof	100	100	✓						
16 Foundation drain									
17 Survey									
18 Flat work labor									
19 Flat work material									
20 Lumber-millwork	4,800	2,385.97	✓	1,757.61		645.05	✓		
21 Steel posts/beams									
22 Windows-sliding doors-sills	2,800			2,800	✓				
23 Framing labor	3,700	1,850	✓	1,850	✓				
24 Siding labor	1,100			1,100	✓				
25 Garage doors									
26 Gutters	375					380	✓		
27 Roof labor	725			645	✓				
28 Roof material	400			480	✓				
29 Plumbing	650			400		175.50	✓		
30 Water-sewer-gas lines									
31 Electric	750			200		475	✓		
32 Heating									
33 Venting	80			68	✓				
34 insulation	850			720	✓				
35 Drywall	2,150			1,600		740	✓		
36 Masonry labor									
37 Masonry material									

Figure 7-8

Cost breakdown for final draw

Item	Budget	Draw I	√	Draw II	√	Draw III	√	Subtotal draws	Dr
38 Stucco									
39 Pre-built fireplace	600					648.48	√		
40 Finish carpentry labor	800					800	√		
41 Ornamental iron									
42 Painting	675					690	√		
43 Decorating									
44 Drapes									
45 Carpet	950					950	√		
46 Hard surface floors	800					775	√		
47 Ceramics									
48 Marble									
49 Cabinets	7,500			5,820		1,800	√		
50 Countertops	800					740	√		
51 Appliances	1,400					1,390.80	√		
52 Mirrors/shower doors									
53 Bath hardware									
54 Light fixtures	600					620	√		
55 Intercom									
56 Central vac									
57 Trash removal	200					200	√		
58 Final grading									
59 Landscaping									
60 Driveway									
61 Retaining wall									
62 Cleaning	100					100	√		
63 Misc. labor									
64 Breakage allowance									
65 Call backs									
66 Tool rental									
67 Const. utilities									
68 Const. interest									
69 HBA fees									
70 VA inspection									
71 Supervision									
72 Overhead									
73 Contingency expense									
74 Real estate commission									
75 Closing costs									
76 Total Draw		11,185.97		17,440.61		11,129.83			
77 Total	39,755								

Figure 7-8 (cont'd)

Cost breakdown for final draw

Contractor Financing

In some parts of the country it's becoming increasingly common for remodelers to not only do the work, but finance it as well. Contractors take two approaches to this option:

1) Some contractors see this as a way to increase their income. They carry the client who can't get money from any other source. Clients like that are willing to pay a higher interest rate and probably even a higher contract price to get the work done. Some contractors make more money on the financing than on the construction itself, if they keep collections current.

2) Others see financing as an additional service. They charge rates comparable to banks and don't charge a higher contract price. Because these contractors offer competitive financing, they get better credit risks, not just the clients who can't get loans elsewhere.

As long as builders don't use high-pressure sales tactics, both approaches are legitimate ways to do business. But most contractors shy away from financing. They're busy enough with the difficulties of contracting.

You'll need a deep pocket to carry financing for your clients. If you don't have it, you may be able to arrange a business loan and make loans to your clients from that source. If you charge higher loan fees and a higher interest rate than you have to pay, there may be a small margin of profit. Of course, you have to be sure your customers are excellent credit risks. Otherwise you'll get into serious trouble very quickly.

If you decide to try contractor financing, be sure to use a legally binding contract and triple-check your clients' credit rating and ability to pay. You'll have to set your own guidelines for acceptable credit risks. In the beginning, at least, it's wiser to err on the side of caution. Protect yourself. Secure the debt with something tangible like a second mortgage or a fully-insured vehicle.

Figure 7-9 is a starting point to determine your clients' ability to pay. Once you have this information, run a thorough credit check. Besides the clients' credit history, consider their accumulated assets and how their financial demands may change during the life of the loan.

The first section covers the clients' net monthly income. *Take-home pay* refers to the amount left after taxes, social security, insurance premiums, and other items have been deducted from the gross pay. Don't list regular deductions such as loan payments or automatic transfers to bank accounts.

Other net income (Line 3) is any money received on a reliable, continuous basis such as business or property income, or stock dividends.

Credit Application

Applicant's name:

Address:

City, Zip:

Telephone:

Monthly income

1	Monthly take-home pay (Applicant)	$
2	Monthly take-home pay (Co-applicant)	$
3	Other net income (List sources)	
	A.	$
	B.	$
4	Total net monthly income (Add lines 1-3)	$
5	Divide amount on line 4 by 2.	$
	(This adjusts the income to allow for typical household expenses such as food, clothing, utilities, gas, entertainment.)	

Monthly expenses

6	Rent or mortgage payment	$
7	Payments for other property or second mortgage	$
8	Regular medical expenses not covered by insurance	$
9	Alimony, child support or child care	$
10	Other expenses such as car payments, insurance, condo maintenance fees, etc.	
11	Total monthly expenses (Add lines 6-10)	$

Estimated creditability

	Enter amount from line 4	$
	Enter amount from line 11	$
12	Subtract line 11 from line 4	$

Payment/net income comparison

13	Loan payment to contractor	$
14	Rent/mortgage payment (Line 6)	$
15	New payment total (Add lines 13 & 14)	$
16	Total net income (Line 4)	$
17	Divide new payment total by total net income (Line 15 by 16)	$

Figure 7-9

Credit application and customer evaluation

The rest of the form is for listing regular expenses and evaluating your clients' ability to repay your loan. If the result in Line 17 of Figure 7-9 is 40 percent (0.40) or less, the clients should be able to handle the payments. If it's 41-45 (0.41-0.45) percent, the clients' ability to repay is questionable. If it's over 45 percent (0.45), the loan may be too risky to make.

Selling Loans

There's another form of contractor financing you should know about. Once the loan papers are signed, you can sell the note to another lender. You'll need an agreement with the lender before signing the loan documents. On this type of financing you're acting as a *loan broker*, a middleman to sell loans. If you broker a loan, it's important to follow the lender's paperwork procedures to the letter. You may arrange to get a fee from the lender for bringing them business.

Many lenders who buy contracts from you will discount the loan total. For example, if your contract is for $12,500, the lender may only pay you $12,000, although he'll be collecting the full $12,500 plus interest. Figure the discount into your job cost.

Contractor financing isn't for everyone. There can be considerable risk involved. We've never tried it because we prefer to be contractors, not bankers. Also, we don't feel much like taking the risk. But the trade publications say if you do it right, it can create business that would otherwise disappear because your prospective customer can't raise the money. You'll have to judge for yourself here.

8

How Much to Charge and How to Bill It

*T*he way you charge for the work you do is often a kind of numbers game. You need enough money to keep the business going and growing. You need enough money to live on. You also need enough money to make the headaches and hassles of owning your own business worth your while. But you can't price yourself out of the market.

How much is enough? How do you charge enough to meet expenses and still have money left over? And, above all, how do you get your client to pay you what you're worth?

The Options

There are three ways to charge for your services.

1) *Time and Materials*— You charge for the hours you work, the materials you buy, and the subcontractors you hire. You either mark up those charges to cover overhead and profit, or charge a percentage of the job total.

2) *Firm Price Contract*— You estimate what a job will cost, including your profit and overhead, and sign a contract with your client for that amount. If your estimate is wrong, you're stuck with the mistake.

3) We'll call the third way the *by the seat of your pants* method. This isn't something we recommend. You guess about what the job will cost and give your client a "ballpark" figure — no written contract, just an oral "understanding." When the job is done, you bill the client for time and materials. If the bill is close to your estimate, and you did a good job, you'll probably get paid. But if your bill is for a lot more than your estimate, a dispute is almost certain. And without a written contract, you'll have to compromise to get any money at all.

"Yes, I did tell Mr. Smith that I could remodel his bathroom for $1000, but that was <u>before</u> he decided he wanted a step-down jacuzzi, tanning salon and built-in rowing machine."

The first two methods are good business. The third can put you out of business in a hurry. At best, contractors who use method three end up working for someone else. At worst, they're forced into bankruptcy.

Most remodelers use either method one or two. Each has its advantages and disadvantages. What you do depends on where you live, the kind of work you do, how good you are, and your reputation in the community. You'll have to decide which method works best for your circumstances. We'll discuss the differences between the two options in the rest of this chapter.

Your Prices Are Based on Your Costs

No matter which method you use, it's important to know what your costs are. All your expenses fall into one of two categories, *direct* and *indirect* costs. Let's look at these costs in detail.

Direct costs are the result of taking on a specific job. Indirect costs, or *overhead*, are the costs of doing business that aren't related to a specific job.

Profit is what's left after you subtract *all* your costs from the total your clients pay you:

Gross income - direct costs - indirect costs = profit

If you only subtract direct costs, you won't have a true picture of your profits. Far too many remodelers make this mistake. They usually don't last long in the construction business, but they make life miserable for themselves and the rest of us while they're around! Because they don't allow for overhead, they bid lower than everyone else. They get the work, but they can't pay their bills, and often leave their clients hanging with unfinished jobs no one wants to complete. As a result, the whole industry gets a black eye.

Identifying Indirect Costs

Overhead, your indirect costs, also falls into two categories. *Fixed* costs stay fairly constant from month to month. *Variable* costs are the ones that come up unexpectedly or that change with the amount of work you do. Rent and loan payments are examples of fixed costs. Tool repair, office supplies, equipment rentals and payroll taxes are variable costs.

Indirect Cost Worksheet

Fixed costs (pro-rated to monthly cost)	Sample Budget	Your estimate
Rent/lease/mortgage	$400	_____
Secretary/bookkeeper	700	_____
Telephone (basic service)	20	_____
Insurance premiums		
Liability	65	_____
Vehicle	75	_____
Licenses & professional fees	30	_____
Depreciation	180	_____
Total fixed costs	**$1470**	_____
Variable costs (estimated)		
Telephone (long distance)	$10	_____
Advertising	75	_____
Interest	50	_____
Utilities	50	_____
Office supplies	10	_____
New equipment	100	_____
Equipment repair	50	_____
Vehicle maintenance	40	_____
Fuel, vehicles and equipment	80	_____
Total variable costs	**$465**	_____
Total overhead	**$1,935**	_____

Figure 8-1

Indirect cost worksheet

Identifying your operating costs is only half the battle. Controlling them is even more important. Just because you don't have paid office staff or a showroom, don't think you don't have overhead. Every time you buy a postage stamp or pay to have a saw blade sharpened, that's overhead.

Fill out Figure 8-1 to identify your overhead expenses. Your line items and numbers may be different from the example, but be as precise as you can when you make your estimate. A low, inaccurate overhead figure is only slightly better than no figure at all.

Working out of your home cuts overhead considerably. If you don't hire an office staff, that saves money too. But if you're just starting out, our sample budget for new tools won't be nearly enough. And loan payments for a new truck will add a lot to your costs.

The bottom line for our sample budget is $1,935 a month, or $23,220 a year. If this company's gross income for the year is $100,000, overhead would be 23.22 percent of gross. That's too much. This company would either have to cut expenses drastically or make a dramatic increase in sales. A better choice would be to do both.

Many of your costs will stay the same whether gross income is $100,000 or $500,000. Profits will usually increase as overhead percentage decreases. In a well-run business, overhead increases proportionally less than sales. Figure 8-2 illustrates this. Find the percentage by dividing overhead by gross income.

You can see from Figure 8-2 that the company operates more efficiently at $150,000 than at $100,000, and even better when the gross sales reach $200,000. The drop in overhead adds 3.25 percent to profits over three years. That's $6,500 in the owner's pocket the third year — money that wouldn't be there if overhead had remained at 15 percent.

Year	Gross income	Overhead	Percentage
1990	$100,000	$15,000	15.0%
1991	$150,000	$20,000	13.3%
1992	$200,000	$23,500	11.75%

Figure 8-2

Overhead percentage decreases as sales increase

The overhead percentage may drop for several reasons:

1) Some costs stay the same whether you gross $10,000 or $100,000. If you lease an office, it costs the same whether you have little work or lots of work. Rent will be about the same until you move to a larger office.

2) Some costs are heavily loaded up front. For instance, if $500,000 worth of liability insurance costs $500, a million dollars' coverage may only cost $100 more.

3) The business manager controls overhead effectively by cutting waste and shopping for better prices.

At some points in a company's growth, the overhead percentage jumps again. An article by Walt Stoeppeolwerth in the March, 1987, issue of *Qualified Remodeler* suggests that profit is a higher percentage of sales (and overhead percentage is lower) when gross income is around $400,000 to $500,000 than when it's $1,000,000. For most remodelers, the profit percentage may not recover until gross receipts reach about $1,500,000.

That's because one person can manage a business that does up to $500,000. Beyond that it takes more labor (both office work and supervision on site), more space, and more equipment. As a result, overhead grows faster than sales for a while.

Once you begin to keep track of overhead, you'll see how it affects profit on *each* job. Don't wait until the end of the year to tally it up. You'll get into the all-too-common cash flow crunch: money pours in during May, only to pour out even faster in July.

Adding Overhead to the Bid

There are two common ways to add overhead expense to your charges. Either add a percentage for overhead on each job, or *allocate* costs between jobs. Allocation is like turning indirect costs into direct costs. For instance, you'd keep close track of your mileage and charge the exact amount to each job. You'd divide your bookkeeper's salary among the jobs you're working on each week and add bookkeeping expense as a cost on each job. That's a very complex way to account for overhead. It's also very hard to be accurate.

It's much easier to add a percentage to each job. Suppose annual gross sales are expected to be $200,000. Overhead will be $24,000 and profit should be $10,000 for the year. What's your bid (including overhead and profit) if direct costs on a job will be $8,300? Here's how to figure the answer:

Overhead should be 12 percent of the selling price and profit should be 5 percent of the selling price. Together, overhead and profit will be 17 percent of the selling price (12% + 5% = 17%). If overhead and profit are 17 percent, the direct cost has to be 83 percent of selling price (100% - 17% = 83%). To find the selling price, divide direct cost by 83 percent: $8,300 divided by 83% = $10,000. Overhead will be 12 percent, or $1,200, and profit will be 5 percent, or $500.

Job number	Direct cost	Overhead percent	Profit percent	Selling price	Over-head	Profit
1	$37,350	12%	5%	_____	_____	_____
2	14,250	18%	7%	_____	_____	_____
3	51,480	8%	4%	_____	_____	_____
4	9,800	20%	10%	_____	_____	_____
5	53,975	10%	5%	_____	_____	_____

Figure 8-3

Figuring the selling price

Use Figure 8-3 to test your knowledge. We've shown direct costs on each job. Fill in the selling price, overhead in dollars, and profit in dollars based on the direct cost, overhead and profit percentages given. When you've finished, turn to the answers at the end of this chapter.

Remember, we're concerned with average figures here. Indirect costs won't be exactly 12 percent of every job, nor do they stay the same from month to month. If all your annual insurance premiums come due in March, overhead will soar that month. The point is, you have to allow for overhead in every job, or you won't have the money to cover it.

Identifying Direct Costs

Direct costs are easier to identify. These are expenses you charge directly to the current job. Materials, subcontractors, labor, and permits are direct costs.

Your bookkeeping system should make it easy to track direct costs. Make out a purchase order or requisition system when you place orders. Ask your suppliers and subcontractors to reference your job name or number on their bills.

When you receive an invoice, post it to your job cost records, or put a copy of the bill in the job file. Then after you pay the bill, keep the original invoice in a file organized by supplier's name.

Contractors just starting out usually have just one job going at a time and probably do most of their own bookkeeping. Larger builders have more jobs going at a time. That makes it harder to keep track of costs.

Form some good job costing habits right from the beginning and you won't have problems later on. Have your employees keep track of their hours by job name or number. Do that even if you work on a contract basis rather than time and materials. That way, you'll have a way to check your estimates of the time it takes to do particular jobs.

Hidden Labor Costs

Don't forget the overhead costs that are part of labor expense. Besides what you pay your employees, remember the employer's share of FICA (social security taxes), workers' compensation, and unemployment tax. If you provide health insurance or retirement benefits, you need to include those, too.

Here's what a $10-per-hour employee actually costs us:

- Basic hourly wage $10.00
- Employer's share FICA (7.65%)   .76
- Workers' compensation (28%)   2.80
- Unemployment insurance (3%)   .30
- Liability insurance (2%)   .20
- Bookkeeping   1.00
- Total hourly rate $15.06

In addition to withholding for income taxes and social security, you have to match the employee's contribution to social security and send it to Uncle Sam at least quarterly along with the withheld taxes. Each state has its own workers' compensation laws and rates. In every state rates vary by trade and from year to year. Our present rate in Colorado is now 28 percent! Last year it was 22. Rates in some states are as low as 2 or 3 percent. Unemployment insurance rates also vary by state. A bookkeeping charge of one dollar per hour will probably cover most of the expense of keeping payroll records, posting costs to job records, and filing the necessary returns.

As you can see, your employee may earn $10 an hour, but his cost to you is over 50 percent more than that. If you offer benefits such as pension and profit sharing, health insurance, vacation pay, or holiday pay, the cost goes up even more.

Suppose you pay $60 per month in health insurance premiums for that employee. Full-time employees work about 176 hours per month, so your insurance for that employee costs you about 34 cents an hour. Now your $10.00 employee costs you $15.40 per hour.

If you use a labor rate of $10.00 an hour when you estimate jobs, you'll spend $5.40 out of your own pocket for every hour your employee works for you. Multiply that by five employees, and it's easy to see why remodeling can be so expensive — to you!

It's easy to simplify figuring hourly labor costs. First, add all the percentages together. Then multiply the employee's hourly rate by the total.

Later in the chapter, you'll see why most remodelers mark their labor charges up even more, especially when billing for time and materials. For now, just be sure you know exactly what your labor is costing you.

Putting Indirect and Direct Costs Together

Now that you know what all your costs are, it's easy to see how much profit you've made. Here's an example:

Job gross	12% Overhead	Materials	Subs	Labor	Profit
$26,000	$3,120	$9,230	$5,480	$6,090	$2,080

Profit is 8 percent of this job. (To find the percentage, divide the profit figure by the job gross, then multiply by 100.)

It's as important to add a percentage for profit into your costs as it is to add a percentage for overhead. This is true whether you work by contract or by charging time and materials.

If you bill for time and materials, there are several ways to add profit and overhead into the job.

1) Agree on the total percentage for overhead and profit and collect it at the end of the job.

2) Add the agreed percentage to each draw as the job progresses.

3) Mark up your labor or materials bills (or both) before you present them to your client.

If you only add a percentage to your labor, remember that you have to use a higher percentage than if you add it to the entire job. Suppose you have a job with the following costs:

Labor	$8,000
Materials	10,000
Subcontractors	5,000
Total costs	$23,000

If you figure 20 percent for overhead and profit, you'll add $4,600 to the job.

23,000 x .20 = 4,600

If you add 20 percent to labor only, you'll only get $1,600. To make $4,600 to cover overhead and profit, you have to add 57.5 percent to the labor charge. To calculate that percentage, divide the profit by the figure you'll mark up to cover it, in this case, labor. Then multiply by 100.

4,600 ÷ 8,000 = .575 = 57.5 percent.

Thus: 8,000 x .575 = 4,600

Remember to use your *actual* labor costs if you're going to add your percentage for overhead and profit to labor only. Here's how that would work:

Hourly wage	*Indirect labor*	*Overhead & profit*	*Total hourly rate*
$10.00	$4.59	$8.39	$22.98

Profit and overhead is 57.5 percent of $14.59. Your billing rate for this employee would be $22.98 per hour.

If you bill time and materials, you might use a lower percentage for jobs where you'll do the work yourself. But you'll also earn less money.

If your job cost is set in a contract and you only manage the job — not do the work yourself — your profit has to be based on the management fee.

The Profit Question

Ask ten different contractors what profit percentage they use, and you'll get ten different numbers. But the ten different numbers may translate into pretty much the same dollar figure. Some contractors add only 2 or 3 percent to their own salaries. Yet, they may earn the same as another builder who allows 30 percent for profit and nothing for his own salary. That's why profit percentages can mean so little.

Is 8 percent in the examples above realistic? That's $8,000 profit on $100,000 in sales. If you include a fair wage for yourself in your selling price, 8 percent is icing on the cake. If not, you'd need a much higher sales volume to live on 8 percent.

Some remodelers claim they make a 50 percent profit on their jobs. (That means they double their costs to arrive at the selling price.) Each $1,000 of costs yields $2,000 in selling price. That may be possible, but only for contractors who have a special niche in the market or have an excellent reputation in the community. They have to be *so* good at their profession that clients are willing to pay the price. For most remodelers starting out, a 100 percent markup isn't very realistic. Unfortunately, when you're just starting out you need profits the most!

According to David Sauer, publisher of *Qualified Remodeler* magazine, pre-tax profits for remodelers averaged 4 to 5 percent in 1985. That's pretty low, but it undoubtedly includes more than a few contractors that lost money in 1985. Clearly, it means that many remodelers don't know what their costs really are, aren't controlling them properly, or aren't charging enough.

On an annual volume of 1 to 1.5 million dollars, a 5 percent profit may be acceptable. That's $50,000 to $75,000, maybe enough to make the headaches worthwhile.

On the other hand, some remodelers make 10, 15, or even 20 percent profit. Even first year remodelers can do that well in an area where demand for remodeling is strong.

Contract vs. Time and Materials

Once you recognize your costs and know how much profit to build into each job, it's easier to select the best way to charge for your work. Your specialty and the way you run your business will help you make this decision. Here are some of the pros and cons you should consider for both contract work and work done on a time and materials basis.

What Are You Charging For?

Contract— Your client pays you for managing the remodeling job. You may do all, some, or none of the actual work, but your job is to see that the job gets done correctly and efficiently. It's your responsibility to pay for all materials, subs, and labor.

Time and Materials— You charge for your labor hours and time to manage the job. You may also charge for materials (with or without a markup), or the owners may buy the materials themselves.

The Risk Factor

Contract— You're locked into a fixed price for the job. Your client doesn't have to pay for your mistakes. Except in rare circumstances, he definitely won't! If you're sure of your overhead costs, estimate accurately, and keep the job running as you've projected, there's little financial risk. You can make even more than you expected if your costs turn out lower than you estimated. Those are all big "ifs." Fortunately, experience and the advice of others can shrink those "ifs."

Time and Materials— You charge for your time on the job and all the materials and subcontract work you pay for. There's almost no risk if you make it clear from the beginning where your profit is included.

"Or we could do it an a time-and-materials basis."

Supplier discounts can work to your advantage here. If you pay your bills within the discount period, you can gain an extra 2 to 5 percent on your materials cost. This is especially true for cabinetwork and floor coverings. You still bill your client for the face amount of the invoice.

Change Orders

Contract— If your client wants a change in the job, you write a change order. You estimate the added cost or credit to the customer in a "mini-contract" that's legal and binding to both you and the client, just like the original contract.

Time and Materials— If your client reduces the work he originally hired you to do, it means only that you'll work fewer hours. If he adds to the job, you'll do the added work and charge the same hourly rate and percentage you agreed to at the beginning of the job.

Bank Financing

Contract— The bank's first concern is whether or not your clients can repay their loans. They may check your references to be sure you finish your jobs for the contract price and that your customers are satisfied with your work.

Time and Materials— Unless you're well known by the lending bank, it's rarely willing to make loans for time-and-materials projects. You may have to give the client a "not-to-exceed" contract. If you exceed the contract amount, your client may have trouble borrowing more money to cover the rest of the job. Time-and-materials remodelers often sell only to clients who can pay cash.

Client Preference

Contract— If the customer picked you out of the phone book or responded to your ad without knowing your skills or reputation, they'll probably prefer a firm contract. Even clients who know you well may prefer a contract. It's easier for them to budget, and they feel more secure when they know a firm price from the beginning.

Time and Materials— Some clients, even those who know you well, prefer a time-and-materials arrangement. Many people think they'll save money that way. They'll still want a ballpark estimate before you begin, but if the job comes in fairly close to that estimate, most clients are satisfied and won't quibble over paying the bill.

Mistakes

It doesn't matter if you work by contract or by time and materials: If you or your employees make a mistake, you have to correct it. If your subcontractor makes a mistake, he has to fix it. If your supplier sends out the wrong material, he must replace it. However, if you *order* the wrong material, the problem is yours. It pays to be competent. The fewer mistakes you make, the more money you'll earn.

The Legal Side

Contract— As we discussed in Chapter 6, a good contract protects you from a client who doesn't honor his end of the deal. And it forces you to uphold your end as well.

Time and Materials— Many remodelers who work by time and materials rely on a handshake. However, to be safe, it's wise to have a contract which covers your hourly wage and your employees' hourly rates, as well as any other arrangements you've made. If you're charging a percentage, a contract describes how much and when you're to be paid. If a client isn't willing to sign such a contract, you should think twice about working for him! Maybe think three times!

Insurance and General Liability

Your insurance needs will be the same no matter which method you use. Some remodelers believe that if you work time and materials and let the homeowner pull the permit and furnish supplies, you're not legally responsible if the work isn't done correctly. Insurance companies and the courts don't see it that way. The client hires you to do a job. Consequently, you're viewed as an expert. That makes you liable for mistakes even if you're hired only for your labor. Anything that doesn't make it past the local building inspector is still your problem.

Bidding or Negotiating for Work

Most remodelers get jobs one of two ways.

1) They bid from a set of specifications against other remodelers.

2) They sit down with the client and negotiate a price, perhaps designing the job as they go.

If you enter a bid, you'll be expected to submit a firm price. The client chooses the remodeler with the best combination of quality and cost. A client who's shopping for a contract probably won't accept a "not-to-exceed" time-and-materials deal because that defeats the purpose of the bid.

If you negotiate a job, your client may still want a firm contract price when the negotiations are finished. A client may be willing to negotiate a time-and-materials contract that specifies your hourly rate and markup percentage and trust that you'll be fair. If you work by contract, you'll negotiate overall price, adding and subtracting details until the job fits the client's price range.

We think it's better to negotiate for work than to bid for it. Too often, clients who take bids for a job are looking only at the bottom line. They forget that quality costs. Build a good reputation and clients will trust you to negotiate a quality job for a fair price. You'll cover all your costs and make a good profit for your hard work in the bargain.

Now here are the answers we promised you for the little quiz earlier in the chapter.

Job number	Direct cost	Overhead percent	Profit percent	Selling price	Overhead	Profit
1	$37,350	12%	5%	$45,000	$5,400	$2,250
2	14,250	18%	7%	19,000	3,420	1,330
3	51,480	8%	4%	58,500	4,680	2,340
4	9,800	20%	10%	14,000	2,800	1,400
5	53,975	10%	5%	63,500	6,350	3,175
Totals	$166,855			$200,000	$22,650	$10,495

Figure 8-4

Answers to Figure 8-3

9

Estimating with Accuracy

No matter how good you are at designing and building, you're not going to make it in this business if you can't estimate costs. Even remodelers who take jobs on a cost-plus-fee basis have to make estimates. Every owner (and lender) needs to know whether the cost will be $10,000 or $25,000 or $50,000. A few bad guesses and you're going to have some angry customers (and maybe a few uncollectible accounts).

Making on-the-spot estimates will help you weed out the tire kickers — the people who expect to get their whole kitchen redone for $5,000. Making a formal, written proposal for those people is a waste of your valuable time.

Estimating construction costs isn't an exact science. For any job there's no one cost that's right for every bidder, even if the work is identified very clearly, the material costs are known and the cost of labor is established. There are too many variables and too many unknowns in construction. And that's especially true for remodeling, where you may not know exactly what's required until the wall is opened up and the subfloor stripped away.

Maybe that's why you'll hear remodelers claim that estimating is all baloney. No one knows what the cost will be, they say, until the work is done. These same remodelers probably insist that they don't bother working up estimates piece by piece. They just *look* at a job and know how much to charge.

That's fine, we say. Maybe there are a few remodelers with so much experience and so much knowledge that they don't have to identify every labor cost, every material needed and all the overhead required. If you fit in that category, fine. Skip on to the next chapter. But for the rest of us (and that should include every remodeler we've ever met), pay very careful attention when someone's passing out tips on pricing jobs and compiling costs. Because that's where the money is made and lost in this business. Estimating is the key — either to a satisfying and financially rewarding career or a quick exit to some other occupation or trade that doesn't require as much care and attention to detail.

In this chapter we're going to explain how to figure any job — right down to the last penny. When we find that figure, is it the *right* price? The only correct figure? The only bid that's low enough to be competitive but high enough to include a fair profit? Of course not! There are many *right* prices, probably as many as there are remodelers bidding the job. But following our system should help you develop consistently good estimates — as good as cost estimates can be, considering the complexity and variables in nearly every construction project.

Good estimating requires a blending of skills — it's a combination of science and art. No two estimators come up with the same numbers in the same way. Just as there is no single *right* price, there is no single right way to estimate. *But there are good estimates and there are bad estimates.* There are good ways to estimate and there are bad ways to estimate. And, of course, there are good estimators and there are bad estimators.

Fortunately, you don't have to settle for bad estimates. Getting it right, consistently, isn't that hard. All it takes is a little knowledge and some patience. If you've got the will to learn and the time, this chapter should help you get it right — and save many times the cost of this book.

Several years ago, *Remodeling* magazine sent identical specs for a small job to three successful estimators. Each used his own costs and his own estimating system. Two of the three estimators insisted that their estimates would be accurate to within 2 percent of actual costs. The third claimed accuracy within 1 percent. How close were they? Not very. The range between low bid and high bid was more than 40 percent. Their prices (excluding overhead and profit), varied from a low of $12,061, to a mid-range of $14,057, to a high of $17,203.

Why the variation? Part of it was because the estimators live in different parts of the country. Material and labor prices vary considerably from one place to another. That explains part of the difference. But there are still some unanswered questions. Look at these costs:

	Bidder 1	**Bidder 2**	**Bidder 3**
Job total	$12,061	$14,057	$17,203
120 SF deck	623	966	1,218
Electrical	1,000	908	986
Insulation	450	530	206

Of course, prices will vary from one community to another. But you'd expect the cost of each line item to vary the same way the job totals vary. The cheapest total price should include insulation at the lowest cost. Look at the figures above. The highest bidder had the lowest insulation cost. That makes us wonder about the claims of accuracy to 1 or 2 percent.

These estimates were for an addition, not a renovation. New work has less of the hitches and surprises we find all the time in remodeling. But, interestingly, the low bid included a 5 percent contingency to cover unanticipated problems. Would you expect any bid to be accurate to within 1 percent if the estimator allowed 5 percent for the unexpected? We wouldn't.

Earlier we talked about variables in project costs. By that we mean the things that can be expected to change from day to day and can't be predicted with much accuracy. For example, have you ever had a bad day when nothing seemed to go right? Everyone has. Every construction crew has days like that. It's inevitable. Everyone works more efficiently some days than others. The more complex the job, the more variables will be involved. Should you include an allowance to cover time spent fixing mistakes on an especially difficult job? How reliable are your suppliers? Do you waste a lot of time and materials to get the quality your client requires? Will you be pressured to finish the job so your clients can have use of the home as quickly as possible? Should you allow for some overtime? These are just a few of the variables in estimating. You can probably think of hundreds more.

It's easy to feel inadequate and confused when bidding your first job. We did. But we won the first job we bid. Amazingly enough, we were within $100 of the next bidder on a $21,000 bid. Even better, we made a reasonable profit on the job. As we look back, we know that bid wasn't a fluke. We spent a long time preparing it, and we rechecked it several times before submitting our proposal. Over the years, we've learned to speed up the process a little. It's possible to create detailed estimates in a limited time without sacrificing accuracy.

Here are the skills you need to be a good estimator:

1) You must be able to read plans and translate measurements. If you've been in construction for any length of time, you probably read blueprints as easily as you swing a hammer. If blueprint reading isn't second nature

to you, buy a good book on the subject and study it. Hundreds are available. Besides knowing how to read plans, you also must be able to visualize what the finished product will look like.

2) You need good math skills. Besides basic arithmetic operations, you'll work with decimals, fractions, and measurement conversions. We've included some useful formulas at the end of this chapter.

3) You must have a working understanding of construction techniques and materials. You need to know not just the process of the job, but the components as well. For instance, the specs may call for new flooring. Will you need underlayment? Floor prep? Pad? Carpet or vinyl?

For a brick patio, don't just estimate the cost of the brick and the labor to lay it. How much ground preparation must you do? Will you need sand for the base? How much sand, lime, mortar? Colored mortar? Leave out these "incidentals" and your estimate will be way too low. Do that several times in a single bid and you may end up paying the homeowner for the chance to do his work.

4) You must be able to translate labor into dollars and cents. How many hours does it take your crew to shingle a square? Set a door? Hang drywall?

5) Most of all, you need common sense. Make sure all your figures — not just the total — are logical. Is it reasonable that the footings will each take 3 yards of concrete? Can you paint the interior of the house with 4 gallons of paint? Can your crew shingle the addition — including valleys and ridges — in a day? Does the total look right? If it doesn't, go back to your take-off form and compare it to your estimate. You may have missed an entire phase or figured one twice.

Estimating Methods

Remodelers estimate by one of two methods: *stick* and *unit* pricing. An estimate can be accurate using either method — when done correctly. With stick pricing (or *stick-by-stick* pricing as it's sometimes called), you try to identify every material and all the labor that will go into the job and put a price on every item. For instance, for wall framing, you figure how many studs (including waste), plates, blocks, braces and nails you need and how much each will cost. Then, you figure how many hours it will take your crew to do the work. The total will probably be fairly close to the actual cost if you remembered to include every item in the estimate.

With *unit pricing* you break job components into measurable units and apply a price to each. For example, you might price wall framing by the square foot or linear foot. You'll have one price for load-bearing walls and another price for partition walls. Wall height, thickness and material will also affect the square foot or linear foot cost. If you decide to use unit prices rather than stick prices, don't get lazy. Be sure your unit prices identify both the labor cost and material cost in each unit.

Of the two pricing methods, the stick method is probably the more accurate, but it takes almost twice as long as unit pricing. We've found stick pricing to be more difficult as well. That's because labor prices are such a large part of most estimates. Even if you use published labor estimating tables, you still have to determine if they're accurate for *your* crew.

Most estimators blend stick and unit pricing for greatest accuracy. For example, you'd be better off using stick pricing for installing a window or ready-made cabinets. But framing or roofing would be easier to estimate with unit prices.

The specs that *Remodeling* magazine gave to their three estimators were all the same. But each of the estimators was free to estimate using his own system. All three did. The estimator who came in at $12,061 used the stick method. It took him a day and a half to prepare the quote. The high bid of $17,203 was prepared with unit pricing and took less than an hour. The estimator who put together the middle bid of $14,057 used a mix of the two and took about half an hour. The last two used a computer. More about that later.

Never try to estimate a job by the square foot of floor. Bathroom jobs can run from $20 to $1,000 a square foot. That's too broad a range. There are far too many variables in remodeling to make guesses by the square foot of floor. It's usually more expensive to remodel a home than it was to build it new. Not only do you have to tear out the old, you have to build the new to blend with the old. Square foot of floor prices are generally useless to remodeling estimators.

Before You Estimate

A good estimate takes good planning. The remodeling estimators who claim to be within 1 or 2 percent of the actual cost have to know exactly what they're bidding. They don't make guesses and assumptions.

The best remodeling job leaves an invisible line between what's old and what's new. The most accurate estimate defines that line exactly and uses it as a starting point. That's why a visit to the site is so important. There's no way to produce an accurate estimate without finding that invisible line. And you can't possibly identify the line without seeing the job.

Most good estimators use checklists, either written on paper or engraved in their minds. Here's why. Making an accurate estimate is a matter of detail — finding every detail that influences cost. Sure, even the best estimators underestimate or overestimate their costs. That's inevitable. This isn't a science. But with a little luck, the high misses and low misses will balance out, leaving the actual cost close to your estimated cost. Leaving something out of the estimate is different. It's a major error. The estimate on anything you forgot is always zero. That's a 100 percent miss. A few of those and your profit is out the window. Very seldom (almost never?) will you include in a cost estimate something that doesn't have to be done. The result: You're left with major oversights (under-estimates) and no over-estimates to balance the scales.

Figure 9-1 is a checklist for interior remodeling. It should save you some time, money and embarrassment. More than once we've spent an evening in a client's turn-of-the-century house and left without some critical detail, something we should have asked about. Later, when you sit down to estimate the job, you're sure to remember that the house has wide baseboards and a base shoe. But you might not remember exactly how wide the baseboards are. Will you need to rip 1x8s to match it? Or can you use ¾ x 5½ material? That can make a big difference in the cost of trim.

Working with Your Subs

Add to our checklists or change them if you like. Every remodeling business is different and needs a customized checklist. Get advice from your subs on what they need to know to estimate a job. They can probably give you fixed prices for standard parts of a job, once they have critical information about the job.

For instance, our electrician charges a flat rate for each opening. He has a set price for changing an electrical panel. For uncomplicated remodeling jobs, we can usually price routine electrical work without consulting him. An arrangement like that helps us make estimates in much less time. Fast turnaround makes your clients happy. It also means you have time for more estimates, which means you'll sell more jobs.

There's a disadvantage to estimating for your subs instead of getting a firm price based on their own bid. You may miss something and be left with charges that are more than the estimate. Remodeling jobs are rarely uncomplicated. You should probably hedge a little on your price to make sure you're covered. But that may present a problem. It works just fine if you're negotiating the price with a client. However, if you're in a bidding war, an inflated bid can throw you out of the running.

To be safe, get a firm price from your subs before you submit a bid. To do that, you'll either need to be able to answer the subs' questions accurately, or you'll have to drag all of them through your client's house. The former is preferable, but the latter is usually necessary.

Save time by anticipating all the subs' questions during your initial consultation. We list five questions under "Electrical" on our checklist. Our subs can price most work when we have answers to those questions. Of course, your best electrical sub may *never* price a job without walking the property himself. We can understand that. It's probably good business. In that case you can leave all questions about electrical work off your checklist.

If you get bids from more than one sub, it's essential that you give each the same clear and complete specs. Some subs will take advantage of loose specs to shoot you a lowball bid, only to drive you nuts later with change orders.

Our second checklist, Figure 9-2, is for exterior work. We combine it with the interior list for room additions. You may question some of the items. For example,

Interior Remodel Checklist

Job number _____ Date _____

Job name _____

Address _____

Walls

Material

___ Plaster/lath

___ Gypboard

___ Other

___ Height

Finish

___ Slick

___ Orange peel

___ Knock down

___ Hand/brush

___ Other

Covering

___ Wall type _____

   ___ painted

   ___ wallpapered

   ___ multiple layers

   ___ paneled

   ___ gypboard backing

   ___ paneling type _____

   ___ other _____

Ceilings

___ Plaster/Lath

___ Gypboard

___ Other

Finish

___ Slick

___ Orange peel

___ Knock down

___ Acoustic

___ Other

Covering

___ Painted

___ Other

Doors and Trim

Doors

___ Style _____

___ Sizes _____

___ Hollow core

___ Solid core

___ Finish _____

Baseboard

___ Style _____

___ Size _____

___ Finish _____

Casing

___ Style _____

___ Size _____

___ Finish _____

Flooring

___ Carpet

___ Vinyl

   ___ subfloor required?

___ Hardwood

   ___ type

   ___ size

Demolition

___ Load bearing walls

___ Joist or trusses

___ Wall type _____

___ Ceiling type _____

___ Access _____

___ Dust walls required?

Electrical

___ Panel location

___ Panel type _____

___ Spaces left _____

___ Wiring type _____

___ Access _____

Plumbing

___ Supply type _____

___ DWV type _____

___ Stack location noted

___ Access _____

Notes _____

_____

_____

_____

_____

_____

Figure 9-1

Interior remodel checklist

noting the heights of vents and chimneys might seem unnecessary. But if you're tying in an addition and didn't notice that vents would be covered by the new roof line, you'll probably have to re-route or extend the vents at your own expense.

No checklist can cover everything, of course. That's why it's especially important to make notes about anything unusual on the job. What may be crystal clear when you do the walk-through may not even come to mind a day later when you sit down to estimate. You'll be sure to forget if you don't get back to the estimate for a week or more. If you're not working from drawings, measure and sketch everything when you first visit the site. The more details you write down, the fewer guesses needed later.

Look for things like possible difficulties in excavation, unusual trim you'll have to match, and plumbing or electrical installations you'll need to upgrade to code. The take-off sheet in Figure 9-3 will help you catch all the details.

Of course, every builder and remodeler is expected to know the local building code and follow it. Your client might prefer that you avoid the expense of doing everything by the book, but if you value your credibility with the building inspector, you'd better not let the owner make that choice. Include all the required upgrades in your bid.

The Estimating Take-Off Form

The most common major estimating nightmare is to forget something altogether. Unless the item is small enough to absorb, this can be a real disaster. We know a contractor who left out all the concrete in a million dollar estimate on a commercial job. He was using a new computer software package and blames the mistake on unfamiliarity with the computer. The result was a major loss. He juggled his work and cash flow to try to cover the mistake but still ended up bankrupt.

It's almost as bad to include part of a job twice. You could be *very* lucky and get the job anyway, and make a sweet profit. But it's much more likely that your bid will be too high and you'll lose the job.

A good take-off form is essential whether you use a computer or pencil and paper. As you study the plans, checklists, and your notes, check the items you'll need to estimate against the take-off form. As you prepare the bid, you'll find additional items to add. Don't make the mistake of thinking an item is too small to bother with. As we pointed out earlier, if you ignore the incidentals, your bid will be way off — in the wrong direction!

Follow the same order to prepare the estimate as you will to do the job. Begin with site preparation and end with hanging mirrors and lighting fixtures. Develop a routine and follow it on every estimate. You'll be less likely to overlook odds and ends if you use the same order all the time.

Exterior Checklist

Job number _____ Date _____
Job name _____
Address _____

Site
___ Shrubs and trees
___ Gas meter and line
___ Telephone
___ Electric
___ Sprinkler system

Structure
___ Foundation
   ___ poured
   ___ block
   ___ stone
   ___ other

Walls
___ Elevation
___ Siding
   ___ hardboard
   lap expos. _____
   ___ brick
___ Corner boards
   size ___

Trim
___ Soffit
   ___ height _____
   ___ width _____
   ___ material _____
___ Fascia
   ___ width _____
   ___ material _____
   ___ mouldings
   cove _____
   crown _____
   bed _____
___ Windows
   ___ window trim _____

Roof
___ Pitch _____
___ Roofing
   ___ type _____
   ___ color _____
   ___ drip edge
___ Guttering

Structural
___ Floor joist _____
___ Subfloor _____
___ Underlayment _____
   ___ rafters _____
   ___ trusses
   ___ length
   ___ pitch
___ Studs _____

Mechanical
___ Vents & chimneys
   ___ height
   ___ extension required

Notes_____
_____
_____
_____
_____
_____
_____

Figure 9-2
Exterior checklist

Take-off Form

Job number _____ Date _____

Job name _____

Address _____

Plans and Permits
___ Architectural fee
___ Engineering fee
___ Soils engineering
___ Tap fees
    ___ water
    ___ sewer
    ___ gas
___ Permits
___ Bonding
___ Re-plat/zoning
___ Temporary electrical
___ Portable toilet
___ Dumpster

Demolition
___ Exterior
    ___ structure
    ___ slabs/sidewalks
    ___ landscaping
    ___ chimney
    ___ walls
    ___ roof
    ___ porch
    ___ skylight
    ___ fencing
___ Interior
    ___ walls
    ___ floors
    ___ stairs
    ___ kitchen cabinets
    ___ plumbing
    ___ electrical
    ___ heating system
    ___ remove insulation

Site Work
___ Landscape protection/relocation
___ Site clearing
    ___ structure
    ___ slabs/sidewalks
    ___ landscape

___ Site grading
___ Excavating and backfill
___ Trenching, backfilling, and
    compacting
___ Finish grading
    ___ raking and seeding
    ___ topsoil
    ___ sodding
___ Areaway prep
___ Perimeter drain
___ Blacktop
    ___ new
    ___ repair

Concrete
___ Footings
___ Foundation
___ Slabs
    ___ basement
    ___ exterior
    ___ driveway
    ___ sidewalks
    ___ patio
___ Screed coat
___ Steps
___ Patch/repair

Brick and Block Masonry
___ Foundation
___ Walls
    ___ solid
    ___ veneer
___ Steps
___ Patch/repair
___ Chimney/fireplace
___ Retaining wall
___ Areaway
___ Patch/repair

Ornamental Metals
___ Stairs
___ Handrails

Wall Coatings & Stucco
___ New
___ Patch/repair

Framing
___ Subfloor
___ Floor
___ Wall
___ Roofing
___ Patch/repair

Roofing
___ Materials _____
___ Tear down
___ Skylights
___ Gutters/downspouts
___ Patch/repair

Exterior Trim, Decks
___ Soffit/fascia
___ Patch/repair
___ Deck/porch
___ Railing
___ Patch/repair

Siding
___ Material _____
___ Patch/repair

Doors
___ Interior
___ Exterior
___ Garage
___ Hardware
___ Patch/repair

Trim
___ Interior
___ Exterior
___ Garage
___ Hardware
___ Patch/repair

Windows
___ New
___ Replacement

Figure 9-3
Estimating take-off form

___ Storms
___ Weatherstripping
___ Trim
___ Patch/repair

Plumbing
___ New lines
___ Laundry hookups
___ Vents/stacks
___ Water heater
___ Bath
    ___ fixtures
    ___ shower
    ___ patch/repair
Kitchen
    ___ fixtures
    ___ patch/repair

Heating
___ Type of heat_____
___ New gas supply lines
___ Ductwork
___ Air conditioner
___ Humidifier
___ Patch/repair

Electrical
___ Light fixtures
___ Appliances
    ___ hookups
___ Doorbell
___ Fans
___ Service
___ Patch/repair

Insulation
___ Blown/batts/blanket
_____
___ Wrap pipes

Drywall
___ Drywall
___ Plaster
___ Patch/repair

Tile
___ Showers
___ Walls
___ Fixtures
___ Patch/repair

Wall Paneling
___ Style_____
___ Cedar closet lining
___ Patch/repair

Ceilings
___ Material_____
___ Patch/repair

Mouldings
___ Style & size_____
    ___ baseboard
    ___ chair rail
    ___ plaster mould
    ___ ceiling
    ___ stairs
    ___ false beams
    ___ other_____
___ Stain/paint
___ Patch/repair

Cabinets
___ Kitchen
___ Bath
___ Other
___ Countertops
___ Soffit

Appliances & Specialty Items
___ Dishwasher
___ Range/oven
___ Range hood
___ Disposer
___ Trash compactor
___ Central vacuum
___ Burglar alarm
___ Smoke detector/fire extinguisher
___ Prefab fireplace

Flooring
___ Hardwood
___ Carpet
    ___ pad
___ Vinyl
___ Tile
___ Floor prep
___ Underlayment
___ Patch/repair

Paint & Wallpaper
___ Exterior
    ___ siding material_____
    ___ trim
    ___ porch
    ___ deck
    ___ doors
    ___ windows
___ Interior
    ___ walls
    ___ trim
    ___ doors
___ Wallpaper
    ___ walls
    ___ ceilings

Cleaning & Hauling
___ Removing debris
___ Final cleaning

Profit & Overhead
___ Contingency
___ Insurance
    ___ liability
    ___ workers' compensation
    ___ unemployment
    ___ vehicle, equipment
___ Office
___ Salaries
___ Other

Figure 9-3 (cont'd)
Estimating take-off form

Figure 9-3 is a very detailed take-off form. We may only use a tenth of the items on any one job. But we use the form on nearly every job. It helps us remember what we're likely to forget.

Putting Your Estimate Together

Once you've completed the checklists and take-off form, you're ready to set up your estimate. Begin by deciding which tasks you'll do and which ones you'll sub out. Here's the breakdown we use:

1) Always subbed out due to licensing requirements:

   ▪ Electrical

   ▪ Plumbing

   ▪ Heating

2) Often subbed out due to practicality:

   ▪ Excavation

   ▪ Site work

   ▪ Concrete

   ▪ Masonry

   ▪ Flooring

   ▪ Drywall

   ▪ Painting

3) Always do ourselves:

   ▪ Demolition

   ▪ Framing

   ▪ Siding

   ▪ Insulation

   ▪ Interior & exterior trim

   ▪ Roofing

The second list varies from job to job. For example, on a 150 square foot addition we'll excavate with our skid loader, set the forms, and paint. On an 800 square foot addition, we'd probably sub those jobs out. On a small interior remodel, we might do the entire job ourselves. Your lists may be very different, depending on your skills, equipment, job size, and amount of other work you have.

Once you decide which jobs to sub out, get the information to your subs. Give them a reasonable length of time to return a price to you. Ten days should usually be enough time. If you're not sure whether you'll use a sub on part of the job, get a price anyway. That way you're covered if you decide later to call him in. Don't overdo this though. If you get too many bids and deliver too few jobs, subs will get tired of bidding.

Next, list the materials your suppliers will have to price. Of course, you don't have to do that for every single item. Even if you use the stick method, you won't call for a current price on 2x4s each time. Your catalogs and price lists should be up-to-date enough to cover those.

You'll need to get a current price on items you use only occasionally, or those that vary depending on size. We always call for prices on doors, windows, and cabinetry. Sometimes we also call for shingles, concrete, and trim materials. When in doubt, get the price. It's pointless — and expensive — to guess, when a quick phone call will yield a precise answer.

On larger jobs where you have architectural drawings, take the prints or your materials list to your lumberyard. Many will do a material take-off for you at no charge. That way you'll have current prices on the entire job. When we have two sets of prints, we give each set to a different lumberyard. When the bids are prepared, we compare more than just the total cost. Each yard has probably missed at least a few items. Compare the two lists and you'll probably find several mistakes.

We once had two lumberyards do a take-off for a new house. The prices came in $15,000 apart. The lower estimate looked like an incredible bargain. The estimator had included everything, including a mailbox, house numbers, even light switch covers. Unfortunately, he didn't include the plywood sheathing for the entire house, or any of the roofing materials. If we'd looked only at the total and then bid based on the yard's material estimate, we would have lost our trucks on that one.

Suppliers will stand behind their quoted cost for every item they price, but they won't guarantee to quote every item on your prints or materials list. If you give suppliers your materials list, insist that they mark the prices on your copy, not a form they make up themselves. That makes it easier to compare quotes.

Choosing an Estimating Book

Whether you estimate with a scratch pad or a computer and whether you use stick or unit pricing, build a reference library of cost estimates. You don't have to reinvent the wheel with every estimate. Trade publishers and bookstores offer a dozen different estimating books. Most are geared to new construction, but several are designed for remodeling. Craftsman Book Company, R.S. Means, and Home-Tech Publications all produce good estimating manuals. Check the order form in the back of this book.

You may have to try several estimating references before you find one that works best for you. They all use slightly different pricing methods and get at least slightly different answers. Even so, they're useful for most of the estimating you'll do. Once you've determined how accurate an estimating book is for your particular crew's efficiency, you don't have to keep track of the standard tasks.

Estimating manuals cover common jobs like site work, demolition, concrete, framing, painting, and trim. You're on your own when it comes to odd jobs like removing a three-story chimney from the inside, or chinking a log wall. Your best bet is to use the stick method for those, and allow yourself some slack.

When you do these uncommon jobs, record your progress carefully. Keep track of your manhours, with comments about the skill levels of your employees. List any special equipment the job required, and write down any observations or comments that will help you if you run into a similar situation later. File the notes in a binder. Develop your own cost records for unusual projects.

No matter what estimating book you buy, cost records on jobs you've completed will be the best guide to costs on jobs you're bidding. There should be two profits in every job. One goes in your pocket. The other is what you learn about doing the work and pricing correctly. Don't let either profit get away from you.

Speed Up Your Estimating

Accuracy is only half the estimating battle. You also have to learn to estimate quickly. Keep your turnaround time from walk-through to final price to a week or less. Two to three days is even better. The faster you can prepare estimates, the more estimating you can do. The more estimates you submit, the more jobs you'll get.

What percentage of jobs you bid should you win? One in ten? One in four? If you get most of the jobs you bid, you're probably pricing your work lower than necessary. If you're winning only 10 percent, it might be because the economy is bad and the competition is stiff. Or maybe you need to slice your prices or trim your overhead. Even in bad times, you should still get your fair share of work.

Estimating requires precision. Most contractors would rather be out building than shuffling price lists and punching a calculator. So how can you speed up the estimating process without sacrificing accuracy?

Computers to the Rescue

A computer running a good software program will cut estimating time by 50 to 75 percent or more. The two estimators who did the higher bids for *Remodeling* used computers. Computers also eliminate computation errors *if* (and that's a big if) you enter the right information in the first place.

Before you rush out and spend a lot of money on computing equipment, there are some things to consider. *Qualified Remodeler* reported in 1988 that only 20 percent of the contractors who invest in estimating software are using it a year later. Many never feel comfortable with it. They buy such sophisticated software that they give up before they can master the programs. If you're not already familiar with computers, learn what you'll be getting into before you decide to invest.

First, decide on the software program. Then buy the computer that's required to run it. Not all programs are available for all kinds of computers.

There are two approaches to computerized estimating. First, you can buy a ready-made estimating program that's designed specifically for estimating. Second, you can buy a general purpose spreadsheet program such as Lotus 1-2-3 or Excel and adapt that program for your use. This second choice is usually much cheaper.

Specialized estimating programs are written to do either unit or stick pricing, not both. Some programs come with some labor and material prices already in the data base. Others require that you enter current prices. Once you've mastered a program and built up the cost data base, you should be able to crank out estimates with amazing speed. No doubt, the two estimators who priced the $14,000 job for *Remodeling* in 30 minutes had a lot of computer experience. But getting that familiar with a sophisticated computer program may take months or even years.

There are disadvantages to specialized estimating software. First, the programs are expensive. Although prices have dropped considerably in the last few years, you can still pay $10,000 or more for an estimating package. Annual cost updates may be as much as $1,000 a year. It's one thing to spend $50 on an estimating book and discover it doesn't suit your needs. It's something else to spend $10,000 and two months on a computer program and discover the same thing.

Another drawback is that most of the software is intended for new construction. And most programs aren't very flexible. They estimate just one way. If that's not your way, you may be better off with a pencil and paper.

Do some research before you choose a software package. Unfortunately, you usually won't be able to take a software package home to try it out. It's too easy to make copies. Spend some time testing the program before you buy. Get the recommendation of a friend or associate who's using a program regularly and likes it.

Some software companies offer demonstration disks. For a fee, usually around $50, you can try a stripped-down version of the program. If you decide to buy that particular program, the fee is applied to the purchase price.

If you have an aptitude for working with computers, or already have a computer, a computer spreadsheet may be a better option than an estimating program. They cost considerably less. You can buy public domain or shareware spreadsheets for as little as $30. *Lotus*, the industry trail-blazer of personal computer spreadsheets, costs several hundred dollars, but a full-featured spreadsheet like this will do other things for you, including bookkeeping.

The disadvantage of a spreadsheet is that you have to program your own estimating formulas into it. But once you've done that, it'll be much faster than estimating with paper and pencil. If you have good programming skills, you can make a spreadsheet program run as fast and efficiently as a specialized estimating package.

A Math Primer for Estimators

No matter how you prepare estimates, we recommend that you work systematically, neatly and consistently. Estimate items in the same order as the work is done. That helps you visualize each step of the project and should eliminate a major omission. Prepare estimates the same way every time — step one, step two, step three, and so on. Being methodical will keep you from missing steps. Work neatly for two reasons. First, it helps you avoid mistakes like a misplaced decimal point. Second, it makes checking easier — both when reviewing your own figures and when you have someone else check your work.

All estimators use abbreviations. There's nothing wrong with that. But use abbreviations consistently. Don't leave any doubt about what you mean. Here are the abbreviations and conversions we use and recommend:

Inches	=	in
Square inches	=	sq in
Linear feet	=	LF
Square feet	=	SF
Square yards	=	SY
Squares	=	sqs
Cubic feet	=	CF
Cubic yards	=	CY
Board feet	=	b ft
Board measure	=	b m

Square measure equivalents (surface measure)

144 square inches	=	1 square foot
9 square feet	=	1 square yard
100 square feet	=	1 square

Cubic measure equivalents (volume measure)

1,728 cubic inches	=	1 cubic foot
27 cubic feet	=	1 cubic yard

Decimal equivalents

Sometimes it's more convenient to use decimal fractions of a foot instead of inches:

Inches	Fraction of a foot	Decimal equivalent
1	1/12	0.083
1½	1/8	0.125
2	1/6	0.1667
2½	5/24	0.2083
3	1/4	0.25
3½	7/24	0.2917
4	1/3	0.333
4½	3/8	0.375
5	5/12	0.417
5½	11/24	0.458
6	1/2	0.5
6½	13/24	0.5417
7	7/12	0.583
7½	5/8	0.625
8	2/3	0.667
8½	17/24	0.708
9	3/4	0.75
9½	19/24	0.792
10	5/6	0.833
10½	7/8	0.875
11	11/12	0.917
11½	23/24	0.958
12	1	1.0

Decimal equivalents of fractions

1/16	=	0.0625
1/8	=	0.125
3/16	=	0.1875
1/4	=	0.25
5/16	=	0.3125
3/8	=	0.375
7/16	=	0.4375
1/2	=	0.5
9/16	=	0.5625
5/8	=	0.625
11/16	=	0.6875
3/4	=	0.75
13/16	=	0.8125
7/8	=	0.875
15/16	=	0.9375
8/8	=	1.0

Formulas

■ **To find the area of a square, rectangle, or parallelogram: Multiply the length by the width or height.**

Example: The area of a wall that's 8 feet high by 12 feet long is 96 square feet (8 x 12 = 96).

What if your measurements aren't in whole feet? First, convert feet and inches to inches, then multiply, and convert back to feet if you want.

To find the area of a slab that's 25 feet, 5 inches long by 14 feet 7 inches wide:

25 feet = 25 times 12 = 300 inches, plus 5 inches = 305 inches long

14 feet = 14 times 12 = 168 inches, plus 7 inches = 175 inches wide

305 x 175 = 53,375 square inches. Since a square foot is 144 square inches, you can change the answer to square feet by dividing by 144 (53,375 ÷ 144 = 370.66 square feet).

■ **To find the area of a triangle, multiply the base by 1/2 the height. (The height is the distance from the base to the top of the angle opposite the base.)**

Example: The area of an end gable that is 30 feet wide and 15 feet high is 225 square feet (30 x 15 = 450 ÷ 2 = 225)

■ **To find the circumference of a circle: Multiply the diameter (the distance across the circle, through the center) by *pi*, written π, which for practical purposes is 3.1416, or 3$\frac{1}{7}$.**

Example: The distance around a circular patio that's 10 feet across is 31.416 feet, or 31 feet, and a little under 5 inches (10 x 3.1416 = 31.416 feet; .416 feet x 12 = 4.99 inches)

■ **To find the area of a circle: Multiply the square of the radius (½ the diameter) by π, (3.1416), or multiply the square of the diameter by 0.7854.**

Example: The area of a round paving stone that's 16 inches in diameter is 201.06 inches, or about 1.4 square feet. (16 ÷ 2 = 8, 8^2 (or 8 x 8) = 64, 64 x 3.1416 = 201.06, 201.06 ÷ 144 = 1.39

or: 16^2 = 256 x .7854 = 201.06)

■ **To find the volume of a circular column: Multiply the area of the base of the column by its height.**

Example: The volume of a concrete pier that's 2 feet, 6 inches in diameter by 5 feet tall is 24.54 cubic feet. First, convert the diameter to inches, 2 x 12 + 6 = 30, then find the area of the base: 15 x 15 x 3.1416 = 706.86 square inches, or 4.90875 square feet, times 5 (the height) = 24.54. You'll need just over 24½ cubic feet of concrete to build the pier.

■ **To find the volume of any rectangular space: Multiply the length by the width (or thickness) by the height.**

Example: You need 1.71 cubic yards of concrete to pour a footing 30 inches deep by 6 inches wide by 37 feet long. First, convert inches to feet, 30 inches = 2.5 feet, and 6 inches = .5 feet. Then 2.5 x .5 x 37 = 46.25 cubic feet. (Remember, there are 27 cubic feet in a cubic yard.)

In most cases, you'll *round* your measurements and calculations. In the example of the concrete pier above, suppose you have six of those to build. Since 24.54 cubic feet is just under a cubic yard (24.54 ÷ 27 = 0.9089), you'd order 6 yards to build six of them, even though the "correct" answer is 5.4533 cubic yards.

Decide how exact your calculations have to be. It's always safe to round up to the next nearest unit (inches, feet, yards). And most operations require that you allow for some waste.

A Sample Estimate

Now let's try a sample project. The Simpsons live in a standard ranch house: living room, kitchen and dining room separated by an eating counter, three bedrooms and a bathroom. Now that the kids are older, Mr. and Mrs. Simpson want a family room. After looking at the house, we decide that the best solution would be a 10 by 12 foot addition off the kitchen for a new dining room. We'll turn the existing dining room into a family room with only minor changes, and add a 10 by 15 foot deck. The Simpsons have a budget of $12,000 to $15,000 — a workable range for the project. We agree to firm up a price and get back to them in a few days.

Back at the office, we put together a bid from the checklists (interior, Figure 9-4, and exterior, Figure 9-5) and the rough sketch we made on graph paper (Figure 9-6).

The Scale Drawing

We start by making a scale drawing based on the on-site sketch (Figure 9-7). A standard scale is ¼ inch = 1 foot. Because this is such a small project, we'll probably enlarge the scale to ½ inch. No matter what scale we use, we always note it on the drawing.

We feel that to put together a good estimate, we need a clear drawing. But if you're like most contractors, your background is in carpentry. You feel a lot more comfortable with a hammer and a framing square than with tracing paper and a T-square. It would be ideal to work with a designer or an architect on every remodeling project, but on small projects it isn't practical to involve outside help. So we've spent many hours at the drawing board.

If you haven't done much drawing, look for materials and templates at architectural and art supply stores. Templates add a polished look to a drawing. They provide guides for drawing door swings, bathtubs, sinks, toilets, and so on, in a variety of scales. Other essential drawing tools include a T-square, scale, pencils, and erasers — and a large, smooth drawing surface.

During the meeting with the Simpsons, we made a sketch on graph paper. That makes it simple to draw a plan quickly and accurately to scale. But we'll do the finished drawing on translucent drafting paper. Translucent paper makes it easier to trace over various job stages instead of redrawing them on each new sheet of paper. On uncomplicated additions we'll do drawings on 11 x 17 sheets because our photocopy machine can copy these. Larger prints can be inexpensively copied by a blueprinting service.

Try to make your drawings as clean and professional as possible. You'll make a better impression on the homeowner and even on the plan checkers at the building department.

Interior Remodel Checklist

Job number ___ 021 ___ Date ___ 7-6 ___

Job name ___ SIMPSON ___

Address ___ 102 PIKES PEAK WAY ___

Walls

Material
- ___ Plaster/lath
- ✓ Gypboard
- ___ Other

8' Height

Finish
- ___ Slick
- ✓ Orange peel
- ___ Knock down
- ___ Hand/brush
- ___ Other

Covering
- ✓ Wall type _____
  - ✓ painted
  - ___ wallpapered
  - ___ multiple layers
  - ___ paneled
  - ___ gypboard backing
  - ___ paneling type _____
  - ___ other _____

Ceilings
- ___ Plaster/Lath
- ✓ Gypboard
- ___ Other

Finish
- ___ Slick
- ✓ Orange peel
- ___ Knock down
- ___ Acoustic
- ___ Other

Covering
- ___ Painted
- ___ Other

Doors and Trim

Doors
- ___ Style _____
- ___ Sizes _____
- ___ Hollow core
- ___ Solid core
- ✓ Finish STAIN

Baseboard
- ✓ Style PINE ANDERSON
- ✓ Size 2 1/4
- ✓ Finish STAIN

Casing
- ✓ Style PINE ANDERSON
- ✓ Size 2 1/4
- ✓ Finish STAIN

Flooring
- ___ Carpet
- ✓ Vinyl (KITCHEN TIE IN)
  - ✓ subfloor required? YES
- ___ Hardwood
  - ___ type
  - ___ size

Demolition
- ___ Load bearing walls   * CLEAN DEMO.
- ___ Joist or trusses   WILL USE SLIDING
- ___ Wall type _____ DOOR OPENING
- ___ Ceiling type _____
- ___ Access _____
- ___ Dust walls required?

Electrical
- ✓ Panel location (GARAGE)
- ___ Panel type SQUARE D 200 AMP
- ___ Spaces left 8
- ___ Wiring type ROMEX
- ___ Access UNFINISHED BASEMENT

Plumbing
- ___ Supply type N/A
- ___ DWV type _____
- ___ Stack location noted
- ___ Access _____

Notes_____
_____
_____
_____
_____
_____

Figure 9-4

Interior remodel checklist

Exterior Checklist

Job number __021__   Date __7 - 6__

Job name __SIMPSON__

Address __102 PIKES PEAK WAY__

Site

☑ Shrubs and trees __SHRUBS TO BE RELOCATED BY OWNER BEFORE EXCAV.__

☑ Gas meter and line __CLEAR__

☑ Telephone __CLEAR__

☑ Electric __METER ON BACK OF GARAGE__

☑ Sprinkler system __OWNER WILL REROUTE BEFORE EXCAVATION__

Structure

☑ Foundation __1'-8" EXPOSED__

  ☑ poured

  ___ block

  ___ stone

  ___ other

Walls

___ Elevation

☑ Siding

  ☑ hardboard

  lap expos. __8"__

  ___ brick

___ Corner boards

  size _____

Trim

☑ Soffit

  ___ height _____

  ___ width __18"__

  ___ material __3/8" A.C.__

☑ Fascia

  ___ width __6"__

  ___ material __RDWD F.J.__

  ___ mouldings

    cove _____

    crown _____

    bed _____

___ Windows

  ___ window trim __B/M__

Roof

___ Pitch __4/12__

___ Roofing __ASPHALT__

  ___ type _____

  ___ color __BLK__

  ___ drip edge

___ Guttering __NO__

Structural

☑ Floor joist __2 x 10__

___ Subfloor __3/4"__

___ Underlayment _____

  ___ rafters _____

  ☑ trusses

  ___ length

  ___ pitch

___ Studs __PRE-CUTS__

Mechanical

___ Vents & chimneys

  ☑ height __CLEAR__

  ☑ extension required

Notes_____

_____

_____

_____

_____

_____

Figure 9-5

Exterior remodel checklist

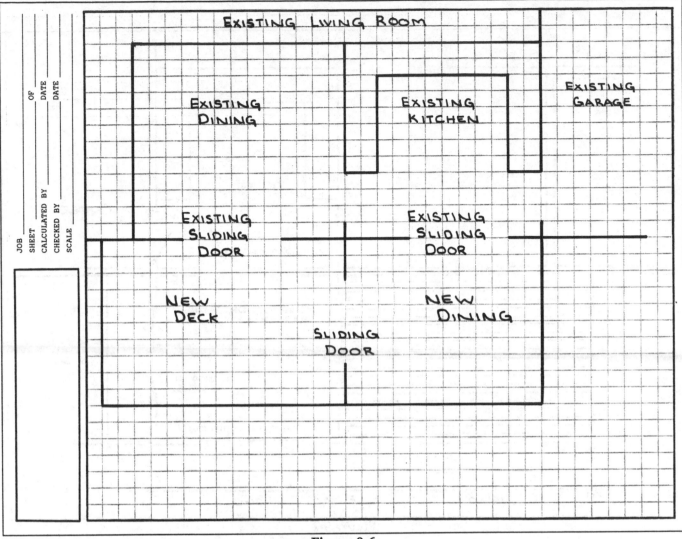

Figure 9-6
Rough sketch

Putting Together the Estimate

Now spread out the plans and spend some time studying them. (If you're working from an architect's drawings, make it easier for yourself by rolling up the drawings with the print out. This will keep the plans from rolling up every time you lay them out to look at them.) With a yellow highlighter, mark any details that need special emphasis. Look for a utility meter that needs to be moved, an odd height ceiling, or an out-of-the-way demolition item. Highlighted items are easy to spot, so you're less likely to overlook them later. Now's the time to decide what parts of the project you'll sub out.

Every estimator has his or her favorite way to lay out an estimate. Do yours the way that's comfortable for you. But it's important to do it the same way every time. We don't have a strong bias on how you do yours, except to recommend you do it the same way every time. If you have a standard routine, you're less likely to omit an item. In our case, we lay each estimate out in three groupings. Within each

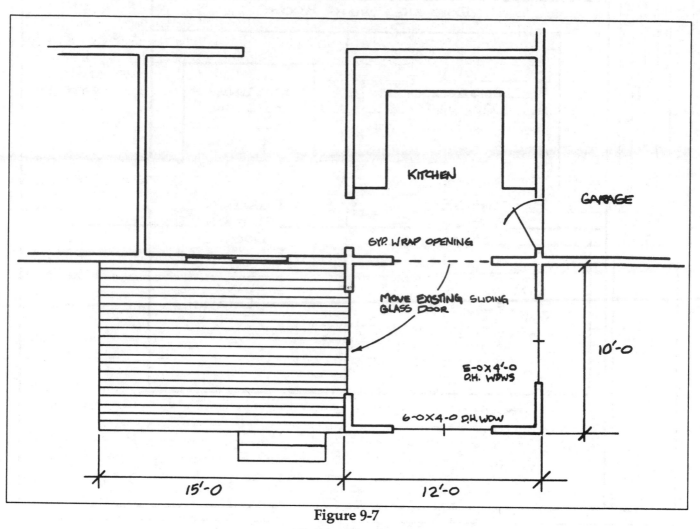

Figure 9-7
Finished sketch

group, we stay in job sequence. That reduces the chance of forgetting or double-pricing an item.

■ Group 1 includes preparation costs, such as design, plans, engineering, and permits.

■ Group 2 includes all the work that our crews will do on the job. These are listed in the actual order of construction: site work, framing, and so on through the final finish work.

■ Group 3 is all subcontractors. For us this generally includes drywall, electrical, and plumbing. For the Simpsons this also includes excavation and foundation.

Let's examine each of these groups in more detail and look at how they fit into stick pricing, unit pricing, or both. From our experience, even in stick pricing the labor ends up being priced by the unit. Whether you've kept cost records, rely on an estimating book for labor, or use a little estimating hocus-pocus (of course we all deny that), you're assigning a dollar amount to a specific unit of work.

Now look at our estimate (Figure 9-8) and see how we've fleshed out those three groups.

Group 1

For items in Group 1, we depend more on our experience than formulas or estimating books.

Planning fee

This includes time spent designing plans, estimating, running down subs' prices, and getting the plans through the building department. Occasionally, we have clients who pay us a flat hourly rate for this leg work. Far more often, we only get paid for this if the job comes through. The Simpson addition is a fairly uncomplicated job. We allow $450 to cover planning costs.

Soils report and foundation engineering

You may not need a soils report at all, but we're required to get one because our area has a wide range of soil conditions. We always leave this cost to the homeowner. There's no other logical way to allow for the $50 to $1,000 report and engineering fees. Pending the soils report, we put in our contract that all foundation prices are based on a standard foundation. Of course, we define in the contract what a standard foundation is.

Engineering

If engineering is necessary, we leave the cost to the homeowner. On most small remodels or additions, only the roof trusses need engineering. The lumberyard that makes our trusses includes engineering as part of its quote.

Permit

Our permit estimate is based on the labor and materials to complete a job. They don't include subs or profit and overhead. From experience, we use 50 percent as a rule of thumb to figure labor and material costs. Although the permit on a job in the $6,000-7,500 range would run us about $50, we allow $150. This covers the paperwork, picking up the permit, and the follow-up for inspections.

The total estimate for Group 1 is $600.00.

Group 2

For items in Group 2, we depend on our database from estimating books we've found to be reliable and job costs we recorded from previous projects. For us, these sources turn practically every estimate into a combination of unit and stick pricing. Again, it's important to stay in job sequence.

	Unit	Material	Labor	Total M&L	Price
Planning fee					450.00
Soils report					by owner
Engineering					by owner
Permit					150.00
Site work					220.00
Excavation					300.00
Foundation					815.00
Backfill					150.00
Floor framing	SF 120			2.58	309.60
Subfloor	SF 120			1.08	130.00
Wall framing	SF 256			1.04	266.00
Wall sheathing	SF 256			0.74	189.00
Roof framing	SF 180			1.67	300.00
Roof sheathing	SF 180			1.08	194.00
Asphalt shingles	SF 180			0.72	129.00
Exterior trim					
Fascia	LF 40			1.35	54.00
Soffit	LF 40			3.22	128.00
Lap siding	SF 256			1.43	366.00
Doors & windows					
Doors (move existing)			90.00	90.00	90.00
Windows					
2 sets double hung		498.00	80.00	578.00	578.00
Interior					
Demo siding	SF 80		0.30	0.30	24.00
Demo sheathing	SF 80		0.22	0.22	17.60
Insulation					
Walls	SF 256	0.21	0.18	0.39	100.00
Ceiling	SF 120	0.47	0.19	0.66	80.00
Drywall					
Walls	SF 352			0.85	299.00
Ceiling	SF 120			0.85	102.00

Figure 9-8
Estimate for Simpson addition

	Unit	Material	Labor	Total M&L	Price
Base/casing	LF 78	0.97	0.52	1.49	116.00
Stain base/casing	LF 78	0.11	0.50	0.61	48.00
Stain windows (2)	Each	2.63	29.90	32.53	65.00
Paint walls & ceiling	SF 472	0.16	0.30	0.46	217.00
Vinyl flooring/underlayment					
Underlayment					91.00
Vinyl					148.00
Electrical					640.00
Heat duct to existing furnace					160.00
Deck					
Piers (3)	Each			60.00	180.00
Pressure-treated					
Beam	Each			45.00	45.00
Joist	SF 150			2.27	340.00
Decking	SF 150			3.45	518.00
Steps (3)	Each			25.00	75.00
Deck railing	LF 25			10.00	250.00
	Subtotal				8334.20
Profit & overhead					
Total					

Figure 9-8 (cont'd)

Estimate for Simpson addition

Site work

This fee covers meeting central locators to check for underground utilities before digging, removing trees or shrubs, staking off the addition, and anything else we have to do to prepare the site before excavation. The best we can do is estimate the number of manhours and equipment hours all of this will take. For the Simpsons, there'll be very little actual site work. We can leave the existing concrete patio without interfering with the job. We've allowed $220 for the small amount of site work.

Floor framing

In using *unit pricing*, we need to first answer several basic questions: What is the total square footage of floor framing we need? And what size of joist is required? On the Simpson project, we're going to use 2x10 joists to match up to the existing house. With a 10- by 12-foot addition, there are 120 square feet of floor area. By checking a reliable unit price estimating book, we find that 2x10 floor joists are priced at $2.58 a square foot, or a total of $309.60 for the addition.

To *stick price* our floor framing, we would look at a joist table and find that with 16-inch spacing, we'll need nine joists for a 10-foot run, or in our case, nine 12-foot 2x10s. To that we'll add two 10-foot 2x10s for the two end rim joists. We'll also need two 12-foot 2x4s and one 10-foot 2x4 in redwood for the sill plate and seal-sill, seven joist hangers to hang the joists from the existing house, and miscellaneous nails. Our concrete subcontractor will provide and set the anchor bolts. We price our material list and add the estimated manhours (multiplied by our current labor rate) it will take to accomplish this task. The result is our stick price for the floor framing.

The rest of the estimate

We use the same process to estimate the T&G plywood flooring, wall framing and sheathing, trusses and rafter tie-in, roof sheathing, roofing, fascia, soffit, windows, doors, siding, and so on. Check our estimates in Figure 9-8.

Group 3

Our final group of prices takes some legwork. We take sets of drawings to all of the subs and suppliers and get them started putting their prices together. For the Simpson's addition, our suppliers' list includes windows and doors, and trusses.

Our sub list looks like this:

Excavation

Foundation

Flooring

Electrical

We finish off the estimate by totaling all the items in our three groups. The total of these prices is our *hard costs*. Now we have to add in profit and overhead. If you have questions about how to figure these items, go back and review Chapter 8.

If the Estimate Is Too High

If your estimate comes in higher than your client can afford, stop to consider a couple of things before you start dropping your price.

First, remember that you're the professional. If your clients have a budget of only $15,000, they have to be realistic about what that will buy. Maybe they can't afford to have everything they want. And that's their problem, *not yours*.

Second, if you do decide to drop your price to save the job, *never* drop the price below your hard costs and your overhead. If you choose to work without any profit, that's your business — although you must love construction more than we do. For your own sake, though, don't pay someone just to have work going.

Finally, have confidence in what you've estimated. We realize this is much easier said than done. But if you've priced every piece of the job and double-checked for logic and accuracy, you're covered.

So dig out your tape measure, calculator and price lists, and start estimating.

10

Scheduling the Job

*H*owever tempted you may be, *don't skip this chapter*! Scheduling is one of those things that most contractors take for granted. They think scheduling is automatic. After you do the site work, you excavate; after you excavate, you run the foundation; after the foundation, you waterproof; and so on. The steps are logical and sequential. Who needs to take time to write it out?

Many contractors — even experienced ones — don't realize that a well-thought-out schedule can be as important as a down-to-the-penny estimate. The more you're in control of the details, the smoother the job and the better your profit. When you schedule in advance, you'll reduce problems, speed up your jobs, increase your profit by reducing overhead per job, and work with your subs more efficiently. Let's look at these benefits one at a time.

Just the process of thinking through each task in the job can help you catch minor problems before they become major crises. This is especially true in remodeling, where there are likely to be far more surprises than in new construction.

Scheduling will also help shorten the overall construction time. A quicker job is usually a more profitable job. True, running a shorter job probably won't lower the direct costs. A window will still cost the same whether a job takes one month or three. A yard of concrete will probably cost the same whether you order next week or next month. But your overhead (indirect costs) will probably be lower. You'll get paid sooner, will spend less time supervising, will have fewer weather problems and can start the next job sooner if the job is well scheduled.

If you can do five jobs in the time you used to do four, your overhead is spread thinner. The phone company won't charge you any more because you're working faster. And your rent won't go up either. That makes your company more competitive and should raise your profits. As a bonus, clients will be happier that the work went so fast. Happy clients generate referrals and that means more business.

A good schedule gives you a clearer picture of where the job stands and what remains to be done. You'll also see which of the remaining activities are critical to finishing on time. You've probably heard this old construction rule of thumb: *It takes 80 percent of the time to do 20 percent of the work*. Scheduling helps you to spot the 20 percent that will slow you down.

Good scheduling helps you work better with subs. You can tell subs precisely when you want them on the job. Instead of a vague "two to three weeks from now," you can confidently schedule a sub for August 16 or 17. As the job progresses, you can narrow it down to the specific day.

When you're still your own foreman, running one job at a time, scheduling may not be a high priority. We don't mean that it's not important, just that you may be able to survive without a formal schedule. But when you're running three or four crews on different jobs, scheduling is essential. Putting it down on paper helps you anticipate — and thus prevent — delays in material delivery and mis-scheduled subs.

There are several ways to schedule jobs. Some are very sophisticated. You probably don't need that. Just noting on a weekly calendar what should be done on each job, and when it needs to be done, will cut your construction time. We guarantee it.

The Basics of Scheduling

No matter what scheduling method you choose, some basics are the same. You'll take these initial steps:

1) Review the estimate and the plans. Divide the job into its logical parts and decide how long each will take. How much work is required? How big will the crew be? How many manhours will be needed for each part of the work? How many subs will you use? How can you schedule the work to use your crew, equipment, and subs most efficiently?

2) Don't try to schedule every single activity on the job — not the studs and joists, for example. Instead, look at the larger picture. Schedule phases

of the job — such as carpentry and drywall. You're trying to get an overall picture of the job, not fitting in a dental appointment for the 23rd between hanging the shower door and setting the bathroom countertops. Schedule in all the subs, even if they'll only be on the job for a few hours.

3) Note items that you'll have to order in advance. Suppliers may not have carpet, windows, wallpaper, appliances, and plumbing fixtures in stock. Use the checklist in Figure 10-1 to jog your memory.

4) What problems do you anticipate? Will weather be a factor? Vacations? Specific deadlines? Is some aspect of the job unusually difficult?

Even if you don't do anything more formal than this, you'll find the job goes smoother. You won't be waiting for windows that are still two weeks away from delivery, or carpet that's six weeks away. You won't be held up by the plumber because you called him at the last minute instead of a week in advance.

The key to good scheduling is *organization*. The more organized *you* are, the more efficient your subs, suppliers, and even your crew can be.

Choosing the Right System for You

Most contractors use one of three basic scheduling systems: the calendar planner, the bar chart, or the critical path method (CPM). And there are plenty of variations and combinations of the three.

The calendar planner uses a simple calendar to note the anticipated start date of key job phases. Right on a calendar you plot the course of the job.

A bar chart uses a grid to show when each job phase should start and finish. It also shows clearly when phases can overlap.

The third method, CPM, shows how each part of the job relates to other parts of the work. The critical path method shows the quickest "path" through a job and the effect delays have on the rest of the project.

We've found that the hardest part of scheduling is estimating how long each phase should take. Experience will teach you whether to plan on two days or ten to paint the exterior of a house. Common sense will help, too. It had better take only one day to pour the footings, or you're in trouble. If you're not familiar with some type of work and don't know how long it should take, check your estimating manual. Most suggest the manhours required per unit of work. You'll have to adjust these figures to accommodate the skill level of your crew, but at least you have a workable place to start.

Don't be afraid to ask a sub how much time he thinks he'll need. If you've never laid carpet, you can't be expected to know how long it will take. Some subs will do their work in phases. Plumbers and electricians will do the rough-in early in the job and then the finish later. Find out how long each phase will take and add them to the schedule.

Items to order

_____ Trusses		_____ Tile	
_____ Windows		_____ Carpet	
_____ Specialty doors		_____ Wallpaper	
_____ Mill work		_____ Plumbing fixtures	
_____ Specialty masonry		_____ Electrical fixtures	
_____ Cabinets		_____ Ornamental iron	
_____ Appliances		_____ Other	

Item	Lead time	Date ordered
_____	_____	_____
_____	_____	_____
_____	_____	_____
_____	_____	_____
_____	_____	_____
_____	_____	_____
_____	_____	_____
_____	_____	_____
_____	_____	_____
_____	_____	_____

Figure 10-1

Ordering checklist

"If it's Tuesday, it must be roofing."

Then add in some extra time as a *fudge factor*. Jobs rarely run as smoothly in real life as they do on paper. The plumber may promise to be there on Tuesday, but if an emergency repair comes up, you may have to wait until Wednesday or even Thursday. Hope for the best, but plan for the hitches.

Should you show the schedule to the client? We don't recommend it. Homeowners have a way of forgetting that the schedule is a goal, not a promise. Tell them what you're aiming for, but don't give them the specifics. They're paying you to worry about delivery dates and whether subs will show up on time.

Sticking to the schedule will be easier if you order the materials you need in plenty of time. If your clients have to select colors or models or designs, give them plenty of time to make those decisions. Provide a list of choices at the beginning of the job. Even if the light fixtures are the last thing to be installed, the homeowners can choose them right away. Schedule with your suppliers just as you'd schedule with a sub. If you order a patio door the first week of February but don't need it delivered until March 10, tell your supplier. That way, if the door isn't delivered on time, it's clear who's responsible.

As your company grows, your scheduling will probably have to become more detailed. For smaller jobs, calendar scheduling may be enough. Larger jobs may require bar charting. But no matter how you schedule, don't start a job without some type of schedule. It's the best way we know of keeping everyone informed of what you want to do and when you want to do it.

To help you get more familiar with each scheduling system, we've created a schedule for a room addition using each of the three basic methods. You can see for yourself the advantages and disadvantages of each system.

Here are the phases scheduled and days we've allowed for each. Asterisks note subcontracted work.

Phase	Days allowed
1) Site work	1
2) Excavation*	1
3) Foundation*	4
4) Waterproof*	0.5
5) Backfill*	0.5
6) Floor frame	2
7) Wall frame	2
8) Roof frame	2
9) Roofing*	1.5
10) Windows	1
11) Exterior trim/siding	2.5
12) Exterior paint	2
13) Gutters*	1
14) Electrical*	1
15) Insulation*	1
16) Drywall*	4
17) Interior paint	2
18) Interior trim stain	2
19) Interior trim	2
20) Electrical finish	1
21) Carpet*	1
22) Close out	2
Total time	**37.0**

Note that the four days allowed for the foundation includes only one day of curing time. Actual curing may take longer than that. But we try to use weekends for curing. That way curing doesn't delay the work.

If each item is done consecutively without any delay between tasks, the job should be finished in 37 working days. That's just under two months, figuring 20 work days a month. Let's see how scheduling can shorten that time.

The Calendar Planner

The calendar planner is the least sophisticated of the three systems. For small jobs and small companies, it works quite well. If you're running only one crew, you can keep a lot of the details in your head. You know your pace and when you'll need materials or subs.

Job address **200 UTE PASS**

Project starting date **AUGUST 2, 1990**

Project completion date **SEPTEMBER 8, 1990**

Monday	Tuesday	Wednesday	Thursday	Friday
1	2 SITE WORK	3 EXCAVATION	4 FOUNDATION (SET FORMS)	5 ⟶ (POUR)
8 ⟶ (STRIP FORMS)	9 WATERPROOF BACKFILL	10 FLOOR FRAME	11 ⟶	12 WALL FRAME
15 ⟶	16 ROOF FRAME	17 ⟶	18 WINDOWS ROOFING ⟶	19 EXT. SIDING AND TRIM ⟶ ELECTRICAL
22 (SIDING AND TRIM) ⟶	23 ⟶	24 EXTERIOR PAINT INSULATION	25 DRYWALL ⟶	26 STAIN INT. TRIM ⟶ GUTTERS
29 STAIN ⟶ DRYWALL ⟶	30 ⟶ ⟶	1 INTERIOR PAINT ⟶	2 ⟶	3 INTERIOR ⟶ TRIM
6 TRIM ⟶ ELECTRICAL	7 CARPET CLOSEOUT	8 ⟶	9	10

Notes

Figure 10-2

Calendar planner

The big disadvantage of calendar planning is that it doesn't show the relationship of phases. It's easy to see that if the weather holds up the foundation work for a week, it will delay the entire job a week. It's not so easy to see the effect of a week's delay by the plumber.

Figure 10-2 shows our hypothetical job scheduled by calendar. Even with this simple method, it's easy to see how phases can overlap, especially those involving subs. According to the schedule, the job should be completed in 27 working days. That's a pretty optimistic estimate, with very little extra time scheduled in.

You can speed up or slow down the job even more, depending on how large your crew is. If you're working by yourself with one helper, it'll probably take several days longer. If you don't use any subs, it'll take considerably more time. However, if you have two or more crews to shift around, you may be able to shorten the job by several days.

*"It's all ready to move into, except for the doors and windows.
They should be delivered in 6 to 8 weeks."*

This schedule assumes you'll be able to get material delivered when you ask for it and will have subs show up when you need them. Recently, our suppliers have cut way back on their stock. We used to be able to get windows delivered from a regional warehouse in three to four working days. Now we wait six to eight weeks for some windows to be built and delivered from the factory. A situation like that can destroy any schedule you put together. If you can anticipate the delay, you can at least put off the start of the job. Or you may be able to talk the client into a different window that's currently in stock.

When the homeowner asks how long the job will take — and it'll be a rare one who doesn't — give yourself six to eight weeks. If you can beat your schedule and finish in five, who will complain? And if problems extend the job to eight and a half weeks, the client will still think that's a reasonable length of time. Only you will know it's not.

The Bar Chart

A bar chart (Figure 10-3) is more useful on a larger job. Write in the days (again ignoring weekends) on the top line. Day 1 would be the start date, day 2 would be the following day, and so on. List job phases down the left margin. Then block out each phase with a series of X's. Start entering X's for each task when you figure

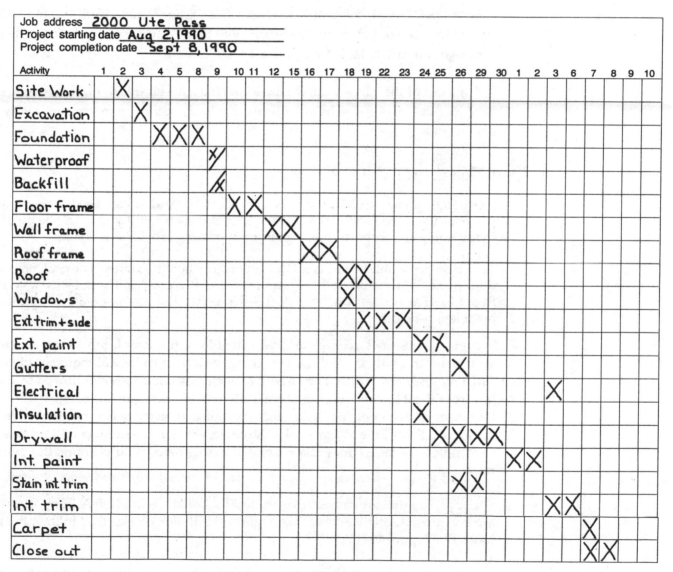

Figure 10-3

Bar chart

that task can begin. As you get more comfortable with the system, you can add letters that represent latest order dates, delivery lags, and so on.

At a single glance, you can see the relationship between the phases. It's also easier to see how you can schedule subs to overlap. And for uncomplicated jobs, the bar chart lets you figure float time. *Float* is the extra time available to complete a task without delaying final completion. For instance, you need a total of five and a half days to do the exterior trim and siding, paint, and gutters. But since they're the final phases for the exterior, there's a week and a half extra that you can use. If the weather's bad and your crew can't paint, you can delay exterior trim a week without setting back the final completion date.

Some portions of the work have zero float time. In fact, until the framing is complete, none of the phases have any float time. When framing is done, there's some extra time available for some tasks, but not all.

For most of the jobs we do, we use a bar chart. It's simple to put together and is easy for our crews and subs to understand. *Quick, easy* and *effective*: that's why we like it.

The Critical Path Method

At first glance, CPM may look complicated. And it can be. For very large projects, the added sophistication can be really useful. But you won't be building many dams and airports. For a typical remodeling job, CPM is a snap.

The theory behind CPM is solid. In every job there's a series of critical tasks that determine the time needed to complete the entire project. These tasks have zero float time. Delay a task on the critical path one day and you've delayed completion by at least one day.

Figure 10-4 shows a complete CPM schedule for the sample job. When you draw your diagram, start as we did by breaking the job into a logical sequence of tasks. Then represent each activity by a square or circle (called a *node*) followed by a line or arrow. That line doesn't represent the length of time a job takes. It just indicates that it must be completed before the next phase or activity can begin. Above the circle, you'll label the phase. Under the circle, write in the number of days needed to complete the task. It may take several drawings before you've found the shortest path.

For phases that are consecutive, the line looks like Figure 10-5 A. For phases that are concurrent, the line looks like Figure 10-5 B. For phases that follow, the line looks like Figure 10-5 C.

Although the example we're using is fairly simple, you can imagine how additional tasks would be added, as illustrated in Figure 10-5 D. When you get this complicated, it simplifies the chart if you use letters instead of writing out the name of the task.

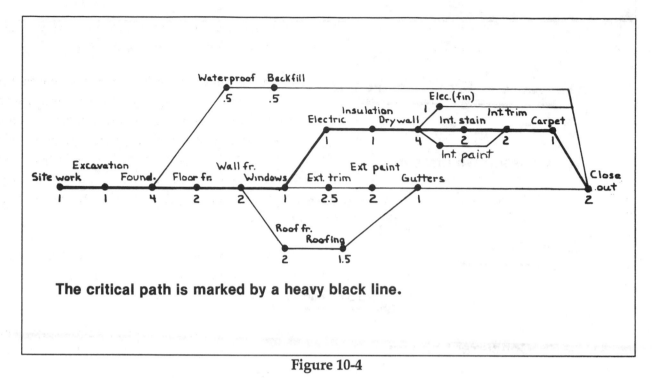

The critical path is marked by a heavy black line.

Figure 10-4

Critical path method schedule

Once you have your job diagrammed, you have to establish which line represents the critical path. To find it, add the number of days it takes to complete the tasks running along each continuous line or path from beginning to end. See Figure 10-6.

Now compare the length of time each path requires. In our example, Path 3 will take the longest time to complete, a total of 24 days. Path 3 is the critical path. As long as all the tasks along that path are completed within the scheduled time, and there aren't any major delays along the other paths, the job can be completed in a total of 24 days.

If a task takes longer than you anticipated, it may mean a change in the critical path. For instance, if the weather turns bad and delays the exterior paint and trim work for a week, then Path 5 would become the critical path.

Mark your critical path with a double line or colored marker. In fact, it's a good idea to use colored markers to highlight all the important parts of your CPM chart.

The more complex your work, the more sophistication your charts will have. If you're scheduling larger jobs, we recommend checking a book on CPM out of your local library. Several good resource books have been written on bar chart and CPM scheduling.

Remember that all scheduling is intended to save time and simplify the job. It's also a goal. But don't get carried away. Be realistic. Your concrete sub's form crew

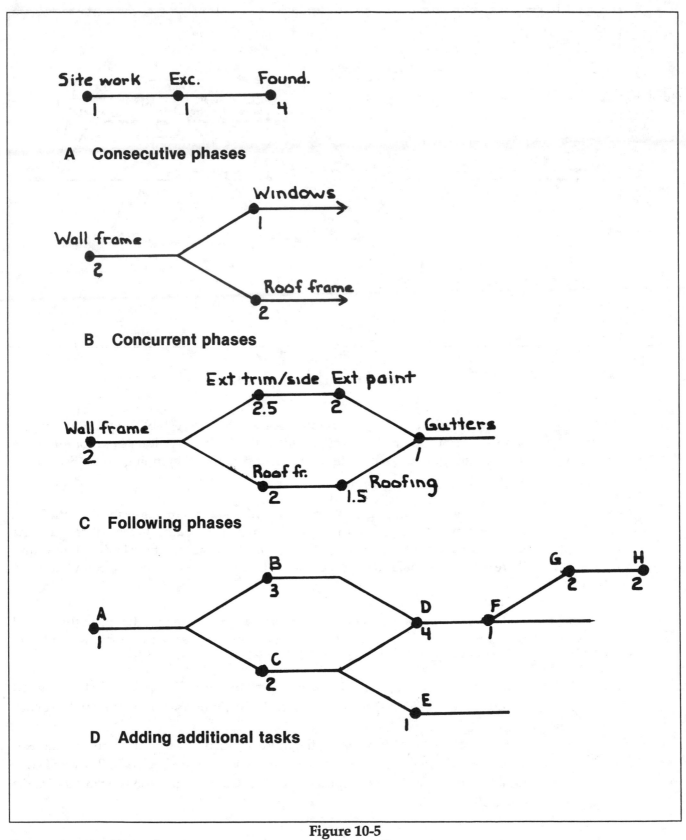

A   Consecutive phases

B   Concurrent phases

C   Following phases

D   Adding additional tasks

Figure 10-5

Breakdown of CPM schedule

	Work phase	Days			Work phase	Days
				Path 4	Site work	1
Path 1	Site work	1			Excavation	1
	Excavation	1			Foundation	4
	Foundation	4			Floor framing	2
	Waterproofing	0.5			Wall framing	2
	Backfill	0.5			Windows	1
	Close out	2			Electrical	1
		9 days total			Insulation	1
					Drywall	4
Path 2	Site work	1			Interior paint	1
	Excavation	1			Interior trim	2
	Foundation	4			Carpet	1
	Floor framing	2			Close out	2
	Wall framing	2				**23 days total**
	Windows	1				
	Electrical	1		Path 5	Site work	1
	Insulation	1			Excavation	1
	Drywall	4			Foundation	4
	Electrical (fin.)	1			Floor framing	2
	Close out	2			Wall framing	2
		20 days total			Windows	1
					Exterior trim	2.5
Path 3	Site work	1			Exterior paint	2
	Excavation	1			Gutters	1
	Foundation	4			Close out	2
	Floor framing	2				**18.5 days total**
	Wall framing	2				
	Windows	1		Path 6	Site work	1
	Electrical	1			Excavation	1
	Insulation	1			Foundation	4
	Drywall	4			Floor framing	2
	Interior stain	2			Wall framing	2
	Interior trim	2			Roof framing	2
	Carpet	1			Roofing	1.5
	Close out	2			Gutters	1
		24 days total			Close out	2
						16.5 days total

Figure 10-6

Locating the critical path

may be able to set all the forms in one day. After all, they do it every day. But *your* crew may form only a half dozen foundations a year. If it'll take your employees two days, admit it from the start and build in the extra day. That's better than falling behind right from the start.

Staying on Schedule

Once you've planned a realistic schedule, the challenge is to stay on it. The key, again, is organization. You need to stay ahead of your crews. Keep them supplied with equipment and materials. Keep subs informed of the schedule and how they fit into it. This is where you'll save real money.

Again, if you're on the job yourself, you can keep your finger on the pulse of the job well enough. But if you depend on a foreman to keep the work rolling, pay him for an extra five or ten minutes to think ahead to the next day's work. We use some simple forms to keep day-to-day operations running smoothly.

Figure 10-7 is a schedule for you to fill out daily and give to the foreman before work starts each day. It should clearly define what the goals are for that working day.

Figure 10-8 is a progress report for the job foreman to complete at the end of the work day. The checklist helps organize what's needed for the next few days.

Scheduling Software

In the last chapter, we talked about computer software for estimating. There are also programs for scheduling. If you have a computer and are comfortable using it, you may want to consider a scheduling program. But most of the scheduling remodelers need to do can be done very easily with pencil and paper. You'll probably find that the software is more a luxury than a necessity. Unless you have several complex jobs going simultaneously (or money to burn), put your money somewhere else.

If you should decide to buy scheduling software, be aware that you'll need either a dot matrix or a laser printer. The software itself starts at around $100 for the simpler programs. The more powerful programs may cost $500 or more.

If you feel the need for more detailed, very complete scheduling and don't have the time to learn the basics yourself, consider using a scheduling service. Most larger cities have companies that offer scheduling services.

In any case, don't underestimate the importance of scheduling. It should be as much a part of your jobs as concrete and lumber.

Daily Schedule

Date_____   Job #_____   Foreman_____

To do:

_____

_____

_____

_____

_____

_____

_____

Subs scheduled:

_____

_____

_____

_____

Materials needed:

_____

_____

_____

_____

_____

_____

Figure 10-7

Daily schedule

Progress Report

Date _____ Job # _____

Job is: _____ on _____ behind _____ ahead of schedule

Notes: _____

_____

_____

_____

_____

_____

_____

Checklist for tomorrow:

_____ materials for tomorrow/coming week

_____ additional equipment for tomorrow

_____ inspections to be called out

_____ equipment/materials to be returned

_____ information needed

_____ call owner

_____ subs to be called/confirmed

_____ potential trouble spots

_____ other

Signed _____

Figure 10-8

Progress report

11

Finding and Keeping Good Employees

No matter how small or how large your company, you'll only be as good as the employees you hire. They're the front line of your operation. They're the ones who make the day-to-day impression that sticks in a client's mind.

One of the hardest things an owner of a remodeling company has to do is grow along with his or her company. It's not easy to go from running a one-man company to running a business with a half dozen crews spread all over town. Many remodelers can't do it. Quality and cost control disappear; with them go referrals and repeat business.

It doesn't have to be this way, though. Carefully chosen and well-trained employees should bring you business, not lose it. Unfortunately, it's not easy to find the right people. The talents you need to hire and run a crew have nothing to do with how well you swing a hammer. In fact, in many ways, they're mutually exclusive skills. Someone who's a good tradesman probably isn't so good at personal relations. And a real charmer is seldom a good tradesman. But we feel that almost anyone can become an effective boss. We did. We expect you'll agree with us after reading this chapter.

Hiring Employees

We won't pretend that this is easy. Hiring the right person for the right job is time consuming, tedious, and difficult. We'd like to give you all the shortcuts — except there aren't any. Any time you try to take one, you'll pay for it down the road.

Good hiring begins with you, the boss. You'd better know what you want from new employees and what you can offer them. When the economy is strong and every builder has plenty of work, the competition for workers is stiff. When work is slow, it's still tough because the best tradesmen are either hanging on to their jobs or have left town to find work elsewhere. No matter what the market is like, it's a challenge to ferret out good employees.

Where Do You Begin?

The classified section of your local paper is the logical place to start. Although you'll get a lot of responses to a help wanted ad, most people who call won't have the qualifications you're looking for. When we run an ad for a laborer, it's not unusual to get 50 or 60 replies the morning after the paper comes out. We used to run an ad three or four days. Now we run it once and are tempted to take the phone off the hook by 10:00 a.m. But even with all those responses, we haven't always found someone who fits our needs and fits smoothly into the assigned crew. Our best — and very worst — employees have come to us through want ads. Unfortunately, we've had more bad than good results. That's why we try to avoid the classifieds when possible.

If you do decide to run an ad, do yourself a favor and include all the important information. Are you looking for a laborer or a carpenter? How much are you paying? Is it a permanent or temporary position? Full or part-time? Where can applicants apply, and for how long? Are references required? Do you have special restrictions such as no smoking? Including it all may raise the cost of the ad two or three dollars, but it saves you hours on the phone answering the same questions over and over. You'll also weed out a lot of people who are looking for a different kind of work.

We've had better luck *networking*. We ask employees, friends, relatives, other contractors, even customers for suggestions. Anyone whose opinion we trust is worth asking. This method has given us by far the best results. Often, it also gives us a chance to discreetly check a reference or two before we even call the person about possible employment. This method won't work in every situation, but it's always the way we begin.

Surprisingly, one of our best employees came from the state unemployment office. By hiring him, we also picked up some healthy tax credits the first year.

Another alternative is to use an employment agency. They do the screening for you and send the most qualified half dozen applicants in for an interview. That saves you the initial screening. Remember, though, that someone has to pay the agency's fee — which may be a month's wages or more. Usually the employer pays.

Handling the Applications and Interviews

Once you have some good applicants, the next step is to focus on those best qualified. We always insist that the applicants apply in person. That gives us a chance to look them all over and make notes on their applications. Even when applicants bring a resume, we still ask them to fill out an application. That's one more chance to observe them. Are they prepared? Did they bring a pencil? Do they have addresses and phone numbers of references handy? Can they write and spell well enough? You don't need a Rhodes scholar, but insist on someone with enough intelligence to fill out a simple form.

We like to get detailed information on each applicant's job history and personal references. Watch out for job hoppers. They'll leave you as quickly as they left their last employer — and probably without notice. Make sure the reference information is complete. If the applicant expects you to get phone numbers and supervisor names on prior jobs, trash the application. It won't be the last thing he's too lazy to do.

We tell applicants we'll be checking their references and job histories. And then we do. We contact as many past employers as are listed, giving the most weight to the most recent employer. When applicants know that you'll be checking on their answers, they're much more likely to respond honestly to your questions. Figure 11-1 is a copy of the employment application we use for our business.

Because our employees are constantly under the noses of our clients, we only hire people with a reasonably neat appearance and the ability to communicate without swearing. We also insist that our employees don't smoke on the job. In ten years, we haven't had anyone quit or create problems because of these rules. Since they're representing us, we can be choosy — and we are.

Here are the hiring basics that work for us:

Application For Employment

Personal Information

Date_____ Social Security #_____

Name_____

        last   first   middle initial

Phone number_____

Present address_____

        street   city   state   zip

Permanent address_____

        street   city   state   zip

Employment Desired

Position_____ Are you employed now?_____

Date you can start_____ Wages desired_____

Education

	School's name and location	Years attended	Date graduated
High school			
Trade/Business school			
College			
Other			

Physical Record

List any physical limitations_____

_____

Have you any problems hearing?_____ Vision?_____

Have you ever been injured?_____ Give details_____

_____

In case of emergency notify_____

                                      name

Address_____

        street   city   state   phone

Figure 11-1

Employment application

Former Employers   (List last 4 employers, last one first)

Date (month/year)	Name and address of employer	Phone	Position	Ending wages	Reason for leaving
From					
To					
From					
To					
From					
To					
From					
To					

References   (Give the names of three persons not related to you, whom you have known at least one year)

Name	Address	Phone	Years known

I authorize investigation of all statements contained in this application. I understand that misrepresentation or omission of facts called for is cause for dismissal. Further, I understand that my employment is not guaranteed for any specific length of time, and regardless of when my wages or salary is to be paid, I can be terminated at any time without notice.

Date_____   Signature_____

FOR OFFICE USE ONLY. DO NOT WRITE BELOW THIS LINE

Interviewed by_____   Date_____

Remarks_____

_____

_____

_____

Neatness_____   Character_____

Personality_____   Ability_____

Hired_____   Position_____

Starting date_____   Wage_____

Signed_____   Date_____

Figure 11-1 (cont'd)

Employment application

1) Have a clear idea of the job you want filled. What skill level do you need? If you need a carpenter, hire a carpenter. If you need unskilled labor, hire a laborer. Hiring overqualified workers can be just as damaging as hiring the underqualified. We've hired workers with more skill than they needed to do the job. It usually didn't take long for them to get frustrated and quit.

2) What pay range does the job call for? It's easy to fall into the trap of hiring a worker for $10 an hour and expecting $20-an-hour performance. If you need a $20-an-hour carpenter, hire someone with $20-an-hour skills and pay $20 an hour. There aren't many $20-an-hour carpenters who will do $20-an-hour work for $10 an hour. Don't look for bargains when hiring. Pay a good wage and expect top quality work.

3) Be realistic in telling the applicants what opportunities they'll have with your company. Be honest about the prospect for future work. If you have jobs lined up for three months and nothing more, let the applicant know the work may last only three months.

4) Explain, too, what the grounds are for dismissal. You'd better know what they are yourself. Anyone who shows up drunk or high on drugs deserves to be dismissed. We'll also fire people who make the same mistake over and over and people who can't get along with members of their crew. We're a little more relaxed about occasional tardiness and even extra time off, as long as it doesn't foul up our schedule. You may feel otherwise. Whatever you do, don't throw a list of new rules at an employee after he's been hired. Put the rules on the table before offering the job.

5) Allow enough time for a complete interview. A bad choice will cause management headaches, raise your unemployment insurance costs, and discourage other employees. Anyone worth hiring is worth an hour of your time. Don't take easy answers. If you have to, interview the applicant a second time. Better to take an extra hour of your time than make a mistake you'll regret. Figure 11-2 shows the questions we ask when interviewing. We remind them we'll be asking similar questions of their former employers and references. This encourages them to be truthful, especially when answering questions 1 and 5.

6) Require at least three references. Unless you're willing to make a few long distance calls, insist on local references. And ask for work-related references. You really don't care what the applicant's brother-in-law thinks of him. You'll be surprised how many can't come up with even two — that should tell you something. Once you get the references, call them all. Make this is a rigid rule. Listen to what they say. If they can't enthusiastically recommend the applicant, move on to your next choice.

1) How long did you work for your last employer? The one before? Why did you leave your last three jobs? What are your long-term goals in construction?

> ☞ *Consider whether the applicant's answers are consistent with the other things you know about: job history, education, and references.*

2) What tools do you own? What brands? Why? How much have you spent on tools in the last year? Do you own a pickup truck?

> ☞ *Are the answers consistent with your expectations for an employee? Are the tool choices logical for a person with the skills claimed?*

3) What did you like about your previous construction jobs? What did you dislike? What changes would you have made if you had been the owner? What would be the ideal construction job for you?

> ☞ *Are the applicant's expectations realistic? Do the complaints sound legitimate? An applicant who can't say anything nice about a former employer won't like anything about your job either.*

4) What will your references praise you for? What will they criticize you for?

> ☞ *How realistic is the applicant's perception of his or her abilities? Does the applicant admit any faults at all? It's hard to give honest answers to questions like these. That's why the answers may be very revealing. Don't be afraid to ask tough questions like these.*

5) How much sick time did you take last year? Have you ever had a job-related accident? What were the circumstances? How often were you late to work in the past month? How often did you leave early? How many personal days off did you request?

> ☞ *Although these are fair questions for you to ask, some applicants may refuse to answer. Weigh that refusal against other qualifications.*

6) Ask a variety of skill questions that relate to the kind of work your company does. If possible, observe the applicant's skill level when doing a task you assign. Note how the applicant handles the tools, approaches the task, finishes the work and how long it takes.

Figure 11-2

Suggested interview questions

"Sorry, I don't do windows."

Traits to Look for (and Avoid)

Ultimately, we look for three things in prospective employees. Most important is *integrity*. This person represents our company to the customer. If we can't trust an employee, why should we ask our clients to trust the same employee? No matter how skilled and how good the references, an employee who will fudge on the time worked, pilfer from a job site, or lie to cover mistakes doesn't belong on our payroll.

Second, we look for *aptitude*. That's a high priority when we hire unskilled labor. We always hope our unskilled workers will learn the trade and stay with us. That builds loyalty and makes for a solid, dependable crew. When we hire carpenters, we're looking for more than skill with a hammer. We also want the mechanical and design skills required on every significant remodeling project. We need tradesmen who can learn whatever it takes to do first rate work on the jobs we handle. We'll give preference to an applicant with a less impressive list of skills if that person shows a willingness to take on additional responsibility. You don't need carpenters who won't help with anything but carpentry. You need tradesmen who can deal with new situations and learn new skills.

Third, we look for a *positive attitude*. A good attitude translates into eagerness to learn and a willingness to do even the dirty jobs. Of course, attitude problems don't always show up during the interview. But when they do, use your common sense and file the application — in the waste basket. Here's a related tip: Don't fall into the trap of hiring the applicant with the biggest sob story. However noble it may be, you aren't running a charity. Do your volunteer social work on the weekends. When you're running a business, run it like a business.

Be especially wary of someone who currently abuses alcohol or drugs. The National Association for the Education and Prevention of Alcohol and Drug Abuse in Construction (NAPADAC) reports that alcohol and drug abusers:

▪ Are 3 times as likely to be late for work and more than twice as likely to request early dismissal or time off.

▪ Have 2-1/2 times as many absences of eight days or more.

▪ Use 3 times the normal level of sick benefits.

▪ Are 5 times as likely to file for workers' compensation benefits.

▪ Are 3 to 6 times as likely to be involved in an accident.

▪ Are 4 times as likely to have an accident on the job.

These statistics are startling. Remember, your first priority is to run a profitable construction company. Protecting alcoholics and drug abusers makes that difficult if not impossible.

It's rarely easy to spot an applicant who's a substance abuser. Your best bet is to check with the applicant's former employers. A reference may not be willing to admit candidly that this person has a problem. But by checking such things as missed days of work, tardiness, and job related accidents, you'll quickly see a pattern emerging.

Employee Paperwork

When you've hired the best applicant, have the new employee fill out Form W-4 (Figure 11-3). We have every employee fill out this form annually so our records stay current. This form stays in your files unless the employee claims 13 or more exemptions. In that case, submit it to the IRS. Let them decide whether they're legitimate.

You should know a few things about the Immigration Act of 1988. Penalties are stiff for knowingly hiring illegal immigrants. The fine for a first offense runs $250 to $2,000. The penalty for subsequent offenses is a fine from $3,000 to $10,000 and a possible prison sentence.

The requirements are simple. Just have every employee fill out Form I-9 (Figure 11-4) within three business days of the hire date. Employees are responsible for proving citizenship or legal residency. Your only responsibility is to review documents to be sure they're genuine. Even if you hire your nephew, you need to see his birth certificate or his original Social Security card. Keep Form I-9 on file for one year after the employee leaves or three years from the hire date, whichever is longer.

As you can see from the sample, the form isn't complicated. It only asks for basic information and document numbers. The problem with the law is that it adds to your paperwork load — which is just what every contractor *doesn't* need.

19**90** Form W-4

Department of the Treasury
Internal Revenue Service

Purpose. Complete Form W-4 so that your employer can withhold the correct amount of Federal income tax from your pay.

Exemption From Withholding. Read line 6 of the certificate below to see if you can claim exempt status. *If exempt, complete line 6; but do not complete lines 4 and 5.* No Federal income tax will be withheld from your pay. This exemption expires February 15, 1991.

Basic Instructions. Employees who are not exempt should complete the Personal Allowances Worksheet. Additional worksheets are provided on page 2 for employees to adjust their withholding allowances based on itemized deductions, adjustments to income, or two-earner/two-job situations. Complete all worksheets that apply to your situation. The worksheets will help you figure the number of withholding allowances you are

entitled to claim. However, you may claim fewer allowances than this.

Head of Household. Generally, you may claim head of household filing status on your tax return only if you are unmarried and pay more than 50% of the costs of keeping up a home for yourself and your dependent(s) or other qualifying individuals.

Nonwage Income. If you have a large amount of nonwage income, such as interest or dividends, you should consider making estimated tax payments using Form 1040-ES. Otherwise, you may find that you owe additional tax at the end of the year.

Two-Earner/Two-Jobs. If you have a working spouse or more than one job, figure the total number of allowances you are entitled to claim on all jobs using worksheets from only one Form

W-4. This total should be divided among all jobs. Your withholding will usually be most accurate when all allowances are claimed on the W-4 filed for the highest paying job and zero allowances are claimed for the others.

Advance Earned Income Credit. If you are eligible for this credit, you can receive it added to your paycheck throughout the year. For details, obtain Form W-5 from your employer.

Check Your Withholding. After your W-4 takes effect, you can use **Publication 919,** Is My Withholding Correct for 1990?, to see how the dollar amount you are having withheld compares to your estimated total annual tax. Call 1-800-424-3676 (in Hawaii and Alaska, check your local telephone directory) to order this publication. Check your local telephone directory for the IRS assistance number if you need further help.

Personal Allowances Worksheet

A Enter "1" for **yourself** if no one else can claim you as a dependent . . . . **A** _____

B Enter "1" if:
  1. You are single and have only one job; or
  2. You are married, have only one job, and your spouse does not work; or
  3. Your wages from a second job or your spouse's wages (or the total of both) are $2,500 or less.
  . . . . . **B** _____

C Enter "1" for your **spouse.** But, you may choose to enter "0" if you are married and have either a working spouse or more than one job (this may help you avoid having too little tax withheld) . . . . **C** _____

D Enter number of **dependents** (other than your spouse or yourself) whom you will claim on your tax return . . . . . . **D** _____

E Enter "1" if you will file as a **head of household** on your tax return (see conditions under "Head of Household," above) . . **E** _____

F Enter "1" if you have at least $1,500 of **child or dependent care expenses** for which you plan to claim a credit . . . . **F** _____

G Add lines A through F and enter total here . . . . ▶ **G** _____

For accuracy, do all worksheets that apply.
- If you plan to **itemize or claim adjustments to income** and want to reduce your withholding, turn to the Deductions and Adjustments Worksheet on page 2.
- If you are **single** and have **more than one job** and your combined earnings from all jobs exceed $25,000 OR if you are **married** and have a **working spouse or more than one job,** and the combined earnings from all jobs exceed $44,000, then turn to the Two-Earner/Two-Job Worksheet on page 2 if you want to avoid having too little tax withheld.
- If **neither** of the above situations applies to you, **stop here** and enter the number from line G on line 4 of Form W-4 below.

------------------- Cut here and give the certificate to your employer. Keep the top portion for your records. -------------------

Form W-4
Department of the Treasury
Internal Revenue Service

Employee's Withholding Allowance Certificate
▶ **For Privacy Act and Paperwork Reduction Act Notice, see reverse.**

OMB No. 1545-0010
19**90**

1 Type or print your first name and middle initial	Last name	2 Your social security number

Home address (number and street or rural route)

City or town, state, and ZIP code

3 Marital status
☐ Single ☐ Married
☐ Married, but withhold at higher Single rate.
Note: *If married, but legally separated, or spouse is a nonresident alien, check the Single box.*

4 Total number of allowances you are claiming (from line G above or from the Worksheets on back if they apply) . . . **4** _____

5 Additional amount, if any, you want deducted from each pay . . . . **5** $ _____

6 I claim exemption from withholding and I certify that I meet **ALL** of the following conditions for exemption:
- Last year I had a right to a refund of **ALL** Federal income tax withheld because I had **NO** tax liability; **AND**
- This year I expect a refund of **ALL** Federal income tax withheld because I expect to have **NO** tax liability; **AND**
- This year if my income exceeds $500 and includes nonwage income, another person cannot claim me as a dependent.

If you meet all of the above conditions, enter the year effective and "EXEMPT" here . . . . . ▶ **6** | 19

7 Are you a full-time student? (**Note:** *Full-time students are not automatically exempt.*) . . . . **7** ☐ Yes ☐ No

Under penalties of perjury, I certify that I am entitled to the number of withholding allowances claimed on this certificate or entitled to claim exempt status.

Employee's signature ▶

Date ▶ , 19

8 Employer's name and address (**Employer:** Complete 8 and 10 **only if sending to IRS**) | **9** Office code (optional) | **10** Employer identification number

Figure 11-3

Form W-4

Form W-4 (1990)　　　　　　　　　　　　　　　　　　　　　　　　　　　　　　Page **2**

Deductions and Adjustments Worksheet

Note: *Use this worksheet only if you plan to itemize deductions or claim adjustments to income on your 1990 tax return.*

1 Enter an estimate of your 1990 itemized deductions. These include: qualifying home mortgage interest, 10% of personal interest, charitable contributions, state and local taxes (but not sales taxes), medical expenses in excess of 7.5% of your income, and miscellaneous deductions (most miscellaneous deductions are now deductible only in excess of 2% of your income)	1 $ _____
2 Enter: { $5,450 if married filing jointly or qualifying widow(er) / $4,750 if head of household / $3,250 if single / $2,725 if married filing separately }	2 $ _____
3 **Subtract** line 2 from line 1. If line 2 is greater than line 1, enter zero	3 $ _____
4 Enter an estimate of your 1990 adjustments to income. These include alimony paid and deductible IRA contributions .	4 $ _____
5 **Add** lines 3 and 4 and enter the total	5 $ _____
6 Enter an estimate of your 1990 nonwage income (such as dividends or interest income)	6 $ _____
7 **Subtract** line 6 from line 5. Enter the result, but not less than zero	7 $ _____
8 **Divide** the amount on line 7 by $2,000 and enter the result here. Drop any fraction	8 _____
9 Enter the number from Personal Allowances Worksheet, line G, on page 1	9 _____
10 **Add** lines 8 and 9 and enter the total here. If you plan to use the Two-Earner/Two-Job Worksheet, also enter the total on line 1, below. Otherwise, **stop here** and enter this total on Form W-4, line 4 on page 1	10 _____

Two-Earner/Two-Job Worksheet

Note: *Use this worksheet only if the instructions at line G on page 1 direct you here.*

1 Enter the number from line G on page 1 (or from line 10 above if you used the Deductions and Adjustments Worksheet) .	1 _____
2 Find the number in **Table 1** below that applies to the **LOWEST** paying job and enter it here	2 _____
3 If line 1 is **GREATER THAN OR EQUAL TO** line 2, subtract line 2 from line 1. Enter the result here (if zero, enter "0") and on Form W-4, line 4, on page 1. **DO NOT** use the rest of this worksheet	3 _____

Note: *If line 1 is **LESS THAN** line 2, enter "0" on Form W-4, line 4, on page 1. Complete lines 4–9 to calculate the additional dollar withholding necessary to avoid a year-end tax bill.*

4 Enter the number from line 2 of this worksheet	4 _____
5 Enter the number from line 1 of this worksheet	5 _____
6 **Subtract** line 5 from line 4	6 _____
7 Find the amount in **Table 2** below that applies to the **HIGHEST** paying job and enter it here	7 $ _____
8 **Multiply** line 7 by line 6 and enter the result here. This is the additional annual withholding amount needed	8 $ _____
9 Divide line 8 by the number of pay periods each year. (For example, divide by 26 if you are paid every other week.) Enter the result here and on Form W-4, line 5, page 1. This is the additional amount to be withheld from each paycheck . . .	9 $ _____

Table 1: Two-Earner/Two-Job Worksheet

Married Filing Jointly		All Others	
If wages from **LOWEST** paying job are—	Enter on line 2 above	If wages from **LOWEST** paying job are—	Enter on line 2 above
0 - $4,000	0	0 - $4,000	0
4,001 - 8,000	1	4,001 - 8,000	1
8,001 - 19,000	2	8,001 - 14,000	2
19,001 - 23,000	3	14,001 - 16,000	3
23,001 - 25,000	4	16,001 - 21,000	4
25,001 - 27,000	5	21,001 and over	5
27,001 - 29,000	6		
29,001 - 35,000	7		
35,001 - 41,000	8		
41,001 - 46,000	9		
46,001 and over	10		

Table 2: Two-Earner/Two-Job Worksheet

Married Filing Jointly		All Others	
If wages from **HIGHEST** paying job are—	Enter on line 7 above	If wages from **HIGHEST** paying job are—	Enter on line 7 above
0 - $44,000	$310	0 - $25,000	$310
44,001 - 90,000	570	25,001 - 52,000	570
90,001 and over	680	52,001 and over	680

Figure 11-3 (cont'd)

Form W-4

EMPLOYMENT ELIGIBILITY VERIFICATION (Form I-9)

1 **EMPLOYEE INFORMATION AND VERIFICATION:** (To be completed and signed by employee.)

Name: (Print or Type) Last	First	Middle	Birth Name

Address: Street Name and Number	City	State	ZIP Code

Date of Birth (Month/Day/Year)	Social Security Number

I attest, under penalty of perjury, that I am (check a box):

☐ 1. A citizen or national of the United States.

☐ 2. An alien lawfully admitted for permanent residence (Alien Number A _____).

☐ 3. An alien authorized by the Immigration and Naturalization Service to work in the United States (Alien Number A _____ . or Admission Number _____ , expiration of employment authorization, if any _____).

I attest, under penalty of perjury, the documents that I have presented as evidence of identity and employment eligibility are genuine and relate to me. I am aware that federal law provides for imprisonment and/or fine for any false statements or use of false documents in connection with this certificate.

Signature	Date (Month/Day/Year)

PREPARER/TRANSLATOR CERTIFICATION (To be completed if prepared by person other than the employee). I attest, under penalty of perjury, that the above was prepared by me at the request of the named individual and is based on all information of which I have any knowledge.

Signature	Name (Print or Type)		
Address (Street Name and Number)	City	State	Zip Code

2 **EMPLOYER REVIEW AND VERIFICATION:** (To be completed and signed by employer.)

Instructions:

Examine one document from List A and check the appropriate box, **OR** examine one document from List B **and** one from List C and check the appropriate boxes. Provide the **Document Identification Number** and **Expiration Date** for the document checked.

List A	List B		List C
Documents that Establish Identity and Employment Eligibility	Documents that Establish Identity	**and**	Documents that Establish Employment Eligibility

List A

☐ 1. United States Passport

☐ 2. Certificate of United States Citizenship

☐ 3. Certificate of Naturalization

☐ 4. Unexpired foreign passport with attached Employment Authorization

☐ 5. Alien Registration Card with photograph

List B

☐ 1. A State-issued driver's license or a State-issued I.D. card with a photograph, or information, including name, sex, date of birth, height, weight, and color of eyes. (Specify State)_____)

☐ 2. U.S. Military Card

☐ 3. Other (Specify document and issuing authority)
_____

List C

☐ 1. Original Social Security Number Card (other than a card stating it is not valid for employment)

☐ 2. A birth certificate issued by State, county, or municipal authority bearing a seal or other certification

☐ 3. Unexpired INS Employment Authorization Specify form
_____

Document Identification

_____

Expiration Date (if any)

_____

Document Identification

_____

Expiration Date (if any)

_____

Document Identification

_____

Expiration Date (if any)

_____

CERTIFICATION: I attest, under penalty of perjury, that I have examined the documents presented by the above individual, that they appear to be genuine and to relate to the individual named, and that the individual, to the best of my knowledge, is eligible to work in the United States.

Signature	Name (Print or Type)	Title
Employer Name	Address	Date

Form I-9 (05/07/87)
OMB No. 1115-0136

U.S. Department of Justice
Immigration and Naturalization Service

Figure 11-4

Form I-9

Employment Eligibility Verification

> **NOTICE:** Authority for collecting the information on this form is in Title 8, United States Code, Section 1324A, which requires employers to verify employment eligibility of individuals on a form approved by the Attorney General. This form will be used to verify the individual's eligibility for employment in the United States. Failure to present this form for inspection to officers of the Immigration and Naturalization Service or Department of Labor within the time period specified by regulation, or improper completion or retention of this form, may be a violation of the above law and may result in a civil money penalty.

Section 1. Instructions to Employee/Preparer for completing this form

Instructions for the employee.

All employees, upon being hired, must complete Section 1 of this form. Any person hired after November 6, 1986 must complete this form. (For the purpose of completion of this form the term "hired" applies to those employed, recruited or referred for a fee.)

All employees must print or type their complete name, address, date of birth, and Social Security Number. The block which correctly indicates the employee's immigration status must be checked. If the second block is checked, the employee's Alien Registration Number must be provided. If the third block is checked, the employee's Alien Registration Number *or* Admission Number must be provided, as well as the date of expiration of that status, if it expires.

All employees whose present names differ from birth names, because of marriage or other reasons, must print or type their birth names in the appropriate space of Section 1. Also, employees whose names change after employment verification should report these changes to their employer.

All employees must sign and date the form.

Instructions for the preparer of the form, if not the employee.

If a person assists the employee with completing this form, the preparer must certify the form by signing it and printing or typing his or her complete name and address.

Section 2. Instructions to Employer for completing this form

(For the purpose of completion of this form, the term "employer" applies to employers and those who recruit or refer for a fee.)

Employers must complete this section by examining evidence of identity and employment eligibility, and:
- checking the appropriate box in List A *or* boxes in both Lists B and C;
- recording the document identification number and expiration date (if any);
- recording the type of form if not specifically identified in the list;
- signing the certification section.

NOTE: Employers are responsible for reverifying employment eligibility of employees whose employment eligibility documents carry an expiration date.

Copies of documentation presented by an individual for the purpose of establishing identity and employment eligibility may be copied and retained for the purpose of complying with the requirements of this form and no other purpose. Any copies of documentation made for this purpose should be maintained with this form.

Name changes of employees which occur after preparation of this form should be recorded on the form by lining through the old name, printing the new name and the reason (such as marriage), and dating and initialing the changes. Employers should not attempt to delete or erase the old name in any fashion.

RETENTION OF RECORDS.

The completed form must be retained by the employer for:
- three years after the date of hiring; or
- one year after the date the employment is terminated, whichever is later.

> Employers may photocopy or reprint this form as necessary.

U.S. Department of Justice
Immigration and Naturalization Service

OMB #1115-0136
Form I-9 (05 07 87)

Figure 11-4 (cont'd)

Form I-9

Hanging On to the Good Ones

Once you've found good employees, your focus shifts to keeping them. Here's the secret behind every good boss-employee relationship: clear communication and mutual respect.

Building that kind of relationship takes effort. It doesn't have to include raises or year-end bonuses — although those help. Here are some small things that don't cost you anything but still build company morale:

- Praise in public, criticize in private. This simple suggestion is solid gold. Compliment freely, but honestly. Empty praise is easily spotted and may actually build resentment. Be sure to share customer compliments as well. In contrast, be cautious in your criticism. Pass on only the valid complaints of your customer. If you find you have more to criticize than compliment, you'd probably be better off without the employee.

- Be a good communicator and a good listener. Don't be afraid of employee suggestions. Even if you suspect the idea won't work, if it won't cost you much, give it a try. We tried a different lumberyard when one of our foremen insisted on it. We only had to use that yard once. He understood immediately that our regular yard was giving us the best quality for the best price. Although it was a hassle, the experiment was worth the effort. The foreman knew we valued him because we listened to his suggestion.

- Learn to delegate. This is especially important in a growing company. We've grown from a two-person company to a business with an office, office staff and several crews. At first, we did all the work ourselves so we *knew* it was done right. Handing the responsibility over to someone else can be painful. But it's essential. If you can't delegate, you can't grow. This doesn't mean you have to lower your standards. You can still insist on the same quality from your crew — as long as they know ahead of time what your expectations are.

- Try creative rewards. Of course, wage increases work, but you've got to handle them fairly. Small tools, an extra vacation day, or restaurant gift certificates will also boost morale. And they won't lock you into a higher weekly paycheck. Be careful about giving a large year-end bonus unless it's tied to specific achievements. Otherwise, the employee may expect at least as much next year even if your cash flow doesn't allow it.

- Offer training or advanced education. Pay for all or a portion of worthwhile seminars. If good construction classes are available locally, offer a small raise for completing specific courses.

Handing responsibility over to someone else can be painful.

▌ Build team spirit. Provide company hats and jackets. Have weekly meetings and do as much listening as you do talking. We like to meet informally for breakfast once a week. Because the emphasis is social rather than business, it's not a requirement that anyone be there. Still, it's a rare employee who misses. We usually manage to get some business done, too.

▌ Be available. As long as your company stays small, it's hard not to be! But as you start running additional crews and become more tied to the office, your employees out in the field can feel abandoned. Make an effort to visit every job site at least once a day. Try to talk with each employee, even if it's only for a few minutes.

▌ Let all employees know you value their work. Don't assume anything. Granted, some employees take more hand-holding than others. But as long as they're doing a good job, it's worth the little extra time and effort it takes to let them know you appreciate it.

Keeping employees happy is an on-going job, one that's never finished. When your employees talk about "our" company instead of "your" company, you'll know you're succeeding.

Firing Employees

We'd like to say that you'll never have to fire an employee if you follow our hiring advice. We'd like to, but we can't. Unfortunately, even if you do your best in hiring and keeping employees happy, you still can make mistakes.

If you've never had to fire anyone, you probably don't know how painful it can be. It's our least favorite task — by a wide margin. But that's just the beginning. Firing someone usually increases your unemployment insurance rates and always creates legal exposure. Most employers will tell you that the unemployment laws are weighted against them. Employees will tell you the opposite. No matter who's right, terminating someone is both unpleasant and risky.

The first rule in firing is to be honest. Be tactful. But you're not doing anyone a favor by lying about the reasons for the termination. If the problem is poor-quality work, say it. If it's a clash of personalities, be frank about it.

Some employees are fired because of something they've done or failed to do. Sometimes it isn't the employee's fault at all. Maybe you don't have enough work to keep everyone busy. Maybe you want to hire lower-skilled (and lower-paid) employees. Maybe two employees have trouble getting along. You might be willing to put up with the more difficult of the two because he's a very productive worker. If you fire employees for reasons like these, be prepared for a confrontation.

But if you handle it right, you can avoid higher unemployment insurance rates when you fire problem employees. Your first line of defense is *documentation*. Keep track of mistakes, unexcused absences and fudged hours. Record days, times, and names. You must also have proof that the employee knew he or she wasn't working up to your standards. Put your complaints in writing. Then have the employee sign a statement that he's been warned that his work or behavior isn't satisfactory. If you decide to fire an employee, call your local unemployment office and find out what they require for evidence of justification.

Working with Subcontractors

Finding and keeping good subs is, in many ways, more difficult than finding and keeping employees. The best subs cost more. They'll be more dependable, responsible, and skillful, but you'll pay for it. In a strong market, that's not much of a handicap. In a weak one, high-priced subs will keep you from winning jobs. Even if your competitor's quality is no match for the quality you're offering, we all know that most work goes to the lowest bidder. You have to find competitive subs who maintain good quality standards. That's never easy.

We look for subs who'll represent us well. We expect our subs to be neat, courteous, and avoid smoking on the job. Obviously, they also have to do the job right the first time.

When subs treat us right, we treat them right. As long as they stay on schedule and do a good job, we pay them promptly. If they hold up the job or have call backs, we hold their check accordingly. Never pay a sub for more work than they've completed. Even if they say the new fixtures are in transit and will be installed by Monday, wait until the job is complete. After all, subs are like the rest of us. If they have their money, it's harder to fit those little details into the schedule.

Unfortunately, you can be held liable for any mistakes a sub makes. That's why your subs *have to* carry workers' compensation and public liability insurance. Any problems they have fall squarely in their laps. Get a little careless about requiring proof of coverage and your insurance carrier may end up paying for their mistakes. That's likely to raise your rates or get your coverage cancelled entirely.

What if the sub goes bankrupt, leaves town, or just throws in the towel while the work is under warranty? Any problems your sub won't take care of become *your* problems. That's a heavy burden to carry and another good reason to be careful when selecting subcontractors.

Generally, we don't cut a final check for a sub's work until we have proof of both workers' compensation and liability insurance. We also require the sub's federal Employer Identification Number (EIN) or his Social Security number, whichever he uses. You'll need it when you fill out Form 1099-MISC — and that's required, at the time of this writing, any time you pay a sub more than $600 in a calendar year. We'll explain more about this in a later chapter.

Remember to get lien waivers from your subs and their suppliers. You need to be protected, just as the homeowner does. If you pay a sub who hasn't paid his supplier, you can end up paying for materials twice. That can trim your profit to nothing — or worse.

Having good employees and subs will make your operation more profitable. But more is required, of course. It takes lots more to run a thriving remodeling business. One thing that's required is an efficient office. That's our subject in the next chapter.

12

Running an Efficient Office

*T*he wisdom in this chapter comes from some hard lessons. Our filing system began as a pile of papers on a desk — and deteriorated from there. For the first few years it was a rare quarter that we didn't have to pay some kind of late penalty. Tax time was a hell all its own. Our record keeping lapses nearly ruined our credit. We finally reached a crisis point when our checkbook and our bank statement were $1,800 apart — in the bank's favor.

Efficiency starts at your desk. You may think that the critical work is done at the job site. And certainly, much of it is. However, if you're disorganized in the office, it affects everything: estimating, scheduling, bookkeeping, cash flow, payroll — you name it!

Only good financial records can tell you if the company is making or losing money.

We've met very few contractors who actually like the paperwork side of construction. Yet a well-run office will make or break a business. That's where you keep track of costs. By itself, being busy doesn't tell you whether or not you're making money. Plenty of contractors have gone bankrupt with six months of work lined up. Only good financial records can tell you if the company is making or losing money. Think of it this way. The history of your company is being written every day in numbers: payables, receivables, assets, liabilities, expenses, income, overhead and profit. If you don't collect those numbers and organize them, you can't possibly understand where your company has been and where it's headed.

The record keeping system explained in this chapter works for us. But it wasn't created in a day. Instead, it's evolved over the last decade — and will continue to evolve as our business grows and changes. Take the parts of our system that you like and adapt them to your needs. Or put together a system of your own that you like better. Just don't make the mistake of thinking that because you're small, you can manage without files or monthly statements. No one is that small!

The Equipment You Need

For a beginning business, you don't need much. But what you do need is vital for survival. As a minimum, you need office space that's well-lit, warm, and can be isolated from other noise and distraction. In other words, the kitchen table is a poor place to start.

If you have a spare bedroom or can afford to rent a small office somewhere, great. But you can get along without them, especially in the remodeling business. You'll always sell jobs on site and have conferences with clients on their job. Even if you had an office, calling meetings there would be a waste of time. Working out of your house is economical and convenient. Set aside a room if you can, or just a corner somewhere if you can't.

If you work out of your house, you'll have to make a decision about the telephone. Installing a second phone line into the house costs very little and helps separate your business from your personal life. Of course, you (or whoever answers it) should be as professional as possible. Unless someone is always around during business hours, either get an answering machine or **an answering service**. If you rely on either of these, always return calls within 24 hours.

Here are the items we found mandatory for a startup remodeling company. You can buy them all for under $1,000 — or far less if you buy used equipment.

- Desk, comfortable chair

- Telephone, answering machine

- Calculator

- Phone index (like a Rolodex™ — a huge time saver!)

- Typewriter

- File cabinet (legal size) with file suspension hangers

- File folders (start with 100 folders)

- Bookcase

- Miscellaneous:

    Phone message book (use it faithfully)

    Typing paper

    Envelopes

    Stapler

    Paper clips

    Rubber bands

    White out correction fluid

    Pens, pencils, erasers

Notice that we didn't include a computer. Computers, as we'll explain a little later in this chapter, are wonderful. We can't imagine running a business without ours. But it's a luxury item, not a necessity. The price will be at least several thousand dollars and learning to use even a few basic programs can take months. Unless you have more startup cash than most, the computer will have to wait. After a year or two of experience, you'll have a better idea of what kind of hardware and software to buy.

Organizing the Files

We try to condense our essential files into one drawer. It keeps the clutter down and reminds us which jobs have priority. We've organized the first drawer into these sections:

1) Bids in progress
2) Jobs in progress
3) Current payroll records
4) Current financial records
5) Accounts payable and receivable
6) Supplier information

A second drawer holds these files:

1) Old bid proposals
2) Completed job records
3) Payroll records for former employees
4) Financial records from previous years
5) Workers' compensation and insurance policies
6) Product information
7) Vehicle maintenance records
8) Miscellaneous items

Let's take a closer look at each of these files.

Bids in progress

Each bid we do, no matter how small, has its own folder. The lead form (Chapter 3) is stapled to the inside for quick reference. It has the client's name, address, phone number, and a brief description of the project. All of the pertinent paperwork goes into the folder: checklists, take-off forms, notes, plans, estimates, subcontractor bids, contracts, and so on. Until we get a final yes or no from a client, the folder stays at the front of the drawer. That way we can tell at a glance what our potential workload is for the next few months.

Periodically, we go through the folders. Just because the client seems to have cooled on a project doesn't mean we throw the bid away. Occasionally a job will be revived. Only when we know the work has been started by another contractor do we move the proposal to the lower drawer. Every year we sort through the folders in the second drawer. We throw out the most obsolete folders unless they have further use as reference when selling or bidding new work.

Jobs in progress

Once we get a firm commitment, we add a second folder to each job. In the original folder we put the contract, change order forms, and payment (draw) information. We also write the building permit number on the lead form. The second folder holds all of the suppliers' invoices and subs' statements. We put these into the folders once a month, after they've been sorted and compared to the monthly statements. Manufacturers' warranties and product information cards go into a third folder we give to the client at the end of the job.

Once the last bill has been paid and the final draw collected on a job, we move the folder to the second drawer. Every January we move files that have been closed for at least a year into accessible storage. This way we keep files available for reference in case problems crop up during the 12-month warranty period.

Current employees

Each employee has his own folder. It holds his application, resume, W-4 and I-9 forms, and all of his time cards. Any warnings or disciplinary actions go into the folder, too.

We've used a variety of time cards. The one we prefer (Figure 12-1) has space for the job number, a description of the work, and start and stop times. We insist that the card is dated and signed. The work description helps us double-check against the time we allowed for the work in our cost estimate. The time worked is checked for accuracy on all time cards. Comparing starting and quitting times on

Time Card

Employee's name ______________________ Rate __________

Pay period beginning ______________ Ending ______________

Job number	Description of work	Time in	Time out
________	______________________	________	________
________	______________________	________	________
________	______________________	________	________
________	______________________	________	________
________	______________________	________	________
________	______________________	________	________

Total regular hours ______________

Total overtime ______________

Employee's signature ______________________ Date ______________

Figure 12-1
Time Card

cards for members on the same crew helps us spot mistakes or a crew member who's padding his time.

When an employee leaves, we move his folder, untouched, to the second drawer. After a year, we throw away the time cards, but everything else we keep. We save time cards for one year because employees can file for unemployment benefits up to one full year after quitting or being fired. Any other information (like unemployment filings or workers' compensation draws) goes in the folder.

We also keep our withholding folders and tax tables in this section. Every month we review the withholding information for each employee. That way, the numbers are complete and handy when we prepare our quarterly tax reports. What used to take an afternoon now takes an hour — even though we have more information to process.

Bookkeeping

Every month we start a new file folder to hold income and expense records for that month. This folder will have a record of all receipts and expenses and job-to-date figures for that month. We'll explain our bookkeeping system in Chapter 14. In addition to the twelve monthly folders, we have a tax folder that holds receipts for donations and other deductible items.

In April each year, the previous year's monthly printouts, the quarterly and year-end information, and Federal and State reports go into a single folder for quick reference. The IRS requires that you keep all paperwork for seven years. If your printouts are concise, they shouldn't take up too much space. You can keep them indefinitely.

It's also helpful to have a folder to hold deposit slips and any other banking transactions. Once you've compared them against the bank statement, they can be filed with the statement. If the bank makes a mistake — which is certainly possible — you'll have proof at your fingertips.

Accounts payable and receivable

This section actually consists of eight or ten folders. The accounts payable folder contains every unpaid bill. Most of our suppliers give a discount if we pay by the tenth of the month, so we pay most of our bills then. We pay bills a second time around the twentieth of the month for those that don't give a discount.

Because of the kind of jobs we do, we don't worry too much about an accounts receivable folder. If we did a lot of small jobs and sent out billings, we'd keep track of those in folders marked *Current*, *30 days*, and *60 days*. By breaking them down into three folders, you can see at a glance where the collection problems are.

The remaining folders hold invoices from suppliers. We break ours down into categories: concrete, paint, drywall, trash, rentals, cash, charge cards (for gas), and miscellaneous. Because we use several lumberyards regularly, we have separate folders for each of them. No invoice is paid until we compare what was ordered to what was delivered and what we're being billed for. We also check to be sure we've been credited for all returns. Our suppliers rarely make mistakes, but when they do, we want to catch them, not pay for them.

Suppliers

After paying the monthly statements, we staple the invoices to the statements and put them in a "Paid Invoice" file. If the supplier sends two invoices, we put one in the job folder and attach the other one to the statement. Most paid invoices are filed by category (such as Rental Equipment or Flooring). But we have a separate file for each of our major suppliers. We also have a separate folder for shop and office invoices.

In January of each new year, we put all the paid statements from the past year into storage along with the year-old completed job folders.

Workers' compensation, liability, and other insurance

These are items that we rarely refer to. Yet the information has to be accessible. In this section, we also have folders for copies of our subcontractors' workers' comp and liability policies.

Product information

There isn't a day that goes by that we don't get some kind of information from manufacturers and suppliers. Some of it gets trashed immediately. The rest we file by product groupings (cabinets, windows, doors, etc.). This section needs to be sorted yearly or it will bury your office very quickly.

Vehicle information

We keep maintenance records on all vehicles. This extra paperwork pays for itself when we sell a truck or piece of machinery.

Miscellaneous items

This is a catch-all section. Occasionally, we get important information from subs that we want to keep. We don't have a folder for each sub because most information that concerns subcontractors is filed elsewhere. For instance, certificates of insurance from subs are filed under "Insurance." We write each sub's EIN or social security number on his card in the telephone file, along with his address and phone number.

Filing is a simple, mindless task. Because it's boring, it's tough to make the time to do it. The worst thing you can do is let a pile of papers collect. Clear your desk every evening so you can start fresh in the morning.

Remember, too, there's nothing sacred about the system we've suggested. If your folders sit empty for a year, you don't need that particular category. If, on the other hand, you collect papers that don't fit into any of these files, create a new file.

Managing Your Time

Long ago we noticed that the more we had to do, the more we got done. If we had two weeks between jobs, we could usually figure on the first job running two weeks behind schedule. But if we had a client pushing us to get started, we'd finish the same job well ahead of schedule. That's just human nature. The time needed to finish the work expands to fill the time available to do the work. Whatever the reason, it's an expensive, inefficient work routine.

Organize Your Tasks

Wise time management is the best defense against lazy work habits. Eliminating time wasters, increasing efficiency, and ending procrastination are all necessary steps. It all comes down to *organization*. And it starts with you.

Begin by making daily and weekly lists of tasks you need to tackle. Note, too, when you want to finish each item. Then set mini-deadlines. If you expect a task will take four hours, break the job into four parts. Plan to finish the first 1/4 in the first hour, the second 1/4 in the second hour and so on. If, at the end of the first hour, you're behind schedule, get serious about finishing more than you had planned in the second hour. Setting realistic intermediate deadlines should improve your motivation early enough to help you finish by the final deadline. Don't be too demanding, though. Don't feel discouraged about the whole day if you miss the first deadline.

When you've completed your list, assign priorities. Most people are tempted to start with the easy tasks and work toward the more difficult. That's backwards. Instead, item number one should be the least liked, most difficult task of the day. Doing it first will accomplish two things. One, you'll be at your freshest and most energetic when you handle it. And two, you'll try to get it done quickly so you can get to the items you enjoy (or at least don't mind doing).

If you need to, break the task into smaller parts and spread them out over several days. By segmenting an item, you can reduce an overwhelming job into manageable parts. Don't worry too much about getting every last detail perfect. Sometimes the drive for perfection can bog you down. It's much easier to come back a second day and check for minor errors.

Before you start any job, think it through. You know it's important to analyze a construction job before you begin. It's just as vital for office tasks. What's the critical path for the pile on your desk? Can any of it be delegated? Is it all essential? Or is some of it busywork you're using to avoid tackling more important but more difficult work?

We know several people who are a little nutty about using their computers. They churn out paperwork by the yard. Most of it's probably a waste of time, like figuring the ratio of every employee's cost to the job total, or how the overhead percentage will drop by a fraction of a percent if they lease a truck instead of buying it outright. But are those things essential? Remember, it takes time to do the calculations and analyze the results. Try to concentrate your time where it's the most productive.

Reduce Paperwork Handling

Because paperwork can pile up so quickly, keep these tips in mind:

1) Handle mail only once. If it's trash when you first look at it, it's still going to be trash two days later. Immediately file all bills in the accounts payable folder. Product information should go into its appropriate file. If you don't know what to do with it, either create a new file or put it in the most logical folder you already have. One way or another, make a decision. Have a logical place for every piece of paper — even if you need a 30-gallon trash can!

2) When you read a letter that needs a response, jot your thoughts on the back. When you sit down to write a formal reply later that day or the next, you'll have a head start.

3) *File daily.* Don't leave your office without a clear desk. It's all right to have a pile prioritized for the next day, but don't leave anything there that you won't finish within 24 hours.

Use Your Time Productively

Too much socializing is a real time waster. Some people waste hours on the phone, others around the coffee pot. Even if you don't think it's a problem for you, try keeping track of your conversation time for a day. Just being conscious of the time you're spending is an incentive to be more efficient. Keep in mind, too, that your visiting should have a purpose and a result. Of course you want to keep in touch with the architect who may send work your way. But that's no excuse for wasting an hour of his time on the phone. A friendly, five-minute conversation will do as much. Jot a few notes before dialing so you stick to the topic.

Remember that you set the example for the company. If you waste time, expect others to do the same. Don't waste time in idle chatter while someone is waiting for your help. That's setting the worst possible example. If you take a two-hour lunch, what does that suggest to your crew? If you feel like taking a half hour instead of a 15 minute coffee break, multiply that by the number of your employees. That 15 extra minutes can inflate into an hour or two each day that you're paying for nonproductive time. Set the example. It's up to you to create a productive atmosphere.

Computers or No Computers

Our computer is a magic machine. We don't use it for everything a computer can do, just for the things a computer does best: bookkeeping, estimating, and word processing. On these tasks our computer has cut the time spent by one-half. Yes, we could survive without it; we did for five years. Although a computer may not be in your first year's budget, sooner or later you'll be smart to take the leap.

It's not easy to know when it's time to buy a computer. Part of the decision depends on you. How willing are you to spend time selecting the right programs and learning to use them? The rest of the decision depends on your business. How much time and effort can you save? What tasks could you handle better on the computer?

To make a good decision on questions like these, you should begin with realistic expectations — knowing what a computer can, and can't, do. Consider these facts before making your decision.

▪ If you're completely disorganized now, a computer will just compound the disorganization. You need to have a working system in place before switching to a computer. A computer won't organize chaos. Humans still have to do their part.

▪ You'll still make mistakes with computers — you'll just make them faster and bigger. If you put the wrong numbers in, you'll get the wrong numbers out.

▪ Computers don't do anything you can't already do. They just do it faster. They can save you so much time you're able to do two or three or ten times as much as you could before. This doesn't mean you can cut back on staff. It only means that your staff should be more productive.

▪ Learning to use a computer takes time. Depending on the size of your company and how many operations you're switching over, it may take years. Furthermore, in the beginning you'll have twice the work — using both the old system and the new system until the new system is reliable. It's deadly to abandon your old way of keeping records before the new system is perfected.

When you finally decide you're ready, the most important thing you need is information. The next section is a starting point. Computer technology changes very quickly. Almost anything we can tell you will be out of date before you read these pages. The best advice is to select a computer and select computer programs the same way you select a doctor or a lawyer. Get the recommendation of someone you know and trust. Ask questions, talk to people, find someone in a business like yours who's using a computer and is satisfied with it. That's the best recommendation possible. If you don't know anyone in that category, pick up a few computer magazines at a news rack. Most include reviews and ratings of computers and programs (software).

Once you have an idea what you need and want, start talking to computer salesmen. Not just one, either. Talk to a half dozen. Explain what your business needs. (Use a form like Figure 12-2 to organize your information.) Describe what your needs will be in the next three to five years. But don't buy more than you really need. Anything you buy will almost certainly be obsolete in three years.

Worksheet for Computer Needs

Number of:	Current	In 3-5 years
Customer accounts	_____	_____
Statements sent per month	_____	_____
Payments received per month	_____	_____
Suppliers/creditors	_____	_____
Checks written per month	_____	_____
General ledger line items/mo.	_____	_____
Employees	_____	_____
Jobs going at one time	_____	_____
Standard documents on file	_____	_____

Figure 12-2
Computer needs worksheet

In case you're a complete neophyte, we've defined some common terms you'll need to know to shop for your first computer.

Hardware — This is the computer, printer, monitor, etc. Hardware alone can't do any of your work, not even word processing.

Central processing unit — The CPU is like the traffic cop at the central crossroads of a computer. It's about the size of your thumb, plugs into the computer and controls the way the computer works. Computers are usually classified by the CPU they use. The first of the modern personal computers (the I.B.M. PC and I.B.M. XT) had 8086 or 8088 CPUs made by Intel. These computers are now obsolete. Next came the AT computer with a 80286 CPU. For most of the work you do, an AT (80286) computer will be good enough. For more speed and larger memory capacity (and a few hundred dollars more), select a computer with a 80386 or

80386SX CPU. The next generation of computers (80486) is faster still. But you need power like that only if you're working with drawing or CAD (computer aided design) programs.

Disk drive — A magnetic storage device which allows the CPU to read data from memory and store it permanently on a disk covered with a magnetic coating. This data isn't lost when the power goes off. Most computers have at least two disk drives, usually a removable 5-1/4" or 3-1/2" floppy disk drive and a hard disk drive that can't be removed. A floppy disk has capacity for a few dozen letters or estimates. Even a small hard disk (20 Mb) can hold thousands — plus the programs needed to create those documents. Floppy disk drives cost about $100. A hard disk will usually cost about $500.

Video terminal or *monitor* — This is the screen the computer uses to display information. It's often called a monitor, a VDT (video display tube) or a CRT (cathode ray tube). You can choose a monochrome (such as black and white) or a color monitor. In many computers, the monitor can only display text. To display graphics such as charts or pictures, you install an additional circuit board called a graphics adapter inside the computer. The modern standard for monitors is called *VGA* and produces an image that's clear and sharp, whether you're displaying letters and numbers or pictures.

Keyboard — This is the part that looks like a typewriter. It often has a separate set of keys with the digits 0-9 arranged like a 10-key adding machine. This is called a numeric keypad. The keyboard also has some special keys which are not on a typewriter: *Control*, *Alt* (alternate), *Option*, and *Esc* (escape). These function something like additional shift keys with some types of software.

Mouse — A mouse is a pointing device. It lets you select things on the screen without using the keyboard. A mouse is usually a small hand-held device with a ball on the bottom and one or more buttons on the top. As you move the mouse across the desk top, it moves a display pointer (or *cursor*) around the display screen. That lets you point at text or select choices on the screen. Just push the mouse buttons to select whatever the cursor is pointing to. Some software programs require a mouse, but most don't.

Printer — There are three kinds on printers: dot matrix, character and laser. The first uses wires or pins to print closely-spaced dots on the paper in a pattern which forms the text characters. It can also print pictures or graphics. The more pins (and hence dots) the printer has, the higher the quality of the text, but the slower the printing. The price also goes up with the number of pins. Common dot-matrix printers have 9 or 24 pins. Prices start around $300.

A character, or letter-quality, printer is a typewriter run by a computer. It usually has a type ball or type wheel, like modern typewriters. The quality of type is excellent, but the printing tends to be slow. Also, a character printer can't produce graphics. High quality dot-matrix printers and laser printers have nearly replaced character printers.

A laser printer can produce type in several different type faces and in many sizes. The type is exceptionally high-quality, like type you would see in a book. In fact, the page you're reading was produced with a laser printer. Most can produce pages faster than you can read them. Laser printers are equally good at reproducing drawings and pictures, although it usually takes longer than producing pages of type. Prices start at about $1,000.

Cables — These connect the different computer parts so they can communicate with each other.

Memory (RAM)— In simple terms, the random access memory (RAM) is the information capacity of a computer. It's the data storage used directly by the CPU. All information used by the CPU must first be transferred into or out of memory. Information in RAM will be lost if the power goes off.

Memory is measured in storage units called bytes. Each byte holds one character of information. One thousand twenty-four bytes is referred to as one kilobyte (KB) of memory, and 1024 times 1024 bytes is called a megabyte (MB) of memory. Most small computers today come with at least one megabyte of memory. If you plan to use programs such as *Lotus 1-2-3, Excel,* or *dBase*, you'll probably want at least 1 or 2 megabytes of additional (expanded) memory.

Software — The programs you buy to run a computer are called software. You can buy packaged software that's sitting on the shelf ready to use. Or you can hire someone to create custom software for you. A third option is to buy a package and have it modified to suit your needs. The first option is by far the cheapest, but you may have trouble finding a program that meets your exact needs. The second should give you the exact program you need, but the price may be more than you can pay. The third is a good compromise. But most powerful, professional-quality programs aren't intended to be modified by the user.

Surge protector — It buffers the computer from power surges that can destroy it. Expensive ones can even provide some backup battery power. A surge protector is the cheapest and most effective insurance you can buy. Consider a UPS (uninterruptable power supply) and surge protection if your power supply isn't reliable and stable.

Documentation — This refers to the instruction manuals for the hardware and the software.

Computer Functions

What will all of this equipment do for you? To begin with, computers will perform four basic functions:

1) Word processing, such as contracts, bids and business letters

2) Calculations, such as bookkeeping

3) Data management, such as keeping track of your receivables

4) Graphics, such as drawing plans and diagrams

You do all of these things anyway. You type a letter, figure an estimate on your calculator, maintain your files and draw your plans. Let's see how you can do them faster on your computer.

Word processing

This is sometimes called text management. The joy of word processing is that you can save the text and change it later without having to retype it. A client wants to make a single change on the contract? Simple. All you do is bring it up on the computer screen, make the change and reprint it. You can also change the layout of a page, check spelling, or move sentences, paragraphs, or even entire pages around within a document. The computer makes it easy to save standard letters and contracts to use over and over.

Numeric calculations

For calculating, you can't beat a computer. One popular computer application is the electronic spreadsheet. Use it to total a column of figures (in an estimate) or a row of numbers (in a bid). The computer never misreads a 7 for a 9, nor does it make computation errors. We use an electronic spreadsheet for accounting, estimating, and job costing.

Data management

We keep an electronic file folder of information on each customer: name, address, bid information, supplies and materials used, billing done, and so on. Our data management program lets us sort the data the way we want and call up any information that's needed. For example, we can sort our clients by zip code and then print mailing labels.

Graphics

Computers are good at creating graphs, charts and drawings. Computer aided design (CAD) programs can produce plans and even three-dimensional pictures. Wouldn't selling be easier if you could "walk" a client through her new addition or show her what kind of space her remodeled kitchen will have?

Buying Right

Too many contractors make the mistake of buying their hardware first and then looking for software. Although most software is either Apple or IBM compatible, plenty of it only works with one computer or the other and some work with neither. If you buy an Apple computer and decide you like programs created for an IBM, you're out of luck. We recommend shopping for software first, then buying the hardware to match.

An industry rule of thumb is to spend 40 percent of your total investment on the hardware and 60 percent on software. That's not what we did, though. We've been very happy with an inexpensive word processing program and an electronic spreadsheet. Combined, they cost around $400. Our hardware cost just under $3,000 when we bought it five years ago. You can see that our ratio was considerably different, and we've still been very pleased with our investment.

Keep in mind that you'll have additional expenses besides hardware and software. Computer paper and ribbons are more expensive than their typewriter counterparts. In addition, you'll need diskettes, tapes, and preprinted checks and stationery to use in your computer printer. The cost of the supplies should be manageable. But maintenance can bust your budget.

You can buy a maintenance contract. In effect, it's an insurance policy. If something goes wrong with your equipment during the contract period, it'll be fixed free. If nothing goes wrong, you're out the money. If you buy a quality piece of equipment, you really shouldn't need the maintenance contract. In five years we haven't had any problems except dust under the keys. We can handle that ourselves.

Reduce maintenance costs by taking good care of your equipment. Buy a dust cover and use it. And don't drink or eat around the equipment. Since dirt and dust are a computer's biggest enemies, an hour of preventive maintenance once a month is a good idea. Cleaning the machine's exterior, printer units, disk drive heads, keyboard, and screen will prevent most problems.

Probably more disasters come from mistreating software than hardware. Follow the manufacturer's suggestions for caring for their products. At least weekly, back up your important files on floppy disk. That way you have an extra copy when the hard disk fails — and eventually every hard disk will fail.

There's so much software on the market it's hard to know where to begin. Fortunately, *Remodeling* magazine carries an annual software directory each May that's loaded with information. Note that it's not a review. It doesn't tell you which have the best features or is the best value. Instead, it gives current costs, applications, systems requirements, and so on, as well as addresses and phone numbers for the software companies.

Before you buy any software, find out what support is provided. Good software should come with a tutorial disk or an easy-to-read manual. The manufacturer should also provide a toll-free number for questions or problems. Your dealer should also back what he sells with a knowledgeable staff. You'll get better prices by buying through the mail. But the little extra you pay to buy through a local dealer may pay dividends when something goes wrong.

Most important, don't be intimidated by what you've bought. It's really just a fancy typewriter/calculator/filing cabinet/drawing tablet that can do more than you ever dreamed possible. You should be comfortable with it in a matter of days. In a few months, you'll probably become an expert!

13

The Paper Shuffle

*B*y nature, we're not violent people. But ten years ago, at the end of every quarter, we'd get an almost uncontrollable urge to load up the pickup with river rock, drive over to the IRS office, and let fly at their picture windows.

Their forms confused us. Our bookkeeping appalled us. Worst of all, during most quarters we had to dip into the money withheld from our employees' checks to pay bills. The result was a financial and emotional crisis at the end of every calendar quarter.

Today, we don't even like to think about those bad old days. And we don't have to. We've changed the way we do business. Good sense prevailed. The IRS office still has their window glass intact. Really, it wasn't their fault. It was our fault. We hadn't learned to shuffle paperwork like every legitimate business must.

"It's almost tax time. I like to be prepared in advance."

Now it's different. We've straightened out our books. We've learned what to do and how to do it. This quarter's forms are about like last quarter's forms. It's all strictly routine. We even take pride in how smooth and easy it is to comply with the law.

If your company is still back where we were ten years ago, take heart. It doesn't have to be that way. Meeting federal, state and local requirements doesn't have to be a headache. You don't have to lie awake nights worrying that your company is going to be shut down for nonpayment of taxes or that an audit is going to bankrupt you. There's a better way. We expect that this chapter will put you on the right road.

Complying with tax regulations requires that you keep accurate payroll, income and expense records. Without these records, there isn't much hope. In the next chapter, we'll cover recording income and expenses. We'll also explain how to record payroll expense and collect the information needed to fill out state and federal tax forms. The subject of this chapter is how to complete the forms themselves.

You might want to consider having a payroll service prepare your payroll and payroll tax forms. The cost is only about $50 a month. Some banks will do it at minimal cost for good customers. But if you decide to do it yourself, here's how.

Depending on your payroll size, you may make tax deposits weekly, monthly, quarterly or annually. Of course, if your payroll is large enough to require weekly deposits, you'll need weekly instead of monthly totals.

In addition to the federal paperwork, you'll have to meet state requirements. Because state tax deposits are much smaller, many remodelers may be able to make state deposits quarterly or even annually, even if you make federal deposits more frequently.

The Federal Tax Forms

You'll have to file a Form 8109 with each deposit, plus several informational forms throughout the year. Here's a summary of what's required on each federal form. Later we'll look at these forms in more detail.

1) Form 8109, Federal Tax Deposit Coupon— This is a check-size form you take to your bank with a check for the amount due. Fill out a separate 8109 for each type of tax being deposited. Deposit the payment and Form 8109 with an authorized financial institution or with a Federal Reserve bank or branch. Almost any bank or savings and loan where you have an account will accept deposits.

2) Form 941, Employer's Quarterly Federal Tax Return— You report three items on the 941: federal taxes and social security taxes (FICA) withheld from employees, your matching FICA taxes, and earned income credit (EIC) payments you make to your employees. Deposits for the 941 may be required weekly, monthly, quarterly, or annually, depending on the size of your payroll.

3) Form 940, Employer's Annual Federal Unemployment Tax (FUTA)— This form is due by January 31 each year. Again, depending on the size of your payroll, you'll make deposits annually or more frequently. This particular tax is sometimes called a "contribution" because you don't withhold anything from the employee's paycheck. The employer pays it all.

4) W-2, Wage and Tax Statement— Every employer has to complete a W-2 annually for each employee. You'll send one copy to the Social Security Administration, one to your state tax department and three to the employee. The sixth copy is for your records.

5) W-3, Transmittal of Income and Tax Statements— The W-3 reports all of the information from the W-2's.

6) Form 1099-MISC, Miscellaneous Income Report— The 1099 is like a W-2 for non-employees. Use it to report the amount you pay to subcontractors each year. Currently, you must report any amount over $600 paid to an unincorporated business or individual. It's a three-part form. Send one copy to the IRS, one to the subcontractor, and keep one for your files.

7) Form 1096, Annual Summary and Transmittal of U.S. Information Returns— This report accompanies and summarizes the information from the 1099. Send it with the IRS's copies.

Make certain you keep copies of each form you file. They're good for quick reference. Even more important, when the IRS has a question about your numbers, you can refer to your own copy.

Also remember that each state will have filing requirements. In Colorado we make deposits for state withholding, state unemployment, and workers' compensation. Check the requirements for your state.

In the next section, we'll show you how to fill out the forms, line by line. Figure 13-1 shows the payroll information we've used for our sample forms. In the next chapter, you'll see that our bookkeeping system keeps track of more information than we show here. In Figure 13-1, we've only included the information needed for the 941, 940, and W-2's. To keep it simple, we've assumed that this company has only three employees, with no turnover for the year.

Form 941, Employer's Quarterly Federal Tax Return

You have to submit a completed 941 by the last day of the month following the end of each quarter:

Quarter Ending	Due Date
March 31	April 30
June 30	July 31
September 30	Oct. 31
December 31	Jan. 31

Your deposits, which include both the federal withholding and social security taxes, are due according to the following schedule:

■ Less than $500 at the end of a quarter— If, at the end of the quarter, your total undeposited taxes for the quarter are less than $500, you don't have to make a deposit. You can pay the taxes to the IRS when you mail Form 941 or deposit them by the 941 due date.

■ Less than $500 at the end of any month— If, at the end of any *month*, your total undeposited taxes are less than $500, you don't have to make a deposit. You can carry over the taxes to the following month within the quarter.

Date	Check #	Emp.#	A Wages	B FICA	C FWT
1/13	2087	200	$800	$120.16	$80
1/13	2088	201	560	84.11	79
1/13	2089	202	640	96.13	68
1/27	2130	200	740	111.14	71
1/27	2131	201	500	75.10	70
1/27	2132	202	640	96.13	68
January totals			**$3,880**	**$582.77**	**$436**
2/10	2178	200	$800	$120.16	$80
2/10	2179	201	560	84.11	79
2/10	2180	202	640	96.13	68
2/24	2254	200	860	129.17	89
2/24	2255	201	595	89.37	82
2/24	2256	202	700	105.14	77
February totals			**$4,155**	**$624.08**	**$475**
3/10	2310	200	$750	$112.65	$71
3/10	2311	201	540	81.11	76
3/10	2312	202	600	90.12	62
3/24	2345	200	800	120.16	80
3/24	2346	201	560	84.11	79
3/24	2347	202	640	96.13	68
March totals			**$3,890**	**$584.28**	**$436**
4/7	2392	200	$800	$120.16	$80
4/7	2393	201	560	84.11	79
4/7	2394	202	640	96.13	68
4/21	2438	200	800	120.16	80
4/21	2439	201	560	84.11	79
4/21	2440	202	640	96.13	68
April totals			**$4,000**	**$600.80**	**$454**
5/5	2498	200	$860	$129.17	$89
5/5	2499	201	595	89.37	82
5/5	2500	202	700	105.14	77
5/19	2562	200	740	111.14	71
5/19	2563	201	500	75.10	70
5/19	2564	202	640	96.13	68
May totals			**$4,035**	**$606.05**	**$457**
6/2	2601	200	$800	$120.16	$80
6/2	2602	201	560	84.11	79
6/2	2603	202	640	96.13	68
6/16	2638	200	800	120.16	80
6/16	2639	201	560	84.11	79

Figure 13-1

Wage and withholding information

Date	Check #	Emp.#	A Wages	B FICA	C FWT
6/16	2640	202	640	96.13	68
6/23	2675	200	400	60.08	40
6/30	2689	201	610	91.62	85
6/30	2690	202	720	108.14	80
June totals			**$5,730**	**$860.64**	**$659**
7/14	2768	200	$400	$60.08	$40
7/14	2769	201	560	84.11	79
7/14	2770	202	640	96.13	68
7/28	2810	200	800	120.16	80
7/28	2811	201	560	84.11	79
7/28	2812	202	640	96.13	68
July totals			**$3,600**	**$540.72**	**$414**
8/11	2859	200	$800	$120.16	$80
8/11	2860	201	560	84.11	79
8/11	2861	202	640	96.13	68
8/25	2912	200	800	120.16	80
8/25	2913	201	560	84.11	79
8/25	2914	202	640	96.13	68
August totals			**$4,000**	**$600.80**	**$454**
9/8	2987	200	$800	$120.16	$80
9/8	2988	201	560	84.11	79
9/8	2989	202	640	96.13	68
9/22	3030	200	740	111.14	71
9/22	3031	201	500	75.10	70
9/22	3032	202	640	96.13	68
September totals			**$3,880**	**$582.77**	**$436**
10/6	3074	200	860	129.17	$89
10/6	3075	201	595	89.37	82
10/6	3076	202	700	105.14	77
10/20	3147	200	800	120.16	80
10/20	3148	201	560	84.11	79
10/20	3149	202	640	96.13	68
October totals			**$4,155**	**$624.08**	**$475**
11/3	3187	200	$800	$120.16	$80
11/3	3188	201	560	84.11	79
11/3	3189	202	640	96.13	68
11/17	3130	200	740	111.14	71
11/17	3131	201	500	75.10	70
11/17	3132	202	240	36.05	22
November totals			**$3,480**	**$522.69**	**$390**

Figure 13-1 (cont'd)
Wage and withholding information

Date	Check #	Emp.#	A Wages	B FICA	C FWT
12/1	3179	200	$740	$111.14	$71
12/1	3180	201	500	75.10	70
12/1	3181	202	640	96.13	68
12/15	3240	200	800	120.16	80
12/15	3241	201	280	42.05	34
12/15	3242	202	640	96.13	68
12/29	3267	200	350	52.57	38
12/29	3268	201	120	18.02	15
12/29	3269	202	320	48.06	34
December totals			**$4,390**	**$659.36**	**$478**

	A Wages	B FICA	C FWT
1) First quarter totals	$11,925	$1,791.13	$1,347
2) Second quarter totals	$13,765	$2,067.49	$1,570
3) Third quarter totals	$11,480	$1,724.29	$1,304
4) Fourth quarter totals	$12,025	$1,806.13	$1,343
5) Yearly totals	$49,195	$7,389.04	$5,564

Notes:

Date— The 941 asks you to note the date wages have been paid. This is only required if your liability is $500 or more in a quarter. As you can see from below, even one full-time employee will put you over the $500 line.

Check #— In case you have a question about your totals, you can quickly refer to the check stub or the cancelled check for clarification.

Emp.# (Employee number)— Our computer systems sorts by a number system, so even if we had only one employee, for bookkeeping purposes, we'd still give him a number rather than use his name. Here's the tax information for each employee:

Employee 200: Married, 2 deductions, wage is $10/hour
Employee 201: Single, 0 deductions, wage is $7/hour
Employee 202: Married, 1 deduction, wage is $8/hour

Wages— This is the total earned in the pay period including overtime.

FICA— This is the amount withheld for social security. Currently, 7.51 percent of the first $50,400 of wages paid in a year is withheld from an employee's check. The employer is required to match the amount, giving the employee a total of 15.02 percent towards his social security.

FWT— (Federal Withholding) This column shows the amount of federal taxes withheld from an employee's paycheck. The IRS will mail you a guide (Circular E) so you know how much to deduct for taxes. The tax amount is determined by three things: the gross wage before deductions, the number of deductions the employee declares, and length of the pay period.

Figure 13-1 (cont'd)

Wage and withholding information

■ $500 or more but less than $3,000 at the end of any month— If your total undeposited taxes are $500 or more but less than $3,000 at the end of any month, you must deposit the taxes within 15 days.

■ $3,000 or more at the end of any eighth-monthly period— An eighth-monthly period is an eighth of a month, or approximately three working days. Look at the chart on the bottom of Form 941. If, at the end of any eighth-monthly period, your total undeposited taxes are $3,000 or more, deposit the taxes within three banking days after the end of that eighth-monthly period.

After you've filed your first 941, the IRS will automatically send you a form every quarter as long as you're in business.

Figure 13-2 shows a completed Form 941 based on the payroll records in Figure 13-1. The figures for lines 1 through 19 on the 941 come from the first quarter totals (line 1), columns A (wages), B (FICA), and C (federal withholding). The bottom portion of the form uses the information broken down by months. Follow along in Figure 13-2 for this line-by-line guide to filling out the 941.

Line 1a)   You only have to answer this question during the first quarter of the year.

Line 2)   This line includes all wages, taxable fringe benefits, and other compensation paid to your employees, even if you don't withhold income or social security taxes on it (Figure 13-1, column A).

Line 3)   This is what you withheld for federal income taxes. It doesn't include social security taxes (Figure 13-1, column C).

Line 4)   This line gives you a chance to correct mistakes from other quarters if you've withheld too much or too little from an employee's check. Either include Form 941c or attach a statement that explains the error and its resolution.

Line 5)   If line 4 is blank, line 5 is the same as line 3. But if you report additional tax withheld, add lines 3 and 4. Subtract line 4 from line 3 if you overpaid withholding taxes in previous quarters.

Line 6)   In this example, the first line of 6 is the same as line 2. The second line is that amount multiplied by 0.1502. At the time of this writing, the social security tax only applied to the first $50,400 of each employee's income per year. If you have employees that gross more than that, you don't include the excess on line 6. For our example, the total on line 6 is from column B of Figure 13-1. You may be off by a few cents when you multiply if you rounded up or down when you did your earlier figuring.

Line 7)   Lines 7a and 7b will not apply to most small construction companies.

Line 8)   Repeat the amount on line 6.

Form **941** Employer's Quarterly Federal Tax Return

(Rev. October 1988)
Department of the Treasury
Internal Revenue Service

4444

► **For Paperwork Reduction Act Notice, see page 2.**
Please type or print.

Your name, address, employer identification number, and calendar quarter of return. (If not correct, please change.)

Name (as distinguished from trade name)   Date quarter ended

Trade name, if any   Employer identification number

Address and ZIP code

OMB No. 1545-0029
Expires: 5-31-91

T	
FF	
FD	
FP	
I	
T	

If address is different from prior return, check here ► ☐

IRS Use

1 1 1 1 1 1 1 1 1 1 1   2   3 3 3 3 3   4 4 4
5 5 5   6   7   8 8 8 8 8 8   9 9   10 10 10 10 10 10 10 10 10

If you do not have to file returns in the future, check here . . ► ☐   Date final wages paid . . . . ►

Complete for First Quarter Only

1a	Number of employees (except household) employed in the pay period that includes March 12th ►	**1a**	3
b	If you are a subsidiary corporation AND your parent corporation files a consolidated Form 1120, enter parent corporation employer identification number (EIN) . . ► | 1b | —		
2	Total wages and tips subject to withholding, plus other compensation . . . . ►	**2**	11,926
3	Total income tax withheld from wages, tips, pensions, annuities, sick pay, gambling, etc. . . ►	**3**	1,347
4	Adjustment of withheld income tax for preceding quarters of calendar year (see instructions) . .	**4**	—
5	Adjusted total of income tax withheld (see instructions)	**5**	1,347
6	Taxable social security wages paid . . . . . $ 11,925 | × 15.02% (.1502) .	**6**	1,791 13
7a	Taxable tips reported . . . . $ _____ × 15.02% (.1502) .	**7a**	
b	Taxable hospital insurance wages paid . . . . $ _____ × 2.9% (.029). . .	**7b**	
8	Total social security taxes (add lines 6, 7a, and 7b)	**8**	1,791 13
9	Adjustment of social security taxes (see instructions for required explanation)	**9**	—
10	Adjusted total of social security taxes (see instructions) . . . . ►	**10**	
11	Backup withholding (see instructions)	**11**	—
12	Adjustment of backup withholding tax for preceding quarters of calendar year . . . . . ►	**12**	—
13	Adjusted total of backup withholding	**13**	1,791 13
14	Total taxes (add lines 5, 10, and 13)	**14**	3,138 13
15	Advance earned income credit (EIC) payments, if any . . . . ►	**15**	—
16	Net taxes (subtract line 15 from line 14). **This must equal line IV below** (plus line IV of Schedule A (Form 941) if you have treated backup withholding as a separate liability).	**16**	3,138 13
17	Total deposits for quarter, including overpayment applied from a prior quarter, from your records ►	**17**	3,138 13
18	Balance due (subtract line 17 from line 16). This should be less than $500. Pay to IRS . . . ►	**18**	—
19	If line 17 is more than line 16, enter overpayment here ► $ _____ and check if to be:		

☐ Applied to next return   **OR**   ☐ Refunded.

Record of Federal Tax Liability (Complete if line 16 is $500 or more.) See the instructions under rule 4 for details before checking these boxes.
Check only if you made eighth-monthly deposits using the 95% rule ► ☐   Check only if you are a first time 3-banking-day depositor ► ☐

Show tax liability here, **not deposits.** IRS gets deposit data from FTD coupons.

Date wages paid		First month of quarter		Second month of quarter		Third month of quarter
1st through 3rd	A		I		Q	
4th through 7th	B		J		R	
8th through 11th	C		K		S	
12th through 15th	D	527.40	L	527.40	T	492.88
16th through 19th	E		M		U	
20th through 22nd	F		N		V	
23rd through 25th	G		O	571.68	W	527.40
26th through the last	H	491.37	P		X	
Total liability for month	I	1018.77	II	1099.08	III	1020.28
IV Total for quarter (add lines *I, II,* and *III*). This must equal line 16 above . . . . . . ►						3138.13

Sign Here

Under penalties of perjury, I declare that I have examined this return, including accompanying schedules and statements, and to the best of my knowledge and belief, it is true, correct, and complete.

Signature ►   Title ►   Date ►

Figure 13-2

Form 941 for first quarter

Line 9) If you've made errors in reporting social security taxes, use this line to report overpayments or underpayments. Again, you'll need to include Form 941c or a statement which explains the mistake and how you've corrected it.

Line 10) If line 9 is blank, line 10 will be the same as line 8. If you report additional social security tax withheld, add lines 8 and 9. Subtract line 9 from line 8 if you overpaid social security taxes in previous quarters.

Line 11) This line reports backup withholding. It usually applies to any non-earned income. You usually won't need to use this line. But there may be rare exceptions. For instance, if a subcontractor asks you to withhold an extra amount from his check to cover his tax liability, you'd note that on line 11.

Line 12) Use line 12 to correct errors in backup withholding tax for earlier quarters of this year.

Line 13) This line also reflects adjusted backup withholding.

Line 14) Add lines 5, 10, and 13 together. Because this example doesn't include any errors from previous quarters, this line should equal the first quarter totals, columns B and C, in Figure 13-1 ($3,138.13).

Line 15) Earned income credit (EIC) is made to eligible employees by advance payments during the year or on their tax returns. To receive EIC, an employee must fill out Form W-5. Most advance EIC payments are made by reducing the amount of taxes withheld from a paycheck. You can deduct EIC payments directly from the amount you owe in withholding and FICA taxes. Because this can be complicated, it's best to work through this with your accountant.

Line 16) Unless you have special circumstances explained on line 9, 11, or 15, this line will be the same as line 14.

Line 17) This line includes all of your deposits for the quarter as well as any overpayments from the previous quarter.

Line 18) If you made your deposits according to the IRS's instructions, the balance due should be less than $500.

Line 19) If for some reason you've deposited more for the quarter than required, you can have the overpayment refunded or applied to your next return.

Record of Federal Tax Liability— Only fill this out if your tax liability (line 16) is $500 or more. This section breaks down your payroll into small parts. For each line, put your tax liability for that time period. Notice that the FICA and federal withholding taxes are combined into a single total.

For instance, the first payroll date for January was the 13th (Figure 13-1). In the first column, lines A, B and C are blank. Line D shows the total FICA and FWT liability for checks written from the 12th through the 15th. The total FWT for that period is $227.00. The total FICA for the same period is $300.40. Combined, the total is $527.40.

No checks were written again until January 27. So lines E, F and G in the first column are blank. The FICA and FWT liability for the checks written on January 27 is $491.37. This number is on line H. The total of the first column is entered on Line I ($1,018.77).

February's tax liability goes in the second column and March's in the third. The total of columns I, II and III goes on line IV. It should be the same as the amount on line 16.

If you're off by a few pennies, it's probably a result of how you multiplied the social security tax and whether you rounded up or down. The IRS is concerned about the amount you actually withheld. So you may have to add or subtract a few cents to make it come out right. If you're several dollars off, check for an entry or a computation error.

Don't forget to sign and date the return. Otherwise, the IRS will bounce it back to you.

We've included three blank 941's for you to practice on (Figure 13-3). Fill them out, using the figures from Figure 13-1 for the second, third and fourth quarters. Then compare them to our completed forms in Figure 13-4.

A word of caution: Make sure you follow the IRS's definition of what's an employee and what's a sub. The IRS uses the following criteria to decide whether or not you need to withhold taxes:

▮ An employee is paid by the hour. A sub may charge by the hour or agree on a contract price.

▮ You, as the employer, set the hours an employee works. A sub will need to work within your schedule, but may choose the specific hours he works.

▮ If you pay any fringe benefits, he or she is an employee, not a sub.

Be careful in following these rules. The IRS can require you to pay what you should have withheld from an employee.

Form 940, Employer's Federal Unemployment (FUTA) Tax Return

You only have to do Form 940 once a year. If your total FUTA tax isn't more than $100, you may make your payment when you file your 940. If it's more than $100, you should deposit your payments on the same schedule as your 941 deposits.

The form is due by February 1, unless you've paid your tax in full through deposits. Then your due date is February 10.

Form **941** Employer's Quarterly Federal Tax Return

(Rev. October 1988)
Department of the Treasury
Internal Revenue Service

4444

▶ For Paperwork Reduction Act Notice, see page 2.
Please type or print.

Your name, address, employer identification number, and calendar quarter of return. (If not correct, please change.)

Name (as distinguished from trade name)

Date quarter ended

Trade name, if any

Employer identification number

Address and ZIP code

OMB No. 1545-0029
Expires: 5-31-91

T
FF
FD
FP
I
T

If address is different from prior return, check here ▶ ☐

IRS Use

1 1 1 1 1 1 1 1 1 1 1   2   3 3 3 3 3 3   4 4 4

5 5 5   6   7   8 8 8 8 8 8   9 9 9   10 10 10 10 10 10 10 10 10 10

If you do not have to file returns in the future, check here . . . ▶ ☐   Date final wages paid . . . . ▶

Complete for First Quarter Only

1a	Number of employees (except household) employed in the pay period that includes March 12th ▶	1a	
b	If you are a subsidiary corporation AND your parent corporation files a consolidated Form 1120, enter parent corporation employer identification number (EIN) . ▶ 1b –		
2	Total wages and tips subject to withholding, plus other compensation . . . . . ▶	2	
3	Total income tax withheld from wages, tips, pensions, annuities, sick pay, gambling, etc. . ▶	3	
4	Adjustment of withheld income tax for preceding quarters of calendar year (see instructions) . ▶	4	
5	Adjusted total of income tax withheld (see instructions)	5	
6	Taxable social security wages paid . . . . $ _____ × 15.02% (.1502) .	6	
7a	Taxable tips reported . . . . . . $ _____ × 15.02% (.1502) .	7a	
b	Taxable hospital insurance wages paid . . . $ _____ × 2.9% (.029) . .	7b	
8	Total social security taxes (add lines 6, 7a, and 7b)	8	
9	Adjustment of social security taxes (see instructions for required explanation)	9	
10	Adjusted total of social security taxes (see instructions) . . . . . ▶	10	
11	Backup withholding (see instructions)	11	
12	Adjustment of backup withholding tax for preceding quarters of calendar year . . . . ▶	12	
13	Adjusted total of backup withholding	13	
14	Total taxes (add lines 5, 10, and 13)	14	
15	Advance earned income credit (EIC) payments, if any . . . . . . ▶	15	
16	Net taxes (subtract line 15 from line 14). **This must equal line IV below** (plus line IV of Schedule A (Form 941) if you have treated backup withholding as a separate liability).	16	
17	Total deposits for quarter, including overpayment applied from a prior quarter, from your records . ▶	17	
18	Balance due (subtract line 17 from line 16). This should be less than $500. Pay to IRS . . . ▶	18	
19	If line 17 is more than line 16, enter overpayment here ▶ $ _____ and check if to be: ☐ Applied to next return **OR** ☐ Refunded.		

Record of Federal Tax Liability (Complete if line 16 is $500 or more.) See the instructions under rule 4 for details before checking these boxes.

Check only if you made eighth-monthly deposits using the 95% rule ▶ ☐   Check only if you are a first time 3-banking-day depositor ▶ ☐

Show tax liability here, **not deposits.** IRS gets deposit data from FTD coupons.

Date wages paid		First month of quarter		Second month of quarter		Third month of quarter
1st through 3rd	A		I		Q	
4th through 7th	B		J		R	
8th through 11th	C		K		S	
12th through 15th	D		L		T	
16th through 19th	E		M		U	
20th through 22nd	F		N		V	
23rd through 25th	G		O		W	
26th through the last	H		P		X	
Total liability for month	I		II		III	

(Do NOT Show Federal Tax Deposits Here)

IV Total for quarter (add lines *I, II,* and *III*). **This must equal line 16 above** . . . . ▶

Sign Here

Under penalties of perjury, I declare that I have examined this return, including accompanying schedules and statements, and to the best of my knowledge and belief, it is true, correct, and complete.

Signature ▶   Title ▶   Date ▶

Figure 13-3
Blank Form 941 for practice

Form **941** — Employer's Quarterly Federal Tax Return

Form **941**
(Rev. October 1988)
Department of the Treasury
Internal Revenue Service

4444

► For Paperwork Reduction Act Notice, see page 2.
Please type or print.

OMB No. 1545-0029
Expires: 5-31-91

Your name, address, employer identification number, and calendar quarter of return. (If not correct, please change.)

Name (as distinguished from trade name)   Date quarter ended

Trade name, if any   Employer identification number

Address and ZIP code

T
FF
FD
FP
I
T

If address is different from prior return, check here ►☐

IRS Use

1 1 1 1 1 1 1 1 1 1 1   2   3 3 3 3 3   4 4 4
5 5 5   6   7   8 8 8 8 8   9 9 9   10 10 10 10 10 10 10 10 10 10

If you do not have to file returns in the future, check here . . ►☐   Date final wages paid . . . . ►

Complete for First Quarter Only

1a Number of employees (except household) employed in the pay period that includes March 12th ►	1a	
b If you are a subsidiary corporation AND your parent corporation files a consolidated Form 1120, enter parent corporation employer identification number (EIN) . . ► |1b| —		
2 Total wages and tips subject to withholding, plus other compensation . . . . . . ►	2	
3 Total income tax withheld from wages, tips, pensions, annuities, sick pay, gambling, etc. . . . ►	3	
4 Adjustment of withheld income tax for preceding quarters of calendar year (see instructions) . . ►	4	
5 Adjusted total of income tax withheld (see instructions)	5	
6 Taxable social security wages paid . . . . $ _____ × 15.02% (.1502) . .	6	
7a Taxable tips reported . . . . $ _____ × 15.02% (.1502) . .	7a	
b Taxable hospital insurance wages paid . . . $ _____ × 2.9% (.029) . . .	7b	
8 Total social security taxes (add lines 6, 7a, and 7b)	8	
9 Adjustment of social security taxes (see instructions for required explanation)	9	
10 Adjusted total of social security taxes (see instructions) . . . . ►	10	
11 Backup withholding (see instructions)	11	
12 Adjustment of backup withholding tax for preceding quarters of calendar year . . . . . ►	12	
13 Adjusted total of backup withholding	13	
14 Total taxes (add lines 5, 10, and 13)	14	
15 Advance earned income credit (EIC) payments, if any . . . . ►	15	
16 Net taxes (subtract line 15 from line 14). **This must equal line IV below** (plus line IV of Schedule A (Form 941) if you have treated backup withholding as a separate liability).	16	
17 Total deposits for quarter, including overpayment applied from a prior quarter, from your records . ►	17	
18 Balance due (subtract line 17 from line 16). This should be less than $500. Pay to IRS . . . ►	18	

19 If line 17 is more than line 16, enter overpayment here ► $ _____ and check if to be:
☐ Applied to next return   **OR**   ☐ Refunded.

Record of Federal Tax Liability (Complete if line 16 is $500 or more.) See the instructions under rule 4 for details before checking these boxes.
Check only if you made eighth-monthly deposits using the 95% rule ►☐   Check only if you are a first time 3-banking-day depositor ►☐

Show tax liability here, **not deposits**. IRS gets deposit data from FTD coupons.

Date wages paid	First month of quarter		Second month of quarter		Third month of quarter	
1st through 3rd	A		I		Q	
4th through 7th	B		J		R	
8th through 11th	C		K		S	
12th through 15th	D		L		T	
16th through 19th	E		M		U	
20th through 22nd	F		N		V	
23rd through 25th	G		O		W	
26th through the last	H		P		X	
Total liability for month	I		II		III	

Do NOT Show Federal Tax Deposits Here

IV Total for quarter (add lines *I, II,* and *III*). **This must equal line 16 above** . . . . ►

Sign Here

Under penalties of perjury, I declare that I have examined this return, including accompanying schedules and statements, and to the best of my knowledge and belief, it is true, correct, and complete.

Signature ►   Title ►   Date ►

Figure 13-3 (cont'd)
Blank Form 941 for practice

Form 941
(Rev. October 1988)
Department of the Treasury
Internal Revenue Service

4444

Employer's Quarterly Federal Tax Return

▶ **For Paperwork Reduction Act Notice, see page 2.**
Please type or print.

Your name, address, employer identification number, and calendar quarter of return. (If not correct, please change.)

Name (as distinguished from trade name)   Date quarter ended

Trade name, if any   Employer identification number

Address and ZIP code

OMB No. 1545-0029
Expires: 5-31-91

T	
FF	
FD	
FP	
I	
T	

If address is different from prior return, check here ▶ ☐

IRS Use

1 1 1 1 1 1 1 1 1 1 1	2	3 3 3 3 3 3	4 4 4
5 5 5 6	7	8 8 8 8 8	9 9 9	10 10 10 10 10 10 10 10 10 10

If you do not have to file returns in the future, check here . . . ▶ ☐   Date final wages paid . . . . ▶

Complete for First Quarter Only

1a	Number of employees (except household) employed in the pay period that includes March 12th ▶	**1a**	
b	If you are a subsidiary corporation AND your parent corporation files a consolidated Form 1120, enter parent corporation employer identification number (EIN) . ▶ **1b** ‒		
2	Total wages and tips subject to withholding, plus other compensation . . . . ▶	**2**	
3	Total income tax withheld from wages, tips, pensions, annuities, sick pay, gambling, etc. . . ▶	**3**	
4	Adjustment of withheld income tax for preceding quarters of calendar year (see instructions) . ▶	**4**	
5	Adjusted total of income tax withheld (see instructions)	**5**	
6	Taxable social security wages paid . . . . . . $ _____ × 15.02% (.1502) .	**6**	
7a	Taxable tips reported . . . . $ _____ × 15.02% (.1502) .	**7a**	
b	Taxable hospital insurance wages paid . . . . $ _____ × 2.9% (.029). . .	**7b**	
8	Total social security taxes (add lines 6, 7a, and 7b)	**8**	
9	Adjustment of social security taxes (see instructions for required explanation)	**9**	
10	Adjusted total of social security taxes (see instructions) . . . . ▶	**10**	
11	Backup withholding (see instructions)	**11**	
12	Adjustment of backup withholding tax for preceding quarters of calendar year . . . . . ▶	**12**	
13	Adjusted total of backup withholding	**13**	
14	Total taxes (add lines 5, 10, and 13)	**14**	
15	Advance earned income credit (EIC) payments, if any . . . . ▶	**15**	
16	Net taxes (subtract line 15 from line 14). **This must equal line IV below** (plus line IV of Schedule A (Form 941) if you have treated backup withholding as a separate liability).	**16**	
17	Total deposits for quarter, including overpayment applied from a prior quarter, from your records . ▶	**17**	
18	Balance due (subtract line 17 from line 16). This should be less than $500. Pay to IRS . . . . ▶	**18**	
19	If line 17 is more than line 16, enter overpayment here ▶ $ _____ and check if to be: ☐ Applied to next return **OR** ☐ Refunded.		

Record of Federal Tax Liability (Complete if line 16 is $500 or more.) See the instructions under rule 4 for details before checking these boxes.
Check only if you made eighth-monthly deposits using the 95% rule ▶ ☐   Check only if you are a first time 3-banking-day depositor ▶ ☐

Show tax liability here, **not deposits.** IRS gets deposit data from FTD coupons.

Date wages paid		First month of quarter		Second month of quarter		Third month of quarter
1st through 3rd	A		I		Q	
4th through 7th	B		J		R	
8th through 11th	C		K		S	
12th through 15th	D		L		T	
16th through 19th	E		M		U	
20th through 22nd	F		N		V	
23rd through 25th	G		O		W	
26th through the last	H		P		X	
Total liability for month	I		II		III	

Do NOT Show Federal Tax Deposits Here

IV Total for quarter (add lines *I, II,* and *III*). This must equal line 16 above . . . . ▶

Sign Here   Under penalties of perjury, I declare that I have examined this return, including accompanying schedules and statements, and to the best of my knowledge and belief, it is true, correct, and complete.

Signature ▶   Title ▶   Date ▶

Figure 13-3 (cont'd)
Blank Form 941 for practice

Form **941** Employer's Quarterly Federal Tax Return

(Rev. October 1988)
Department of the Treasury
Internal Revenue Service

4444

▶ For Paperwork Reduction Act Notice, see page 2.
Please type or print.

OMB No. 1545-0029
Expires: 5-31-91

Your name, address, employer identification number, and calendar quarter of return. (If not correct, please change.)

Name (as distinguished from trade name)

Trade name, if any

Address and ZIP code

Date quarter ended

Employer identification number

| T |
| FF |
| FD |
| FP |
| I |
| T |

If address is different from prior return, check here ▶ ☐

IRS Use

```
1 1 1 1 1 1 1 1 1 1 1   2   3 3 3 3 3 3   4 4 4
5 5 5   6   7   8 8 8 8   9 9   10 10 10 10 10 10 10 10 10
```

If you do not have to file returns in the future, check here . . . ▶ ☐   Date final wages paid . . . ▶

Complete for First Quarter Only

1a Number of employees (except household) employed in the pay period that includes March 12th ▶ | **1a** |

b If you are a subsidiary corporation AND your parent corporation files a consolidated Form 1120, enter parent corporation employer identification number (EIN) . ▶ | **1b** | –

2	Total wages and tips subject to withholding, plus other compensation . . . . . . ▶	**2**	13,765
3	Total income tax withheld from wages, tips, pensions, annuities, sick pay, gambling, etc. . . . ▶	**3**	1,570
4	Adjustment of withheld income tax for preceding quarters of calendar year (see instructions) . . ▶	**4**	
5	Adjusted total of income tax withheld (see instructions)	**5**	1,570
6	Taxable social security wages paid . . . . . $ 13,765	× 15.02% (.1502)	**6**	2,067 49
7a	Taxable tips reported . . . . $ _____	× 15.02% (.1502)	**7a**	
b	Taxable hospital insurance wages paid . . . . $ _____	× 2.9% (.029) . .	**7b**	
8	Total social security taxes (add lines 6, 7a, and 7b)	**8**	2,067 49
9	Adjustment of social security taxes (see instructions for required explanation)	**9**	
10	Adjusted total of social security taxes (see instructions) . . . . ▶	**10**	
11	Backup withholding (see instructions)	**11**	
12	Adjustment of backup withholding tax for preceding quarters of calendar year . . . . . ▶	**12**	
13	Adjusted total of backup withholding	**13**	
14	Total taxes (add lines 5, 10, and 13)	**14**	2,067 49
15	Advance earned income credit (EIC) payments, if any . . . . ▶	**15**	
16	Net taxes (subtract line 15 from line 14). **This must equal line IV below** (plus line IV of Schedule A (Form 941) if you have treated backup withholding as a separate liability).	**16**	
17	Total deposits for quarter, including overpayment applied from a prior quarter, from your records . ▶	**17**	3,637 49
18	Balance due (subtract line 17 from line 16). This should be less than $500. Pay to IRS . . . . ▶	**18**	

19 If line 17 is more than line 16, enter overpayment here ▶ $ _____ and check if to be:
☐ Applied to next return   **OR**   ☐ Refunded.

Record of Federal Tax Liability (Complete if line 16 is $500 or more.) See the instructions under rule 4 for details before checking these boxes.
Check only if you made eighth-monthly deposits using the 95% rule ▶ ☐   Check only if you are a first time 3-banking-day depositor ▶ ☐

Show tax liability here, **not deposits.** IRS gets deposit data from FTD coupons.

Date wages paid		First month of quarter		Second month of quarter		Third month of quarter
1st through 3rd	A		I		Q	527.40
4th through 7th	B	527.40	J	571.68	R	
8th through 11th	C		K		S	
12th through 15th	D		L		T	
16th through 19th	E		M	491.37	U	527.40
20th through 22nd	F	527.40	N		V	
23rd through 25th	G		O		W	100.00
26th through the last	H		P		X	364.76
Total liability for month	I	1,054.80	II	1,063.05	III	1,519.64

IV Total for quarter (add lines **I, II,** and **III**). **This must equal line 16 above** . . . . ▶   3,637.49

(Do NOT Show Federal Tax Deposits Here)

Sign Here Under penalties of perjury, I declare that I have examined this return, including accompanying schedules and statements, and to the best of my knowledge and belief, it is true, correct, and complete.

Signature ▶   Title ▶   Date ▶

Figure 13-4

Form 941 for second quarter

Form **941**
(Rev. October 1988)
Department of the Treasury
Internal Revenue Service

4444

Employer's Quarterly Federal Tax Return

▶ For Paperwork Reduction Act Notice, see page 2.
Please type or print.

Your name, address, employer identification number, and calendar quarter of return. (If not correct, please change.)

Name (as distinguished from trade name)

Date quarter ended

Trade name, if any

Employer identification number

Address and ZIP code

OMB No. 1545-0029
Expires: 5-31-91

T	
FF	
FD	
FP	
I	
T	

If address is different from prior return, check here ▶ ☐

IRS Use

1 1 1 1 1 1 1 1 1 1 1 1   2   3 3 3 3 3   4 4 4

5 5 5   6   7   8 8 8 8 8   9 9 9   10 10 10 10 10 10 10 10 10 10

If you do not have to file returns in the future, check here . . . ▶ ☐   Date final wages paid . . . ▶

Complete for First Quarter Only

1a	Number of employees (except household) employed in the pay period that includes March 12th ▶	**1a**		
b	If you are a subsidiary corporation AND your parent corporation files a consolidated Form 1120, enter parent corporation employer identification number (EIN) . . ▶ **1b** ⎸ –			
2	Total wages and tips subject to withholding, plus other compensation . . . . ▶	**2**	11,480	
3	Total income tax withheld from wages, tips, pensions, annuities, sick pay, gambling, etc. . . ▶	**3**	1,304	
4	Adjustment of withheld income tax for preceding quarters of calendar year (see instructions) . . ▶	**4**		
5	Adjusted total of income tax withheld (see instructions)	**5**	1,304	
6	Taxable social security wages paid . . . . . $ __11,480__ × 15.02% (.1502) .	**6**	1,724	29
7a	Taxable tips reported . . . . $ _____ × 15.02% (.1502) .	**7a**		
b	Taxable hospital insurance wages paid . . . . $ _____ × 2.9% (.029). .	**7b**		
8	Total social security taxes (add lines 6, 7a, and 7b)	**8**	1,724	29
9	Adjustment of social security taxes (see instructions for required explanation)	**9**		
10	Adjusted total of social security taxes (see instructions) . . . . ▶	**10**		
11	Backup withholding (see instructions)	**11**		
12	Adjustment of backup withholding tax for preceding quarters of calendar year . . . . . ▶	**12**		
13	Adjusted total of backup withholding	**13**		
14	Total taxes (add lines 5, 10, and 13)	**14**		
15	Advance earned income credit (EIC) payments, if any . . . . ▶	**15**		
16	Net taxes (subtract line 15 from line 14). **This must equal line IV below** (plus line IV of Schedule A (Form 941) if you have treated backup withholding as a separate liability). . . . . . ▶	**16**		
17	Total deposits for quarter, including overpayment applied from a prior quarter, from your records ▶	**17**	3,028	29
18	Balance due (subtract line 17 from line 16). This should be less than $500. Pay to IRS . . . ▶	**18**		
19	If line 17 is more than line 16, enter overpayment here ▶ $ _____ and check if to be:			

☐ Applied to next return   **OR**   ☐ Refunded.

Record of Federal Tax Liability (Complete if line 16 is $500 or more.) See the instructions under rule 4 for details before checking these boxes.
Check only if you made eighth-monthly deposits using the 95% rule ▶ ☐   Check only if you are a first time 3-banking-day depositor ▶ ☐

Show tax liability here, **not deposits.** IRS gets deposit data from FTD coupons.

Do NOT Show Federal Tax Deposits Here

Date wages paid		First month of quarter		Second month of quarter		Third month of quarter
1st through 3rd	A		I		Q	
4th through 7th	B		J		R	
8th through 11th	C		K	527.40	S	527.40
12th through 15th	D	427.32	L		T	
16th through 19th	E		M		U	
20th through 22nd	F		N		V	491.37
23rd through 25th	G		O	527.40	W	
26th through the last	H	527.40	P		X	
Total liability for month	I	954.72	II	1054.80	III	1018.77

IV Total for quarter (add lines *I*, *II*, and *III*). **This must equal line 16 above** . . . . ▶

Sign Here

Under penalties of perjury, I declare that I have examined this return, including accompanying schedules and statements, and to the best of my knowledge and belief, it is true, correct, and complete.

Signature ▶   Title ▶   Date ▶

Figure 13-4 (cont'd)
Form 941 for third quarter

Form 941
(Rev. October 1988)
Department of the Treasury
Internal Revenue Service

4444

Employer's Quarterly Federal Tax Return

▶ For Paperwork Reduction Act Notice, see page 2.
Please type or print.

OMB No. 1545-0029
Expires: 5-31-91

Your name, address, employer identification number, and calendar quarter of return. (If not correct, please change.)

Name (as distinguished from trade name)   Date quarter ended

Trade name, if any   Employer identification number

Address and ZIP code

| | T | FF | FD | FP | I | T |

If address is different from prior return, check here ▶ ☐

IRS Use

| 1 1 1 1 1 1 1 1 1 1 | 2 | 3 3 3 3 3 | 4 4 4 |
| 5 5 6 7 8 8 8 8 8 8 | 9 9 | 10 10 10 10 10 10 10 10 10 10 |

If you do not have to file returns in the future, check here . . ▶ ☐   Date final wages paid . . . . ▶

Complete for First Quarter Only

1a Number of employees (except household) employed in the pay period that includes March 12th . ▶ | 1a |

b If you are a subsidiary corporation AND your parent corporation files a consolidated Form 1120, enter parent corporation employer identification number (EIN) . ▶ | 1b | –

2 Total wages and tips subject to withholding, plus other compensation . . . . . ▶	2	12,025
3 Total income tax withheld from wages, tips, pensions, annuities, sick pay, gambling, etc. . . ▶	3	1,343
4 Adjustment of withheld income tax for preceding quarters of calendar year (see instructions) . ▶	4	
5 Adjusted total of income tax withheld (see instructions)	5	1,343
6 Taxable social security wages paid . . . . . $ 12,025 ___ × 15.02% (.1502) .	6	1,806 13
7a Taxable tips reported . . . . $ ___ × 15.02% (.1502) .	7a	
b Taxable hospital insurance wages paid . . . . $ ___ × 2.9% (.029). .	7b	
8 Total social security taxes (add lines 6, 7a, and 7b)	8	1,806 13
9 Adjustment of social security taxes (see instructions for required explanation)	9	
10 Adjusted total of social security taxes (see instructions) . . . . ▶	10	
11 Backup withholding (see instructions)	11	
12 Adjustment of backup withholding tax for preceding quarters of calendar year . . . ▶	12	
13 Adjusted total of backup withholding	13	
14 Total taxes (add lines 5, 10, and 13)	14	
15 Advance earned income credit (EIC) payments, if any . . . . ▶	15	
16 Net taxes (subtract line 15 from line 14). **This must equal line IV below** (plus line IV of Schedule A (Form 941) if you have treated backup withholding as a separate liability).	16	
17 Total deposits for quarter, including overpayment applied from a prior quarter, from your records . ▶	17	3,149 13
18 Balance due (subtract line 17 from line 16). This should be less than $500. Pay to IRS . . ▶	18	
19 If line 17 is more than line 16, enter overpayment here ▶ $ ___ and check if to be:		

☐ Applied to next return   **OR**   ☐ Refunded.

Record of Federal Tax Liability (Complete if line 16 is $500 or more.) See the instructions under rule 4 for details before checking these boxes.
Check only if you made eighth-monthly deposits using the 95% rule ▶ ☐   Check only if you are a first time 3-banking-day depositor ▶ ☐

Show tax liability here, **not deposits.** IRS gets deposit data from FTD coupons.

Date wages paid		First month of quarter		Second month of quarter		Third month of quarter
1st through 3rd	A		I	527.40	Q	491.37
4th through 7th	B	571.68	J		R	
8th through 11th	C		K		S	
12th through 15th	D		L		T	440.34
16th through 19th	E		M	385.29	U	
20th through 22nd	F	527.40	N		V	
23rd through 25th	G		O		W	
26th through the last	H		P		X	205.65
Total liability for month	I	1,099.08	II	912.69	III	1,137.36

(Do NOT Show Federal Tax Deposits Here)

IV Total for quarter (add lines **I, II,** and **III**). **This must equal line 16 above** . . . . ▶   3,149.13

Sign Here   Under penalties of perjury, I declare that I have examined this return, including accompanying schedules and statements, and to the best of my knowledge and belief, it is true, correct, and complete.

Signature ▶   Title ▶   Date ▶

Figure 13-4 (cont'd)
Form 941 for fourth quarter

For the 940, you'll need information from the wages column in Figure 13-1. The amount taxed and the percentage of the tax may change yearly. In 1989, the rate was 0.008 percent of the first $7,000 of each employee's annual income. That gives you some incentive to keep employee turnover to a minimum. Notice that the payroll for the year is $49,195 (line 5, column A). If you'd had seven employees come and go with none of them earning over $7,000, you'd have to pay the tax on the entire amount. If three employees stayed all year, you only pay on the first $21,000 (3 employees x $7,000). With the low FUTA rate of 0.008 percent, liability on a $49,000 payroll would still only be $392. But that's more than twice as much as you pay for only three employees — $168.

In addition, most states will give you a similar advantage for low turnover. Presently in Colorado an employer pays unemployment tax on the first $10,000 in wages.

You can quickly see from Figure 13-5 that the 940 is far less complicated than the 941. If you pay all your contributions to your state unemployment fund when they're due and you only work in one state, you can fly through it. Here's what belongs on each line, and why.

Part I

Line 1) Use line 5, column A in Figure 13-1. This includes the total payments you made to employees during the year, even if they're not taxable. Include bonuses, clothing, commissions, and so on.

Line 2) For a small construction company the only exempt payments will probably be on benefits paid for sickness or injury under a workers' compensation law and certain family employment, like a spouse or child employed by the company.

Line 3) Enter the total amounts of more than $7,000 you paid each employee. In our example, the same three employees worked the entire year. The excess paid over $7,000 to each one is a total of $28,195.

Line 4) Add lines 2 and 3.

Line 5) This should give you a maximum of $7,000 for each employee. Most likely you won't have any exempt wages, but ask your accountant just to be sure.

Line 6) This is your total Federal Unemployment Tax. The rate for 1989 was .8 percent of your taxable payroll — you multiply the taxable amount by .008. If the total on this line is more than $100, you must fill out Part II of the form. The rest of the lines on the form are self-explanatory.

Part II

Complete this part if your total tax is over $100. If line 5 in Part I is $12,500 or more, your liability will be over $100. In the example we're using, the liability will be due the first half of the year because of low employee turnover.

Form **940-EZ**

Department of the Treasury
Internal Revenue Service

**Employer's Annual Federal
Unemployment (FUTA) Tax Return**

OMB No. 1545-1110

1989

T	
FF	
FD	
FP	
I	
T	

If incorrect, make any necessary changes. ▶

Name (as distinguished from trade name)   Calendar year

Trade name, if any

Address and ZIP code   Employer identification number —

Before beginning, follow the chart under "Who Can Use Form 940-EZ" on page 2. If you cannot use Form 940-EZ, you must use Form 940 instead.

A Enter the amount of contributions paid to your state unemployment fund. (See instructions for line A on page 4.) . . ▶ $ _____ |

B (1) Enter the name of the state where you have to pay contributions . . . . ▶ COLORADO

(2) Enter your state reporting number(s) as shown on state unemployment tax return. ▶ _____

Part I   Taxable Wages and FUTA Tax

1	Total payments (including payments shown on lines 2 and 3) during the calendar year for services of employees . .	1	49,195

	Amount paid	
2	Exempt payments. (Explain all exempt payments, attaching additional sheets if necessary.) ▶ _____ _____ _____	2	
3	Payments for services of more than $7,000. Enter only amounts over the first $7,000 paid to each employee. Do not include any exempt payments from line 2	3	28,195

4	Total exempt payments (add lines 2 and 3)	4	28,195
5	**Total taxable wages** (subtract line 4 from line 1) . . . . ▶	5	21,000
6	**FUTA tax.** Multiply the wages on line 5 by .008 and enter here. (If the result is over $100, also complete Part II.) . .	6	168
7	Total FUTA tax deposited for the year, including any overpayment applied from a prior year (from your records) . .	7	
8	**Amount you owe** (subtract line 7 from line 6). This should be $100 or less. Pay to IRS . . . . ▶	8	
9	**Overpayment** (subtract line 6 from line 7). Check if it is to be: ☐ Applied to next return, or ☐ Refunded. . ▶	9	

Part II   Record of Quarterly Federal Unemployment Tax Liability (Do not include state liability.) Complete only if line 6 is over $100.

Quarter	First (Jan. 1 – Mar. 31)	Second (Apr. 1 – June 30)	Third (July 1 – Sept. 30)	Fourth (Oct. 1 – Dec. 31)	Total for Year
Liability for quarter	95.40	72.60			

If you will not have to file returns in the future, write "Final" here (see *Who Must File a Return* on page 2) and sign the return. ▶

Under penalties of perjury, I declare that I have examined this return, including accompanying schedules and statements, and, to the best of my knowledge and belief, it is true, correct, and complete, and that no part of any payment made to a state unemployment fund claimed as a credit was, or is to be, deducted from the payments to employees.

Signature ▶   Title (Owner, etc.) ▶   Date ▶

For Paperwork Reduction Act Notice, see page 2.   Form **940-EZ** (1989)

Figure 13-5
Form 940

Form W-2, Wage and Tax Statement

A W-2 is required for any employee if you:

∎ Withheld income or social security taxes

∎ Would have withheld taxes if the employee hadn't claimed exemption on Form W-4.

∎ Paid them $600 or more.

∎ Paid any employee compensation other than money, such as tools, vehicles, trips, prizes and so on.

∎ Gave them any advance EIC payment.

You're required to give all employees copies of their W-2 by January 31. The Social Security administration must receive their copy by February 28.

Although you can fill out Forms 941 and 940 with a ballpoint pen, you must type Form W-2. It's important to use good, clean carbons and a typewriter with clean keys. Optical scanning machines read the forms and they're much pickier than human readers. If the form can't be read by the machine, the IRS will send it back to you to do over.

The W-2 is fairly easy to figure out. The hard part is completing it without a mistake. As you'll quickly learn, typing an error-free page is a real challenge. Somehow, even getting the carbons in and facing the right direction can seem like an impossibility.

Look at Figure 13-6. We've filled out the first W-2 for employee number 200 using the information from Figure 13-7 (columns D, E, and F of lines 6, 7, and 8). Notice that the FICA column (E) is a total of the social security taxes withheld from your employee and the employer's contribution. But on the W-2, only enter the amount withheld, not the combined total.

Box 1)   The control number is optional. It's for your own convenience.

Box 3)   Put your EIN here. If you don't have one, use your social security number.

Box 4)   If you have a state I.D. number, it goes here. If you don't, leave it blank. It's not necessary to repeat your federal EIN even if this is what you use for your state I.D. number.

Boxes 5 and 6)   Normally, you can ignore these two.

Box 7)   Enter how much you've given the employee in EIC payments.

1 Control number 22222 | For Paperwork Reduction Act Notice, see separate instructions OMB No. 1545-0008 | For Official Use Only ▶

2 Employer's name, address, and ZIP code	3 Employer's identification number	4 Employer's state I.D. number

Best Construction
111 Peak View Blvd.
Colorado Springs, CO 80909

5 Statutory employee	Deceased	Pension plan	Legal rep.	942 emp.	Subtotal	Deferred compensation	Void

6 Allocated tips	7 Advance EIC payment

8 Employee's social security number	9 Federal income tax withheld 1,931.00	10 Wages, tips, other compensation 19,380.00	11 Social security tax withheld 1,455.43

12 Employee's name (first, middle, last) Edward D. Barlow	13 Social security wages 19,380.00	14 Social security tips

612 E. Uintah
Colorado, Springs, CO
80909

16 (See Instr. for Forms W-2/W-2P)	16a Fringe benefits incl. in Box 10

17 State income tax 755.82	18 State wages, tips, etc. 19,380.00	19 Name of state CO

15 Employee's address and ZIP code	20 Local income tax	21 Local wages, tips, etc.	22 Name of locality

Form **W-2 Wage and Tax Statement 1989**

Copy A For Social Security Administration   Dept. of the Treasury—IRS

Do NOT Cut or Separate Forms on This Page

---

1 Control number 22222 | For Paperwork Reduction Act Notice, see separate instructions OMB No. 1545-0008 | For Official Use Only ▶

2 Employer's name, address, and ZIP code	3 Employer's identification number	4 Employer's state I.D. number

5 Statutory employee	Deceased	Pension plan	Legal rep.	942 emp.	Subtotal	Deferred compensation	Void

6 Allocated tips	7 Advance EIC payment

8 Employee's social security number	9 Federal income tax withheld	10 Wages, tips, other compensation	11 Social security tax withheld

12 Employee's name (first, middle, last)	13 Social security wages	14 Social security tips

16 (See Instr. for Forms W-2/W-2P)	16a Fringe benefits incl. in Box 10

17 State income tax	18 State wages, tips, etc.	19 Name of state

15 Employee's address and ZIP code	20 Local income tax	21 Local wages, tips, etc.	22 Name of locality

Form **W-2 Wage and Tax Statement 1989**

Copy A For Social Security Administration   Dept. of the Treasury—IRS

Do NOT Cut or Separate Forms on This Page

---

1 Control number 22222 | For Paperwork Reduction Act Notice, see separate instructions OMB No. 1545-0008 | For Official Use Only ▶

2 Employer's name, address, and ZIP code	3 Employer's identification number	4 Employer's state I.D. number

5 Statutory employee	Deceased	Pension plan	Legal rep.	942 emp.	Subtotal	Deferred compensation	Void

6 Allocated tips	7 Advance EIC payment

8 Employee's social security number	9 Federal income tax withheld	10 Wages, tips, other compensation	11 Social security tax withheld

12 Employee's name (first, middle, last)	13 Social security wages	14 Social security tips

16 (See Instr. for Forms W-2/W-2P)	16a Fringe benefits incl. in Box 10

17 State income tax	18 State wages, tips, etc.	19 Name of state

15 Employee's address and ZIP code	20 Local income tax	21 Local wages, tips, etc.	22 Name of locality

Form **W-2 Wage and Tax Statement 1989**

Copy A For Social Security Administration   Dept. of the Treasury—IRS

Figure 13-6

W-2 for employee 200

Employee number: 200
Name: Edward D. Barlow
Address: 612 E. Uintah
City, 80909
Social security number: 505-87-2018

Date	Check #	D Wages	E FICA	F FWT
1/13	2087	$800	$120.16	$80
1/27	2130	740	111.14	71
2/10	2178	800	120.16	80
2/24	2254	860	129.17	89
3/10	2310	750	112.65	71
3/24	2345	800	120.16	80
4/7	2392	800	120.16	80
4/21	2438	800	120.16	80
5/5	2498	860	129.17	89
5/19	2562	740	111.14	71
6/2	2601	800	120.16	80
6/16	2638	800	120.16	80
6/23	2675	400	60.08	40
7/14	2768	400	60.08	40
7/28	2810	800	120.16	80
8/11	2859	800	120.16	80
8/25	2912	800	120.16	80
9/8	2987	800	120.16	80
9/22	3030	740	111.14	71
10/6	3074	860	129.17	89
10/20	3147	800	120.16	80
11/3	3187	800	120.16	80
11/17	3130	740	111.14	71
12/1	3179	740	111.14	71
12/15	3240	800	120.16	80
12/29	3267	350	52.57	38
6) Emp. 200 totals		**$19,380**	**$2,910.83**	**$1,931**

Figure 13-7
Payroll totals

Employee number: 201
Name: Frank E. Crocker
Address: 1988 N. Tejon Apt. 6b
City, 80903
Social security number: 688-22-1765

Date	Check #	D Wages	E FICA	F FWT
1/13	2088	$560	$84.11	$79
1/27	2131	500	75.10	70
2/10	2179	560	84.11	79
2/24	2255	595	89.37	82
3/10	2311	540	81.11	76
3/24	2346	560	84.11	79
4/7	2393	560	84.11	79
4/21	2439	560	84.11	79
5/5	2499	595	89.37	82
5/19	2563	500	75.10	70
6/2	2602	560	84.11	79
6/16	2639	560	84.11	79
6/30	2689	610	91.62	85
7/14	2769	560	84.11	79
7/28	2811	560	84.11	79
8/11	2860	560	84.11	79
8/25	2913	560	84.11	79
9/8	2988	560	84.11	79
9/22	3031	500	75.10	70
10/6	3075	595	89.37	82
10/20	3148	560	84.11	79
11/3	3188	560	84.11	79
11/17	3131	500	75.10	70
12/1	3180	500	75.10	70
12/15	3241	280	42.05	34
12/29	3268	120	18.02	15

7) Emp. 201 totals $13,675 $2,053.95 $1,912

Figure 13-7 (cont'd)
Payroll totals

Employee number: 202
Name: Samuel J. Jones
Address: 17955 Rampart Road
Cascade, 80929
Social security number: 557-72-1100

Date	Check #	D Wages	E FICA	F FWT
1/13	2089	$640	$96.13	$68
1/27	2132	640	96.13	68
2/10	2180	640	96.13	68
2/24	2256	700	105.14	77
3/10	2312	600	90.12	62
3/24	2347	640	96.13	68
4/7	2394	640	96.13	68
4/21	2440	640	96.13	68
5/5	2500	700	105.14	77
5/19	2564	640	96.13	68
6/2	2603	640	96.13	68
6/16	2640	640	96.13	68
6/30	2690	720	108.14	80
7/14	2770	640	96.13	68
7/28	2812	640	96.13	68
8/11	2861	640	96.13	68
8/25	2914	640	96.13	68
9/8	2989	640	96.13	68
9/22	3032	640	96.13	68
10/6	3076	700	105.14	77
10/20	3149	640	96.13	68
11/3	3189	640	96.13	68
11/17	3132	240	36.05	22
12/1	3181	640	96.13	68
12/15	3242	640	96.13	68
12/29	3269	320	48.06	34
8) Emp. 202 totals		$16,140	$2,424.26	$1,721

Figure 13-7 (cont'd)
Payroll totals

Box 8)   Put in the employee's social security number.

Box 9)   Enter the total employee's federal income tax here.

Box 10)   The employee's total wages go here.

Box 11)   Put only the employee's social security taxes that you've withheld here. Don't include your matching portion.

Box 12)   Make sure you spell the employee's name correctly.

Box 13)   The amount here will match the amount in box 10, unless the employee made more than $50,400. In that case the amount would be $50,400.

Box 14)   Ordinarily this wouldn't apply to a small construction company.

Box 15)   Enter the employee's address and ZIP code. If the employee has quit and moved without leaving a forwarding address, mail the form to the best address you have. If it's returned, leave it in your file, unopened, for four years so you have proof that you tried to transmit the form.

Boxes 16 and 16a)   Apply only to deferred income and certain benefits. See your accountant about these.

Box 17)   Enter the employee's state income tax.

Box 18)   Normally, this box should be the same as the number in box 10.

Box 19)   The name of your state goes here.

Boxes 20, 21, and 22)   If you have local taxes, fill in these boxes. Otherwise, don't waste your typewriter ribbon.

If you want some practice, finish doing W-2's for employees number 201 and 202. Compare your answers to those in Figure 13-8.

Form W-3, Transmittal of Income and Tax Statements

Mail the W-3 (Figure 13-9) with your W-2's. And be sure to leave the W-2's in 8-1/2 by 11 sheets. Don't cut them apart. Like the W-2, the W-3 should be clearly typed.

Box 1)   Again, the control number is for your use.

Box 2)   Since you'll file a 941, that's the box you check.

1 Control number	22222	For Paperwork Reduction Act Notice, see separate instructions OMB No. 1545-0008	For Official Use Only ▶		
2 Employer's name, address, and ZIP code			3 Employer's identification number	4 Employer's state I.D. number	
Best Construction 111 Peak View Blvd. Colorado, CO 80909			5 Statutory employee ☐ Deceased ☐ Pension plan ☐ Legal rep. ☐	942 emp. ☐ Subtotal ☐ Deferred compensation ☐	Void ☐
			6 Allocated tips	7 Advance EIC payment	
8 Employee's social security number	9 Federal income tax withheld 1,931.00		10 Wages, tips, other compensation 19,380.00	11 Social security tax withheld 1,455.43	
12 Employee's name (first, middle, last) Edward D. Barlow	13 Social security wages 19,380.00			14 Social security tips	
612 E. Uintah Colorado Springs, CO 80909	16 (See Instr. for Forms W-2/W-2P)			16a Fringe benefits incl. in Box 10	
	17 State income tax 755.82	18 State wages, tips, etc. 19,380.00		19 Name of state CO	
15 Employee's address and ZIP code	20 Local income tax	21 Local wages, tips, etc.		22 Name of locality	

Form **W-2** **Wage and Tax Statement** **1989**　　Copy A For Social Security Administration　　Dept. of the Treasury—IRS

Do NOT Cut or Separate Forms on This Page

1 Control number	22222	For Paperwork Reduction Act Notice, see separate instructions OMB No. 1545-0008	For Official Use Only ▶		
2 Employer's name, address, and ZIP code			3 Employer's identification number	4 Employer's state I.D. number	
Best Construction 111 Peak View Blvd. Colorado, CO 80909			5 Statutory employee ☐ Deceased ☐ Pension plan ☐ Legal rep. ☐	942 emp. ☐ Subtotal ☐ Deferred compensation ☐	Void ☐
			6 Allocated tips	7 Advance EIC payment	
8 Employee's social security number	9 Federal income tax withheld 1,912.00		10 Wages, tips, other compensation 13,675.00	11 Social security tax withheld 1,026.97	
12 Employee's name (first, middle, last) Frank E. Crocker	13 Social security wages 13,675.00			14 Social security tips	
1988 N. Tejon Apt. 6b Colorado Springs, CO 80903	16 (See Instr. for Forms W-2/W-2P)			16a Fringe benefits incl. in Box 10	
	17 State income tax 533.32	18 State wages, tips, etc. 13,675.00		19 Name of state CO	
15 Employee's address and ZIP code	20 Local income tax	21 Local wages, tips, etc.		22 Name of locality	

Form **W-2** **Wage and Tax Statement** **1989**　　Copy A For Social Security Administration　　Dept. of the Treasury—IRS

Do NOT Cut or Separate Forms on This Page

1 Control number	22222	For Paperwork Reduction Act Notice, see separate instructions OMB No. 1545-0008	For Official Use Only ▶		
2 Employer's name, address, and ZIP code			3 Employer's identification number	4 Employer's state I.D. number	
Best Construction 111 Peak Blvd. Colorado, CO 80909			5 Statutory employee ☐ Deceased ☐ Pension plan ☐ Legal rep. ☐	942 emp. ☐ Subtotal ☐ Deferred compensation ☐	Void ☐
			6 Allocated tips	7 Advance EIC payment	
8 Employee's social security number	9 Federal income tax withheld 1,721.00		10 Wages, tips, other compensation 16,140.00	11 Social security tax withheld 1,212.13	
12 Employee's name (first, middle, last) Samuel J. Jones	13 Social security wages 16,140.00			14 Social security tips	
17955 Rampart Rd. Cascade, CO 80929	16 (See Instr. for Forms W-2/W-2P)			16a Fringe benefits incl. in Box 10	
	17 State income tax 629.46	18 State wages, tips, etc. 16,140.00		19 Name of state CO	
15 Employee's address and ZIP code	20 Local income tax	21 Local wages, tips, etc.		22 Name of locality	

Form **W-2** **Wage and Tax Statement** **1989**　　Copy A For Social Security Administration　　Dept. of the Treasury—IRS

Figure 13-8
Completed W-2's

Box 5)　This is the number of completed forms you're sending, not the number of pages. If you have three employees, as in our example, then the number is "3" even though they're on a single sheet.

Box 6)　You can ignore this box.

Box 7)　Enter the total advance EIC payments you made. If three of your employees received EIC payments, put the total in box 7.

Box 9)　This is the total amount of income tax withheld from all the employees. See line 5, column C.

Box 10)　This is the total amount you paid in wages to your employees. See line 5, column A at the end of Figure 13-1.

Box 11)　This is the total social security tax withheld from all of your employees. It doesn't include the portion you matched. It should be half of the figure in line 5, column B in Figure 13-1.

Box 12)　If you have a state I.D. number, enter it here. If not, leave it blank.

Box 13)　Enter the total wages on which social security was paid. If none of your employees made more than $50,400, it should be the same number as the one in box 10.

Box 14)　Leave this box blank.

Box 15)　Your EIN (Employer Identification Number) goes here if you're doing business as a corporation. If you don't have an EIN, use your social security number instead.

Box 16)　Ordinarily, a small construction business would not use more than one EIN during the year.

Box 17)　Your name goes here. It should match the name used on Forms 941 and 940.

Box 18)　Leave it blank.

Box 19)　Your address and ZIP go here. Once the government has found you, they'll send you preaddressed labels.

1 Control number 33333	For Official Use Only ► OMB No. 1545-0008		

| ☐ Kind of Payer ► | 2 941/941E ☒ Military ☐ 943 ☐ CT-1 ☐ 942 ☐ Medicare gov't. emp. ☐ | 3 | 4 | 5 Total number of statements 3 |

6 Allocated tips	7 Advance EIC payments	8 Establishment number

9 Federal income tax withheld 5528	10 Wages, tips, and other compensation 49195	11 Social security tax withheld 3694.52

12 Employer's state I.D. number	13 Social security wages 49195	14 Social security tips

15 Employer's identification number	16 Other EIN used this year

17 Employer's name	18 Gross annuity, pension, etc. (Form W-2P)

	20 Taxable amount (Form W-2P)

	21 Income tax withheld by third-party payer

19 Employer's address and ZIP code (If available, place label over boxes 15, 17, and 19.)

Under penalties of perjury, I declare that I have examined this return and accompanying documents, and to the best of my knowledge and belief they are true, correct, and complete.

Signature ►

Title ►

Date ►

Telephone number (optional) _____

Form **W-3 Transmittal of Income and Tax Statements 1989**   Department of the Treasury Internal Revenue Service

Please return this entire page with the accompanying Forms W-2 or W-2P to the Social Security Administration address for your state as listed below. **Household employers filing Forms W-2 for household employees should send the forms to the Albuquerque Data Operations Center.** Note: Extra postage may be necessary if the report you send contains more than a few pages or if the envelope is larger than letter size. Do NOT order forms from the addresses listed below. You may order forms by calling 1-800-424-FORM (3676).

If your legal residence, principal place of business, office or agency is located in ▼	Use this address ▼
Alaska, Arizona, California, Colorado, Hawaii, Idaho, Iowa, Minnesota, Missouri, Montana, Nebraska, Nevada, North Dakota, Oregon, South Dakota, Utah, Washington, Wisconsin, Wyoming	Social Security Administration Salinas Data Operations Center Salinas, CA 93911
Alabama, Arkansas, Florida, Georgia, Illinois, Kansas, Louisiana, Mississippi, New Mexico, Oklahoma, South Carolina, Tennessee, Texas	Social Security Administration Albuquerque Data Operations Center Albuquerque, NM 87180
Connecticut, Delaware, District of Columbia, Indiana, Kentucky, Maine, Maryland, Massachusetts, Michigan, New Hampshire, New Jersey, New York, North Carolina, Ohio, Pennsylvania, Rhode Island, Vermont, Virginia, West Virginia	Social Security Administration Wilkes-Barre Data Operations Center Wilkes-Barre, PA 18769
If you have no legal residence or principal place of business in any state	Social Security Administration Wilkes-Barre Data Operations Center Wilkes-Barre, PA 18769

Paperwork Reduction Act Notice.—We ask for this information to carry out the Internal Revenue laws of the United States. We need it to ensure that taxpayers are complying with these laws and to allow us to figure and collect the right amount of tax. You are required to give us this information.

The time needed to complete and file this form will vary depending on individual circumstances.

The estimated average time is 25 minutes. If you have comments concerning the accuracy of this time estimate or suggestions for making this form more simple, we would be happy to hear from you. You can write to the **Internal Revenue Service,** Washington, DC 20224, Attention: IRS Reports Clearance Officer TR:FP; or the **Office of Management and Budget,** Paperwork Reduction Project (1545-0008), Washington, DC 20503.

Figure 13-9

Form W-3

Box 20)   Leave it blank.

Box 21)   This only applies to income tax withheld from your employee's paycheck by someone else. Unless an employee has been paid by a third party for sick pay, it's unlikely that this would apply to you.

Form 1099-MISC, Miscellaneous Income Report

Form 1099-MISC is probably the simplest of the federal forms. The purpose of the 1099 is to make sure that unincorporated businesses are accurately reporting all of their income.

You must file a 1099-MISC on any individual or unincorporated business that you've paid $600 or more in the calendar year. Mail one copy to the business or individual by January 31. And like the W-2, it should be clearly typewritten.

Figure 13-10 is an example of a 1099-MISC with the top portion completed. Figure 13-11 lists subcontractor information you can use to practice filling out the other two forms.

Payer— Type your name, address, city, state, and ZIP code in this box.

Payer's Federal identification number— Type your EIN (or social security number) here.

Recipient's identification number— The subcontractor's EIN goes here. If the sub doesn't have an EIN, use a social security number instead. To avoid chasing EIN or social security numbers down in January, request the number before you cut a sub's final check.

Recipient's name and address— The subcontractor's name and address go here. For both the W-2 and the 1099, if you don't have a current address for the sub, mail a copy to the best address you have. If it comes back to you undeliverable, keep it in your files, unopened, for four years.

Account number— This space is for your bookkeeping and isn't required.

Boxes 1-6)   Leave blank. The exception to this would be if you've withheld any federal income tax. That amount should be put in box 4.

9595 ☐ VOID ☐ CORRECTED For Official Use Only

Type or machine print PAYER'S name, street address, city, state, and ZIP code	1 Rents	OMB No. 1545-0115	**Miscellaneous Income**
Best Construction 111 Peak View Blvd. Colorado Springs, CO 80909	$	**1989** Statement for Recipients of	
	2 Royalties $		

PAYER'S Federal identification number	RECIPIENT'S identification number 84--0869821	3 Prizes and awards $	4 Federal income tax withheld $	**Copy A** **For Internal Revenue Service Center**
Type or machine print RECIPIENT'S name (first, middle, last) Peak Drywall		5 Fishing boat proceeds $	6 Medical and health care payments $	For Paperwork Reduction Act Notice and instructions for completing this form, see Instructions for Forms 1099, 1098, 5498, 1096, and W-2G.
Street address 1400 Pike Ave.		7 Nonemployee compensation $ 3890	8 Substitute payments in lieu of dividends or interest $	
City, state, and ZIP code Colorado, CO 80909		9 Payer made direct sales of $5,000 or more of consumer products to a buyer (recipient) for resale . . . ▶ ☐		
Account number (optional)		10 Crop insurance proceeds $		

Form **1099-MISC**

Do NOT Cut or Separate Forms on This Page   Department of the Treasury · Internal Revenue Service

---

9595 ☐ VOID ☐ CORRECTED For Official Use Only

Type or machine print PAYER'S name, street address, city, state, and ZIP code	1 Rents $	OMB No. 1545-0115	**Miscellaneous Income**
	2 Royalties $	**1989** Statement for Recipients of	

PAYER'S Federal identification number	RECIPIENT'S identification number	3 Prizes and awards $	4 Federal income tax withheld $	**Copy A** **For Internal Revenue Service Center**
Type or machine print RECIPIENT'S name (first, middle, last)		5 Fishing boat proceeds $	6 Medical and health care payments $	For Paperwork Reduction Act Notice and instructions for completing this form, see Instructions for Forms 1099, 1098, 5498, 1096, and W-2G.
Street address		7 Nonemployee compensation $	8 Substitute payments in lieu of dividends or interest $	
City, state, and ZIP code		9 Payer made direct sales of $5,000 or more of consumer products to a buyer (recipient) for resale . . . ▶ ☐		
Account number (optional)		10 Crop insurance proceeds $		

Form **1099-MISC**

Do NOT Cut or Separate Forms on This Page   Department of the Treasury · Internal Revenue Service

---

9595 ☐ VOID ☐ CORRECTED For Official Use Only

Type or machine print PAYER'S name, street address, city, state, and ZIP code	1 Rents $	OMB No. 1545-0115	**Miscellaneous Income**
	2 Royalties $	**1989** Statement for Recipients of	

PAYER'S Federal identification number	RECIPIENT'S identification number	3 Prizes and awards $	4 Federal income tax withheld $	**Copy A** **For Internal Revenue Service Center**
Type or machine print RECIPIENT'S name (first, middle, last)		5 Fishing boat proceeds $	6 Medical and health care payments $	For Paperwork Reduction Act Notice and instructions for completing this form, see Instructions for Forms 1099, 1098, 5498, 1096, and W-2G.
Street address		7 Nonemployee compensation $	8 Substitute payments in lieu of dividends or interest $	
City, state, and ZIP code		9 Payer made direct sales of $5,000 or more of consumer products to a buyer (recipient) for resale . . . ▶ ☐		
Account number (optional)		10 Crop insurance proceeds $		

Form **1099-MISC**   Department of the Treasury · Internal Revenue Service

Figure 13-10
Form 1099-MISC

1) Peak Drywall $3,890
ID # 84-0869821
1400 Pike Ave.
Colorado Springs, CO 80909

2) AAA Concrete $4,021
ID # 84-0993569
1800 S. Nevada
Colorado Springs, CO 80906

3) Kuhns Painting $1,485
ID # 87-7990872
654 Cascade
Colorado Springs, CO 80903

Figure 13-11
Subcontractor information

Box 7)   The money you pay subs is *nonemployee compensation*. Put the total amount paid to each sub for the calendar year. Include payments for both material and labor. Type the amount without using commas or dollar signs. It's 14500, not $14,500.

Boxes 8-10)   These don't apply.

Form 1096, Summary and Transmittal of U.S. Information Returns

Form 1096 (Figure 13-12) compiles the information on the 1099-MISC. It's fairly simple. Type it clearly and file no later than February 28.

Filer's name— If you don't have a preprinted label, type your name and address in this space.

Employer identification number— You only need to fill this in if you're not using a preprinted label.

Social security number— If you're not using a preprinted label and don't have an EIN, put your social security number here. Otherwise, leave it blank.

Total number of documents— This refers to the number of completed forms you're sending, not the number of pages. If you've filled out forms for six subcontractors, then the number is 6, even though they fill two pages.

DO NOT STAPLE   6969   ☐ CORRECTED

Form **1096** Department of the Treasury Internal Revenue Service	**Annual Summary and Transmittal of U.S. Information Returns**	OMB No. 1545-0108 19**89**

Type or machine print FILER'S name (or attach label)

Street address   PLACE LABEL HERE

City, state, and ZIP code

If you are not using a preprinted label, enter in Box 1 or 2 below the identification number you used as the filer on the information returns being transmitted. Do not fill in both Boxes 1 and 2.	Name of person to contact if IRS needs more information Telephone number ( )	**For Official Use Only**

1 Employer identification number	2 Social security number	3 Total number of documents	4 Federal income tax withheld $	5 Total amount reported with this Form 1096 $

Check only one box below to indicate the type of forms being transmitted.   If this is your FINAL return, check here . . . . . ☐

W-2G 32	1098 81	1099-A 80	1099-B 79	1099-DIV 91	1099-G 86	1099-INT 92	1099-MISC 95	1099-OID 96	1099-PATR 97	1099-R 98	1099-S 75	5498 28
☐	☐	☐	☐	☐	☐	☐	☐	☐	☐	☐	☐	☐

Under penalties of perjury, I declare that I have examined this return and accompanying documents and, to the best of my knowledge and belief, they are true, correct, and complete.

Signature ▶ .... Title ▶ .... Date ▶ ....

Please return this entire page to the Internal Revenue Service. Photocopies are NOT acceptable.

Instructions

Purpose of Form.—Use this form to transmit Forms W-2G, 1098, 1099, and 5498 to the Internal Revenue Service.

Completing Form 1096.—If you received a preprinted label from IRS with Package 1099, place the label in the name and address area of this form inside the brackets. Make any necessary corrections to your name and address on the label. However, do not use the label if the taxpayer identification number (TIN) shown is incorrect. If you are not using a preprinted label, enter the filer's name, address, and TIN in the spaces provided on the form. **The name, address, and TIN you enter on this form must be the same as those you enter in the upper left area of Form 1099, 1098, 5498, or W-2G.** A filer includes a payer, a recipient of mortgage interest payments, a broker, a barter exchange, a person reporting real estate transactions, a trustee or issuer of an individual retirement arrangement (including an IRA or SEP), and a lender who acquires an interest in secured property or who has reason to know that the property has been abandoned. Individuals not in a trade or business should enter their social security number in Box 2; sole proprietors and all others should enter their employer identification number in Box 1. However, sole proprietors who are not required to have an employer identification number should enter their social security number in Box 2.

Group the forms by form number and submit each group with a separate Form 1096. For example, if you must file both Forms 1098 and Forms 1099-A, complete one Form 1096 to transmit your Forms 1098 and another Form 1096 to transmit your Forms 1099-A.

In Box 3, enter the number of forms you are transmitting with this Form 1096. Do not include blank or voided forms in your total. Enter the number of correctly completed forms, not the number of pages, being transmitted. For example, if you send one page of three-to-a-page Forms 5498 with a Form 1096 and you have correctly completed two Forms 5498 on that page, enter 2 in Box 3 of Form 1096. Check the appropriate box to indicate the type of form you are transmitting.

No entry is required in Box 5 if you are filing Form 1099-A or 1099-G. For all other forms, enter in Box 5 of Form 1096 the total of the amounts from the specific boxes of the forms listed below:

Form W-2G	Box 1
Form 1098	Box 1
Form 1099-B	Boxes 2, 3, and 6
Form 1099-DIV	Boxes 1a, 5, and 6
Form 1099-INT	Boxes 1 and 3
Form 1099-MISC	Boxes 1, 2, 3, 5, 6, 7, 8, and 10
Form 1099-OID	Boxes 1 and 2
Form 1099-PATR	Boxes 1, 2, 3, and 5
Form 1099-R	Boxes 1 and 8
Form 1099-S	Box 2
Form 5498	Boxes 1 and 2

If you will not be filing Forms 1099, 1098, 5498, or W-2G in the future, either on paper or on magnetic media, please check the "FINAL return" box.

If you are filing a Form 1096 for corrected information returns, enter an "X" in the CORRECTED box at the top of this form.

For more information about filing, see the separate Instructions for Forms 1099, 1098, 5498, 1096, and W-2G.

For Paperwork Reduction Act Notice, see separate Instructions for Forms 1099, 1098, 5498, 1096, and W-2G.   Form **1096** (1989)

Figure 13-12

Form 1096

Federal income tax withheld— Unless you've withheld federal income taxes from the sub, leave this blank.

Total amount reported with this Form 1096— Add up the total amount listed in box 7 of all the 1099-MISC forms.

The next line has a series of boxes and numbers. Put a check in the box above 1099-MISC/95 to indicate which forms you're filing.

Form 8109, Federal Tax Deposit Coupon

When you make deposits for either Form 941 or 940, you'll need a tax deposit coupon (Figure 13-13). You'll get a coupon book with your name, address, and EIN preprinted on it. You'll need to complete only three items on the form: the amount of deposit, the type of tax, and the tax period.

Use separate checks and coupons for each kind of tax, even if you're making them at the same time. Hand print the money amount without using dollar signs, commas, or a decimal. Be sure to fill out the stub for your own records.

In identifying the tax period, remember to mark the quarter *it's owed for*, not the quarter in which you are paying. For instance, if the liability is incurred in March and is being paid in April, darken the first quarter box.

Figure 13-14 shows a completed coupon for the first quarter.

The Last Word

The government expects you to know what forms to fill out, when they're due, and never make a mistake in the process. Penalties can be stiff if you don't comply.

Our advice is simple: Don't make mistakes. If you do, however, your best bet is to respond to inquiries courteously and promptly. Whatever information they ask for, give it to them in full. The less time they spend nosing around your books, the less likely it is they'll find more mistakes.

One more thing. In the unlikely event you get audited, be cautious in answering questions, either written or oral. Keep your answers short and to the point. Give them what they need and no more. Internal Revenue Service agents are trained to draw out information. They love exploratory questions. They'll gradually lead you from one point to the next until, without realizing it, you've raised additional issues for them to probe. There's no advantage in that — not for you at any rate.

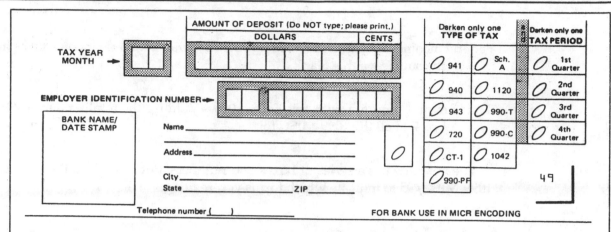

Federal Tax Deposit Coupon
Form **8109-B** (Rev. 1-87)

------- SEPARATE ALONG THIS LINE AND SUBMIT TO DEPOSITARY WITH PAYMENT -------

OMB NO. 1545-0257

IMPORTANT

Read instructions carefully before completing Form 8109-B Federal tax deposit coupons.

Note: The entries other than in the name and address section and the telephone number are processed by optical scanning equipment and must be completed by hand in the manner specified. The name and address section and the telephone number may be completed other than by hand. When completing the hand entries, we suggest you use a soft lead pencil (for example, a #2 pencil) so that the entries can be read more accurately by the optical scanning equipment. Do **NOT** use photocopies of the coupons to make your deposits.

Paperwork Reduction Act Notice.—We ask for this information to carry out the Internal Revenue laws of the United States. We need it to ensure that taxpayers are complying with these laws and to allow us to figure and collect the right amount of tax. You are required to give us this information.

Purpose of Form.—Use Form 8109-B deposit coupons to make tax deposits only in the following two situations:

(1) You have reordered your preprinted deposit coupons (**Form 8109**) but you have not yet received them; or

(2) You are a new entity and have already been assigned an employer identification number (EIN), but have not yet received your initial supply of preprinted deposit coupons (Form 8109).

Note: *You should get your reordered coupons (or your initial supply) within 5-6 weeks of the reorder (or receipt of your EIN). If you do not, please contact your local IRS office.*

If you have applied for an EIN, have not received it, and a deposit must be made, send your payment to your Internal Revenue Service Center. Make your check or money order payable to IRS and show on it your name (as shown on Form SS-4, Application for Employer Identification Number), address, kind of tax, period covered, and date you applied for an EIN. Do NOT use Form 8109-B in this situation.

Do not use Form 8109-B to deposit delinquent taxes for which you have been assessed by the IRS. Pay those taxes directly to the IRS.

How To Complete Form 8109-B.—Enter your name exactly as shown on your return or other IRS correspondence, address, and employer identification number in the spaces provided. If you are required to file a Form 1120, Form 990-C, Form 990-PF (with net investment income), Form 990-T, or Form 2438, enter the month in which your tax year ends in the "TAX YEAR MONTH" boxes. For example, if your tax year ends in January, enter 01; if it ends in June, enter 06; if it ends in December, enter 12. Please make your entries for employer identification number and tax year month (if applicable) in the manner specified in *Amount of Deposit* below. Darken one box each in the "Type of Tax" and "Tax Period" columns as explained below.

Amount of Deposit.—

Enter the amount of the deposit in the space provided.

Enter amount legibly, forming the characters as shown below:

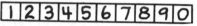

Handprint money amounts without using dollar signs, commas, a decimal point, or leading zeros. The commas and decimal point are already shown in the entry area.

For example, a deposit of $7,635.22 would be entered like this:

If the deposit is for whole dollars only, enter "00" in the "CENTS" boxes.

Types of Tax.—

Form 941	— Withheld Income and Social Security Taxes. (Includes Form 941 series of returns.)
Form 940	— Federal Unemployment (FUTA) Tax. (Includes Form 940PR.)
Form 943	— Agricultural Withheld Income and Social Security Taxes. (Includes Form 943PR.)
Form 720	— Excise Tax.
Form CT-1	— Railroad Retirement and Railroad Unemployment Repayment Taxes.
Form 990-PF	— Excise Tax on Private Foundation Net Investment Income.
Schedule A	— Backup Withholding. (Reported on Forms 941 and 941E.)
Form 1120	— Corporation Income Tax. (Includes Form 1120 series of returns and Form 2438.)
Form 990-T	— Exempt Organization Business Income Tax.

Form 990-C	— Farmers' Cooperative Association Income Tax.
Form 1042	— Withholding at Source.

How To Determine the Proper Tax Period.—

(a) Payroll Taxes and Withholding:
  (Forms 941, Schedule A (Form 941), 940, 943, 1042, and CT-1)

If your liability was incurred during:

- January—March, darken the 1st quarter box
- April—June, darken the 2nd quarter box
- July—September, darken the 3rd quarter box
- October—December, darken the 4th quarter box

Note: *If the liability was incurred during one quarter and deposited in another quarter, darken the box for the quarter in which the tax liability was incurred. For example: If the liability was incurred in March and deposited in April, darken the 1st quarter box.*

(Continued on back of page.)

Department of the Treasury
Internal Revenue Service

Form 8109-B (Rev. 1-87)

Figure 13-13
Blank form 8109

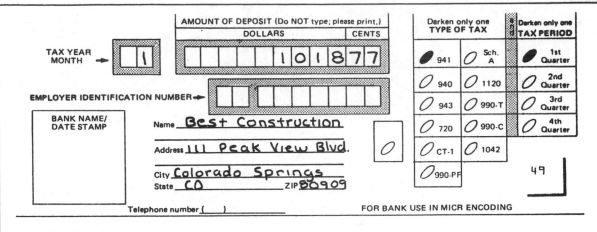

TAX YEAR MONTH → 1

AMOUNT OF DEPOSIT (Do NOT type; please print.)

DOLLARS	CENTS
1 0 1 8	7 7

EMPLOYER IDENTIFICATION NUMBER →

BANK NAME/ DATE STAMP

Name **Best Construction**

Address **111 Peak View Blvd.**

City **Colorado Springs**

State **CO**   ZIP **80909**

Telephone number ( )

Darken only one TYPE OF TAX: ● 941

Darken only one TAX PERIOD: ● 1st Quarter

49

FOR BANK USE IN MICR ENCODING

Federal Tax Deposit Coupon
Form 8109-B (Rev. 1-87)

← SEPARATE ALONG THIS LINE AND SUBMIT TO DEPOSITARY WITH PAYMENT →

OMB NO. 1545-0257

IMPORTANT

Read instructions carefully before completing Form 8109-B Federal tax deposit coupons.

Note: The entries other than in the name and address section and the telephone number are processed by optical scanning equipment and must be completed by hand in the manner specified. The name and address section and the telephone number may be completed other than by hand. When completing the hand entries, we suggest you use a soft lead pencil (for example, a #2 pencil) so that the entries can be read more accurately by the optical scanning equipment. Do NOT use photocopies of the coupons to make your deposits.

Paperwork Reduction Act Notice.—We ask for this information to carry out the Internal Revenue laws of the United States. We need it to ensure that taxpayers are complying with these laws and to allow us to figure and collect the right amount of tax. You are required to give us this information.

Purpose of Form.—Use Form 8109-B deposit coupons to make tax deposits **only** in the following two situations:

(1) You have reordered your preprinted deposit coupons (Form 8109) but you have not yet received them; or

(2) You are a new entity and have already been assigned an employer identification number (EIN), but have not yet received your initial supply of preprinted deposit coupons (Form 8109).

Note: *You should get your reordered coupons (or your initial supply) within 5-6 weeks of the reorder (or receipt of your EIN). If you do not, please contact your local IRS office.*

If you have applied for an EIN, have not received it, and a deposit must be made, send your payment to your Internal Revenue Service Center. Make your check or money order payable to IRS and show on it your name (as shown on **Form SS-4,** Application for Employer Identification Number), address, kind of tax, period covered, and date you applied for an EIN. Do NOT use Form 8109-B in this situation.

Do not use Form 8109-B to deposit delinquent taxes for which you have been assessed by the IRS. Pay those taxes directly to the IRS.

How To Complete Form 8109-B.—Enter your name exactly as shown on your return or other IRS correspondence, address, and employer identification number in the spaces provided. If you are required to file a Form 1120, Form 990-C, Form 990-PF (with net investment income), Form 990-T, or Form 2438, enter the month in which your tax year ends in the "TAX YEAR MONTH" boxes. For example, if your tax year ends in January, enter 01; if it ends in June, enter 06; if it ends in December, enter 12. Please make your entries for employer identification number and tax year month (if applicable) in the manner specified in *Amount of Deposit* below. Darken one box each in the "Type of Tax" and "Tax Period" columns as explained below.

Amount of Deposit.—

Enter the amount of the deposit in the space provided.

Enter amount legibly, forming the characters as shown below:

Handprint money amounts without using dollar signs, commas, a decimal point, or leading zeros. The commas and decimal point are already shown in the entry area.

For example, a deposit of $7,635.22 would be entered like this:

DOLLARS	CENTS
7 6 3 5	2 2

If the deposit is for whole dollars only, enter "00" in the "CENTS" boxes.

Types of Tax.—

Form 941 — Withheld Income and Social Security Taxes. (Includes Form 941 series of returns.)

Form 940 — Federal Unemployment (FUTA) Tax. (Includes Form 940PR.)

Form 943 — Agricultural Withheld Income and Social Security Taxes. (Includes Form 943PR.)

Form 720 — Excise Tax.

Form CT-1 — Railroad Retirement and Railroad Unemployment Repayment Taxes.

Form 990-PF — Excise Tax on Private Foundation Net Investment Income.

Schedule A — Backup Withholding. (Reported on Forms 941 and 941E.)

Form 1120 — Corporation Income Tax. (Includes Form 1120 series of returns and Form 2438.)

Form 990-T — Exempt Organization Business Income Tax.

Form 990-C — Farmers' Cooperative Association Income Tax.

Form 1042 — Withholding at Source.

How To Determine the Proper Tax Period.--

(a) Payroll Taxes and Withholding:
(Forms 941, Schedule A (Form 941), 940, 943, 1042, and CT-1)

If your liability was incurred during:

● January—March, darken the 1st quarter box

● April—June, darken the 2nd quarter box

● July—September, darken the 3rd quarter box

● October—December, darken the 4th quarter box

Note: *If the liability was incurred during one quarter and deposited in another quarter, darken the box for the quarter in which the tax liability was incurred. For example: If the liability was incurred in March and deposited in April, darken the 1st quarter box.*

(Continued on back of page.)

Department of the Treasury
Internal Revenue Service

Form 8109-B (Rev. 1-87)

Figure 13-14
Form 8109

14

Keeping the Books

*I*f you have a degree in accounting, you can skip this chapter. But if you're like we were, with barely a business class between us, you'll want to read it carefully. The system we describe keeps our accountant happy at tax time and has survived workers' compensation, liability insurance, and IRS audits. It doesn't have any bells or whistles — it just tells you whether you're making or losing money and where it's happening.

If you want more information, there are plenty of good bookkeeping and accounting books available at your local library or bookstore. Just make sure you understand the basic bookkeeping system we describe before you start improving on it.

We began our formal bookkeeping by picking up some standard forms from an office supply store. The set we bought was designed for manufacturers and contractors. It included spreadsheets for cash disbursements, payroll records, and job costs, plus another half dozen spreadsheets that didn't apply to construction or we didn't find necessary. The forms came with printed headings like *Materials & Supplies*, *Subcontractor Costs*, and *Cash Discount Taken*. Not all the column headings fit our business, but they gave us a place to start.

Ideal is the only company we know that publishes printed spreadsheets. You can contact them at:

> *Ideal*
> Esselte Pendaflex Corporation
> 71 Clinton Road
> Garden City, New York 11530
> 516-741-3200

If you don't like their system, you can buy ledger sheets and make up your own column headings. While it takes longer to label each column, you can customize the information you record.

The entire *Ideal* system cost us only about $15 ten years ago. (The cost will be about $25 today.) That investment brought order to the untidy piles on our desk. When we computerized our bookkeeping, we continued with much the same format. Over the years we keep refining, adding and dropping columns as our information needs change. Still, it's basically the same system we bought a decade ago.

If we hadn't decided to get a computer, we probably would have gone to a "one-write" system. As its name implies, this is a shortcut system for doing the books. Time savings come from the check-writing system. When you write a check, it makes carbon copies directly into the ledgers. That saves a step and reduces entry errors. Check writing takes a little longer, but overall, the system saves considerable time. If you're interested in a peg board or one-write system, you can get more information from *Wilmer Service Line* or *Safeguard Business Systems*.

> Wilmer Service Line
> Murlin & Pine Streets
> Celina, OH 45822
> 1-800-537-7793 (eastern division)
> 1-800-562-6555 (western division)
>
> or
>
> Safeguard Business Systems
> 1220 National Avenue
> Addison, IL 60101
> 1-800-523-2422

Any manual bookkeeping system carries the risk of computation errors. In fact, that may be where our computer saves us the most time. No longer do we spend hours adding and re-adding columns trying to find mistakes. We know that if our books don't balance, it comes from an entry error, not a mistake in arithmetic.

Breaking the System into Parts

We use a computer to keep our books. But whether you use a computer or paper and pencil, bookkeeping works the same way. Once you've perfected almost any manual record keeping system, converting to a computer is relatively easy. The system is the same. The computer just sorts information and accumulates totals much more quickly. We don't have to post the same items twice. And we can pull out the information we need at the touch of a key.

No matter whether you use a computer, *Ideal* forms, a one-write system, or your own spreadsheets, you'll need to accumulate information the same way. As we pointed out earlier, we have three basic components in our system:

Cash disbursements

This is a record of every check we write. The information we post includes:

1) date of the check

2) to whom it was written

3) check number or "cash" designation

4) the check amount

5) the job to which it applies (a single check may be posted to several jobs)

6) the purpose of the check (material, labor, office, equipment, etc.)

With a one-write system, you enter the first five items only one time — when you write the check. You record item 6 in a separate column when you write the check. Figure 14-1 is a sample cash worksheet.

Payroll records

For each employee, you'll need to keep a separate ledger sheet that shows quarterly and annual totals. The employee records have columns for:

1) pay period

2) employee's name

3) check number

4) pay rate

5) hours worked

6) amount earned

7) withholding deducted

8) net amount to employee

9) other costs (matching FICA, unemployment insurance, workers' compensation, health insurance, etc.)

10) employee's gross cost to employer

1	2	3	4	5	6	7	8	9	10	11	12	13
					Cash	Rec'd.	Job	Perm./			W/H &	Gross
Date	Paid to	Ck. #	Amt Pd.	Mat'ls	Disc.	on Acc't	Name	Lic.	Rentals	Subs	E.C.	Labor
3	Ed's Hardware	2756	6.80	6.80			Maple					
3	Safeway	Cash	3.20	3.20			Maple					
3	AAA Plumbing	2757	215.66				Brown			215.66		
5	Case Tile	2758	27.80	27.80			Maple					
6	Draw #3 (final)					840.00	Maple					
6	Draw #2					7138.50	Brown					
8	Ins. Center (health) *	2759	216.00				Shop					
9	Home Lumber	2760	177.22	186.55	-9.33		Simms					
9	Home Lumber	2760	547.83	576.66	-28.83		Brown					
9	Peak Lumber	2761	306.04	311.90	-5.86		Brown					
9	Peak Lumber	2761	31.13	31.73	-0.60		Shop					
9	K & P Paints	2762	41.01	41.84	-0.83		Maple					
9	Mt. Tools	2763	112.91				Simms					
9	CS Supply	2764	61.27	62.52	-1.25		Brown					
9	Center Rental	2765	132.44		-2.70		Brown		135.14			
9	CS Concrete	2766	476.28	486.00	-9.72		Brown					
9	Baker Electric	2767	240.00				Brown			240.00		
14	Ed Barlow	2768	315.46				Var.				-250.58	566.04
14	Frank Crocker	2769	412.84				Var.				-365.22	778.06
14	Sam Jones	2770	499.84				Var.				-384.22	884.06
14	IRS Deposit (941) *	2771	1495.44				Shop					
18	Post Office	2772	25.00				Shop					
20	Insurance Ctr. (Truck)	2773	214.00				Shop					
20	Tool repair	2774	18.09				Shop					
21	Draw #1					6521.00	Dale					
22	City Utilities	2775	26.49				Shop					
22	Mountain Bell	2776	64.51				Shop					
22	Texaco	2777	109.25				Shop					
22	Springs Lumber	2778	110.42	110.42			Simms					
22	Circle Drywall	2779	442.00				Simms			442.00		
22	West-Central Paging	2780	25.00				Shop					
22	Dollar office supply	2781	8.14				Shop					
22	AAA Concrete	2782	940.00				Brown			940.00		
22	Kuhn's Painting	2783	340.00				Simms			340.00		
24	City Building Dep't.	2784	45.00				Dale	45.00				
26	Haley Management	2785	350.00				Shop					
27	Pella Windows	2786	1685.00	1685.00			Simms					
27	Checker Auto	2787	12.06				Shop					
27	Timberline Hardwoods	2788	60.48	60.48			Simms					
27	Draw					6800.00	Simms					
28	County Treas. (truck tags)	2789	85.20				Shop					
28	State w'holding - 2nd qtr *	2790	521.24				Shop					
28	Workers' comp - 2nd qtr *	2791	2940.30				Shop					
28	IRS - 941 bal. - 2nd qtr *	2792	48.37				Shop					
28	Ed Barlow	2793	630.92				Var.				-465.16	1096.08
28	Frank Crocker	2794	412.84				Var.				-365.22	778.06
28	Sam Jones	2795	499.84				Var.				-384.22	884.06
	TOTALS		14933.32	3590.90	-59.12	21299.50		45.00	135.14	2177.66	-2214.62	4986.36

Figure 14-1

Cash worksheet

14	15	16	17	18	19	20	21	22	23	24	25	26	27	28	29
	Job	Shop					Intr.	Intr.							
Ck. #	Equip.	Equip.	Repairs	Truck	Office	Rent	Exp.	Inc.	Insur.	Adver.	Tele.	Taxes	Cont.	Other	Desc.
2756															
Cash															
2757															
2758															
2759									216.00						
2760															
2760															
2761															
2761															
2762															
2763	112.91														
2764															
2765															
2766															
2767															
2768															
2769															
2770															
2771												1495.44			
2772					25.00										
2773				214.00											
2774			18.09												
2775															
2776						26.49				18.00	46.51				
2777				109.25											
2778															
2779															
2780											25.00				
2781					8.14										
2782															
2783															
2784															
2785						350.00									
2786															
2787				12.06											
2788															
2789				85.20											
2790												521.24			
2791									2940.30						
2792												48.37			
2793															
2794															
2795															
	112.91		18.09	420.51	33.14	376.49			3156.30	18.00	71.51	2065.05			14933.32

Figure 14-1 (cont'd)
Cash worksheet

With the one-write system you can insert an employee's ledger page when you write the check. That way you'll post all this information to the employee's check stub, the payroll ledger, and the employee's ledger sheet, all at the same time. Figure 14-2 is a sample page from a payroll worksheet.

Job costs

This section keeps track of the profit and loss on each job. It repeats some of the information from the disbursement section of the cash worksheet, but you separate it out by each job. The important items are:

1) date of check

2) to whom the check was written

3) check number (or "cash" designation)

4) the amount of the check

5) cash received on the account

6) account balance

With a one-write system, you insert a job cost record between your check and the cash worksheet. As you write the check, the information is copied to the job cost record and the cash worksheet, all at the same time. Of course, for this to work, the format of the various forms must be the same. You'll notice that our illustrations aren't identical, but you can see the similarity. You'll see sample job cost records in Figure 14-3.

Let's look at each of these sections in more detail.

Cash Disbursements

Figure 14-1 is a sample cash worksheet that shows all cash transactions, including checks, cash purchases, and money received from customers. If you don't understand any of our explanation, referring to the sample should help.

Over the years, we've fine-tuned the column headings of this section. While our list might work for you, it probably won't be perfect. You may decide to break some headings down into several more specific headings. Or you may combine several headings that you don't use a lot. Each January we review the efficiency of our books and combine or delete columns to make the records more useful. Here are the headings we're currently using:

Date— This column is a waste of time — until, of course, you want to track a bill or an invoice. The time you save by omitting the date isn't worth the confusion a dateless entry can cause.

Employee earnings, 3rd quarter, 1989

				Hours worked		Earnings			Withholding					Employer Costs					
1	2	3	4	5	6	7	8	9	10	11	12	13	14	15	16	17	18	19	20
Pay Period	Employee	Ck. #	Rate	Regular	Overtime	Regular	Overtime	Total Earnings	FICA	FWT	SWT	Total Deduct.	Employee Net	FICA	Workers' comp. (22%)	Health Ins.	Other Taxes (3%)	Tot. Add'l Costs	Employer Gross
7/3-7/14	Ed Barlow	2768	10.00	40	--	400.00	--	400.00	30.04	40.00	14.50	84.54	315.46	30.04	88.00	36.00	12.00	166.04	566.04
7/17-7/28		2793	10.00	80	--	800.00	--	800.00	60.08	80.00	29.00	169.08	630.92	60.08	176.00	36.00	24.00	296.08	1096.08
7/31-8/11		2859	10.00	80	--	800.00	--	800.00	60.08	80.00	29.00	169.08	630.92	60.08	176.00	36.00	24.00	296.08	1096.08
8/14-8/25		2912	10.00	80	--	800.00	--	800.00	60.08	80.00	29.00	169.08	630.92	60.08	176.00	36.00	24.00	296.08	1096.08
8/28-9/8		2987	10.00	80	--	800.00	--	800.00	60.08	80.00	29.00	169.08	630.92	60.08	176.00	36.00	24.00	296.08	1096.08
9/11-9/22		3030	10.00	74	--	740.00	--	740.00	55.57	71.00	25.30	151.87	588.13	55.57	162.80	36.00	22.20	276.57	1016.57
Totals:				434.0		4340.00		4340.00	325.93	431.00	155.80	912.73	3427.27	325.93	954.80	216.00	130.20	1626.93	5966.93
7/3-7/14	Frank Crocker	2769	7.00	80	--	560.00	--	560.00	42.06	79.00	26.10	147.16	412.84	42.06	123.20	36.00	16.80	218.06	778.06
7/17-7/28		2794	7.00	80	--	560.00	--	560.00	42.06	79.00	26.10	147.16	412.84	42.06	123.20	36.00	16.80	218.06	778.06
7/31-8/11		2860	7.00	80	--	560.00	--	560.00	42.06	79.00	26.10	147.16	412.84	42.06	123.20	36.00	16.80	218.06	778.06
8/14-8/25		2913	7.00	80	--	560.00	--	560.00	42.06	79.00	26.10	147.16	412.84	42.06	123.20	36.00	16.80	218.06	778.06
8/28-9/8		2928	7.00	80	--	560.00	--	560.00	42.06	79.00	26.10	147.16	412.84	42.06	123.20	36.00	16.80	218.06	778.06
9/11-9/22		3031	7.00	71.5	--	500.50	--	500.50	37.59	70.00	23.60	131.19	369.31	37.59	110.11	36.00	15.02	198.72	699.22
Totals:				471.5		3300.50		3300.50	247.89	465.00	154.10	866.99	2433.51	247.89	726.11	216.00	99.02	1289.02	4589.52
7/3-7/14	Sam Jones	2770	8.00	80	--	640.00	--	640.00	48.06	68.00	24.10	140.16	499.84	48.06	140.80	36.00	19.20	244.06	884.06
7/17-7/28		2795	8.00	80	--	640.00	--	640.00	48.06	68.00	24.10	140.16	499.84	48.06	140.80	36.00	19.20	244.06	884.06
7/31-8/11		2861	8.00	80	--	640.00	--	640.00	48.06	68.00	24.10	140.16	499.84	48.06	140.80	36.00	19.20	244.06	884.06
8/14-8/25		2914	8.00	80	--	640.00	--	640.00	48.06	68.00	24.10	140.16	499.84	48.06	140.80	36.00	19.20	244.06	884.06
8/28-9/8		2989	8.00	80	--	640.00	--	640.00	48.06	68.00	24.10	140.16	499.84	48.06	140.80	36.00	19.20	244.06	884.06
9/11-9/22		3032	8.00	80	--	640.00	--	640.00	48.06	68.00	24.10	140.16	499.84	48.06	140.80	36.00	19.20	244.06	884.06
Totals:				480.0		3840.00		3840.00	288.36	408.00	144.60	840.96	2999.04	288.36	844.80	216.00	115.20	1464.36	5304.36

Figure 14-2
Payroll worksheet

Job Cost Record					
Customer: Fred & May Brown					
				Rec'd on	
Date	Paid to	Ck. #	Amount	Acc't	Balance
Balance forward, June 30:					3682.91
3	AAA Plumbing	2757	215.66		
6	Draw #2			7138.50	
9	Home Lumber	2760	576.66		
9	Peak Lumber	2761	311.90		
9	CS Supply	2764	62.52		
9	Center Rental	2765	135.14		
9	CS Concrete	2766	486.00		
9	Baker Electric	2767	240.00		
14	Frank Crocker	2769	286.91		
14	Sam Jones	2770	359.15		
22	AAA Concrete	2782	940.00		
28	Ed Barlow	2793	616.55		
28	Frank Crocker	2794	389.01		
28	Sam Jones	2795	442.03		
	Totals:		5061.53	7138.50	5759.88

Job Cost Record					
Customer: Tim & Martha Simms					
				Rec'd on	
Date	Paid to	Ck. #	Amount	Acc't	Balance
Balance forward, June 30:					2611.45
9	Home Lumber	2760	186.55		
9	Mt. Tools	2763	112.91		
14	Ed Barlow	2768	396.23		
14	Frank Crocker	2769	393.89		
14	Sam Jones	2770	364.67		
22	Springs Lumber	2778	110.42		
22	Circle Drywall	2779	442.00		
22	Kuhn's Painting	2783	340.00		
27	Pella Windows	2786	1685.00		
27	Timberline Hardwoods	2788	60.48		
27	Draw			6800.00	
28	Ed Barlow	2793	260.32		
28	Frank Crocker	2794	233.43		
28	Sam Jones	2795	265.22		
	Totals:		4851.12	6800.00	4560.33

Figure 14-3

Job cost records

Job Cost Record					
Customer: Barbara Maple					
				Rec'd on	
Date	Paid to	Ck. #	Amount	Acc't	Balance
Balance forward, June 30:					3981.17
3	Ed's Hardware	2756	6.80		
3	Safeway	Cash	3.20		
5	Case Tile	2758	27.80		
6	Draw #3 (final)			840.00	
9	K & P Paints	2762	41.84		
14	Ed Barlow	2768	169.81		
14	Frank Crocker	2769	97.26		
14	Sam Jones	2770	160.24		
	Totals:		506.95	840.00	4314.22

Job Cost Record					
Customer: Anna Dale					
				Rec'd on	
Date	Paid to	Ck. #	Amount	Acc't	Balance
Balance forward:					0.00
21	Draw #1			6521.00	
24	City Building Dep't.	2784	45.00		
28	Ed Barlow	2793	219.21		
28	Frank Crocker	2794	155.61		
28	Sam Jones	2795	176.81		
	Totals:		596.63	6521.00	5924.37

Figure 14-3 (cont'd)
Job cost records

Paid to— This, of course, is the business or individual to whom the check was written. When we write a check using our computer, we use numbers to identify employees and subs. Employees have numbers in the 200's, and subs are 300's. When you keep books by hand, it's most efficient to use a name for the person or company.

Check Number— Write either the check number or "cash" if you've paid in cash. If you have more than one checking account, you'll need to designate which account the check is from, or you can keep a separate worksheet for each account. Another option would be to use a check numbering separation system to identify different operations. For instance, you could start at number 1000 for your remodeling work, and at number 9000 in the same account for your earth moving business.

"We identify employees and subs by numbers."

Amount Paid— The amount you wrote the check for, or the amount of cash you spent.

Materials— Enter here the *full invoice amount* for materials you buy for jobs or shop inventory, even if you received a discount off the bill.

Cash Discount— If you receive a discount from your supplier for a quantity purchase or prompt payment, write that amount in this column as a negative (minus) amount. When you balance the cash worksheet, the number in this column subtracted from the total of any cash distribution columns for the same purchase (such as material or office expense) will equal the check amount.

Received on Account— Generally, only the amount clients pay you goes into this column. On the rare occasion when you have income from other sources — such as when you sell a piece of equipment — put the amount in this column and make a brief note in the *Description* column at the end of the worksheet to remind you at tax time where that income came from. Post earned interest in its own column.

Job Number or Name— Our computer sorts by number. We use numbers in the 100's to identify jobs. If you're using the pencil and paper method, and you have no more than a handful of jobs going, just use the client's name or street.

Permits & Licenses— Enter your costs for any permits and licenses here. If you prefer, you can use this column just for job-related permits (which are direct costs) and record your general permits and licenses elsewhere, as overhead or shop expense.

Rentals— It's helpful to keep track of your equipment rentals in a separate column. By checking your rental costs, you can see when it's more cost-effective to buy a tool.

Subcontractors— Break down your subcontractor costs by the job. In most cases, they'll bill you that way. But if they bill you for more than one job on a single invoice, be sure to separate the charges when you post your job cost records. (We covered that in Figure 14-3.)

If your sub gives you a discount for paying the bill by a certain date, write the amount of your check in the *Amount* column, the amount of the discount in the *Cash Discount* column (as a minus number), and the full amount of the invoice in the *Subs* column.

W/H & E.C. (Withholding & Employer Contributions)— If you're not using a computer, the number in this column will be the sum of column 13 (*Total deductions*) and column 19 (*Total added costs*) from the payroll worksheet which we'll discuss in the next section. A computerized payroll system calculates all this for you.

Gross Labor— This is the total of your employee's salary before deductions, plus your related payroll costs. It comes from column 20 on the payroll worksheet. This column, and the previous one, are for bookkeeping purposes only. You'll record the actual expenses in other columns when you write the checks.

Ck. #— We've copied the check number column to make it easier to stay on the correct line when you're posting to a wide spreadsheet, or one that's divided between two pages the way our example is in this book.

Job Equipment— This column identifies tools and equipment you buy for a specific job. For tax purposes, you can write off inexpensive items which you replace frequently as expenses in the current year. But when you buy a major piece of equipment that you'll use a long time on many jobs, you'll *depreciate* the item over several years. Your accountant will suggest how long the depreciation period should be, and which purchases fit this category.

As an example, you'd put drywall stilts in the *Job Equipment* column as a current expense like labor and material. If you bought a dump truck, that would be an *asset*, not a current expense, and you'd depreciate it over several years.

Shop Equipment— Use this column for equipment (other than major tools) that you use regularly, but that you don't want to bother charging to a specific job. For instance, suppose you build cabinets in your own shop. You wouldn't want to keep track of every saw blade or sheet of sandpaper on a job-by-job basis, but you still need to keep track of all this equipment for tax purposes.

Repairs— Whenever equipment needs replacement parts or repair, post the cost here. Even if you do the repair yourself, note any cost you incur. And note in the *Description* column what's being repaired. That makes it easy to look back and tell when it's no longer cost-effective to maintain a piece of equipment, but better to buy a new one.

Truck— Truck and car expenses include gas, maintenance, repair, insurance, and taxes. We lump it all together in one column rather than spread it over several. You can do it either way. If you separate it out, you may want to make a notation in the *Description* column that the taxes and insurance are for vehicle expenses.

Office— Enter here postage, paper, file folders, or anything else you need to run the office.

Rent— You can only deduct rent you actually pay. If you don't pay rent, don't enter any cost here. If you work out of your house, you can deduct a percentage of your mortgage, utilities, and depreciation on your tax return. But the IRS scrutinizes home-office expenses *very* carefully, so check with your accountant.

Interest Expense— If you have a business loan, whether it's for equipment purchase, a mortgage, or to cover cash flow, post the interest paid in this column. You can add a column for *Notes* or *Loans Payable* to record the principal when you make your payment, or you can post it in the *Other* column at the end of the worksheet.

Interest Income— Post any interest you've earned from business funds here, if it's deposited directly into your checking account.

Insurance— We list all our insurance, including workers' comp, employee health plans, business liability insurance, fire, and theft insurance in this column. In the payroll worksheet, there's a column for workers' compensation, also. Of course, you don't write a check to your insurance carrier each time you write a payroll check. Instead, you make periodic payments based on a percentage of your payroll.

If you deduct the workers' comp as a percentage of wages and then deduct the actual premium when you pay it, you'll deduct twice for the same expense. That'll make the IRS very unhappy when they discover the truth, and they'll make sure they share that unhappiness with you. Health insurance for your employees also works this way. We use an asterisk (*) to mark those items on our cost records, and separate them from other shop expenses. We'll explain that later on, in the section on Job Costs.

Advertising— Besides the cost of ads and phone book listings, we include in this column any entertaining we do in the line of business. The IRS only allows you to deduct 75 percent of the cost of meals and the first two alcoholic beverages per person. So that's what we put here.

Telephone— We also include truck phone and radio repeater charges in this column.

Taxes— Enter all tax payments here, whether they're taxes you've withheld from employees' pay checks, or those you have to pay yourself. Keep the breakdown between the two in your payroll records. If you're required to collect sales tax, you'll include your reimbursement to the state or local agencies in this column, also.

Note: There's another way to handle tax payments to government agencies, if your cash worksheet is cumulative (with a running balance from month to month). Post your checks for payroll-related taxes, withholding, and matching payments to the *Withholding and Employer Costs* column (as a positive number). That way, whenever you balance the cash worksheet, you'll know exactly how much of the money in your checking account really belongs to the government.

Contributions— Post only actual money contributions in this column. But keep track of all donations, whether money, services, or material. Collect your receipts for contributions and keep them in a separate folder. Your accountant will make sure they're deducted properly on your tax return.

Other— Post entries here that don't fit any of the other columns, and write the purpose of the payment in the *Description* column that follows this one.

We've put the first eight columns in Figure 14-1 in the order shown, because those are the ones we use most often. But you might prefer to put the *Materials* and *Cash Discount* columns after the *Job Name* with the rest of the expense distribution columns, or move the *Received on Account* column to the end of the worksheet. Arrange the sheet to suit your own requirements, but make it detailed enough so you'll see right away if an expense category is getting out of hand.

Payroll Records

We've incorporated all the following column headings into our computer system, but you'll need the same information for a manual system. Let's look at each of the payroll column headings.

Pay Period— Use beginning and ending dates — like 3/6-3/17 for March 6 to March 17. Also, identify the year on the first line. If you need to go back and double-check records, you'll be able to scan for the right year quickly and easily.

Employee— Employee's name

Check Number— This is essential for quick reference. Copy this number from your cash worksheet or check register when you write the payroll checks.

Rate— Hourly rate for hourly workers, or periodic rate for salaried employees (weekly, monthly, etc.).

Hours worked: Regular Time— For hourly employees, 40 hours a week is the maximum that you can pay at regular time. You aren't required to pay salaried workers overtime, even if they work 60 hours a week.

Hours worked: Overtime— You have to pay hourly employees time-and-a-half for every hour beyond 40 hours a week.

Regular Time Earnings— Multiply the regular hours worked by the rate per hour.

Overtime Earnings— Multiply the overtime hours by 1.5 times the hourly rate.

Total Earnings— Total regular and overtime earnings. If you have only salaried employees, this is the only column you need. You can ignore the previous four columns. You'll need to add columns for vacation or sick leave time, if you pay for those.

FICA— Multiply the employee's gross earnings by the withholding factor. (It was 0.0751 for 1989; it's 0.0765 for 1990).

Federal Withholding— Use the IRS publication Circular E to figure withholding. Be sure to deduct the correct amount for the pay period, marital status, and number of deductions for each employee.

State Withholding— Your state should have a publication similar to Circular E to determine state withholding taxes.

Total Deductions— These include FICA, federal and state withholding, and any insurance premiums the employee pays.

Employee Net— This is the amount of the check you write to the employee. It equals the amount posted in the Total Earnings column minus the amount under Total Deductions.

FICA— Employer's share of Social Security contributions. At this writing, this amount is the same as the employee's withholding.

Workers' Compensation— Workers' comp premiums can add up fast. In Colorado, the rate starts at 28 percent for construction and goes up from there, depending on the company's specialty. If you forget to keep track of this cost, you'll get a very distorted picture of your job profits, and a real shock when you get the bill from your workers' comp carrier.

Insurance— If you pay for group insurance or other benefits, post those costs here. If you pay part of a benefit and the employee pays the rest, you'll need two columns: one to deduct from the employee's gross pay, and this one to add to your gross payroll cost.

Other Taxes— Figure a single percentage to use in this column. It should include federal and state unemployment taxes, and any other employer contributions you're required to make, besides FICA which appears earlier.

Total Add'l Costs— Add up your portion of FICA, workers' compensation, the insurance premiums you pay, and other taxes.

Gross Cost to Employer— This is what your employee really costs you. It equals the amount in the *Total Earnings* column plus the *Total Add'l Costs* column entries. You post this amount in column 13 (*Gross Labor*) of the cash worksheet.

Job Costs

You'll use the totals from your cash worksheet to reveal your overall profit or loss for the year. Your job cost records break that larger picture down into smaller parts. When you know whether you've made or lost money on a *particular* job, you can track the various parts of the job to see where the profit or loss came from. Figure 14-3 shows the job cost records posted from the cash worksheet in Figure 14-1.

Any time you lose money on a job, you should find out why. You may need to change your estimating system, trim labor costs, or use materials more efficiently. The job cost breakdown is where you begin analyzing cost overruns.

You've already posted all this information in the cash worksheet. It's simply arranged differently here to help you track job costs. We use only six column headings for the job cost records in Figure 14-3:

Date— Enter the date of the transaction here.

Paid To— The company or person to whom you wrote the check.

Check Number— The check number is useful when you want to refer back to the cash worksheet or checkbook register.

Amount— Enter the *gross* amount of the invoice, not the net amount you actually paid after discounts. You may want to break this column down into separate ones for materials, labor, and sub costs. This would be especially helpful if you include a breakdown of your contract price by the same categories on the cost sheet.

Each pay period, figure out how much of your total payroll costs you must allocate to each job. Here's how to do that:

1) Have your workers fill out their time sheets according to which job they're working on, then total the hours for each job.

2) Fill out the payroll worksheet to find out what your total cost is for that employee and that payroll period (payroll worksheet, column 20).

3) Use the following formula to find each employee's cost per job:

hours on job x total employer cost ÷ total pay period hours = cost per job

Putting numbers to it, it looks like this:

Frank Crocker (in our payroll worksheet example) worked on three jobs during the period of 7/3–7/14, for a total of 80 hours. His time sheet shows that he worked 29½ hours on Brown, 10 hours on Maple, and 40½ hours on Simms. Figure 14-4 is a sample time sheet that shows Frank's hours. He cost us a total of $778.06 for the period.

	Best Construction Company			
Employee's name: FRANK CROCKER			Pay period: 7-3 – 7-14	
Date	Job 1 BROWN	Job 2 MAPLE	Job 3 SIMMS	Total
7-3			8	8
7-5	4	5		9
7-6		5	4	9
7-7			8	8
7-8			7	7
7-10	4 1/2		3 1/2	8
7-11	8			8
7-12	8			8
7-13	5		2	7
7-14			8	8
TOTAL	29 1/2	10	40 1/2	80

Figure 14-4
Employee time sheet

To figure what Frank cost us for each job:

Brown: 29.5 x 778.06 ÷ 80 = 286.91

Maple: 10 x 778.06 ÷ 80 = 97.26

Simms: 40.5 x 778.06 ÷ 80 = 393.89

Total: 778.06

Now, look back to the job cost sheets in Figure 14-3. You can see the respective amounts posted on the 14th for each of the three jobs.

Received on Account— There may only be two or three numbers in the entire column, but they'll be the most important ones.

Balance— Subtract the items in the *Amount* column(s) from the numbers in the *Received on Account* column. Keep your running total current so you know whether your customer's payments are keeping up with your job expenses.

Notice that our examples show only one month. In practice, you may prefer to keep a cumulative job cost record for the duration of the job.

We also keep a job cost sheet for our shop expenses. We use that to keep track of our overhead costs. Our shop expense cost sheet is Figure 14-5.

The size of your company will determine how detailed the job cost records need to be. It'll also indicate how often you need to balance the account. If you keep the books and run the jobs, you'll probably have a fair idea whether a job is over or

Shop Expenses					
Date	Paid to	Ck. #	Amount	* Items	Total
8	Ins. Center (health)	2759		216.00	
9	Peak Lumber	2761	31.73		
14	IRS Deposit (941)	2771		1495.44	
18	Post Office	2772	25.00		
20	Insurance Ctr. (Truck)	2773	214.00		
20	Tool repair	2774	18.09		
22	City Utilities	2775	26.49		
22	Mountain Bell	2776	64.51		
22	Texaco	2777	109.25		
22	West-Central Paging	2780	25.00		
22	Dollar office supply	2781	8.14		
26	Haley Management	2785	350.00		
27	Checker Auto	2787	12.06		
28	County Treas. (truck tags)	2789	85.20		
28	State withholding - 2nd qtr	2790		521.24	
28	Workers' comp - 2nd qtr	2791		2940.30	
28	IRS - 941 bal. - 2nd qtr	2792		48.37	
	Totals:		969.47	5221.35	6190.82

Figure 14-5

Shop cost records

below budget. If someone else writes the checks and keeps track of the bills, you may have more trouble. We recommend you run a total at least once a week.

Putting It All Together

Balance your worksheets and checkbook each month to be sure you haven't made any posting or math mistakes. To balance the cash worksheet, first total each column, then combine all the columns except the *Amount Paid* and the *Received on Account* columns. Be sure to *subtract* the *Cash Discount* and *Withholding* and *Employer Contribution* totals from the rest. The combined total of all the distribution columns should equal the total in *Amount Paid*. (The *Received on Account* total should equal your bank deposits for the period.)

If these don't balance, it's time to look for your mistake. Begin by finding the difference between the column totals and the *Amount Paid* total. If you've made an entry error, it'll often show up here. Look in the *Amount Paid* column to see if the difference equals any item there. It's possible you forgot to copy it to the proper distribution column. Or if an item is split between several columns, you may have entered only part of the amount instead of all of it. If all of the entries match correctly, start looking for addition or subtraction errors.

Of course, if the columns don't balance out to the exact penny, your company won't go under within the next 30 days. But it's a good idea to try to find every mistake, even a nickel. Of course, it's hardly cost effective to spend an entire evening doing it. Use your common sense on this one.

Managing Cash Flow

Knowing where the money is coming from and where it's going is the bottom line for any company. Timely cash flow can make or break your business. The money has to come in before it can go out.

Of course, if there aren't any jobs in progress, tips on cash flow aren't very helpful. But even when you're booked solid for the next six months, income and expenses may not be running parallel.

There are many ways to avoid a cash shortage. If your client is working with a lender, try to set up your draws to cover you on the tenth and the end of the month, the two most critical times for bill paying.

Even if you can't set up specific draws, you can still adjust the construction schedule to cover bill-paying on the tenth. If you're due for a draw at the start of framing, be ready for it by the first week of the month so you can get your draw by the tenth. Keep in mind, too, that most suppliers start a new billing cycle around the 25th. They won't bill anything ordered after that date until the following month.

Be sure to take advantage of the discounts that suppliers give. Most will give at least 1, perhaps 2 percent; some will go as high as 5 percent. A few percent doesn't sound like much until you see how it adds up. It's not unusual for us to have discounts of $50 to $100 a month.

There are two advantages to taking supplier discounts. The first is the money you save. The second isn't so obvious. Large suppliers usually have several price structures. In a paint store, for example, the homeowner pays list price, a general contractor may get a 10 percent discount, and painting contractors pay even less. If you always pay by the tenth, the supplier recognizes you as a good credit risk. They may repay your faithfulness by moving you to a better discount rate. Even when we operated at a fairly small scale, most suppliers had us on their best discount schedule because we paid by the tenth. In effect, we were able to save twice.

Totaling Up for the Year

Year-end financial statements and tax returns depend on good record keeping throughout the year. Our accountant prepares both for us, but his work is only as good as the information we give him.

The first step in compiling your year-end statements is to total all the columns on the cash disbursement worksheets for each month, and calculate a grand total for each column (unless you've kept a running total throughout the year).

Your Profit and Loss Statement

■ *Gross Income—* Your total income from sales — that's all the money you received from customers. It's column 7 on the cash worksheet.

■ *Job Costs—* Include *gross labor* from column 13 of the cash worksheet (or column 20 of the payroll worksheet), *materials*, column 5, *rentals*, column 10, *subcontractor costs*, column 11, *job equipment costs*, column 15, and any other costs that are directly job-related. Notice that you must adjust this total by subtracting the *cash discounts* in column 6. (Your costs are what you actually paid, not what you were billed.)

■ *Gross Profit—* Subtract *Job Costs* from *Gross Income*.

■ *Other Income—* Add interest income from column 22, and any other business-related income that doesn't come directly from jobs. An example would be rent you receive for part of a warehouse your company owns.

■ *Gross Income—* Add *Other Income* to *Gross Profit*.

■ *Net Profit—* The other columns in your cash worksheet (except contributions) are business expenses which you deduct from *Gross Income* to find your *Net Profit* (or sometimes, unfortunately, *net loss*).

Expenses - Special considerations

Vehicle Expense— If you occasionally use a personal vehicle for business — seeing clients, making bank deposits, or picking up materials — keep a record of the mileage. The IRS allows mileage deductions.

Insurance— Don't include insurance payments which you've already subtracted as part of *Gross Labor* costs. Only your building insurance, general liability, and vehicle insurance goes here.

Taxes— Again, the taxes that have been deducted under payroll should not be deducted a second time here.

Contributions— You can't deduct contributions you make from your business as a business expense, but keep track of them. They're deductible from your personal income tax return. Your accountant will handle that for you.

Your Balance Sheet

To compile a balance sheet you'll need some additional information. It takes a little work, but it's a good idea to put one together annually. Most banks require a financial statement that includes both a profit and loss (income) statement and a balance sheet for loan approval or to extend you a line of credit. Even if your bank doesn't ask for it, you should have a financial statement for your own information. It will give you an idea of your financial health.

A balance sheet is divided into two parts: assets, and liabilities and equity (or net worth). Assets are what you own or what is owed to you. Liabilities are what you owe. For instance, your truck is an asset. The loan against it is a liability. If the value of the truck is greater than the loan amount, the difference is an asset. If the loan amount is more than the value, the difference is a liability. Naturally, the idea is to have more assets than liabilities, because assets, less liabilities, equal the equity you have in your business. Your equity indicates your financial strength.

Assets and liabilities

- *Current Assets* are cash on hand and in the bank.

- *Fixed Assets* are vehicles, equipment, real estate, life insurance cash value, etc.

- *Other Assets* are accounts, loans, or mortgages that other people owe you.

- *Liabilities* are money you owe — accounts payable, loans, notes and mortgages.

You can submit financial statements either with or without an audit. An unaudited financial statement usually carries a disclaimer saying that it was prepared from figures furnished by the subject. Your accountant will charge more to prepare an audited statement. You'll also face some inconvenience while he or she plows through your invoice files and canceled checks, but your banker or lender will take an audited statement more seriously.

That's a brief look at the bookkeeping system that's kept us afloat for ten years. We're not saying that this is one you should adopt, or one that's legal for the kind of business you do, or the state that you're in. But it's been working for us. With the tax laws constantly changing, it's important that you have a competent accountant. You can't afford to make mistakes in this area.

In the next chapter, we'll share some of the hard lessons we've learned about buying insurance.

15

Buying Insurance

*I*f we had written this book five years ago, this chapter would be considerably different. In 1985 and 1986, the insurance industry went through troubled times. Interest rates had skyrocketed the previous decade. To cash in on the earning opportunity, insurance carriers went after all the business they could, however risk-laden. When interest rates dropped at the same time settlement costs rose, it spelled trouble for the insurance companies — and the consumers.

A 1986 survey by the National Association of Home Builders revealed a depressing trend. Eighty percent of the contractors questioned had insurance rate increases in the previous year. Eighteen percent had increases between 50 and 100 percent. Even more unsettling: 20 percent reported that their policies were canceled within the past year even though almost two-thirds of them had never filed a claim.

Now we're all paying much higher premiums than we were a few years ago. But the risk of cancellation or huge annual price increases has diminished. And unless you have a poor history or work in a high-risk specialty like roofing, coverage is fairly easy to get.

Within the next few years, however, the insurance industry predicts that this may change again as carriers readjust premiums to cover ever higher settlements. There are no easy solutions to the insurance escalation. It will probably take legislation to keep affordable insurance available.

In the meantime, if you're in business, you need insurance.

Kinds of Insurance

A new contractor needs a variety of coverage. One agent can probably provide everything you need, but you may not get the lowest price. You can usually save if you price-shop with several agents. Only you can decide if the money you save is worth the time it takes to deal with several agents and companies. If you decide to stay with one agent, use one who handles several different insurance lines. Then she can at least compare prices and coverage for vehicle, liability, or other kinds of insurance.

There are six common kinds of coverage you should have.

1) Property Insurance
2) General Liability
3) Builder's Risk
4) Vehicle
5) Workers' Compensation
6) Umbrella Policy

The last one is optional. Only in the last few years has it even been necessary for the small business. We'll take a closer look at all six kinds of coverage.

Property Insurance

Property insurance covers your property against fire, storm, theft, and vandalism. Most likely you already have homeowner's or renter's insurance. If you work out of your garage, your residential policy may or may not provide adequate coverage. If you have a separate place of business, you'll need a separate policy. A good property insurance policy should also cover you at the job site. Go over your coverage with your agent. You can't afford any gaps in your protection.

No matter what kind of property policy you have, it won't cover your employees' tools. Make sure they carry their own insurance for them.

"On second thought, maybe some insurance would be a good idea after all."

Property insurance rates depend on the amount of coverage and the deductible. If you only want $10,000 worth of coverage, you'll pay more per dollar of coverage than if you have a million dollar policy. And for the smaller policies, raising the deductible won't reduce the premiums as much as they will for a larger policy.

General Liability

General liability policies are also sometimes called "broad form" insurance. You may need general liability insurance to get your contractor's license. Although the required coverage varies, you'll probably need at least $300,000.

General liability has a variety of components designed to protect you from problems with a client. Hazards arising from contractual liability, personal slander, bodily injury, and property damage are all automatically part of a general liability policy.

Of these, the property damage clause can be the most confusing. General liability insurance covers damage caused by poor workmanship, but not the poor workmanship itself. For example, let's assume an employee sets a cabinet wrong. It falls off the wall and breaks against the counter, chipping the counter. Your insurance will cover the repair or replacement of the counter, but not the broken cabinet. In other words, if you or your crew produces poor quality work, you pay for it.

There are two kinds of general liability policies available for contractors: *occurrence form* and *claims made*. Occurrence form is the more common of the two. It covers you for anything that may have happened while the policy was in force, even if you're no longer insured by that company.

Claims made policies, on the other hand, cover you only for incidents that happen while the policy is in force. Once the policy period has ended, any claim that's filed against you or your work comes out of your pocket.

Consider this example. In 1987, due to the negligence of an employee, a client is hit by a falling 2 x 4, injuring his shoulder. Initially, the client takes responsibility for being in the wrong place at the wrong time. Two years later, however, when his doctor tells him he's going to need surgery on that shoulder, the last of his good will disappears and he calls his lawyer.

The company that held your occurrence form policy in 1987 would be required to defend you, even if you'd changed insurance companies in 1988. But if you had a claims made policy in force in 1987, you wouldn't have coverage when the claim was made in 1989. While you can buy a rider to cover you for previous years, the rider becomes more and more expensive for each year it goes back. After four or five years, the rider may be more expensive than the policy itself.

For obvious reasons, insurance companies like *claims made* policies. And the lower initial premiums may look like a good way to keep down your overhead. But like everything else, you get what you pay for. One of these policies just doesn't offer you much protection. We recommend spending the extra money for the safety of occurrence form insurance.

Builder's Risk

General contractors should carry a builder's risk policy. It's less common for remodelers, but on some jobs it's a good idea. Builder's risk covers you for losses due to theft, vandalism, storm, and fire during the entire period of construction. Even if the clients are technically responsible for the loss, their homeowner's policy will rarely cover it.

Vehicle Insurance

In most states, liability insurance is required for all vehicles. If you're in an accident, you'll be able to cover the damages you cause. Optional comprehensive and collision insurance covers your own vehicle. If you're willing to pay for damage to your own vehicle, you can carry only liability.

Most policies will include a rider that covers your employees as they drive between jobs. You should have this even if the employee carries his own vehicle insurance. If he's in an accident going from one site to another, you'll be named in the lawsuit because the employee was acting on your orders.

Unfortunately, you may also be considered to have the "deep pockets." In other words, the victim (and his lawyer) will assume that you have more money than the employee. So even if you aren't really at fault, you still may end up paying the largest portion of the settlement.

You don't need to carry any special liability insurance for trailers that are under 2,000 pounds. If you have an accident in your truck while pulling a trailer, and the trailer breaks loose and damages another vehicle, the liability insurance covering your truck will take care of the other vehicle. However, the comprehensive and collision insurance on your truck does not extend to the trailer. You should have the cargo of the trailer covered separately.

Trailers over 2,000 pounds should be insured separately for liability. That insurance will also cover whatever you're carrying in the trailer. For instance, the liability insurance on the trailer that hauls your backhoe from your shop to the job site would also cover your backhoe while in route. Once on the site, if the brakes on the backhoe fail during the night and it rolls into the neighbor's garage, your business liability insurance will cover the damage. But both the backhoe and the trailer would need their *own* comprehensive and collision insurance. These are optional insurance policies, however. You have to decide whether you can afford the additional premiums, or take a chance on having to come up with replacement or repair costs if your equipment is damaged.

Workers' Compensation

Workers' comp insurance is a requirement in every state. And more than any other kind of insurance, the cost will vary dramatically from state to state. That's because the state sets the rate. There may be some variance from the state's official rate, but rarely will a private carrier be cheaper than the state-run insurance fund.

In some states, you can buy only from the state. In others, workers' comp is sold only by private companies. Where the state is the only provider, the rates are often lower. But the compensation is lower as well.

For example, the rate for construction workers in Kentucky is currently 12.45 percent. That means 12.45 cents is paid to the workers' comp fund for each dollar paid in labor. Across the river in Ohio, the rate is 3.45 percent. Why the difference? It comes out in the benefits paid. If a carpenter lost his thumb in a work-related accident in Kentucky, workers' comp would pay him two-thirds of his salary for 400 weeks. If he made $10 an hour, that's over $100,000. If the same worker lost his thumb in Ohio, he'd get $3,500. Period! So if you're going to lose your thumb, it's better to lose it in Kentucky than Ohio.

The higher premium translates to real protection for the employee. The trouble is, the higher premium is also a real problem for the employer. Many contractors can't afford the same protection for themselves that they provide for their crew.

You can't be in business without workers' comp. However, you can lower your costs by beginning with the minimum premium you think you'll need. If you end up with a bigger crew than you expected, be sure to set money aside for the added premium you'll owe. You can also pay quarterly or more frequently, which helps with cash flow. Call your underwriter when you have a problem or a question.

Umbrella Policy

An umbrella policy provides coverage above and beyond the rest of your insurance. Its purpose is to give you the deeper pockets that people think you have, if you're faced with a major lawsuit. This kind of policy is most valuable when you have a high degree of exposure — and a lot to lose. If you're just starting out, it has a low priority. You need your limited capital for other, more immediate, needs.

An insurance company will only write an umbrella policy for a company that has an adequate amount of insurance for normal situations. For example, for a million dollar umbrella policy, you'd be expected to carry a million dollar general liability policy.

Handling Claims

If you suspect that a claim may be filed against you, your best defense is to document everything. Work to keep the situation from getting worse, even if you feel you're clearly in the right.

Once a claim is made against you, report it immediately to your agent. She, in turn, will hand it over to the company's adjusters and lawyers. The sooner this is done, the more quickly a settlement can be made. And quick settlements usually mean a lower cost to the carrier.

Unfortunately, even if your insurance company pays a claim filed against you, you still may not be in the clear. If the problem was caused by obvious negligence on your part, or by something you'd been warned about by the insurance company, the company may turn around and sue you.

For example, if one of your employees has a bad driving record, the insurance company may cover you as long as he's not allowed to drive while working for you. If he drives anyway and causes an accident, the company may pay the claim and then sue you for their loss. This is likely to happen only on large settlements. But if the carrier feels it had to pay for your clear negligence, at the very least you'll probably find yourself without an insurer.

You carry insurance so your company will survive and even grow larger and more profitable in the future. In the next chapter, we'll talk about planning for that growth.

16

Looking Ahead

Most remodeling companies start small. It's a rare one, though, that doesn't plan to grow. Unless the growth is well managed, however, success is likely to be brief and expensive. We recently read of a remodeler who, in less than a decade, rode a business roller coaster. He started as a manual laborer, built up his own company with over 100 employees, plunged to near bankruptcy, then soared to ownership of a new company with $1,000,000 in annual sales. He may be on another boom or bust path.

Sound growth comes slowly, after advance planning. Every business should have a five-year plan. Although it may change from year to year, you need to have a road map to where you're going. And the plan has to be realistic. To help you write your business plan, you can order a copy of *Contractor's Growth and Profit Guide* from the order form at the back of this book.

Very simply, a good business plan has two important steps: defining strengths and goals, and analyzing how to capitalize on your strengths and the market conditions to achieve the goals.

Define who you are and what you do best. What area or areas of construction do you do best? Who are your clients? What value do you offer to your clients that makes you unique? What sets you apart from all the other names in the Yellow Pages?

Next, define your goals. Do you want better cash flow? Higher profits? Expanded market share?

With your goals in mind, analyze what you've done in the past and your potential for the future. Suppose one of your goals is better cash flow. In the past, were your draws based on the calendar or the job phase? A simple change here might make a sizable difference. Other goals may take more planning — and perhaps help from other professionals, such as an accountant.

You'll need to analyze the market and economy in your area, your crew's strengths and weaknesses, and most of all, your own skills and energy for achieving your goals.

Of course, it's possible to grow at the rate that roller-coaster remodeler did. But if you've absorbed what we've been advising in this book, you'll know it's not wise. How can you hire good people and manage them without trained, experienced supervisors? How can you possibly keep track of all those jobs?

There's nothing wrong with a business as large as the one we described here — as long as it will still be around in another year or another five years. And it probably won't be unless there's strong experience at the top.

What's a realistic growth pattern? It depends on your skills and goals. Doubling a company in a year's time means one thing when you have four employees, another thing entirely when you have 40.

In the end, a company's success isn't judged by its size, but by its profitability and stability. If you can make as much money with five employees and a $500,000 gross as you can with 20 employees and a $2,000,000 gross, why would you want the headaches of the latter?

It's good to feel pride in your company — especially if that pride stems from high quality, good value, and the respect of your clients and employees. Just being the biggest in town is hardly anything to brag about.

You're on Your Own

Ultimately, all of the information in this manual can only give you the mechanics for starting your own construction business. What we can't give you are the personal qualities that make or break any business: honesty, integrity and competence.

In building your company, you can't go wrong by imitating what you most admire in other businesses. Think how you've been treated by suppliers and subs. What makes you use the same ones a second time, or every time, even if their prices are a little higher? Those same qualities in your company will sell you to your clients again and again. This is true even in a poor economy.

What is it about your business that makes clients refer you to others? What's your strong point? Is it your competence? Your reliability? Your crew? Whatever it is, build on it. By capitalizing on your strengths, you'll build a rock-solid business.

For Further Information

The learning doesn't stop here. Fortunately, there are plenty of books and magazines geared toward the contractor. And there are dozens of associations, covering every facet of the industry, trying to educate anyone who has enough interest to request information.

We'll give you the names and addresses of publications and groups which may interest you. Most of the national associations also have state and local groups. Check in your business white pages.

Organizations

National Association of the Remodeling Industry— The NARI has a solid reputation as the only national organization that's strictly for remodelers. It's very much in tune with the problems unique to our segment of the construction industry. It provides educational seminars and trade shows for members and non-members. It also wields some political clout. NARI works to get favorable legislation created and passed for the remodeling industry.

National Association of the Remodeling Industry (NARI)
1901 N. Moore St., Suite 808
Arlington, VA 22209
(703) 276-7600

National Association of Home Builders— NAHB is probably the best-known organization in the construction industry. Its lesser-known offspring, NAHB Remodelor's Council, is rapidly growing. Like NARI, NAHB and the Remodelor's Council provide educational seminars and trade shows. Even more than NARI, NAHB's main thrust seems to be political. Both associations increase public awareness and interest. NAHB publishes a magazine, *Builder*, for its members.

> National Association of Home Builders (NAHB)
> NAHB Remodelor's Council
> 15th & M Streets, N.W.
> Washington, D.C. 20005
> (800) 368-5242

National Kitchen and Bath Association— The NKBA is one of the largest of the specialty organizations. Its certification programs for kitchen and bath remodelers are designed to add skill and professionalism to the industry.

> National Kitchen and Bath Association (NKBA)
> 124 Main St.
> Hackettstown, NJ 07840
> (201) 852-0033

In addition to these three, there are well over a hundred smaller organizations which represent all aspects of the industry. There's probably an association that serves your specialty, whatever it may be. *Qualified Remodeler* publishes a page of association information every month. It also publishes a list of associations in its annual product buying guide. Watch for the areas you're most interested in, or call them directly to find out if there's an organization for your specialty.

Magazines

> *Architectural Digest*
> P.O. Box 10040
> Des Moines, IA 50340
> (213) 937-4740

> *The Journal of Light Construction*
> P.O. Box 686
> Holmes, PA 19043-9969
> (800) 345-8112

The following magazines are free to anyone in the remodeling or construction industry:

Remodeling
Hanley-Wood Publications
655 15th Street N.W., Suite 475
Washington D.C. 20005
(202) 737-0717

Qualified Remodeler, Commercial Renovation, and
Kitchen and Bath Concepts are all available from:

20 E. Jackson Blvd., Suite 700
Chicago, IL 60604
(312) 922-5402

Professional Builder
44 Cook St.
Denver, CO 80206
(303) 388-4511

Kitchen & Bath Design News
KBC Publications
2 University Plaza
Hackensack, NJ 07601
(201) 487-7800

Index

Other Practical References

Fences & Retaining Walls

Everything you need to know to run a profitable business in fence and retaining wall contracting. Takes you through layout and design, construction techniques for wood, masonry and chain link fences, gates and entries, including finishing and electrical details. How to build retaining walls and rock walls. Also includes chapters on how to get your business off to the right start, keep the books, stay within the law and estimate accurately. If your state requires a contractor's exam, you'll appreciate the chapter on contractor's math. **400 pages, 8½ x 11, $23.25**

Plumbers Handbook Revised

This new edition shows what will and what will not pass inspection in drainage, vent, and waste piping, septic tanks, water supply, fire protection, and gas piping systems. All tables, standards, and specifications are completely up-to-date with recent changes in the plumbing code. Covers common layouts for residential work, how to size piping, selecting and hanging fixtures, practical recommendations and trade tips. This book is the approved reference for the plumbing contractors exam in many states. **240 pages, 8½ x 11, $18.00**

Roof Framing

Frame any type of roof in common use today, even if you've never framed a roof before. Shows how to use a pocket calculator to figure any common, hip, valley, and jack rafter length in seconds. Over 400 illustrations take you through every measurement and every cut on each type of roof: gable, hip, Dutch, Tudor, gambrel, shed, gazebo and more. **480 pages, 5½ x 8½, $22.00**

Video: Roof Framing 1

A complete step-by-step training video on the basics of roof cutting by Marshall Gross, the author of the book *Roof Framing*. Shows and explains calculating rise, run, and pitch, and laying out and cutting common rafters. **90 minutes, VHS, $80.00**

Video: Roof Framing 2

A complete training video on the more advanced techniques of roof framing by Marshall Gross, the author of *Roof Framing*. Shows and explains layout and framing an irregular roof, and making tie-ins to an existing roof. **90 minutes, VHS, $80.00**

National Construction Estimator

Current building costs in dollars and cents for residential, commercial and industrial construction. Prices for every commonly used building material, and the proper labor cost associated with installation of the material. Everything figured out to give you the "in place" cost in seconds. Many time-saving rules of thumb, waste and coverage factors and estimating tables are included. **544 pages, 8½ x 11, $22.50. Revised annually**

Audio: Estimating Remodeling

Listen to the "hands-on" estimating instruction in this popular remodeling seminar. Make your own unit price estimate based on the prints enclosed. Then check your completed estimate with those prepared in the actual seminar. After listening to these tapes you will know how to establish an operating budget for your business, determine indirect costs and profit, and estimate remodeling with the unit cost method. **Includes seminar workbook, project survey and unit price estimating form, and six 20-minute cassettes, $65.00**

Spec Builder's Guide

Explains how to plan and build a home, control your construction costs, and then sell the house at a price that earns a decent return on the time and money you've invested. Includes professional tips on the time and money you've invested. Includes professional tips to ensure success as a spec builder: how government statistics help you judge the housing market, cutting costs at every opportunity without sacrificing quality, and taking advantage of construction cycles. Every chapter includes checklists, diagrams, charts, figures, and estimating tables. **448 pages, 8½ x 11, $27.00**

Wood-Frame House Construction

From the layout of the outer walls, excavation and formwork, to finish carpentry and painting, every step of construction is covered in detail, with clear illustrations and explanations. Everything the builder needs to know about framing, roofing, siding, insulation and vapor barrier, interior finishing, floor coverings, and stairs — complete step-by-step "how to" information on what goes into building a frame house. **240 pages, 8½ x 11, $14.25. Revised edition**

Cabinetmaking From Design to Finish

Every aspect of cabinetmaking is covered from layout, through joinery, to finishing techniques. Gives illustrated instructions for designing cabinets to fit the kitchen workcenter, creating dado, mortise, tenon, lap & dowel joints, making frames and panels, to the actual construction of cabinets and installing cabinet hardware. **416 pages, 5½ x 8½, $22.00**

Building Cost Manual

Square foot costs for residential, commercial, industrial, and farm buildings. In a few minutes you works up a reliable budget estimate based on the actual materials and design features, area, shape, wall height, number of floors and support requirements. Most important, you include all the important variables that can make any building unique from a cost standpoint. **240 pages, 8½ x 11, $14.00. Revised annually**

Estimating Home Building Costs

Estimate every phase of residential construction from site costs to the profit margin you should include in your bid. Shows how to keep track of manhours and make accurate labor cost estimates for footings, foundations, framing and sheathing finishes, electrical, plumbing and more. Explains the work being estimated and provides sample cost estimate worksheets with complete instructions for each job phase. **320 pages, 5½ x 8½, $17.00**

Rafter Length Manual

Complete rafter length tables and the "how to" of roof framing. Shows how to use the tables to find the actual length of common, hip, valley and jack rafters. Shows how to measure, mark, cut and erect the rafters, find the drop of the hip, shorten jack rafters, mark the ridge and much more. Has the tables, explanations and illustrations every professional roof framer needs. **369 pages, 5½ x 8½, $15.75**

Contractor's Survival Manual

How to survive hard times in construction and take full advantage of the profitable cycles. Shows what to do when the bills can't be paid, finding money and buying time, transferring debt, and all the alternatives to bankruptcy. Explains how to build profits, avoid problems in zoning and permits, taxes, time-keeping, and payroll. Unconventional advice includes how to invest in inflation, get high appraisals, trade and postpone income, and how to stay hip-deep in profitable work. **160 pages, 8½ x 11, $16.75**

Illustrated Guide to the National Electrical Code

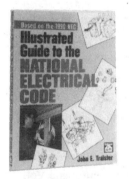

This fully-illustrated guide to the National Electrical Code offers a quick and easy visual reference for installing electrical systems. Whether you're installing a new system or repairing an old one, you'll appreciate the simple explanations written by a code expert, and the detailed, intricately-drawn and labeled diagrams. They say that a picture is worth a thousand words, so this fully-illustrated reference should save you hours of time trying to understand the current NEC. **256 pages, 8½ x 11, $24.00**

Handbook of Construction Contracting Vol. 1

Volume 1: Everything you need to know to start and run your construction business; the pros and cons of each type of contracting, the records you'll need to keep, and how to read and understand house plans and specs to find any problems before the actual work begins. All aspects of construction are covered in detail, including all-weather wood foundations, practical math for the jobsite, and elementary surveying. **416 pages, 8½ x 11, $24.75**

Handbook of Construction Contracting Vol. 2

Volume 2: Everything you need to know to keep your construction business profitable; different methods of estimating, keeping and controlling costs, estimating excavation, concrete, masonry, rough carpentry, roof covering, insulation, doors and windows, exterior finish, specialty finishes, scheduling work flow, managing workers, advertising and sales, spec building and land development, and selecting the best legal structure for your business. **320 pages, 8½ x 11, $24.75**

Profits in Buying & Renovating Homes

Step-by-step instructions for selecting, repairing, improving, and selling highly profitable "fixer-uppers." Shows which price ranges offer the highest profit-to-investment ratios, which neighborhoods offer the best return, practical directions for repairs, and tips on dealing with buyers, sellers, and real estate agents. Shows how to determine your profit before you buy, what bargains to avoid, and simple, inexpensive upgrades that will charm your buyers and ensure your profits. **304 pages, 8½ x 11, $19.75**

Contractor's Guide to the Building Code Revised

This completely revised edition explains in plain English exactly what the Uniform Code requires and shows how to design and construct residential and light commercial buildings that will pass inspection the first time. Suggests how to work with the inspector to minimize construction costs, what common building shortcuts are likely to be cited, and where exceptions are granted. **544 pages, 5½ x 8½, $24.25**

Stair Builders Handbook

If you know the floor to floor rise, this handbook will give you everything else: the number and dimension of treads and risers, the total run, the correct well hole opening, the angle of incline, the quantity of materials and settings for your framing square for over 3,500 code approved rise and run combination — several for every 1/8 inch interval from a 3 foot to a 12 foot floor to floor rise. **416 pages, 5½ x 8½, $15.50**

Estimating Electrical Construction

A practical approach to estimating materials and labor for residential and commercial electrical construction. Written by the A.S.P.E. National Estimator of the Year, it explains how to use labor units, the plan take-off and the bid summary to establish an accurate estimate. Covers dealing with suppliers, pricing sheets, and how to modify labor units. Provides extensive labor unit tables, and blank forms for use in estimating your next electrical job. **272 pages, 8½ x 11, $19.00**

Builder's Comprehensive Dictionary

Never let a construction term stump you. Here you'll find almost 10,000 construction term definitions, over 1,000 detailed illustrations of tools, techniques and systems, and a separate section containing most often used legal, real estate, and management terms. **532 pages, 8½ x 11, $24.95**

Builder's Guide to Accounting Revised

Step-by-step, easy-to-follow guidelines for setting up and maintaining an efficient record keeping system for your building business. Not a book of theory, this practical, newly-revised guide to all accounting methods shows how to meet state and federal accounting requirements, including new depreciation rules, and explains what the tax reform act of 1986 can mean to your business. Full of charts, diagrams, blank forms, simple directions and examples. **304 pages, 8½ x 11, $20.00**

Remodeling Contractor's Handbook

Everything you need to know to make a remodeling business grow: Identifying a market for your business, inexpensive sales and advertising techniques that work, and how to prepare accurate estimates. Also explains building a positive company image, training effective sales people, placing loans for customers, and bringing in profitable work to keep your company growing. **304 pages, 8½ x 11, $18.25**

How to Sell Remodeling

Proven, effective sales methods for repair and remodeling contractors: finding qualified leads, making the sales call, identifying what your prospects really need, pricing the job, arranging financing, and closing the sale. Explains how to organize and staff a sales team, how to bring in the work to keep your crews busy and your business growing, and much more. Includes blank forms, tables, and charts. **240 pages, 8½ x 11, $17.50**

Running Your Remodeling Business

Everything you need to know about operating a remodeling business, from making your first sale to insuring your profits: how to advertise, write up a contract, estimate, schedule your jobs, arrange financing (for both you and your customers), and when and how to expand your business. Explains what you need to know about insurance, bonds, and liens, and how to collect the moeny you've earned. Includes sample business forms for your use. **272 pages, 8½ x 11, $21.00**

Estimating Tables for Home Building

Produce accurate estimates in minutes for nearly any home or multi-family dwelling. This handy manual has the tables you need to find the quantity of materials and labor for most residential construction. Includes overhead and profit, how to develop unit costs for labor and materials, and how to be sure you've considered every cost in the job. **336 pages, 8½ x 11, $21.50**

Craftsman

Craftsman Book Company
6058 Corte del Cedro
Carlsbad, CA 92008
(619) 438-7828

In a hurry?
We accept phone orders
charged to your MasterCard,
Visa or American Express.
Call 1-800-829-8123
FAX (619) 438-0398

✉

Mail Orders
We pay shipping when you
use your charge card or when
your check covers your order in full

Name

Company

Address

City   State   Zip

Total enclosed _____ (In Calif. add 6% tax)
If you prefer, use your ☐ Visa ☐ MasterCard ☐ AmEx
Card number_____
Expiration date_____Initials_____

10 Day Money Back GUARANTEE

☐ 65.00 Audiotape: Estimating Remodeling
☐ 24.95 Builder's Comprehensive Dictionary
☐ 20.00 Builder's Guide to Accounting, Revised
☐ 14.00 Building Cost Manual
☐ 22.00 Cabinetmaking: Design to Finish
☐ 24.25 Contractor's Guide to Building Code
☐ 16.75 Contractor's Survival Manual
☐ 19.00 Estimating Electrical Construction
☐ 17.00 Estimating Home Building Costs
☐ 21.50 Estimating Tables for Home Building
☐ 23.25 Fences and Retaining Walls
☐ 24.75 Handbook of Construction Contracting Vol. 1
☐ 24.75 Handbook of Construction Contracting Vol. 2
☐ 17.50 How to Sell Remodeling
☐ 24.00 Illustrated Guide to National Electrical Code
☐ 22.50 National Construction Estimator
☐ 18.00 Plumber's Handbook Revised
☐ 19.75 Profits in Buying & Renovating Homes
☐ 15.75 Rafter Length Manual
☐ 18.25 Remodeling Contractor's Handbook
☐ 22.00 Roof Framing
☐ 21.00 Running Your Remodeling Business
☐ 27.00 Spec Builder's Guide
☐ 15.50 Stair Builder's Handbook
☐ 80.00 Video: Roof Framing, 1
☐ 80.00 Video: Roof Framing, 2
☐ 14.25 Wood-Frame House Construction
☐ 19.50 How to Succeed w/ Own Construction Business

Craftsman Book Co
6058 Corte del Cedro
P.O. Box 6500
Carlsbad, CA 92008

In a hurry
We accept phone orders
charged to your MasterCard,
Visa or American Express
Call 1-800-829-8123
FAX (619) 438-0398

Name _____

Company _____

Address _____

City/State/Zip _____

Send check or money order
Total enclosed _____
(In California Add 6% tax)
Use your ☐ Visa ☐ MasterCard or ☐ AmEx
Card # _____
Exp. date _____ Initals _____

10-Day Money Back GUARANTEE

☐ 95.00 Audio: Const. Field Supervision
☐ 65.00 Audio: Estimating Remodeling
☐ 19.95 Audio: Plumbers Examination
☐ 22.00 Basic Plumbing with Illust.
☐ 30.00 Berger Building Cost File
☐ 11.25 Bluprt Reading for Bldg Trades
☐ 19.75 Bookkeeping for Builders
☐ 24.95 Blder's Comp. Dictionary
☐ 20.00 Blder's Guide to Account. Rev.
☐ 15.25 Blder's Guide to Const. Financ.
☐ 15.50 Blder's Office Manual Revised
☐ 14.00 Building Cost Manual
☐ 11.75 Building Layout
☐ 22.00 Cabinetmaking: Design - Finish
☐ 25.50 Carpentry Estimating
☐ 19.75 Carpentry for Resid. Const.
☐ 19.00 Carpentry in Com. Const.
☐ 16.25 Carpentry Layout
☐ 17.75 Computers: Blder's New Tool
☐ 14.50 Concrete and Formwork
☐ 20.50 Concrete Const. & Estimating
☐ 26.00 Const. Estimating Refer. Data
☐ 22.00 Construction Superintendent
☐ 19.25 Const. Surveying & Layout
☐ 19.00 Cont. Growth & Profit Guide
☐ 24.25 Cont Guide to Bldg Code Rev.
☐ 16.75 Contractor's Survival Manual
☐ 16.50 Cont. Year-Rd Tax Guide
☐ 15.75 Cost Records for Const. Est.
☐ 9.50 Dial-A-Length Rafterule
☐ 18.25 Drywall Contracting
☐ 13.75 Electrical Blueprint Reading
☐ 25.00 Electrical Const. Estimator

☐ 19.00 Estimating Electrical Const.
☐ 17.00 Estimating Home Blding Costs
☐ 28.00 Estimating Painting Costs
☐ 17.25 Estimating Plumbing Costs
☐ 21.50 Est. Tables for Home Building
☐ 22.75 Excav. & Grading Hndbk Rev.
☐ 9.25 E-Z Square
☐ 23.25 Fences & Retaining Walls
☐ 15.25 Finish Carpentry
☐ 24.75 Hdbk of Const. Contr. Vol. 1
☐ 24.75 Hdbk of Const. Contr. Vol. 2
☐ 15.00 Home Wiring: Improv. Ext. Rep.
☐ 17.50 How to Sell Remodeling
☐ 19.50 How Succed w/ Own Const Co.
☐ 24.50 HVAC Contracting
☐ 24.00 Illustrated Guide to NE Code
☐ 20.25 Manual of Electrical Contr.
☐ 19.75 Manual of Prof. Remodeling
☐ 17.25 Masonry & Concrete Const.
☐ 26.50 Masonry Estimating
☐ 22.50 National Const. Estimator
☐ 19.25 Paint Contractor's Manual
☐ 21.25 Painter's Handbook
☐ 27.50 Painting Cost Guide
☐ 23.50 Pipe & Excavation Contracting
☐ 13.00 Plan & Design Plumb. Systems
☐ 19.25 Planning Drain, Waste & Vent
☐ 21.00 Plumber's Exam Prep. Guide
☐ 18.00 Plumber's Handbook Revised
☐ 19.75 Profits in Buy & Renov Homes
☐ 15.75 Rafter Length Manual
☐ 23.00 Remodeler's Handbook
☐ 18.25 Remodeling Contr. Handbook

☐ 26.25 Remodeling Kitchens & Baths
☐ 11.50 Residential Electrical Design
☐ 16.75 Residential Electr. Hndbk.
☐ 18.25 Residential Wiring
☐ 22.00 Roof Framing
☐ 14.00 Roofers Handbook
☐ 17.00 Rough Carpentry
☐ 21.00 Run. Your Remodeling Bus.
☐ 27.00 Spec Builder's Guide
☐ 15.50 Stair Builder's Handbook
☐ 15.50 Video: Bathroom Tile
☐ 15.50 Video: Contracting a Home 1
☐ 15.50 Video: Contracting a Home 2
☐ 32.00 Video: Design Your Kitchen
☐ 24.75 Video: Drywall Contracting 1
☐ 24.75 Video: Drywall Contracting 2
☐ 15.50 Video: Electrical Wiring
☐ 15.50 Video: Exterior Painting
☐ 15.50 Video: Finish Carpentry
☐ 15.50 Video: Hanging an Ext Door
☐ 15.50 Video: Int. Paint & Wallpaper
☐ 15.50 Video: Kitchen Renovation
☐ 24.75 Video: Paint Contractor's 1
☐ 24.75 Video: Paint Contractor's 2
☐ 15.50 Video: Plumbing
☐ 80.00 Video: Roof Framing, 1
☐ 80.00 Video: Roof Framing, 2
☐ 15.50 Video: Rough Carpentry
☐ 24.75 Video: Stair Framing
☐ 15.50 Video: Windows & Doors
☐ 15.50 Video: Wood Siding
☐ 7.50 Visual Stairule
☐ 14.25 Wood-Frame House Const.

Craftsman Book Co
6058 Corte del Cedro
P.O. Box 6500
Carlsbad, CA 92008

In a hurry
We accept phone orders
charged to your MasterCard,
Visa or American Express
Call 1-800-829-8123
FAX (619) 438-0398

Name _____

Company _____

Address _____

City/State/Zip _____

Send check or money order
Total enclosed _____
(In California Add 6% tax)
Use your ☐ Visa ☐ MasterCard or ☐ AmEx
Card # _____
Exp. date _____ Initals _____

10-Day Money Back GUARANTEE

☐ 95.00 Audio: Const. Field Supervision
☐ 65.00 Audio: Estimating Remodeling
☐ 19.95 Audio: Plumbers Examination
☐ 22.00 Basic Plumbing with Illust.
☐ 30.00 Berger Building Cost File
☐ 11.25 Bluprt Reading for Bldg Trades
☐ 19.75 Bookkeeping for Builders
☐ 24.95 Blder's Comp. Dictionary
☐ 20.00 Blder's Guide to Account. Rev.
☐ 15.25 Blder's Guide to Const. Financ.
☐ 15.50 Blder's Office Manual Revised
☐ 14.00 Building Cost Manual
☐ 11.75 Building Layout
☐ 22.00 Cabinetmaking: Design - Finish
☐ 25.50 Carpentry Estimating
☐ 19.75 Carpentry for Resid. Const.
☐ 19.00 Carpentry in Com. Const.
☐ 16.25 Carpentry Layout
☐ 17.75 Computers: Blder's New Tool
☐ 14.50 Concrete and Formwork
☐ 20.50 Concrete Const. & Estimating
☐ 26.00 Const. Estimating Refer. Data
☐ 22.00 Construction Superintendent
☐ 19.25 Const. Surveying & Layout
☐ 19.00 Cont. Growth & Profit Guide
☐ 24.25 Cont Guide to Bldg Code Rev.
☐ 16.75 Contractor's Survival Manual
☐ 16.50 Cont. Year-Rd Tax Guide
☐ 15.75 Cost Records for Const. Est.
☐ 9.50 Dial-A-Length Rafterule
☐ 18.25 Drywall Contracting
☐ 13.75 Electrical Blueprint Reading
☐ 25.00 Electrical Const. Estimator

☐ 19.00 Estimating Electrical Const.
☐ 17.00 Estimating Home Blding Costs
☐ 28.00 Estimating Painting Costs
☐ 17.25 Estimating Plumbing Costs
☐ 21.50 Est. Tables for Home Building
☐ 22.75 Excav. & Grading Hndbk Rev.
☐ 9.25 E-Z Square
☐ 23.25 Fences & Retaining Walls
☐ 15.25 Finish Carpentry
☐ 24.75 Hdbk of Const. Contr. Vol. 1
☐ 24.75 Hdbk of Const. Contr. Vol. 2
☐ 15.00 Home Wiring: Improv. Ext. Rep.
☐ 17.50 How to Sell Remodeling
☐ 19.50 How Succed w/ Own Const Co.
☐ 24.50 HVAC Contracting
☐ 24.00 Illustrated Guide to NE Code
☐ 20.25 Manual of Electrical Contr.
☐ 19.75 Manual of Prof. Remodeling
☐ 17.25 Masonry & Concrete Const.
☐ 26.50 Masonry Estimating
☐ 22.50 National Const. Estimator
☐ 19.25 Paint Contractor's Manual
☐ 21.25 Painter's Handbook
☐ 27.50 Painting Cost Guide
☐ 23.50 Pipe & Excavation Contracting
☐ 13.00 Plan & Design Plumb. Systems
☐ 19.25 Planning Drain, Waste & Vent
☐ 21.00 Plumber's Exam Prep. Guide
☐ 18.00 Plumber's Handbook Revised
☐ 19.75 Profits in Buy & Renov Homes
☐ 15.75 Rafter Length Manual
☐ 23.00 Remodeler's Handbook
☐ 18.25 Remodeling Contr. Handbook

☐ 26.25 Remodeling Kitchens & Baths
☐ 11.50 Residential Electrical Design
☐ 16.75 Residential Electr. Hndbk.
☐ 18.25 Residential Wiring
☐ 22.00 Roof Framing
☐ 14.00 Roofers Handbook
☐ 17.00 Rough Carpentry
☐ 21.00 Run. Your Remodeling Bus.
☐ 27.00 Spec Builder's Guide
☐ 15.50 Stair Builder's Handbook
☐ 15.50 Video: Bathroom Tile
☐ 15.50 Video: Contracting a Home 1
☐ 15.50 Video: Contracting a Home 2
☐ 32.00 Video: Design Your Kitchen
☐ 24.75 Video: Drywall Contracting 1
☐ 24.75 Video: Drywall Contracting 2
☐ 15.50 Video: Electrical Wiring
☐ 15.50 Video: Exterior Painting
☐ 15.50 Video: Finish Carpentry
☐ 15.50 Video: Hanging an Ext Door
☐ 15.50 Video: Int. Paint & Wallpaper
☐ 15.50 Video: Kitchen Renovation
☐ 24.75 Video: Paint Contractor's 1
☐ 24.75 Video: Paint Contractor's 2
☐ 15.50 Video: Plumbing
☐ 80.00 Video: Roof Framing, 1
☐ 80.00 Video: Roof Framing, 2
☐ 15.50 Video: Rough Carpentry
☐ 24.75 Video: Stair Framing
☐ 15.50 Video: Windows & Doors
☐ 15.50 Video: Wood Siding
☐ 7.50 Visual Stairule
☐ 14.25 Wood-Frame House Const.

Craftsman Book Co
6058 Corte del Cedro
P.O. Box 6500
Carlsbad, CA 92008

In a hurry
We accept phone orders
charged to your MasterCard,
Visa or American Express
Call 1-800-829-8123
FAX (619) 438-0398

Name _____

Company _____

Address _____

City/State/Zip _____

Send check or money order
Total enclosed _____
(In California Add 6% tax)
Use your ☐ Visa ☐ MasterCard or ☐ AmEx
Card # _____
Exp. date _____ Initals _____

10-Day Money Back GUARANTEE

☐ 95.00 Audio: Const. Field Supervision
☐ 65.00 Audio: Estimating Remodeling
☐ 19.95 Audio: Plumbers Examination
☐ 22.00 Basic Plumbing with Illust.
☐ 30.00 Berger Building Cost File
☐ 11.25 Bluprt Reading for Bldg Trades
☐ 19.75 Bookkeeping for Builders
☐ 24.95 Blder's Comp. Dictionary
☐ 20.00 Blder's Guide to Account. Rev.
☐ 15.25 Blder's Guide to Const. Financ.
☐ 15.50 Blder's Office Manual Revised
☐ 14.00 Building Cost Manual
☐ 11.75 Building Layout
☐ 22.00 Cabinetmaking: Design - Finish
☐ 25.50 Carpentry Estimating
☐ 19.75 Carpentry for Resid. Const.
☐ 19.00 Carpentry in Com. Const.
☐ 16.25 Carpentry Layout
☐ 17.75 Computers: Blder's New Tool
☐ 14.50 Concrete and Formwork
☐ 20.50 Concrete Const. & Estimating
☐ 26.00 Const. Estimating Refer. Data
☐ 22.00 Construction Superintendent
☐ 19.25 Const. Surveying & Layout
☐ 19.00 Cont. Growth & Profit Guide
☐ 24.25 Cont Guide to Bldg Code Rev.
☐ 16.75 Contractor's Survival Manual
☐ 16.50 Cont. Year-Rd Tax Guide
☐ 15.75 Cost Records for Const. Est.
☐ 9.50 Dial-A-Length Rafterule
☐ 18.25 Drywall Contracting
☐ 13.75 Electrical Blueprint Reading
☐ 26.00 Electrical Const. Estimator

☐ 19.00 Estimating Electrical Const.
☐ 17.00 Estimating Home Blding Costs
☐ 28.00 Estimating Painting Costs
☐ 17.25 Estimating Plumbing Costs
☐ 21.50 Est. Tables for Home Building
☐ 22.75 Excav. & Grading Hndbk Rev.
☐ 9.25 E-Z Square
☐ 23.25 Fences & Retaining Walls
☐ 15.25 Finish Carpentry
☐ 24.75 Hdbk of Const. Contr. Vol. 1
☐ 24.75 Hdbk of Const. Contr. Vol. 2
☐ 15.00 Home Wiring: Improv. Ext. Rep.
☐ 17.50 How to Sell Remodeling
☐ 19.50 How Succed w/ Own Const Co.
☐ 24.50 HVAC Contracting
☐ 24.00 Illustrated Guide to NE Code
☐ 20.25 Manual of Electrical Contr.
☐ 19.75 Manual of Prof. Remodeling
☐ 17.25 Masonry & Concrete Const.
☐ 26.50 Masonry Estimating
☐ 22.50 National Const. Estimator
☐ 19.25 Paint Contractor's Manual
☐ 21.25 Painter's Handbook
☐ 27.50 Painting Cost Guide
☐ 23.50 Pipe & Excavation Contracting
☐ 13.00 Plan & Design Plumb. Systems
☐ 19.25 Planning Drain, Waste & Vent
☐ 21.00 Plumber's Exam Prep. Guide
☐ 18.00 Plumber's Handbook Revised
☐ 19.75 Profits in Buy & Renov Homes
☐ 15.75 Rafter Length Manual
☐ 23.00 Remodeler's Handbook
☐ 18.25 Remodeling Contr. Handbook

☐ 26.25 Remodeling Kitchens & Baths
☐ 11.50 Residential Electrical Design
☐ 16.75 Residential Electr. Hndbk.
☐ 18.25 Residential Wiring
☐ 22.00 Roof Framing
☐ 14.00 Roofers Handbook
☐ 17.00 Rough Carpentry
☐ 21.00 Run. Your Remodeling Bus.
☐ 27.00 Spec Builder's Guide
☐ 15.50 Stair Builder's Handbook
☐ 15.50 Video: Bathroom Tile
☐ 15.50 Video: Contracting a Home 1
☐ 15.50 Video: Contracting a Home 2
☐ 32.00 Video: Design Your Kitchen
☐ 24.75 Video: Drywall Contracting 1
☐ 24.75 Video: Drywall Contracting 2
☐ 15.50 Video: Electrical Wiring
☐ 15.50 Video: Exterior Painting
☐ 15.50 Video: Finish Carpentry
☐ 15.50 Video: Hanging an Ext Door
☐ 15.50 Video: Int. Paint & Wallpaper
☐ 15.50 Video: Kitchen Renovation
☐ 24.75 Video: Paint Contractor's 1
☐ 24.75 Video: Paint Contractor's 2
☐ 15.50 Video: Plumbing
☐ 80.00 Video: Roof Framing, 1
☐ 80.00 Video: Roof Framing, 2
☐ 15.50 Video: Rough Carpentry
☐ 24.75 Video: Stair Framing
☐ 15.50 Video: Windows & Doors
☐ 15.50 Video: Wood Siding
☐ 7.50 Visual Stairule
☐ 14.25 Wood-Frame House Const.

BUSINESS REPLY MAIL

FIRST CLASS PERMIT NO. 271 CARLSBAD, CA

POSTAGE WILL BE PAID BY ADDRESSEE

Craftsman Book Company
6058 Corte Del Cedro
Box 6500
Carlsbad, CA 92008-0992

NO POSTAGE
NECESSARY
IF MAILED
IN THE
UNITED STATES

BUSINESS REPLY MAIL

FIRST CLASS PERMIT NO. 271 CARLSBAD, CA

POSTAGE WILL BE PAID BY ADDRESSEE

Craftsman Book Company
6058 Corte Del Cedro
Box 6500
Carlsbad, CA 92008-0992

NO POSTAGE
NECESSARY
IF MAILED
IN THE
UNITED STATES

BUSINESS REPLY MAIL

FIRST CLASS PERMIT NO. 271 CARLSBAD, CA

POSTAGE WILL BE PAID BY ADDRESSEE

Craftsman Book Company
6058 Corte Del Cedro
Box 6500
Carlsbad, CA 92008-0992

NO POSTAGE
NECESSARY
IF MAILED
IN THE
UNITED STATES